The Judge

The Judge

William P. Clark,
Ronald Reagan's Top Hand

BY

Paul Kengor
&
Patricia Clark Doerner

IGNATIUS PRESS   SAN FRANCISCO

Cover photograph: From the Clark family archives

Cover design by Roxanne Mei Lum

© 2007 Ignatius Press, San Francisco
All rights reserved
ISBN 978-1-58617-183-4
Library of Congress Control Number 2007927194
Printed in the United States of America ∞

To the examples of

Robert E. Clark, grandfather

William Pettit Clark, father

And to the greater honor and glory of God

The very good never believe themselves very good,
because they are judging themselves by the Ideal.

Fulton J. Sheen, *Peace of Soul*

CONTENTS

PREFACE

He has lived by Teddy Roosevelt's credo "Keep your eye on the stars, but your feet on the ground", doing his best to stay true to himself and the cherished tenets of his father, his grandfather, and his God. He persevered in this determination through years of stunning success in the public sector. Given the opportunity, however, he would deny it all.

William P. Clark has never lived up to his own expectations. His achievements are surpassed only by his humility, a humility based on firm religious beliefs rather than a lack of confidence. Those beliefs took him across the country to an Augustinian seminary in upstate New York when he was a young Stanford student. Within the year, however, it became clear to him that the religious life was not his calling, at least at that time.

Throughout his youth Bill developed indissoluble bonds with the men in the extended Clark clan: Westerners all, soft spoken but tough and quick to act, devout subscribers to TR's speak-softly-and-always-be-prepared philosophy. "Integrity" was never spoken; it was universally assumed.

As the first-born of thirty-one grandchildren, Bill shared a particularly close relationship with his grandfather, Ventura County's most colorful sheriff and, later, the "last of the frontier marshals". It was four-year-old "Billy Boy" who pinned the badge on Shirley Temple's vest as she was "officially" deputized by Marshal Clark. Fifty years later, the two would serve together in the U.S. Department of State: he, as second in command; she, as foreign affairs officer.[1]

---

[1] Richard Nixon appointed Shirley Temple Black U.S. Representative to the United Nations in 1969; she served under Gerald Ford as Ambassador to the Republic of Ghana, then as White House Chief of Protocol. After serving as foreign affairs officer with the State Department under Ronald Reagan, she was appointed Ambassador to Czechoslovakia by George H. W. Bush.

As first-born and only son, Bill was his father's top hand, spending many hours in the saddle, herding cattle, roping, branding, on Rancho Chismahoo, Battle Creek Ranch, and Slagger Camp—the lonely life that breeds independence of thought, integrity of being and limited use of the spoken word, if we are to believe in the Code of the West.

The life of the cowhand leaves time to dream. Countering atheistic communism and one day having some land of his own were foremost among Bill's dreams. Both hopes have been achieved—both dreams have been realized. The Soviet empire has been dismantled; Bill has his thousand-acre ranch near Paso Robles, California, where he spends his sunset years with Joan, alongside children and grandchildren, as they rope and brand their cattle, compete in rodeos, and play Mozart.

He is still on a quest, his mission in life having devolved to finding the mystical peace of the mythical cowboy hero. The dream of peace fades, however, in the glare of social and moral causes calling out for attention now that he has retired from formal government service. The peaceful serenity of the contemplative may never be his—but he is living as happily-ever-after as his restless soul will allow.

Lest one think these the partial ramblings of a fond "favorite cousin",[2] I offer some facts as well as a couple of opinions in addition to my own. Bill Clark was with Ronald Reagan from the beginning—from his first campaign for governor of California through the retirement years. During the most crucial period in the first administration—from 1981 through 1983—when a host of policy directives was conceived and crafted with the intent of defeating the Soviet empire, Clark, next to the President, held the chief role.

Reagan's official biographer, Edmund Morris, lists Clark as a man who made "an art form of taciturnity," yet "the most impressive advisor" within the White House inner circle, "in fact the only person in the entire two terms who had any kind of spiritual intimacy with the President."[3]

As further described by Morris: "Tall, handsome, expressionless, and slow moving in black alligator boots, [Clark] stood out among

---

[2] There is no cousin of Bill's who has *not* been designated "favorite".
[3] Edmund Morris, "The Pope and the President", *Catholic World Report*, November 1999, p. 54.

conservative Washingtonians like the proverbial Stranger come to town, his pinstripe suits too well cut, his gold-rimmed half-moons too thin for Beltway comfort." [4] A telling description, it calls to mind the cowboy hero of early western movies, the champion who rides in to the rescue, defeats the bad guys, then rides off into the sunset.

Yet the celluloid cowboys never deliberated in the hallowed halls of national power. Bill Clark did, and when he did, he stayed true to form in all ways. One instance: His usual routine, most mornings before Washington awoke, was to lope through Georgetown, past Roosevelt Island and up Capitol Mall astride Amadeus, the magnificent white Lipizzaner stallion, a gift to President Reagan from the Austrians. [5]

His National Park Police riding companions affectionately dubbed the self-effacing fifth generation California rancher "the masked man on the white horse", conjuring images of knights errant throughout the history of Western Civilization. The Code of Chivalry meets the Code of the American West.

Congratulations to those park police riding companions for correctly assessing the character of the man. Congratulations to Paul Kengor for convincing Bill that his is a story worth the telling. And thank you, Paul, for inviting me to join you in writing this book.

— *Patricia Clark Doerner*

---

[4] Edmund Morris, *Dutch: A Memoir of Ronald Reagan* (New York: Random House, 1999), p. 455.

[5] Dale Russakoff, "Mornings on Horseback", *Washington Post*, February 11, 1985, p. B1. Clark admits to frequent temptations to swim his horse to Roosevelt Island during these years, as TR had done before him. What stopped him? For one, he figured he'd probably be arrested; secondly, he didn't want to arrive at the office in wet clothing.

INTRODUCTION

The Mission

On a spring day in 1988, William P. Clark—known by friends and associates as "The Judge"—taxied into position on the dirt landing strip of his thousand-acre ranch near Paso Robles, the heart of California's Central Coast wine country. At age fifty-six, he was substantially finished with government service and looking forward to life at the ranch, working cattle, planting olive trees, and developing a vineyard. Both orchard and vineyard would complement a Spanish mission-style chapel—at this point no more than a dream, yet to be designed.

Judge Clark, whose request to be called Bill goes mostly unheeded, had left the Reagan administration three years earlier. He had served Ronald Reagan for more than twenty years, beginning when Reagan ran for governor of California. During his two years as Reagan's national security advisor, Clark was—next to the President—probably the most powerful man in America, and thus among the most powerful men in the world. Though no longer a regular presence at Reagan's side, Clark continued to serve his country from the background and to advance causes he had been unable to address during his public life.

On this day, as he prepared his tandem-seat Super Cub for takeoff, his public career was mostly behind him. The night before, Clark had returned from a trip to Europe. He felt jet-lagged, not especially sharp, but his desk at the office in town was piled high with work.

Early into takeoff, the plane got caught in a crosswind. "I knew right away that I was in trouble", says Clark. "I lost control." At about sixty miles per hour, the plane veered into a supply building to the right of the runway, missing the above-ground fuel tanks outside the building. Clark slumped unconscious in a mangled mess of smoking

13

metal. Ribs broken, shoulder separated, skull fractured, and soaked in blood and fuel, he was alive but hardly out of danger.

The engine, simmering hot, was pushed back against his legs, while fuel from the fractured wing tank sprayed onto the unconscious pilot. For some reason, the plane failed to burst into flames. "It should have lit up", Clark says, pausing. "Statistically, it should have lit up—but it didn't."

A briefcase on the seat next to Clark contained a Dictaphone that was somehow activated in the course of the crash. The audiotape still survives; Clark and his sons have listened to it, but wife Joan refuses. On the recording, listeners can hear the unconscious Clark groaning and calling for help.

Clark's only coherent plea, "God, please help me!" is followed by the sound of ripping metal. Jesús Muñoz, longtime ranch hand and friend, had happened upon the crash and yanked the door from its hinges. Clark's feet were entangled in the two rudder panels, jammed beneath the engine. As Muñoz struggled to pull Clark free, fuel spilled over both men. Finally, pulling with all of his strength, Muñoz tugged Clark from the wreckage.

Clark remained unconscious for an hour-and-a-half before waking in the intensive care unit at a hospital forty-five minutes from the scene. While his sons watched, he cautiously moved his legs and feet, rotated his fingers and arms, and winced at the sharp pain in his shoulder and head. He offered thanks to God that he had survived, that he had been alone on the flight, and then he made a decision: He would no longer delay building the chapel. That brush with death, said Clark, was "a little wake-up call in my life. . . . God's wake-up call." [1]

"Look," he says, "I'm no Saint Paul, but the incident helped me decide to go ahead and build the chapel." Within a few years, the chapel, financed solely by Clark, was completed on top of a grassy hill at the entrance to his ranch. Incorporating a surplus ceiling and stone remnants from the William Randolph Hearst collection at nearby San Simeon and containing sacred art collected by Bill and Joan from fourteenth- to seventeenth-century European monasteries, the chapel hosts a number of religious services and cultural events throughout the year. "Chapel Hill", as it is known locally, is open to those of all

---

[1] Clark, "Alumni Spotlight/Q&A", *Vista Magazine*, p. 19.

faiths and is the pride of the local community, to which Clark has donated it.

Clark has come full circle. He started life as a young man on a California ranch, and now closes it as a man in his seventies on a California ranch, where he proudly struggles with the progression of Parkinson's disease. "God gave Parkinson's to such saints as John Paul II and my father," he said, "and now he has gotten around to the sinners, such as myself."

These sunset years are a time for reflecting on the past, as well as for accepting what lies ahead. Though not without some regrets, Judge Clark may be allowed a proper amount of satisfaction in his public record. During the Sacramento years, Clark was appointed Governor Reagan's chief of staff at a time of scandal and crisis and helped to right the ship of state. When he thought his work done, he decided it was time to return to his ranch. The Governor then named him superior court judge, later elevated him to the court of appeal and, finally, appointed him justice of the California Supreme Court. After Reagan ascended to the presidency, he requested that Clark go with him to Washington, where Clark became his deputy secretary of state, then national security advisor and, lastly, secretary of the interior.

Official Reagan biographer Edmund Morris dubbed Clark the "most impressive" advisor in the Reagan White House and "the most important and influential person in the first administration". An August 1983 *Time* magazine cover story entitled "The Man with the President's Ear", informed the public that next to Reagan, Clark was the "most powerful man in the White House", so close to Reagan, and so loyal to and trusted by the President, that White House staff called him Uncle Bill.[2]

"He was always there when my Dad needed him", says the former President's oldest son, Michael. "He was very important to my dad's career. And their relationship was more than political; they were good friends."[3]

President Reagan himself told the press that Clark was "one of my most trusted and valued advisers."[4] Again, "no one has given me more

---

[2] Maureen Dowd, "The Man with the President's Ear", *Time*, August 8, 1983.

[3] Interview with Michael Reagan, May 9, 2005.

[4] Ronald Reagan, "Remarks Announcing the Appointment of Robert C. McFarlane as Assistant to the President for National Security Affairs", *Public Papers of the Presidents of the United States: Ronald Reagan*, October 17, 1983, p. 1471.

faithful service above and beyond the call of duty." [5] When Reagan had a tough task, he called upon Clark, his troubleshooter, his right-hand man.[6] As photographs illustrate, Bill Clark was often literally at Reagan's right side, and always trying to fulfill the adage that he coined, "Let Reagan be Reagan." No one was more inclined to let Reagan act on his instincts.

Nowhere was this more true than in determining policy in regard to the Soviet Union. During two critical years as Reagan's national security advisor, Clark helped lay the groundwork for the administration's remarkable effort to undermine Soviet communism and win the Cold War. Another cover story at the time, in the *New York Times Magazine*, noted that Clark was not only "the most influential foreign-policy figure in the Reagan administration", but also "the president's chief instrument" in confronting Soviet influence in the world. The two of them, often alone, met to discuss some of the boldest and most successful actions of the entire Cold War. As the *New York Times'* White House correspondent reported, colleagues observed Clark returning from his private meetings with Reagan and prepared themselves for the "important decisions" to come.[7]

Roger W. Robinson, Jr., a senior staff member at Clark's National Security Council, stated categorically: "More than any others, Ronald Reagan and Bill Clark won the Cold War. Period." [8] Thomas C. Reed,

---

[5] Reagan wrote this to Clark in a February 8, 1985 letter on White House letterhead.

[6] Floyd Brown, who is West Coast director of the Young America's Foundation, which owns and manages the Reagan Ranch, notes that next to Nancy Reagan, Clark was Reagan's "single closest friend and confidant—and everyone knows that! ... Whenever the president had a tough job, look who got it—Bill Clark." Peter Dailey, a Reagan-appointed U.S. Ambassador to Ireland who has known Clark since high school, agrees: "Whenever the going got tough, Reagan always wanted Bill Clark around." Interviews with Floyd Brown, October 5, 2005, and with Peter Dailey, January 17, 2006.

[7] The article stated: "Colleagues observe Mr. Clark ambling back from his private meetings with Mr. Reagan and wonder what important decisions are coming that might catch them by surprise." Steven R. Weisman, "The Influence of William Clark", *New York Times Magazine*, August 14, 1983.

[8] Interview with Roger Robinson, June 6 and 8 and July 7, 2005. Robinson adds: "That's not to say that Cap Weinberger, Bill Casey, Ed Meese, Jeane Kirkpatrick and others were not major, integral players.... There were many who were crucial to this huge enterprise. But at the end of the day you really had to rely on Bill to carry the water with the president. The extraordinary relationship and implicit trust between these two men was the force multiplier that implemented a secret multipronged strategy that led to the collapse of the Soviet Union and its empire. No question about it." Interviews with Roger Robinson, June 6 and 8, 2005.

another NSC staff member, agrees that Clark was "utterly essential" to the strategy to prevail over the USSR. He says that Clark "put the pieces in place to bring the Cold War to a conclusion.... Clark was absolutely key to that."[9] Norman A. Bailey, yet another NSC staffer, went so far as to say that America "owes a very great debt" to Clark, who "did more than any other individual to help the President change the course of history and put an end to an empire that was, indeed, 'the embodiment of evil.' "[10] Ronald Reagan himself told Clark at the height of the Cold War: "All of us owe you a great debt.... Thanks for being there, as you always are."[11]

And yet, the indispensable Clark became the forgotten man—as Edmund Morris recorded, "so private, quiet, and unflamboyant that he's now largely forgotten".[12] He was forgotten in part because he never promoted himself. Said former Secretary of Defense and long-time Reagan aide Caspar Weinberger: "He was one of the most influential people in Washington, enormously important to Reagan's goals and success, as governor and then as president, but you'd never hear that from Bill or even know it in the way he acted."[13]

Reagan biographer Lou Cannon also remarked on Clark's self-effacing nature. "[Clark] did more for Reagan ... while calling less attention to himself than anyone else I know."[14] In its 50th anniversary issue, *National Review* listed Clark among a select group of leading "unsung conservatives", while emphasizing that Clark was "the most significant Reagan ally not to have written a memoir".[15]

What is the reason Clark has neglected to record his accomplishments for posterity? Clark is the prototypical man of the West who one day saddled his horse and drifted off into the sunset, exiting Washington with no fanfare and no one watching.

---

[9] Interview with Tom Reed, April 6, 2005.

[10] Norman A. Bailey, *The Strategic Plan That Won the Cold War: National Security Decision Directive 75* (McLean, VA: The Potomac Foundation, 1999), p. i.

[11] This November 7, 1983 statement from Reagan on White House letterhead is held by Clark in his files.

[12] Edmund Morris interviewed by *The American Enterprise*, November/December 1999.

[13] Interview with Cap Weinberger, April 14, 2005.

[14] Cannon quoted in: "Unsung Conservatives: Fifteen Who Made a Difference", *National Review*, December 19, 2005, p. 33.

[15] "Unsung Conservatives: Fifteen Who Made a Difference", *National Review*, December 19, 2005, p. 33.

As he had no interest in promoting himself, Clark's contributions have not been fully reported. Many of his actions in the 1980s have remained secret, particularly his Cold War communications with Pope John Paul II and his meetings with Margaret Thatcher, François Mitterrand, Saddam Hussein, and others.

Bill Clark and his mission have gone unheralded, which was the way he wanted it. At long last, this is the story.

CHAPTER I

The Clarks of Ventura County

The story of William Patrick Clark must begin with his California pioneering family of ranchers and lawmen. As Irish Catholic immigrants, the Clarks found more in common with the native Californio[1] culture than that of the sedate English Protestant immigrants to the area. Like their Californio *amigos*, the Clarks, men and women alike, were more at home on horses than on the ground, more given to competing in rodeos than growing the largest pumpkin for the annual county fair.

Clark's paternal grandfather, a man he admired from his earliest years, was named for the Irish patriot Robert Emmet, who led the notoriously unsuccessful rebellion against British rule in 1803. Following his arrest, the twenty-five-year-old Protestant was hanged, drawn, and quartered, which might have passed unnoticed but for his speech at the dock, recited to this day by the school children of Ireland: "When my country takes her place among the nations of the earth, then and only then let my epitaph be written."

One of the many epitaphs for Robert Emmett Clark of Ventura County, California can be found in a 1964 issue of *PC: The Weekly Magazine of Ventura County*. The title itself encapsulates the public life of Bill Clark's grandfather: "Cattleman, Poor Man, Coachman, Sheriff, Ranger, Marshal, Living Myth."[2]

---

[1] Californio: A person of Spanish descent living in California before the discovery of gold and the subsequent arrival of the Americans and others.

[2] The cover photograph, taken in 1921, features the newly elected sheriff and "pioneer Ventura County lawman" in white hat, bandana, leather chaps, fringed leather cuffs, sitting

Known for being honest and playing by the rules, Robert "Bob" Clark initially hailed from Fair Play, Wisconsin. Throughout his life, he made much of the name of his birthplace and the date of his birth, 1876, the centennial of his country's founding. He wore his patriotism as proudly as did the Irish national hero for whom he was named. Each Clark residence was incomplete until the flagpole was in place and Bob had initiated the daily American flag ceremony.

Bob's grandfather, Bernard Clarken, emigrated from Ireland in 1858, leaving behind painful memories of the Great Famine and the death of his young wife. Bernard and children Michael Hugh, Thomas, and Winefred went to Liverpool, England, and boarded the Calhoun, bound for the United States, determined to establish a better life in the new country. The family found its way to New Diggins, Wisconsin, where the Clarkens became the Clarks.

Within a few years of their arrival, Michael Hugh was inducted into the Union Army, captured shortly thereafter, and spent the duration of the Civil War in, as one family member described it, a hellhole of a prison camp.[3] On his release at war's end in 1865, he returned to Wisconsin and married his sweetheart, Margaret Lynch. Margaret gave birth to ten children, eight of whom survived to adulthood, including youngest son, Robert Emmett Clark.

Michael Hugh's younger brother, Thomas, was the first sibling to head west, eventually settling in the Ojai Valley, eighty miles north of Los Angeles.[4] According to historian Yda Addis Storke, the Clarks were the fourth American family to arrive in the area.

---

at a card table behind a stack of poker chips; his left hand was in possession of the infamous Dead Man's hand, while his right hand rested on his lap in possession of a six-shooter. His lips are pursed, his eyes stare directly ahead. He means business—as he did throughout his career as a lawman—but it was business always leavened by humor, as the photo implies.

[3] Interview with Clare Clark Whitley, 1984. One branch of the family is certain that Michael Hugh's incarceration was in Andersonville; another, that he was repeatedly inducted into the Union Army in various recruiting centers, collecting the $300 bounty each time. If so, he would have served his time as a Union prisoner of war. There seems to be no concrete evidence either way; however, the latter scenario would understandably be shrouded in the mists of history.

[4] Ojai is actually west of Los Angeles—very confusing to those who do not understand the peculiar geography of the state. As it "seems" to be north—about as close to the coastline as is Los Angeles—we bow to common perception in this description.

Michael Hugh followed his brother shortly after the completion of the transcontinental railroad. By 1881, he had earned enough money to establish a home and send for his family. Wife Margaret with their seven children arrived at the railroad terminus in the town of Newhall, from where their journey was recommenced by stagecoach. Thus, little Bob first experienced California by stagecoach, a mode of transportation that would one day become his livelihood, but not until he first herded cattle and worked a ranch.

Bob Grows Up

By his early twenties, Bob Clark was driving the stage himself, accompanied by the occasional passenger, a six-gun, and the six horses that pulled his coach over the old Casitas Pass Road between Ojai and Santa Barbara, back in the days when the only passersby were mountain lions, rattlesnakes, and the occasional bandit. Each day was an adventure, given the narrow dirt roads carved along rushing rivers and steep mountainsides. Frequently, the already treacherous byways were washed out by mudslides. Even so, Bob delivered the U.S. mail in timely fashion.

Bob's escapades made their way into bestselling books, including those of Harold Bell Wright, and fired the imaginations not only of his grandson Bill, but also of a boy in Dixon, Illinois, named Ronald Wilson Reagan. In 1922, the eleven-year-old Reagan read a book by Wright titled *That Printer of Udell's*. The moment he finished the novel, young Ronald set it down and told his mother that he wanted to be "like that man" in the book and be baptized. More than fifty years after reading *Udell's*, Reagan reminisced that it and other books from his youth left him with "an abiding belief in the triumph of good over evil". These books, he said, contained "heroes who lived by standards of morality and fair play"—men like Fair Play Bob.[5]

On his stagecoach route Fair Play Bob met many prominent people of the day, including John D. Rockefeller, Andrew Carnegie, Mrs. James A. Garfield, President William Howard Taft's sister, and Senator Mark Hanna's daughter, but he found none as impressive as a pretty girl from Missouri named Alice Barnett.

---

[5] See Paul Kengor, *God and Ronald Reagan: A Spiritual Life* (New York: ReganBooks, 2004), pp. 18–19.

Born in 1886, Miss Barnett was ten years younger than Bob. The shy, serious young lady was thought to have contracted tuberculosis while training to become a nurse in St. Louis. Alice's worried parents sent her all the way to California, with her sister, Clara, as chaperone, to recover her health. After disembarking from the train in the Ojai Valley, Clara asked to ride on the seat with the dashing stagecoach driver.[6] Bob did not turn her down, but it was Alice, huddled miserably inside the coach, who caught his eye.

Alice's parents were not sure which shocked them more: their daughter's rapid recovery or the fact she had learned to ride a horse "clothespin-style". When Alice informed them that she wanted to marry this wild cowboy named Bob, they were distressed.[7] Frantic letters poured westward, but to no avail. Alice and Bob wed three months later at Mission San Gabriel.

The union of Bob and Alice added another branch to Bill Clark's colorful lineage. According to family lore, Alice's ancestry included such personages as Martha Custis Washington, Robert E. Lee, and John Wilkes Booth, thereby linking Bill Clark to some of the seminal and most traumatic moments in American history: the nation's founding and its near undoing.[8]

Bob the Ranger

Alice decided that Bob's vocation was a bit risky for the future father of her children. Bob agreed, and became one of the first forest rangers hired for Teddy Roosevelt's new U.S. Forest Service. This was hardly a move in a safe direction. The federal rangers, embodying the spirit and constitution of the Rough-Rider-turned-President they proudly served, were charged with the duty of bringing law and order to the

---

[6] Interview with William Pettit Clark, conducted October 12, 1979, by the Ventura County Historical Museum.

[7] Pat Clark Doerner, "The Life and Times of Judge Bill Clark", Presentation to Ventura County Republican Hall of Fame, June 1, 2000. Alice's parents were especially upset that they had not been informed of their prospective son-in-law's last name and that he had not the presence of mind to write to them "concerning the matter" himself.

[8] While these links remain undocumented, they were set in concrete by Bill Clark's great aunt, Clara Barnett Hoeller. "Aunt Clara", a devout Daughter of the Confederacy, was particularly proud of the connection to John Wilkes Booth.

Wild West. Bob's first assignment, and his and Alice's first home, was the dusty, chaparral-covered Saugus-Castaic area of Los Angeles County.

Bob met Roosevelt when the President's Great White Fleet anchored in Santa Barbara for the Fourth of July celebration in 1908.[9] Later TR gave Bob a pearl-handled Colt .45 revolver called the Peacemaker in appreciation for service against lawlessness, especially in temporarily suspending the Jenkins-Chormicle feud in his first assignment as a ranger.

Mr. Jenkins and Mr. Chormicle and their kin had been fighting over cattle rustling, mining rights, water rights, grazing rights, and rights to roadways. Bob explained the situation this way:

> The chief feuders weren't complicated. Jenkins was a great knife-thrower, always wore a vest with a throwing knife in a holster under it. He generally rode in a buggy and let his six-shooter lie on the seat beside him. Old man Chormicle was an uncomplicated fellow, too. He wore two six-guns and usually carried a rifle in case any argument started at long range.[10]

The bickering led to more than twenty deaths between the two families, so Bob "tried out [his] guns for some of the people up there".[11] The antagonists were dutifully impressed with his sharp shooting and decided they should end their hostilities. The legendary story set an unforgettable example of "peace through strength" for grandson Bill.

Bob the Sheriff

Bob resigned from the forest service in 1914 to return to the land, running cattle on the Casitas Ranch and in the Ventura back country; but in 1922 he was urged to run for sheriff of Ventura County. The previous elected sheriff had been shot dead.[12]

---

[9] Interview with William Pettit Clark, conducted October 12, 1979. Other accounts say that Bob took the train to Washington to meet with TR.

[10] Quote published in article on Bob Clark: "Cattleman, Poor Man, Coachman, Sheriff; Ranger, Marshal, Living Myth", *PC: The Weekly Magazine of Ventura County*, March 21, 1964, p. 3.

[11] "A Living Legend of the Old West", *Fortnight: California's Own Newsmagazine*, May 5, 1954, page 5.

[12] Interview with William Pettit Clark, conducted October 12, 1979. Patricia Clark Callachor, "The Sheriffs of Ventura County", *Ventura County Historical Society Quarterly*, vol. 30, no. 4, p. 5.

Bob won the election in a landslide. His eleven years as county sheriff coincided with Prohibition, which made Bob's job even livelier and could have made him a lot richer, if he had compromised his principles. As sheriff, Bob rounded up hundreds of bootleggers. He also apprehended seventeen murderers.

Bob Clark was not only handy with his gun but also with his fists. His steely blue eyes could stare down any gangster. These gifts came in handy while cleaning up the infamous "China Alley". This lawless section of Oxnard was full of criminals, prostitutes, violence, and opium. It seemed as though there was a murder there every Saturday night.[13] One evening in February 1926, Sheriff Clark descended on China Alley with the district attorney, fifty search warrants, and his pearl-handled revolver. Bob refrained from firing his gun, but later confessed to using the lesser end of his pistol when someone held a knife to his chest, nicking the skin several times, attempting to convince him of "the merits of looking the other way". As Bob later related, "I had to bop him over the head with that old gun."[14] When the operation was over, there were seventy-two new residents in the Ventura County jail.

In July 1933, Franklin Delano Roosevelt tapped Clark to serve as U.S. marshal for the District of Southern California. In that role, Bob busted more bootleggers, murderers, and mobsters. In one particularly colorful case, he boarded Tony Cornero's floating casino and tossed all the slot machines into the ocean before turning the ship over to the Coast Guard.

One of Bob Clark's traits that most impressed his grandson Bill was the respectful way he treated his prisoners. "He was", says Bill "tremendously humane to his prisoners; he treated them with kindness and dignity, refusing to handcuff them, instead relying on their integrity as human beings."

One day while transporting prisoners to San Quentin, Bob Clark's charity came full circle. The automobile he was driving careened out of control, rolled over an embankment, and caught fire. Marshal Clark was knocked unconscious. The prisoners, because they were not manacled to the interior of the car, were able to free themselves; but, rather than escape, they pulled Bob from the car, saving his life.

---

[13] Interview with William Pettit Clark, conducted October 12, 1979.
[14] *Fortnight*, p. 5.

As a little boy, Bill was often his grandfather's companion when after Sunday Mass he visited the Ventura County jail to have breakfast with the inmates. Bill enjoyed their white rice pudding with raisins and brown sugar, and the prisoners seemed gratified by the boy's presence as well as the sheriff's implicit trust in them.

In 1949, Bob retired to an orange and avocado ranch in Santa Paula, just over the hill from Ojai. At last, wrote a local scribe, he could retire in peace, having given the "city bads" a dose of his "vigorous brand of justice; all of which made him a legend in his day and allowed him to bask in his past."[15]

Bob the Survivor

Looking back, it seems providential that Bob survived all he did, never tumbling to his doom down a mountainside or stumbling to his death from a bullet to the back in China Alley. Perhaps it was God's protection that saved him. As his grandson would say, it was part of the "DP"—the Divine Plan—that Bob always lived for another day, spending his final days in peaceful retirement.

In Memoriam

After Bob's death in 1956, Grandmother Alice gave Bill his grandfather's prayer book, a gift to the marshal from the Reverend John J. Cantwell, Archbishop of Los Angeles. As he was paging through, Bill noticed one particularly well-worn page, the corners yellowed by Bob's nicotine-stained fingertips. On it was this prayer:

> O my God, I constantly refer all my actions to your greater glory and suffer willingly whatever you shall appoint. . . .
> Lord, please enlighten my understanding. . . .
> Grant that I be not puffed up with pride. . . .
> Let me always remember to be submissive to my superiors, humble to my inferiors, faithful to my friends and charitable to my enemies. . . .

---

[15] Quote taken from cover story in PC: The Weekly Magazine of Ventura County, March 21, 1964, p. 3.

O my God, make me prudent in my undertakings, courageous in dangers, patient in afflictions, and humble in prosperity....

Help me to obtain holiness of life by sincere confession of my sins, by devout reception of the Body of Christ, by a continual recollection of mind, and by a pure intention of heart.

The words so captured his grandfather's spirit that Bill had them reproduced onto small prayer cards with a handsome crimson border and a tiny photo of Marshal Bob in his trademark look—black western hat and tie. The title has been amended by Bill to: "Prayer of Clement XI and Robert Emmett Clark". A stack of these cards sits in Clark's law office in Paso Robles, available to anyone who passes by. He distributes them at family gatherings and at religious services on Chapel Hill.

Bob served nearly forty years as a lawman. He is remembered by the United States Marshals Service as "one of the West's most colorful and widely known early law enforcement officers" and "the last of the Frontier Marshals".[16]

The First Bill Clark: William Pettit Clark

Among Bob and Alice's ten offspring was another lawman: William Pettit Clark, a future Ventura County deputy sheriff, under-sheriff, and City of Oxnard police chief.[17] Born in Ojai in 1907, he was named for his maternal great grandfather, William McAfee Pettit, a pioneer doctor of southeast Missouri who was killed by a shotgun blast to the chest by a man he had "thrashed" for beating a crippled slave the previous day.[18]

"Bill Sr." began his formal education in the Santa Ana School in a rural area of Ventura County now under the man-made Lake Casitas.[19] There were fourteen students in the school, and all relied on

---

[16] See "Last of the Frontier Marshals", on the website of the U.S. Department of Justice.

[17] Note: Despite what has been reported elsewhere, William Pettit was never a full sheriff. The sheriff position was an elected position. He did run for the position once, but lost to Sheriff Bill Suytar.

[18] Interview with William Pettit Clark, conducted October 12, 1979; additional information from Pat Clark Doerner archives.

[19] Ojai's William Pettit was known as "Bill" and was often (and still is) mistakenly referred to as "Bill Clark Sr.", an easy mistake given that his abbreviated name reads "William P. Clark", just like his son's. That said, to mitigate confusion, this book will likewise refer to the elder Bill as "Bill Sr.".

horses for transportation, as did Sue Beam, their teacher, who boarded at the Clark home. Bill Sr. finished the eighth grade across the river at Mill School when he was thirteen, graduating, as he told his children, at the head of his class, later confessing with a grin that he was the *only* person in his class.

As a teen, Bill Sr. herded cattle in the lonely back country of Ventura County, a line of work that included plenty of adventure. One day thirteen-year-old Bill Sr. and *vaqueros* John Dent and Felipe Melandrez were moving cattle from the low country up to better grazing on the Alamar, a long expanse of meadowlands across the county line into Santa Barbara County. They were in the highest part of the mountains, an isolated area near the headwaters of the Sespe River. "We had about forty head of horses in a string, so we were going to stay there", said Bill later. The problem was that they were clean out of supplies. So, John was selected to go to town; Felipe had a toothache and considered joining him. Bill Sr. said he would be okay alone and told the pair to go ahead.[20]

The next day, a brush and timber fire, driven by an east wind, broke out in the mountains. Felipe and John could not get back in to help their stranded partner. Bill Sr.'s father had advised him that if ever he were caught in a fire, snowstorm, or flood, if he was in a safe place, he should stay put. "Do not try to move, because you'll get in trouble", was Ranger Bob's advice.

Word spread that Clark was in danger. His father, however, spoke of his son with confidence: "Don't worry about it. Bill will find a safe place and he'll never move." He didn't. Bill spent ten days in that spot, next to a stream with a pool of water. He ate fish and the remaining cheese and tortillas until it was safe to ride out.

Bill Sr. spent four years at Ventura High School, where he was elected class president and captain of the 1925 football team, a record that won him a scholarship to St. Mary's College in the San Francisco Bay area. He received some serious injuries playing ball for St. Mary's, and after three years there he was forced to withdraw from the team, thus losing his scholarship. He was not devastated by the loss, for it allowed him to return to his first love: working cattle in Ventura County.

---

[20] Interview with William Pettit Clark, conducted October 12, 1979.

"The only thing I ever thought about from the time I was knee-high to a grasshopper", he said, "was getting into the cow business or working with cattle. When I got out of college that's where I headed." [21]

But not right away. His father, Bob, called upon him, in an emergency situation, to become his deputy in the Ventura County sheriff's office. He resisted—he wanted ranch work—but he fulfilled his father's request, as he had always done.

For three years, Bill Sr. worked as Bob's deputy and with distinction. During that time, in 1932, he helped capture Fulton Green, an escapee from the Arkansas State Penitentiary and one of America's ten most wanted men. He went through Green's front door unannounced and met him face to face. Green reached for his gun, but was grabbed from behind by one of Bill Sr.'s fellow lawmen.[22] Green was lucky: Lawman Clark, like his father before him, was a good shot. Also like his father, he never killed a man.[23]

A Ranch and a Family

For Bill Sr. this was a time not only for a new career but also for a new life entirely. In high school, he had dated Bernice Gregory, and they had stayed in a close relationship, even as they attended separate colleges. They married in January 1931 at Mission San Buenaventura, and their first child, William Patrick Clark, was born on the following October 23. He was followed by two daughters: Molly in 1933 and Cynthia in 1935.

Bill Sr. Heads to the Ranch

When his father was appointed U.S. marshal in Los Angeles in 1933, Bill Sr. left the deputy post to become under-sheriff of Ventura County. "I enjoyed it," he said later, "but I was always looking over the [barbed-wire] fence." [24]

---

[21] Ibid.

[22] Dave White, "The Clark Family", PC: The Weekly Magazine of Ventura County, August 19, 1973.

[23] Quote taken from cover story in PC: The Weekly Magazine of Ventura County, March 21, 1964, p. 3.

[24] Interview with William Pettit Clark, conducted October 12, 1979.

Then one day in 1937 Bill Charnley, an eastern stockbroker who wintered in Ojai, walked into the sheriff's office and announced, "Well, I got my ranch. Are you ready to go to work?" Clark asked: "When do you want me to start?" Charnley replied: "Tomorrow." The under-sheriff announced he was resigning and starting a ranching job the next morning.[25]

Bill Sr. and owner Bill Charnley ran cattle on the Chismahoo Ranch and on National Forest land until the 1940s, when the government claimed the heart of "the most beautiful ranch in Ventura County", as Bill Sr. called it, for a portion of its impending water preservation project, damming up the Ventura River to form Lake Casitas. Charn-ley sold what was left of the ranch to a group that renamed the remaining territory the Coca Cola Ranch. He died shortly thereafter.

While working the Chismahoo, Bill Sr. became involved in Ran-cheros Visitadores, the invitation-only men's riding group that makes an annual week-long, sixty-mile trek through the Santa Ynez Valley ranch land after assembling at Mission Santa Ynez. The first ride was organized in 1930 by John J. Mitchell, who owned a twelve-thousand-acre ranch along the Santa Ynez River. After being a guest at the elite Bohemian Grove north of San Francisco, Mitchell wanted to create a horseback version of the men's camp experience. It was the perfect solution for the "old-timers", as Bill Sr. called them, who longed for the "good old days" when there were no fences, and neighbors rode from ranch to ranch helping one another gather and brand cattle. It was a period of time that engendered a camaraderie that none wished to lose, but with the changing times, it was slipping away.

In 1933 Bob Clark, with Adolfo Camarillo, helped found Campo Adolfo, one of the oldest camps in Rancheros. Bill Sr. made his first ride in 1937 and was quickly voted trail boss. He completed over forty rides, holding "probably every office there is to hold", while repeatedly winning most of the Rancheros awards for horsemanship.

At the time of the breakup of Chismahoo Ranch, Bernice's uncle L. D. Fox called with a question similar to Bill Charnley's: "You want to get on a ranch? Come up here and I'll help you out.... You run the ranch. I want to go fishing." Fox was calling from Tehama County, about 130 miles from Sacramento.

---

[25] Ibid.

Together, Clark and Fox purchased Tehama County's Battle Creek Ranch, on the fertile floor of the Sacramento Valley. Their total operation, including the summer range and leased federal land, covered sixty thousand acres with an "appropriate complement" of sheep and cattle. Eventually, Bill Sr. bought out Fox's interest. It was a "super ranch", Bill Sr. later reflected.[26] The years on the Chismahoo, on Battle Creek, on the summer range, were idyllic not only for Bill Sr. but for his children as well.

Different Pastures

Ten years of ranching had passed when one day in 1947 a forest ranger drove thirty miles through the mountains in a pickup to say there was an emergency call for Bill Clark. "I was afraid something had happened to some of the family", Bill later related. He rushed to the ranger station to find that the call was from old friend Ed Carty, the mayor of Oxnard, offering Bill Sr. the job of chief of police. Carty told him: "We're having trouble with our police department. Will you come down and take over?" As Clark mulled it over, Bob Livingston got on the phone to encourage the right answer, followed by Bill's close friend Bob Doud. "Well," said Bill Sr., "I'll go see what the family thinks about it."[27]

The Divine Plan must have been in order, for Bill Sr. had just received what he considered "a real good offer" for the range and cattle. Additionally, the ranch was not doing well, nor providing the living Bill Sr. wished for his family. He laid out everything to the family and said, "You think about it and talk it over, and tomorrow at breakfast time we'll have a vote—by secret ballot." In his mind, Bill Sr. surveyed the voters: He knew his son loved ranch life, but his son had already announced that he wanted to study law. He knew if Bill Jr. was to realize that goal, he needed to upgrade his high school education to college preparatory level.

Bill Sr. made five ballots and declared he would not vote unless there was a tie. There was no tie; although his heart wasn't in it, Bill

---

[26] Ibid.

[27] White, "The Clark Family", *PC: The Weekly Magazine of Ventura County*, August 19, 1973; and Interview with William Pettit Clark, conducted October 12, 1979.

Jr. voted with the ladies to return to family, old friends, and educational opportunity in Oxnard.[28]

Oxnard's New Police Chief

Bill Sr. stepped into a difficult position: the three previous police chiefs, as he later put it, "had gotten fouled up".[29] They had been receiving payoffs in exchange for "looking the other way" when the law was broken in Oxnard. With corruption in the police department to sweep clean and a staff of eighteen police officers to sort out, William Pettit Clark went to work "practically 24 hours a day".[30]

One day the new police chief was walking down the boulevard with Dan Davidson, a "great old-timer". Davidson pointed to a black Cadillac: "Bill, that fellow over there is one of the guys." The individual ran a house of ill repute, which the police chief's crew had shut down the night before, apprehending five prostitutes.

Chief Clark confronted the man: "We knocked over your house last night. You're through in Oxnard and you might just as well pack up and get out. Things are going to be different around here." As Bill later related, "We never saw him in Oxnard again."[31]

There were other well-known lawbreakers, such as Sol Finklestein, alias Charlie King, who had gotten into trouble in New York and had fled to California. King was trying to consolidate and control crime in and around Oxnard. He had bribed local officials, including police chiefs, in the past and approached Clark's deputy telling him there was plenty of money for everyone, including Chief Clark. Everyone on "The Hill", as King referred to the courthouse, was on the take, he said, and he was the guy providing the goods.

Clark saw King's offer coming and made a quick run to Sacramento before King had the chance to act. He met with Governor Earl Warren, future chief justice of the U.S. Supreme Court, whom Clark knew well. "I told him what was up", said Clark. "I didn't tell him who was involved, but I told him I was going to get an

---

[28] Ibid.
[29] Interview with William Pettit Clark, conducted October 12, 1979.
[30] Ibid.
[31] Ibid.

offer." Governor Warren sent Clark to Warren Olney, secretary of the crime commission.

Clark drove to San Francisco and met with the shrewd Olney, who warned that once King was charged with bribery, his defense attorney—Jerry Geisler, a famous criminal lawyer of the period who represented Marilyn Monroe in her divorce from Joe DiMaggio, as well as Lana Turner in the stabbing of Johnny Stompanato[32]—would stroll into the courtroom and contend that Clark had eagerly agreed to take the money but at the last minute got cold feet and backed out. Olney told Clark to return to his Oxnard office and write down every detail of any future meetings with King.[33]

Clark did just that. Not long after, King entered Clark's office and handed him three thousand dollars in twenty-dollar bills, adding, "I'll guarantee you seventy-five thousand a year as long as you don't knock over any of my places. After we get started, there is no limit to where we can go." The taciturn Clark responded, "Well, Mr. King, you play your game and I'll play mine",[34] as a photographer stepped out of a closet and snapped a photo. A stenographer stepped from another closet, having recorded every word. King was placed under arrest.

Clark put together a case and took it to the district attorney, who brought charges against King. He was put on trial, convicted, and served a lengthy term.

California Pioneers

The descendants of Bernard and Anne Clarken were among the California pioneer families that built Ventura County and the surrounding area. There was Marshal Bob's brother Tom, who was a county supervisor for a record thirty-two years, beginning in 1904, during which time he built the roads in Ventura County. A world record established by Tom was the best time for four-abreast chariot racing—achieved in 1926. An equally impressive equestrian was Bob's sister Peg, regarded for her bravery and as the Mother of Horsemanship at

---

[32] Interview with Dan McGovern, April 1, 2005.
[33] Interview with William Pettit Clark, conducted October 12, 1979.
[34] Ibid.

the prestigious Thacher School of Ojai, where she taught for thirty-five years starting in 1908. She shocked the locals by riding astride (divided skirt)—and ran her own riding stable, which she operated successfully for years. Peg spoke several Indian dialects and knew the backcountry as well as anyone.[35]

Bill Sr. once said of these early Clarks and their cousins: "At one time ... [they] owned practically all of the upper Ojai valley." [36] They were brave, law-abiding, and patriotic. They constituted, as Ronald Reagan described his own upbringing, Bill Clark's "inheritance". These people and places forged Bill Clark into the boy, the man, and the public figure he eventually became.

---

[35] Pat Clark Doerner, "Horsemen of the Ojai", September 2004.

[36] At the least, they owned much of it, along with a few other early families. Interview with William Pettit Clark, conducted October 12, 1979.

CHAPTER 2

Influence and Inspiration

William Clark Jr. was born at the height of the Great Depression on October 23, 1931. Growing up, he and his two younger sisters were unaware of the money shortages that must have troubled their parents. Country living allowed the family to be largely self-sufficient, producing its own milk, butter, beef, pork, and vegetables.

Clark's mother had studied journalism at the University of Southern California. On her return to Ventura County, she worked as court clerk, then in the law offices of Judge Walter Fourt. When she and Bill Sr. married, she exchanged a career and the comforts of small-town life to play the part of pioneer wife—riding the range, canning fruits and vegetables, and cooking on a wood stove. After a long day of hard work, she would find refuge in her treasured *New Yorker*, often by light of a kerosene lamp.

While the family was living on the Chismahoo Ranch in the Santa Ana Valley, across the river from Ventura proper, young Bill went to first grade in the two-room schoolhouse his father had attended. This institution of six grades and forty students was staffed by one school marm, Sue Beam Edwards, who had taught Clark's father, aunts, and uncles. Bill Jr. rode Dynamite, the first horse of his own, to school and back.

Bernice had not been raised Catholic, as her husband had, but she converted to join him in his faith, with the promise to raise their children as Catholics. When the children reached school age, she oversaw their education and motivated them to work hard and aim high. She joined the local school board and did what she could to improve the educational opportunities at Santa Ana School.

With the help of a local government representative, Bernice planned a field trip to the State Capitol in Sacramento. It was an ambitious plan for the small, rural school, but she made it happen. The tour guide for the group of twenty students was the executive secretary to Governor Olson—a job Bill Jr. would one day hold with Governor Reagan. As for the tour guide himself, a friendly young man named Stanley Mosk, he would later be Bill's colleague and friend on the California Supreme Court. The kids from Santa Ana School not only learned the workings of state government, but also enjoyed their first restaurant meal and elevator ride.

Introducing country children to the political process might have been out of the ordinary for the time, but it was not out of character for Bernice Clark. She and her husband were Democrats, Jeffersonian Democrats. While Bill Sr. was quiet in his choice of political affiliation, Bernice embraced her beliefs with great vigor. She became involved in the Ventura County Democratic Party, heading it occasionally, and would continue to be a devoted Democrat after her son moved to the Republican Party.

A true Californian, Bernice appreciated the Californio culture and was fluent in the Spanish language. She consistently battled bigotry, particularly against those of Spanish heritage. One small example: during World War II, she studied the list of draftees published in the local newspaper and concluded that a disproportionately high number of men with Spanish surnames were being drafted. Angry, she appeared before the Ventura County draft board to issue a complaint, no doubt with effectiveness.

She was "a natural leader", says Ventura County's Richard Doerner, who once served with Bernice on a jury in a murder case. There was no question who would be foreman, he recalls: "She was the strongest person in the group."

A natural leader given to outspoken pronouncements does not make for the tenderest of mothers. "She was a good mother," says Bill, "but she was not a warm person." While he recalls his mother's strong personality, he also remembers her talent for words. "She could turn a phrase as well as anyone—a brilliant woman and a wit", he says. Yet that wit was often used to devastating effect, deflecting attempts to establish close relationships—with everyone—everyone but her beloved husband.

For reasons unknown to Clark, his mother had not been raised by her parents, but by her maternal grandparents, who brought her to Ventura from Portland when she was five years of age. "I know she had a difficult childhood", he says, adding he regrets he never was able to learn much about it. Although he often attempted to have a closer relationship with his mother, it proved to be difficult, even to the time of Bernice's death.

While Bernice would not discuss her own childhood, she was happy to speak of her more distant ancestors: William Johnson who fought on the side of independence in the Revolutionary War, and Johnson descendant L. D. Roberts who laid the first plat for the town of Ojai. She was not only proud of but grateful to the grandfather who raised her, J. B. Fox, who moved north to Oregon in 1907, when the town of Nordhoff (Ojai) became too crowded for his comfort.[1] It was the failure of his business ventures in Fremont that prompted his move back to Ventura County, with little Bernice and wife, Rebecca.

However difficult her own upbringing, Bernice made a stable and happy home for her children. For birthdays, they got cake, ice cream, and basic clothing. Christmas meant more clothes and one new toy. Bill has fond memories of receiving a red wagon one year and a bow and arrow the next.

Every once in a while a special gift would arrive: often a puppy, a kitten, or, most special of all, a new horse. On one memorable occasion, P. K. Wrigley of Wrigley Chewing Gum fame sent little Billy one of his Catalina Island goats. Billy loved that goat, naming him P. K., and feeding him three times a day. One afternoon, something startled P. K.; he panicked, sprinting full speed into a block wall, breaking his neck. "This was the first time I questioned the goodness of God", Bill says. "It took me a long time to get over P. K.'s death."

Handing down clothing sibling-to-sibling and cousin-to-cousin was a time-honored tradition in the family. A second cousin, somewhat older and a size or two larger, kept Bill supplied with the wool jackets he wore to Mass each Sunday in town.

---

[1]Bob Clark always claimed that J. B. left in 1907 as that was the year that Bill Sr. was born. Before J. B. left, he donated the land for the depot in Nordhoff. As a consequence, the street was named in his honor. Although the depot is gone, Fox Street remains.

With the move north to Battle Creek Ranch, the family's isolation increased, with the nearest neighbors three miles distant. Bill fondly remembers *Juguete*, "Baby Toy", the pinto mare that delivered him to the bus stop each morning, the last stop on the twenty-mile line. On several occasions, she slipped and fell on the icy trail, sending her young rider, his books and violin into orbit—but she would patiently wait until he climbed back on board to finish the trip. Once she saw or heard the bus, the remarkable animal whinnied, turned, and galloped full speed back to the barn through creeks and hills, as dependable as the best driver in Washington.

Bernice continued her community activism, spotting for enemy planes at a neighboring ranch. Her cooking guaranteed that Battle Creek Ranch got "the very best crews, as Mom served the absolute best meals in northern California", recalls Bill's sister, Molly.

Bill Jr. hunted deer, geese, ducks, and small game for the family table. Bill Sr. smoked ham, bacon, and salmon in an old shed out back, cured olives and sauerkraut and made bread. They slaughtered pigs, including a scraping and scalding process neither son nor father enjoyed, usually calling in neighbors to help finish the grim procedure.

"Each animal had a specific purpose in our lives", Clark says. At Battle Creek Ranch, he watched over 4,400 sheep on the northeastern slopes of Mount Shasta and knew each of the belled leaders by name. The dogs not only herded sheep, he says, but also kept "me warm at night in winter and gave me someone to talk to. . . . I thought of them all as my faithful four-legged friends; I lived and worked with them and grew to love them as well."

Often weeks would elapse between visits from Bill's dad bringing supplies or the occasional stops by a forest ranger. The solitude, the quiet and the natural surroundings gave Clark time to think, to pray, to develop an interior life. On the days he thought might be Sunday, he recited the prayers of the Mass—either alone, or with Martin Iriguoin, the French Basque ranch hand.

On horseback Bill patrolled the summer range—sixty thousand acres of federal land that his father leased for three cents an acre. He corralled and doctored sheep and cattle, galloping through valleys and clambering over peaks, always with a dog at his side and a rifle nearby to protect the livestock from bear and coyotes. His sister Cynthia fondly remembers her summer months at Slagger Camp, when she and her brother saddled up the horses at dawn and circled the unfenced cattle and sheep to keep them from straying too far in the search for feed. It was an "incredible" childhood, she says. "Not much unfenced range to roam these days."

Ranching life instilled a work ethic that accompanied Clark throughout his life. "We all worked hard", he says. "There was no play time. There was no such thing as vacation. Everyone was expected to work at least six days a week, dawn to dusk on most days, with morning and evening chores even on school days."

His sisters, however, remember some playful episodes. They laugh at the memory of Molly driving a pickup truck as fast as she dared, to airlift the glider constructed by their fledgling aviator brother. Little Cynthia ran behind for as long as she could, holding up the tail so the craft would not drag on the ground at takeoff. This was the maiden and the final flight of the aircraft, pilot Clark's first unscheduled landing, *sine* fractures.

Villanova Prep

The 1947 move back to Oxnard gave Bill Clark the opportunity he needed to prepare for the future. The long hours of ranch work in Red Bluff left little time for study and, because of the seasonal nature of grazing, Bill attended school only about six months of the year. If law school was to be his educational goal, he knew he needed to increase his studies during his last two years of high school.

With help and encouragement from his parents, Clark enrolled at Villanova Preparatory School in the Ojai Valley. A private institution founded in 1924 by the Order of Saint Augustine, Villanova was noted for its rigorous academics and its enthusiastic athletic teams. Many of Clark's antecedents (his great aunts and uncles) were involved in the founding of the school.

There was one problem, however: The Clarks could not afford the tuition at Villanova. Father Kennedy, the tough, Irish headmaster, was impressed by the young man and arranged for Bill to work for his tuition in the kitchen. Clark returned the priest's investment by becoming the school's most famous graduate, lending his name to fundraising events, and donating a substantial sum for the construction of a gym, which the Augustinians insisted on naming for him. Clark was also instrumental in securing for the school the $3,000,000 Clare Boothe Luce bequest establishing a scholarship fund for women—both staff and students—who major in math and science.

As his parents settled affairs in Red Bluff, Bill Jr. stayed at the Doud home in Oxnard until classes began. He and Chuck Doud had known each other since they were toddlers. Through the Red Bluff years, Chuck spent several summers with the Clarks at Slagger Camp. One summer he and Bill dismounted their horses long enough to buy an old, beat-up Model T, which they towed home, tore apart, and got running.

Doud remembers how well the Villanova priests prepared the boys for college. "They were all tough", he says. One who particularly sticks in Chuck's mind was Father Monte, who had survived the Bataan Death March.

Bill played offense and defense on the football team, catching passes and making tackles—or "at least I tried to", he says. Doud played left tackle next to left end Clark and was recruited to play for Notre Dame, which boasted a thirty-nine-game winning streak in Doud's freshman year. Freshman Doud got no playing time under legendary coach Frank Leahy and thus transferred from South Bend to UCLA, where he became an all-American tackle. After college, Doud became a successful stockbroker.

At right end was John Gavin, whose classmates claim he received the highest grade nationally on the Naval ROTC exam. He became an actor, starring opposite Lana Turner, Julie Andrews, and other screen beauties, as well as following Ronald Reagan as president of the Screen Actors Guild. Under President Reagan, John Gavin was named U.S. Ambassador to Mexico, reporting frequently to National Security Advisor Clark.

Peter Dailey starred on the Villanova team as quarterback. He became an all-American running back at UCLA, where he played with Doud against Michigan State in the 1954 Rose Bowl. Asked if his team won the game, Dailey says with a grin: "We won the first half." Dailey became an ambassador in the same year as Gavin—to Ireland. As for his career, Dailey built one of the largest advertising firms in the United States.

Teammate Doud remembers Clark as having "never jumped out in front of the crowd for acclamation or anything", except for one occasion: the final football game of their senior year. The annual game against Nordhoff High School was the highlight of the season, and the prize was a bronze water bucket with football shoes dangling from the rim. "The Bucket" was the most esteemed of all trophies.

Villanova lost the game by a hair, and quietly Clark plotted his revenge. As Nordhoff was celebrating the victory at their home gym, Clark jumped out on stage in front of the crowd, snagged The Bucket, and dashed out the door. He ran nearly four miles cross country back to Villanova with angry Nordhoff players in hot pursuit.

He returned to his dorm room, battered and bloodied from cutting through the brush. His teammates gathered around. "What in the world happened to you?" Clark hoisted the trophy and did a small victory dance, as Doud recalls with great satisfaction. "None of us knew what he was up to! No one put him up to it. He decided on his own, quietly, and then he just did it. He had no fear." Amid handshakes and laughter, Clark returned the trophy to his pursuers. Clark, Gavin, Dailey, and Doud—the Augustinian fathers at Villanova, student population 110 in 1948–1949, graduated four exceptional young men.

Clark received solid religious formation at Villanova. Mass was celebrated daily, though attendance was not mandatory, and the fathers taught the doctrines of the faith, as well as the social teachings of the Church.

At Villanova, and later at the seminary, Clark read papal encyclicals such as *Rerum Novarum, Quadragesimo Anno,* and *Divini Redemptoris,* all of which provided him with a healthy combination: antipathy for communism and sympathy for the working man and the poor.

Divini Redemptoris left a deep impression on the young man. Penned by Pope Pius XI in 1937, during the Spanish Civil War, the encyclical identified communism as a materialistic, atheistic ideology. "According to this doctrine there is in the world only one reality, matter ... there is no room for the idea of God; there is no difference between matter and spirit, between soul and body; there is neither survival of the soul after death nor any hope in a future life" (DR, no. 9).

Yet like a messianic religion, communism promises man a future redemption. It claims that through material evolutionary forces, man is inexorably moving toward a perfect society of radical equality, in which there will be no private property, or authority, or even marriage and family. "There is no recognition of any right of the individual in his relations to the collectivity; no natural right is accorded to human personality, which is a mere cog-wheel in the Communist system. In man's relations with other individuals, besides, Communists hold the principle of absolute equality, rejecting all hierarchy and divinely-constituted authority, including the authority of parents" (DR, no. 9).

For communists, the mechanism of social progress is class conflict; hence, they "endeavor to sharpen the antagonisms which arise between the various classes of society. Thus the class struggle with its consequent violent hate and destruction takes on the aspects of a crusade for the progress of humanity. On the other hand, all other forces whatever, so long as they resist such systematic violence, must be annihilated as hostile to the human race" (DR, no. 10).

Since before the Bolsheviks took power in Russia in 1917, the Catholic Church had been targeted for destruction by the communist movement. By 1937, countless numbers of Catholics and other Christians had been sent to prison or killed for resisting communism in those countries already under communist rule or undergoing communist revolutions. In the Soviet Union, Mexico, and Spain, Catholic clergy, in particular, were singled out for arrest and execution. Catholic churches, monasteries, schools, and hospitals were confiscated, closed, or destroyed.

Divini Redemptoris was not the first papal document to address communism, but with renewed urgency it called upon Catholics and all believers to join forces in order to prevent its spread. Figures within the Church would heed the call and join the cause, from Pope Pius XII, Francis Cardinal Spellman, and Bishop Fulton Sheen to a high school student named Bill Clark.

Uncle Ned, Maureen, and Stanford

When Bill Clark graduated from Villanova as salutatorian in 1949, he was awarded the only degree he would ever receive. His high school education was perhaps the most significant schooling of his life, formative and central to all he accomplished later in Sacramento and Washington. Because of his failure to earn a college diploma, Clark determined that it would be inappropriate to accept the honorary degrees he was later offered.

His high school record, as well as an entrance exam, qualified Clark for admission to Stanford University, where he enrolled in the fall of

1949. Stanford appealed to him because of its excellent reputation and because his Uncle Ned, a Stanford graduate, so loved the school.

James Edward "Ned" Clark was Bill Sr.'s brother and young Bill's godfather. At this point in Bill's life, he was unsure of his goals, though he knew he was attracted to law, to ranching and, possibly, the religious life. Uncle Ned, his mentor, suggested Bill study law in order to accrue the necessary capital for a ranch; with any luck and a lot of hard work, he could have both career and ranch, as Ned himself had done.

All four of Marshal Bob Clark's sons had dreams of owning their own land on which they could run cattle. Ned, his third son, put himself through Stanford University, starting his career with Shell Oil Company by hoeing weeds in their Ventura oil fields during summer break. In 1947, he made the down payment on his eight hundred acres above Ojai and spent the next ten years or so paying off his student loans and his ranch through his continued work for Shell. He ended his career at Shell as executive vice president, dodging the bullet of the presidency of the company by retiring early to his ranch in Ojai.

Ned was not the only person to influence Bill's decision to study law at Stanford; high-school sweetheart Maureen Maxwell had a great deal to do with his choice as well. Two years younger than Bill, Maureen planned to follow him to Stanford and did, but there was a problem: her parents were not convinced that Clark was the man for their daughter. Accordingly, they sent Maureen off to Paris for a year, giving her the opportunity to sever or at least to slow her long relationship with Bill.

The highlight of Bill's time at Stanford was meeting Clare Boothe Luce, who became a lifelong friend and advisor. The cause of their meeting was a tragic event that had happened some years before. From her first marriage, Clare had a daughter, an only child named Ann. On January 11, 1944, Ann, a Stanford senior only months shy of graduating *summa cum laude*, was killed in an automobile accident.

In 1950, Clare and her second husband, Henry Luce,[2] began construction of a memorial chapel in Ann's memory in Palo Alto. As one

---

[2] Henry Luce was a tough conservative, considered to be the most influential magazine publisher in the U.S. Luce was co-founder and editor-in-chief of *Time* magazine and founder of *Life, Fortune, House & Home, Sports Illustrated*, as well as producer of *March of Time* for radio and cinema. At the time of his death, he was reputed to be worth $1 million in Time Inc. stock.

of Stanford's serious Catholics, Bill Clark was attuned to these developments, and when the exquisite chapel was completed, Clare asked the young man to help her move the dedication project along.

At the time of her daughter's death, no one knew that Clare Boothe Luce, actress, writer, U.S. ambassador, and congresswoman,[3] was interested in Catholicism. A Jesuit priest who had been in contact with Luce relayed her grief to Bishop Fulton Sheen, who called her one day in 1945 and invited her to dinner. After dinner, when the dishes were cleared, the Bishop turned to the subject of religion. "Give me five minutes to talk to you about God, and then I will give you an hour to state your own views", he said. When he got to the issue of the goodness of God, Clare cut in: "If God is good, why did he take my daughter?" Sheen answered: "In order that through sorrow, you might be here now starting instruction to know Christ and His Church." [4]

"Fulton Sheen was responsible, or certainly the catalyst, for the material part of Clare's conversion", says Bill. Clare Boothe Luce became one of America's most famous converts. She decided not to run for re-election to Congress and to return to writing. In 1947, she wrote a series of articles describing her conversion for *McCall's*.

Saint Ann's Chapel was dedicated at Stanford on October 21, 1951. On the day of the memorial, Clark borrowed a car to pick up Clare and Henry at San Francisco's United Air terminal. He remembers their appearances as he pulled up: "She was, of course, beautiful, and impeccably dressed; he was grumpy and rumpled." During the Mass, which Clark served as lead acolyte, Presbyterian Luce, editor and publisher of *Time*, *Life*, and *Fortune*, appeared "disinterested, grouchy", remembers Clark. Yet in spite of his distaste for the Catholic Church, Henry acquired a priceless medieval ivory Madonna and Child from the Whitney Museum in honor of his wife's conversion. Many years later, Clare would present the Madonna to Clark.[5]

---

[3] Clare Boothe Luce was an accomplished woman. In addition to those occupations listed, she worked in various fields: as managing editor of *Vanity Fair*, author of *The Women* and a number of other successful plays, as Ambassador to Italy under President Eisenhower. She was known to be witty—and articulate to the point of being considered outspoken.

[4] Thomas C. Reeves, *America's Bishop* (San Francisco: Encounter Books, 2001), p. 176.

[5] Bill commissioned a replica of the treasure. It sits at the family gravesite in Ventura as there was no other image of the Blessed Virgin at Ivy Lawn Cemetery.

Fulton Sheen and other well-known Catholics and dignitaries such as Bernard Baruch and Admiral Nimitz attended the ceremony. The dedication plaque reads:

> Thy beauty, now, is all for the King's delight;
> He is Thy Lord, and worship belongs to Him.
> In memory of my daughter Ann Clare Brokaw.
> Clare Boothe Luce.

Merton and Sheen

When asked which writers influenced him as a young man, Clark cites Augustine, Saint Francis, and G. K. Chesterton, but, most of all, Thomas Merton and Fulton Sheen.

Merton's autobiography, *The Seven Storey Mountain*, published in October 1948, was fundamental to Clark's decision to consider the priesthood, as it was for a generation of young men. "That book was quite influential on me during that period of my life," says Clark, "and it still is."

Merton was born in France in 1915. His parents were artists and expatriates; his Quaker mother was from America and his Anglican father from New Zealand. At the outbreak of World War I, the family fled to New York, where Merton's mother died of stomach cancer in 1921. During the next several years Merton stayed with different family members and attended three different boarding schools, one in France and two in England. In 1931, when Merton was sixteen years old, his father died of a brain tumor.

Left to tackle the world alone, Merton went on a search for the meaning and purpose of life that led him through hedonism and communism and ultimately to Catholicism. He eventually entered a Trappist monastery, where his restless heart found solace in those "four walls of my new freedom".

Merton's account was riveting to young men like Bill Clark struggling through a similar quest for Truth. Merton also struck a responsive chord with Clark in his understanding of human fallibility. In the book's first paragraph, Merton described his fallen state and that of all men: "Free by nature, in the image of God, I was nevertheless the prisoner of my own violence and my own selfishness, in the image of the world into which I was born. That world was the picture of Hell, full of men like myself, loving God and yet hating Him."

Clark owns a rare ink and charcoal drawing of Saint Clare by Merton, the only known work of graphic art that Merton signed. It is inscribed:

> To Clare Boothe Luce on her feast day
> August 12th 1950
> from Father Louis Merton, OCSO.[6]

The drawing was a gift to Clark from Clare Boothe Luce, who supported Merton's work, including the writing of *Seven Storey Mountain*. She wrote an endorsement that ran on the dust jacket of the original edition, as did contemporaries Evelyn Waugh, Graham Greene, and Fulton Sheen.

Peace of Sheen

Fulton Sheen influenced Clark more than any other writer. Born in 1895, Sheen was one of the most remarkable and eminent American Catholics of the twentieth century. Throughout most of the 1950s, Sheen's television show, *Life Is Worth Living*, was immensely popular as were his *Catholic Hour* radio broadcasts that started in 1928. Sheen was also a prolific and popular writer, producing innumerable newspaper columns, speeches, and books.[7] By April 1952, Sheen was on the cover of *TIME* magazine. He won the 1952 Emmy Award for "Most Outstanding Television Personality", besting superstars such as Jimmy Durante, Edward R. Murrow, Lucille Ball, and Arthur Godfrey.

It was through the written word that Bill Clark found Sheen.[8] To this day, when asked if there was a single book that influenced him more than any other, Clark cites Sheen's 1949 work *Peace of Soul*,[9]

---

[6] "Louis" was Thomas Merton's religious name; O.C.S.O. stands for Order of Cistercians of Strict Observance.

[7] Reeves, *America's Bishop*, p. 176.

[8] Clark today does not recall watching Sheen on TV as a young man, because he and his family did not own a TV; perhaps Bill, like his brother Ned, was opposed to that decadent time-stealing contraption and wouldn't allow it in the house.

[9] Fulton J. Sheen, *Peace of Soul* (New York: McGraw-Hill, 1949). The book has recently been republished by Liguori/Triumph Press (Liguori, MO).

which he first read when he was eighteen years old. The work reinforced what he was already observing at home with his father's unspoken spirituality, particularly in regard to Sheen's teachings on the necessity of humility.

Peace of Soul has never left Bill Clark's side. Copies sit on bookshelves at his home and office and at Chapel Hill. "It is a significant work", says Clark. "I occasionally will give it to someone who is having difficulty."

Sheen's *Communism and the Conscience of the West*[10] also influenced Clark. Sheen relies on Marx and Lenin in making his core point: "The truth on the subject is that communism and atheism are intrinsically related and that one cannot be a good Communist without being an atheist and every atheist is a potential Communist." As Marx himself stated: "Communism begins where atheism begins."

Sheen lays out the religious nature of communism, the "preaching" of Lenin, the "apostles of Marx", and the manner in which Stalin was treated like a god. He advises that the Russian people—for whom, he observes, "atheism is not natural"—take heart that Christ's tomb is empty, while Lenin's tomb is not.

The Seminary

After freshman year at Stanford, Clark left the university. Stanford was not right for him, socially or academically, and a call to the priesthood began to ring out above all else. Father John Tierney of the Stanford Newman Club counseled Clark that he needed to determine whether or not he had a vocation to the religious life.

In the fall of 1950, Clark entered the Augustinian seminary in New Hamburg, New York, beside the Hudson River, amid rolling hills covered with small farms, and snow and toboggans in the winter.

His mother was not in favor of his decision, for reasons he never knew,[11] but his friends approved, and were not surprised. Peter Dailey says that in addition to reverence, Clark always had the "quiet, thoughtful demeanor" common to both priest and judge.

---

[10] Fulton J. Sheen, *Communism and the Conscience of the West* (Indianapolis and New York: Bobbs-Merrill, 1948).

[11] Cousin Pat's guess is that Bernice wanted Bill's family line—and name—to continue.

The novitiate was an important time for Clark, a period of even further soul-searching and reflection, "not unlike my earlier life," he says, "except in this case, silence was mandatory, aside from two hours in the afternoon". The reading was demanding, requiring him to study Aquinas, Augustine, and other Church Fathers. "Even at meals, we had a reader." [12]

After five hours of sleep at night, for the Novices the day began with divine office, Mass, and meditation, followed by breakfast, which finished at 8:15. Then, each student did his assigned "house job" before classes started at 9:00. They sat for three classes before dismissal for lunch and midday prayer. In the afternoon, they worked as a group caring for the seminary's one hundred acres of land. [13]

The winter that year was one of the coldest on record and, as the only Californian, Clark was assigned the task of rising one hour ahead of everyone else and shoveling coal into the furnace to keep the ancient place warm—a good-natured initiation he good-naturedly accepted.

In Clark's class, forty men began the program, and roughly twenty stayed on. Among those who became priests and lifetime friends of Clark were Tom Behan, who ended up at Our Mother of Good Counsel Church on Vermont Avenue in Hollywood, and Robert Burke, who joined the faculty at Merrimack College in North Andover, Massachusetts. Both priests found their home in the Order of Saint Augustine.

Behan was from Staten Island, New York. Like Clark, he was "very influenced" by the writings of Merton, particularly by *The Seven Storey Mountain*. Behan recalls that Clark was especially moved by *The Seeds of Contemplation*, also written by Thomas Merton. "Bill was very interested in monasticism and the spiritual life," says Behan. [14] He also remembers how "Clarkie" stood out when it came to working the land in the afternoons: "He was the most skilled in all that stuff. He was on the tractor all the time. The agriculture and the animals were foreign to a city boy like me, but not to Clarkie. He knew how to do it all."

---

[12] Weisman, "The Influence of William Clark", p. 18.
[13] Interview with Tom Behan, December 1, 2005.
[14] Ibid.

He also knew how to pull off a practical joke. During a pig roast, Clark surreptitiously arranged for Behan to be served a pig's nose sandwich. Behan lunged in, only to quickly draw back once he was informed of the contents of his meal.[15]

After months of thoughtful prayer, as well as constant counsel from Father McCaffrey and Father Judson, the novice master, Clark discerned that a calling to the religious life had not materialized. Father Judson stated that he should not be disappointed in that conclusion for there was clearly Divine Purpose in his having come to New Hamburg.

Clark left the novitiate in February, midway through the one-year program. He packed his belongings into an old Navy duffel bag, put on the black overcoat his godfather had given him, said his goodbyes, and hitched rides from upstate New York to California, sleeping in trucks and eating at truck stops along the way.

Cousin Pat Clark, Uncle Ned's daughter, recalls what Bill told her when she asked him why he left the seminary: he said he felt he could fight communist oppression better as a layman.

Though he did not pursue the priesthood, the novitiate was an integral part of the Divine Plan, informing the remainder of his life. "It was crucial that I was there", he says. "My time at the novitiate added an important dimension to my time on earth; it was probably the most personally constructive year of my life. God put me there for a reason—what I learned at the novitiate, as a disciple, I would attempt to carry forward through all my life."

On his return to the family home in Oxnard, Clark's sister Cynthia asked her brother what he had learned in the seminary. The high school sophomore never forgot his answer: "I learned the meaning of prayer."

---

[15] Ibid.

CHAPTER 3

East Meets West

The Cold War Becomes Personal

Returning home from the novitiate, Bill Clark, whether he knew it or not, had edged closer to finding his place in the world. He hopped on a tractor and worked the ranch—meditation time, as it had been throughout his life.

After a few months, he decided to give Stanford another try, but he found the studies less than edifying and the social life frivolous, other than his dates with Maureen, who was also enrolled.

Unlike Clark, Maureen adapted readily to life at Stanford, earning top grades and a place at the center of the social whirl. The periphery of the popular set was about as much as Bill could handle. Even though Maureen was wearing his SAE fraternity pin, he soon came to the conclusion it was time to move on. Dean Balch recommended that he consider "some other line of activity", such as ranching or farming, or perhaps, he added, Clark should try another school. Remembering Uncle Ned's advice on pursuing law in order to provide the means to own a ranch, Clark applied to another university, one that promised to prove a better fit, yet was still near Maureen.

Clark registered to study pre-law under the Jesuit fathers at the University of Santa Clara, California's oldest institution of higher learning. He completed two years of undergraduate work, bringing his grades up to a respectable level, sufficient to be admitted to Loyola Law School in Los Angeles. He headed back to Southern California in his 1931 Model A Ford and spent the rest of 1952 and most of 1953 at Loyola, while clerking at the Los Angeles firm of Gibson, Dunn & Crutcher.

Clark had no choice when it came to his next move, a move that would provide him with his first experience beyond the borders of California and outside the confines of the monastery. Uncle Sam called him, as he did so many other young Americans during the Korean War. Clark spent eight weeks at Fort Ord for basic training, then eight weeks at Hunter Leggett for advanced infantry training. In late 1953, soldier Clark was assigned to the U.S. Army's Counter Intelligence Corps. His papers listed him as 6 feet 2 inches, 180 pounds, with brown hair, brown eyes, and type A blood.

After seventeen weeks of training at Fort Holabird, Maryland, Clark graduated from the Army Counter-Intelligence Corps as a plain-clothes agent, and was given the assignment of running security reviews of various military posts in Europe, including Mannheim/Feudenheim, West Germany.

Bill Meets Joan

Clark took up residence in a three-story compound in Mannheim, sharing quarters with five other men also involved in intelligence and surveillance. He spoke the German language, ate his meals in German restaurants, and enjoyed a three-hundred-dollar civilian clothing allowance. He and his fellow agents tracked the whereabouts of KGB agents and communist operatives, who drove their souped up BMWs far into West German territory. The Americans followed in less conspicuous and slower Opels, doing their best to behave like indigenous Germans.

In the course of his investigation, Clark had cause to question Johanna "Joan" Martha Brauner—an Austrian beauty with high cheek bones, dark brown hair, and blue eyes—as she was principal secretary to the commanding officer of the Mannheim/Feudenheim ordinance depot. Before long, the two were conversing frequently, but always in the line of duty, to comply with the non-fraternization rule imposed during the occupation. They discovered a mutual love of Mozart, a common dedication to Christian beliefs, with Joan's Lutheran convictions providing counterpoint to Bill's Roman Catholic certainty, and her sparkling personality proving an antidote to Bill's sometimes somber spirits. Additionally, the communists had confiscated her home and driven her family into exile. Joan Brauner despised communism even more than did Clark.

Clark's investigation revealed sensitive documents relating to nuclear materials to be out of place, unaccounted for, perhaps even missing. As a consequence, the commanding officer of the Mannheim ordinance depot was removed from his position—but Clark's conversations with Joan continued.

Joan's mother, Nina, was Austrian. Nina's father had served as a major general in the Austrian army under Emperor Franz Josef. Joan's father, Eduard, an Austrian of Polish and German ancestry, had grown up near Krakow, Poland. He spoke four languages: Polish, Czech, German, and a smattering of Russian. He also had been in the Austrian military, serving in the cavalry on the eastern front during World War I.

When the Hapsburg monarchy crumbled in 1918, the Brauners were made citizens of the newly founded Republic of Czechoslovakia. German-speaking people made up more than a quarter of Czechoslovakia's population, and the presence of this minority led to ethnic tensions within the new country and would be used by Germany as a pretext for further war.

Joan grew up in a German-speaking home in Troppau, in the former Austrian principality of Silesia, near the Polish border. Troppau was a proud town, one of the host cities for the historic Congress of Vienna in the early nineteenth century.

Nina and Eduard gave their children plenty of time and love, says Joan, the best gifts any parent can give a child. Joan adored her sister, Helena, five years her senior and "would do absolutely anything" she asked her to do. Paul, "the pampered", was youngest, the only son, favored not only for the traditional reasons, but also because he had suffered a near fatal illness—scarlet fever—in early life.

Joan's best friend was Gabrielle, "Gaby", with whom she swam, skated, and sang. Both girls enjoyed reading and exchanged all the books in their respective collections. As Joan grew older, she developed a romance with classical music, theatre, and opera. The ideal birthday present was a ticket to a performance—but just when Joan reached the age when she could fully appreciate her cultural heritage, Central Europe was again torn apart by war.

Joan first saw Nazis in her hometown in 1938, when they began filling the government ministries after England and France agreed to let Hitler take control of Silesia and the other German-speaking areas of Czechoslovakia. In 1939, German troops marched into Prague and conquered the rest of the country. Two years later, at the age of ten, Joan was forced to join the female equivalent of the *Hitler-Jugend*, the *Bund Deutscher Mädchen*: "You had no choice," she explains. "Everyone had to join.... As a child, you couldn't even go to school unless you were a member."

"Generally," she says, "you were largely okay [under Nazi rule] if you didn't bring attention to yourself in any way." The same could not be said for the Jewish people. Joan recalls the day she stared aghast as a beautiful old synagogue burned to the ground. "My mother was shocked, but what could she do? If she had spoken up, she would have put our entire family in jeopardy. We would have been arrested or maybe just disappeared." Within a short period of time, there were no Jews left in Troppau. Those who had not fled had been sent to the death camps.

With World War II well underway, Joan's father feared for his family's safety. He sold the business he had worked hard to build, a factory that made precision hand tools, and waited. The authorities then placed him in a civil post to run the town air-raid system.

The Nazis' fortunes began to sour when their offensive against Russia ended in defeat in early 1943. Over the next two years, the Russians pushed the German army out of Eastern Europe, sparking a new set of fears. The people around her "were very fearful of the Russians", says Joan. Most Czechs of German or Austrian heritage fled, leaving all behind.

The Brauners—mother Nina with children Helena, Joan, and Paul—sought refuge with Tante Elsa, Nina's eldest sister who lived in Teplitz at the foot of the Bohemian Mountains near the German border. Eduard stayed behind, manning the air-raid system, activated now most every night. As the war ended in 1945, Joan and her family celebrated somewhat tentatively; surely they would now return home—to whatever was left in Troppau. The Russians, however, stayed in the country as victorious occupiers, imposing curfews, rationing food, and tightening their grip over the people. Eduard, despairing of his beautiful city ever being safe enough to bring his wife and children home, abandoned all and joined his family in Teplitz.

The family was not safe for long. Czech authorities began encouraging hostility against those of German or Austrian ancestry. A Czech communist official showed up one day at Tante Elsa's home and announced, "You have until tomorrow morning to pack all your bags and leave." The next morning the Brauner family, now joined by Tante Elsa, placed their bags on a hand cart and set out over the mountains to the Province of Saxony, Germany, to the home of Tante Martha, Nina and Elsa's middle sister.

During their trek through the mountains, the family endured many hardships. The climb up the mountains was suffocating for Joan, who wore three layers of clothing as her body had to serve as her "suitcase". She and her family drank from creeks and streams along the ascent and, after one such stop, turned the corner of the serpentine road to discover putrefying bodies floating at the top of the stream from which they had just quenched their thirst.

At one stop along the way, they stayed with a family friend of Tante Elsa's, enjoying a brief respite from the horrors of their flight. After all had retired for the night, leaving their few bags in the hallway, Russian soldiers pounded on the front door, demanding schnapps and vodka. "It was well known that Russians raped girls and women of any age", explains Joan. The frightened Eduard, the only man present, quickly pushed the women and children to the roof of the house before admitting his "guests". Thanks to the Russian language he had learned during World War I, he was able to explain that he had no alcohol—not what the soldiers wanted to hear. Angry, they pushed their way into the house, locked Eduard in a room, and began ransacking the house—all of which the frightened women and children could hear clearly from their hiding place.

Finally, all fell silent. The women were too terrified to call out. After he felt it was safe to do so, Eduard climbed out the window of the room in which he had been locked, and helped Nina, Tante Elsa, their hostess and the children to the ground. When they entered the house, they found that the few things they had managed to carry up the mountain were now gone, including the one suitcase with all their vital documents—their precious identities, affirming birth and citizenship.

The following evening, the Brauners arrived, weary and dispirited, at Tante Martha's home in Waldkirchen, Germany. The communists had taken everything from them, but the Brauners still had their lives. Gaby's father, a respected pediatrician, waited too long to leave Troppau. When he finally realized the danger of Russian occupation, he took his family to a heavily Czech settlement, but the full-blooded

Czechs would not abide anyone with German ancestry. To save his wife and four daughters from the torture and rape being inflicted upon German-speaking Czechs, Dr. Dietrich fed his family poison, then shot himself.

Many years later, as Bill and Joan were wandering through the antique shops in Los Angeles, in search of a dining room table large enough to accommodate their growing family, Joan let out a cry. "That's it! There it is!" Bill turned, expecting to see the perfect dining room set. What he saw was a perfect copy of the Brauner family hand cart, as battered as the original, and imported from Europe.[1] Bill and Joan immediately bought this metaphor of the Brauner family losses to communism, and have ever since placed it in a location of honor at the entrance to their home.

Looking to Escape

Joan lived for the next few years in the refuge of Waldkirchen, where she finished her high-school education. It was a three-mile walk to the nearest school; Joan's only winter shoes were the heavy combat boots she inherited from her favorite cousin, Klaus. The boots were among the personal effects mailed home to his mother, Martha, after Klaus was killed fighting for the Germans on the eastern front.

Joan graduated in 1949, the same year Clark did, and shortly thereafter became a teacher in the eastern German village of Rathendorf. "There were Latvians, Lithuanians, Ukrainians—people from everywhere who had tried to escape the Russians," says Joan. They had not succeeded. By the end of the 1940s, the Russians had complete control over eastern Germany and the east side of Berlin. As a teacher, Joan was required to swear allegiance to the new communist government of East Germany; she did not, however, join the Communist Party.

Joan and her family watched and waited patiently for the opportunity to escape into West Germany. As the borders were sealed, the only way out was through the west side of Berlin that was still held by the Western Allies. Joan's chance came in 1952 when she took a train to East Berlin, crossed into West Berlin, and then bluffed her way aboard a plane to Hamburg.[2]

---

[1] Series of interviews with Joan Clark, July 2006.
[2] Some accounts list the time of Joan's escape as 1951 rather than 1952.

Eventually, one by one, each member of her family made his way to freedom in the West. Because so many people were fleeing from East Germany through West Berlin, in 1961 the communists constructed a fortified and guarded wall to prevent passage from one side of the city to the other. The Brauners—Eduard and Nina, Helena, Joan and Paul—had made their way out of East Germany while their escape was still possible.

Joan went to England to work and study at Saint Hugh's College, Oxford University, a year she remembers as "fabulous, wonderful, unforgettable". She paid her bills by working as a chamber and serving maid while taking private English lessons, attending as many Shakespearean plays as she could. "The contrast between this amazing freedom and my life of the previous twenty years was almost incomprehensible at times", she says.

After she finished her studies, Joan went to work for the U.S. military in Mannheim, where she met Clark during the course of his investigation. Eventually their interviews came to an end, and the two began discreetly dating. A couple of months later, on May 5, 1955, they were married in a private ceremony at Santa Clara Catholic Church in Basel, Switzerland.

The following September, when Clark was discharged from the service, Joan flew all the way west—to Ventura County, California. Bill Sr. and Bernice warmly welcomed their veteran son and his new bride with a family gathering and the traditional barbecue at their Camarillo home.

Joan was not the only East European refugee in West Germany whom Clark met and helped resettle in America. Under Bill's watch in the Counter Intelligence Corps (CIC) were a number of Polish refugees, including roughly thirty officers who formed a front group to help the Americans monitor subversive communist activities along the Iron Curtain. Some of these officers had missed by only a few hours the Katyn Woods massacre of 1940—the incident in which the NKVD,[3] Russia's infamous Main Directorate for Soviet State Security, executed fifteen thousand captured Polish military officers, from the rank of colonel to general.[4]

---

[3] *Narodnyi Komissariat Vnutrennikh Del*, the Main Directorate for Soviet State Security.
[4] On this, see David Remnick, *Lenin's Tomb* (New York: Random House, 1994), p. 3.

Clark helped as many Polish officers as possible find jobs in America so they could emigrate. "They were good men", says Clark. "Devout men. I did what I could." Among these were Walter Straszak and Theodor "Teddy" Obzrut and his wife, Christina, who had also collected intelligence for Clark. With his sponsorship, they eventually made it to California.

Counselor Clark

At twenty-four years of age, Clark returned to his goal of becoming a lawyer. He enrolled at Loyola Law School, taking evening classes, and worked full time during the day, earning income as an insurance adjuster for USF & G Insurance Company in downtown Los Angeles. He also performed odd jobs when he could get them. He exchanged grounds maintenance for their first home, a garage apartment in Glendale.[5]

As costs mounted to an uncomfortable level, Clark left Loyola before completing the requirements for a degree; he had, however, earned enough credits to qualify for the bar exam. After studying on his own for a year, he passed the California bar on a second try in 1958.

In March 1958, after admission to both the California and federal bars, Counselor Clark and his wife moved to Oxnard, where he represented the third generation of Clarks to uphold law and order in Ventura County. Unsuccessful in obtaining a position with the legal establishment of the town, he opened his own one-room firm "and waited for the phone to ring".[6]

His practice was slow in that first year, with the exception of appointments in criminal defense at fifteen dollars per hour. The locals remembered him as "little Billy Clark" who had failed to graduate from law school, but Clark remained undaunted. He kept busy, particularly by accepting pro bono cases representing the poor and indigent of the community, many of whom became his good friends. The successful among them graduated to paying-client status as soon as they were

---

[5] The Clarks lived in the apartment on Kenneth Road from December 1955 to November 1956.

[6] Quotes taken from Clark's testimony to the Senate Foreign Relations Committee, February 2, 1981.

able. Clark truly enjoyed small town practice; within a few years his one-man firm expanded into a successful partnership, Clark, Cole and Fairfield.[7]

These years as a young lawyer forged a new bond between Clark and the father he so admired. By 1950, Bill Sr. had served as police chief for three hectic years, and he longed to return to the cattle business. He not only began running cattle again, but also obtained a real-estate license and began overseeing the purchase of ranch properties. He and his son constructed The Clark Building in Oxnard to house the law practice and the Clark Land and Cattle Company. Both endeavors thrived, and Bill Sr. achieved the financial security he, and especially his wife, had always longed for.

During this time when Clark and his father worked so closely together, Bill Jr. joined his grandfather, father, and Uncle Ned as a member of Rancheros Visitadores, becoming its first third-generation member. In the setting of the annual rides, he connected informally with old friends and family in the easy camaraderie of life on the trail.

Family Gains and Goodbyes

Bill and Joan started their family in 1956, first, with the arrival of Monica, named for the mother of Saint Augustine and in recognition of the Augustinian novitiate in upstate New York. More little Clarks added to the family: Peter was born in 1957, followed by Nina in 1958, Colin Dominick in 1959, then Paul four years later in 1963. The Clarks welcomed each child as a blessing; each new birth brought them joy.

In 1956, the same year Bill and Joan began their family, Clark lost his beloved grandfather, his *compañero*, Robert Emmett Clark. Marshal Bob, who had become as much a legend in these parts as his patriotic eponym had been in Ireland, died on August 18, 1956, a few days before his eightieth birthday. "I believe he just wore out", said Clark of his death. "I adored him. We all adored him." Bob was survived by his widow, Alice, seven children, and twenty-six grandchildren.

---

[7] The Clarks' first home in Oxnard: 340 K Street; first home purchased: 12 Carriage Square where they lived from January 1957 to January 1967.

The Mindszenty Factor

Though Eastern Europe seemed a world away from Ventura County, Clark closely followed events behind the Iron Curtain. Nikita Khrushchev, the man who had replaced Stalin as the leader of the Soviet Union, seemed to be promising a "peaceful co-existence" with the West. Led by reformer Imre Nagy, the Hungarian people hoped that this was their chance to break free from Soviet domination.

In October 1956 what began as a student uprising turned into a mass demonstration in Budapest. Retribution from the communists was swift and fierce. The Russians sent in soldiers and tanks; over a two- to three-day period, thirty thousand Hungarians were slaughtered.

It was an event that Clark, along with a fellow Californian he had not yet met, watched very carefully and never forgot. Separately, Clark and Ronald Reagan lamented that President Dwight Eisenhower did not defend the Hungarians.

During the Hungarian uprising, Jozsef Cardinal Mindszenty, whom Clark calls "the most significant Christian of the twentieth century", was freed from house arrest. The ailing sixty-four-year-old Archbishop was hailed by the reform movement as a national hero for his resistance first against fascism and then communism.

Shortly after being made a bishop in 1944, Mindszenty was imprisoned by the Nazi occupiers of Hungary for protesting their roundup of Hungarian Jews. In October 1945, when Pope Pius XII placed the Cardinal's hat on his head, the Pontiff prophesied: "Among the thirty-two, you will be the first to suffer the martyrdom whose symbol this red color is." [8] Only ten months later, on December 26, 1946, the communists celebrated the Christmas season by arresting Cardinal Mindszenty for urging his flock to resist their confiscation of Hungarian lands and Catholic schools. He endured torture as he refused to plead guilty to trumped-up charges of treason, conspiracy, and other crimes. He told his fellow Hungarians that if he ever made any type of confession, they should assume it was under duress.

During a sensational show trial, Mindszenty pleaded guilty before his accusers, a confession widely believed to have been obtained through drugging and five weeks of torture. He was sentenced to life in prison;

---

[8] Quoted in literature provided by the Cardinal Mindszenty Foundation.

Pope Pius XII responded by excommunicating all individuals involved in the conviction.

Mindszenty spent the next eight years in a solitary confinement that nearly killed him. He was released in 1955 because of ill health, but kept under surveillance. When he was freed during the 1956 revolution, rather than flee, he took residency in the U.S. embassy, refusing to leave his country unless the communist government rescinded his conviction, which, under pressure from the Kremlin, it would not do. He offered up his suffering on behalf of Christians living under the tyranny of communism. In a 1957 television broadcast, Bishop Sheen named him the "Dry Martyr of Hungary".[9]

Mindszenty's story had a profound effect on both Bill and Joan Clark. His *Memoirs* were released by Macmillan Publishing on November 15, 1974—the perfect Christmas gift for her husband, Joan decided. "On Christmas morning, Bill opened his gift and had this funny look on his face", recalls Joan. "I said, 'Don't you like it?' Then he reached around under the Christmas tree and pulled out the copy he had gotten for me."

There is a parallel between the crystallizing effect of Mindszenty's *Memoirs* on Clark and the similar effect of Whittaker Chambers's memoirs, *Witness*, on Ronald Reagan. "To me," said Clark, "Mindszenty was the crime fighter—a quiet, rugged fighter; the foremost clergyman in the fight against communism."

Was it Cardinal Mindszenty that most influenced Clark's determination to take on communism, was it Bishop Sheen, or was it another source? "I can't put my finger on the exact source, on a single source", answers Clark. "Certainly Sheen fought communism and was a major influence on me. Mindszenty even more so because he lived it." Regardless, the fate of the Hungarians further convinced Clark that the West needed to battle against communism, not simply contain it behind the Iron Curtain. "I knew that communism lived a lie", he says. "It had to be defeated—and its 300,000,000 slaves set free."

---

[9] "Dry", said Sheen, because he primarily suffered mental torture rather than being physically annihilated like martyrs of old.

CHAPTER 4

Sacramento

The Partnership Begins

These were good years, when the Clarks settled into Oxnard. Joan became a U.S. citizen, and Clark enjoyed the work at his law firm—Clark, Cole & Fairfield,[1] though he was a rancher at heart. He wore his western hat, made the annual Rancheros trek, joined the Ventura County Sheriff's Posse, and felt more comfortable as a member of the Cattlemen's Association than as a member of the Bar Association.

He longed for a ranch, and a ranch beckoned three hours north of Oxnard in San Luis Obispo County. He made a small down payment on a one-thousand-acre grain and cattle ranch twenty-five miles east of Paso Robles in Shandon, population one hundred and forty.

Clark became interested in politics during this period of Lyndon Johnson's Great Society. He harbored "doubts about its greatness" as he saw the Democratic Party abandon its traditional values of family, labor, and religion in its push for government welfare programs. In 1964, Clark completed his journey to the Republican Party and voted for Barry Goldwater—as did Ronald Reagan, agreeing with Reagan's assessment: "I didn't leave the Democratic Party; it left me."

It was the Goldwater campaign that provided Clark with his introduction to Ronald Reagan. Not a moviegoer, he had never seen a Reagan film, but he had caught an episode or two of GE Theatre, the number-one-rated television show that Reagan hosted. When Clark

---

[1] Carl Cole and Bill Fairfield.

and his wife attended a Goldwater rally at the Los Angeles Sports Coliseum, where Reagan was pinch-hitting, they were immediately impressed. "We turned to each other and said, 'This is it; this is the man'", says Joan. They decided that if Reagan ever ran for office, they would not only support him, they would also volunteer for his campaign.

Before Clark could enlist in a Reagan campaign, Reagan called him—in 1965. Reagan told Clark that he had been studying state politics and hoped Clark would consider a run for state assembly. A number of Ventura County Republicans had been encouraging Clark to file for the next election; nevertheless, Reagan's call came as a surprise. "I was honored that he asked", says Clark. "I thanked him profusely . . . but it wasn't the right time." He declined Reagan's request, explaining that he had a young family and a new law practice. "Well," said Reagan, "if I should ever run for office myself, from what I've heard about you, I'd like to meet you again and maybe have your assistance."

The following year, Reagan ran for governor of California, and he called on Clark again. This time Clark accepted Reagan's request and became his Ventura County campaign chairman. "My mother and I don't discuss politics these days", said Clark in an interview at the time.[2] His father understood his decision, yet remarked that his son "had always said he'd never be in a political job, but Ronald Reagan talked him into it".[3]

The Reagan campaign had simple beginnings. Planning meetings were held on Wilshire Boulevard in Los Angeles at a small storefront office with one piece of furniture—a table. Franklyn (Lyn) Nofziger, a reporter for the San Diego Union, was Reagan's press director and led the meetings. Described fondly by Clark as a big bear of a man, Nofziger sat in the middle of the table, while Clark and the others stood. "Our first campaign office", he says, "was definitely bare bones."

After Reagan won the primary, his team geared up for the general election against Edmund G. "Pat" Brown, the tough and popular incumbent governor. Reagan ran a polished, sophisticated campaign, striking the electorate as a nice guy, a handsome guy, with equally attractive ideas. He spoke of "fiscal responsibility", of a "Creative Society" looking

[2] White, "The Clark Family", PC: The Weekly Magazine of Ventura County, August 19, 1973.

[3] Phil Pattee, "Honored Ex-Rancher", Oxnard Press, October 5, 1983.

for new ways to resolve old problems, not the same shopworn big-government approaches. He promised changes in California's troubled tax system, including a moratorium on property taxes for the elderly, and addressed issues ranging from smog to education to open-housing legislation.[4] Reagan won by a landslide—with one million votes, taking 55 of 58 counties, and carrying 400,000 Democrat defectors. Many Republican legislators were swept into office on his coattails.

Clark likes to point out the role his longtime friend Tom Reed, chairman of the northern California campaign, played in the victory. Phil Battaglia, chairman of the campaign statewide, "said the whole thing could be won in southern California, and he was right," says Clark, "but they wrote off northern California. They couldn't find anyone to take northern California. They thought it was hopeless." The job went to Reed. "Tom ended up winning every county in northern California except for San Francisco", says Clark—a stunning victory for Reagan.

After the election, Reagan asked Clark to be one of a team of three men and proceed to Sacramento to determine the problems he would face as new governor. Taking leave of his law practice, Clark accepted on a ninety-day commitment. From the November 1966 election to the January 1967 inauguration, Clark served on Reagan's Task Force on Reorganization of the Executive Branch, eventually becoming its chairman. The team reported to Reagan a dim fiscal picture; the state was spending in excess of one million dollars per day above revenue. Upon hearing Clark's report, the Governor-elect responded with a smile, "Do you think we can ask for a recount?"

When January arrived and Clark was about to return home, Reagan asked him to stay on and become his cabinet secretary to organize his communication structure. Clark was content with his life as a country lawyer; yet, he was struck by Reagan's commitment to address not only state concerns, from taxes to education, but also issues beyond California's borders, issues important to Bill Clark, such as U.S.-Soviet relations, the Vietnam War, and other geopolitical topics.

Reagan was "a man of truth and integrity", Clark concluded, "whose philosophy made sense". These were the qualities of a good leader, the characteristics Clark had seen in the other men he had admired,

---

[4] See "Up from Death Valley", *Time*, June 17, 1966; and Lou Cannon, *Governor Reagan* (New York: Public Affairs, 2003), pp. 144–45.

such as his father, grandfather, and godfather. The ranch tugged, but so did Ronald Reagan. Clark accepted his offer and moved his family to a rental apartment in Sacramento in June, at the end of the children's school year.

The Office of the Governor

The new Governor, says Clark, felt the enormity of his responsibility but his underlying philosophy and vision allowed him to approach his task with gusto. Fast-growing California, with twenty million citizens, was the most populous state in the union and the world's sixth-largest economy. The state government consisted of 115,000 employees and was spending, as Budget Director Caspar Weinberger soon discovered, more than $5 billion annually. By cutting his teeth on California's enormous budget and bureaucracy, and in learning the importance of delegation, Reagan was receiving an education in managing a massive economy that would serve him well in Washington.

Relying on an agenda prepared by Clark, Reagan presided over regular meetings of his "inner cabinet" consisting of Secretary Battaglia, Cabinet Secretary Clark, Press Secretary Nofziger, and four executive directors—Spencer Williams, Norman "Ike" Livermore, Gordon Luce, and Earl Coke. At thirty-two, Battaglia was the youngest of a cabinet that averaged only forty-one years of age. Reagan was fifty-five.

The four executive directors, all of whom ran a state agency or department, convened with Clark Monday through Friday at 5 P.M. to address the issues of the day. On Monday, Wednesday, and Friday the five men met in the morning for an hour to prepare issues for the Governor prior to the scheduled cabinet meeting. Out of this process came a well-known contribution established by Clark: the Reagan "mini-memo".

Every issue taken to the Governor was presented in a one-page, four-paragraph memo with one paragraph each devoted to the statement of the issue, the facts in the case, a discussion (pro and con), and a recommendation: ISSUE, FACT, DISCUSSION, RECOMMENDATION. At the cabinet meetings, Reagan read the memos, asked questions, made any decisions required, then sealed them with his trademark "OK, RR" at the bottom of the page. Lou Cannon, the San Jose Mercury-News reporter who later became the definitive biographer of Reagan's governorship, said the mini-memos worked well, in part because Clark was "scrupulously fair" in representing all sides of an issue, in order not "to cook" a decision.[5]

From the outset, the mini-memos were criticized as "mini-minded". Some argued that complex issues could not be boiled down to a four-paragraph, issue-fact-discussion-recommendation formula.[6] While there might be some truth to the criticism, Clark used the memos to avoid overwhelming the chief executive with time-consuming reports. As he later explained to a reporter, "[I]t has been found that almost any issue can be reduced to a single page. . . . [I]f the governor wants to go into the thing in more depth, he will request more detailed reports." The only way the Governor can "operate efficiently", added Clark, "is to ration his time".[7]

Cabinet Secretary Clark described the decision-making process as "an inverted funnel in which facts move upward and decisions downward"—a system he would later employ as director of President Reagan's National Security Council. Reagan also preferred a system that he and Clark called "round-tabling". Whatever the issue, the Governor wanted comments from everyone around the table. Clark told a reporter that Reagan was "a good listener and a decisive executive", and that the Governor had "never once . . . failed to reach a decision on the issues we have presented him".[8] Reagan enjoyed making decisions, especially if the issue was ripe, and did not defer matters. "He was like a good judge", says Clark. "He would rule from the bench as often as he could."

Even with a method of delegation in place for handling the affairs of state, Reagan and his team were nearly overwhelmed by the amount of work facing them. Clark was putting in twelve to eighteen hour days at the office. Asked by a journalist what impressed him most during the first one hundred days of state government, Clark replied: "That's easy. The magnitude of it all." The first few months had brought

---

[5] See Cannon, *Governor Reagan*, pp. 187 and 400.

[6] For an early example, see Carl Ingram, "Aide Defends 'Mini-Memos'", *Sacramento Union*, June 16, 1967.

[7] Quoted in Lee Edwards, *Reagan: A Political Biography* (San Diego, CA: Viewpoint Books, 1967), pp. 205–6. See pages 203–4 for a more detailed schedule of the Governor's day.

[8] Lou Cannon, "Reagan's 'Inner Cabinet' at Work: County's Clark in Key Role", *Ventura County Star-Free Press*, February 26, 1967, p. D7.

"crisis after crisis on what seems like an hourly basis". At one time during an interview with a reporter, Clark had a caller waiting in his outer office and was talking on two telephones at once. "That's the way things go most of the time," said Clark, "although I try not to take too many calls while talking to someone." [9]

The Abortion Decision

Abortion was one of the big issues confronting Reagan during his first few months in office. In the mid-1960s, abortion was not the national controversy it became after the 1973 *Roe v. Wade* Supreme Court decision. Polite society, as a rule, did not discuss such personal matters. So when the Therapeutic Abortion Act was being debated in the state assembly, Reagan was not sure what to think about it. He later admitted that abortion had been "a subject I'd never given much thought to".[10] Additionally, his aides were divided on the question.[11]

Reagan turned to his trusted advisor Clark: "Bill, I've got to know more—theologically, philosophically, medically." Clark loaded up the Governor with reading materials, and Reagan spent a weekend in semi-seclusion. Years later, Reagan remarked that he did "more studying and soul searching" on abortion than on any other issue as governor.[12] Edmund Morris, the official Reagan biographer, said that "by the time the Therapeutic Abortion Act reached him on June 13, Reagan was quoting Saint Thomas Aquinas."

Nonetheless, Reagan signed the legislation, having been convinced by some among his own party and staff that the bill only allowed abortions in rare cases, where pregnancy would gravely impair the

---

[9] Bob Lauffer, "Ventura Countian among Top Aides to Gov. Reagan", *Daily News* (Camarillo, CA), March 27, 1967.

[10] Ronald Reagan, radio broadcast, "Abortion Laws", April 1975, in Kiron Skinner, Annelise Anderson, and Martin Anderson, eds., *Reagan, in His Own Hand: The Writings of Ronald Reagan That Reveal His Revolutionary Vision for America* (New York: Free Press, 2001), p. 384.

[11] See Cannon, *Governor Reagan*, p. 211.

[12] See Edmund Morris, *Dutch: A Memoir of Ronald Reagan* (New York: Random House, 1999), p. 352; Reagan, "Abortion Laws", p. 380; Cannon, *Governor Reagan*, p. 212; and Sitman, "The Conscience of a President", in Paul Kengor and Peter Schweizer, eds., *The Reagan Presidency* (Lanham, MD: Rowman-Littlefield, 2005), p. 88.

physical or mental health of the woman or resulted from rape or incest. Further, Reagan assumed a veto would be overridden.[13]

After the Therapeutic Abortion Act of 1967 became law, the number of legal abortions in California boomed from 518 in Reagan's first year in office to an average of 100,000 per year from 1968 to 1974, the remaining years of his governorship.[14] As would happen in the years ahead with nearly every other state abortion law, the mental-health provision was abused by patient and doctor alike. Even the bill's Democrat sponsor later confessed to being surprised that physicians so liberally interpreted the law.[15]

Reagan was shocked at the unintended consequences of his signature and left with an "undefinable sense of guilt" after abortions skyrocketed in California. It was the "the only time as governor or president that Reagan acknowledged a mistake on major legislation". Clark called the incident "perhaps Reagan's greatest disappointment in public life".[16]

As noted by scholar Matt Sitman, Reagan's signing of the abortion bill was an inauspicious political beginning for a man that reporter Fred Barnes later labeled the "father of the pro-life movement".[17] Yet it was his experience of being duped by the advocates of abortion that crystallized Reagan's commitment to protecting the sanctity of human life. "It is impossible to understand his later staunchly pro-life positions without grasping the lessons he learned from this early political battle." Reagan came away from his mistake with "a cogent understanding", politically and morally, of abortion and its implications.[18]

A repentant and wiser Reagan emerged ready for battle, declaring, "When this subject arises again, we shall be prepared." [19] Clark was

---

[13] See Morris, *Dutch*, p. 352; Cannon, *Governor Reagan*, pp. 210–14; Sitman, p. 88; and William Clark, "Ronald Reagan, Lifeguard", foreword to *Abortion and the Conscience of the Nation*, by Ronald Reagan (Sacramento, CA: New Regnery Publishing, 2000), pp. 9–10.

[14] Among others, data cited in Dinesh D'Souza, *Ronald Reagan: How an Ordinary Man Became an Extraordinary Leader* (New York: Free Press, 1997), p. 67.

[15] Cannon, *Governor Reagan*, pp. 210–14.

[16] See Morris, *Dutch*, p. 352; Cannon, *Governor Reagan*, p. 213; and Clark, Foreword to *Abortion*, p. 9.

[17] For the definitive examination of this subject, see: Sitman, "The Conscience of a President". Also see: Fred Barnes, "American Conservatism: Ronald Reagan, Father of the Pro-Life Movement", *Wall Street Journal*, November 6, 2003, p. A14.

[18] Sitman, "The Conscience of a President", p. 88.

[19] Clark, Foreword to *Abortion*, p. 10.

already prepared. From this point forward, he and Ronald Reagan would be of one mind and would act accordingly, in regard to the subject of the sacredness of all human life, as history and this narrative demonstrate.

The Scandal

By late summer of 1967 things were calming down a bit at the Governor's office. The administration was in less of a day-to-day emergency mode and more attuned to the big picture. Cabinet Secretary Clark felt he was easing into a steady, more relaxed "plateau". Just then, an internal crisis erupted, with serious potential to derail Reagan's governorship, and, thereby, his presidential prospects.

A scandal emerged involving Executive Secretary Battaglia, suspected of being involved in an illicit sexual affair with another Reagan aide. Even more explosive, particularly given social views at the time, were allegations that the affair was homosexual. When certain reporters first wanted to expose such sensational specifics, both Reagan and Clark dissuaded them. Both said, "Think of his children."

Several senior Reagan aides began investigating the rumors, which culminated in a dramatic meeting with Reagan on Friday, August 25, 1967. Eleven of Reagan's top aides and supporters gathered in the governor's suite at the Del Coronado Hotel in San Diego, where they revealed to the Governor that Battaglia stood accused of inappropriate conduct. Reagan's counselors recommended that he fire Battaglia.[20]

There was more to his advisors' concerns than the sexual charges. Members of the administration had been dissatisfied with Battaglia's management, including his frequent and lengthy absences. Reagan was unsure how to react—he liked Battaglia; he liked everyone. He considered the evidence and the various alternatives, and on Saturday Battaglia was asked by Holmes Tuttle to resign.

Tuttle and Henry Salvatori, two prominent members of the Kitchen Cabinet—the wealthy group of California conservative businessmen poised to make Ronald Reagan president—were worried the Battaglia affair would harm Reagan's chances for the presidency. Reagan had been identified as a leading presidential candidate, but what were his

---

[20] See Cannon, *Governor Reagan*, p. 238.

chances once his top staff person, the man who ran his victorious gubernatorial campaign, left after only eight months on the job?

On top of that, the expected negative publicity could undermine Reagan's credibility. As predicted, the September 15 *San Francisco Examiner* ran a double headline about the resignation across the top of the fold. The *Sacramento Bee* political writer wrote that Battaglia's departure was the "puzzlement of 1967 for Sacramento".[21] Other articles ran with titles like "Mystery Cloaks Battaglia Exit" and "Mystery Still Shrouds Battaglia Resignation". Finally, on October 31, gossip columnist Drew Pearson broke the full story in the *Los Angeles Times*, asking whether Governor Reagan could "survive" the "discovery that a homosexual ring has been operating in his office". Pearson claimed that he knew of a "tape recording" of a "sex orgy" that had allegedly occurred in a Lake Tahoe cabin purchased by two male Reagan aides.[22]

The New Chief of Staff

The Kitchen Cabinet knew that a reliable man of integrity was needed immediately to replace Battaglia, and Clark was the unanimous choice of Reagan and his staff. As cabinet secretary, Clark had run the shop during Battaglia's absences.[23] He already had proved himself capable of performing chief of staff duties. Clark's new position was confirmed on August 26, 1967 in a letter handwritten by Ronald Reagan:

> All papers, documents and other property of the Governors offices (the executive wing) are hereby placed under the custody & control of Wm. P. Clark Jr. and/or such other persons as he may designate in writing, and nothing shall be removed from these offices without the permission of Wm. P. Clark Jr.
>
> Ronald Reagan

> Witnessed by—Arthur F. Van Court 8/26/67
> Arnold E. Nielsen 8/26/67

---

[21] Richard Rodda, "Battaglia's Departure Is Capitol's 1967 Puzzlement", *Sacramento Bee*, September 3, 1967.

[22] See Cannon, *Governor Reagan*, p. 248.

[23] Ibid., p. 239.

The letter had been written the same day Kitchen Cabinet member Tuttle informed Battaglia that he had to go.

On the morning after Labor Day, Clark quietly moved into the offices vacated by Battaglia. His salary was raised to $24,000, still substantially less than he made practicing law. The unimpressive amount failed to convey that next to the Governor, he was the most powerful man in Sacramento, a position to which he had never aspired. His picture was on the front page of every newspaper in the state, and for the first time, he was featured in the nation's major dailies and weeklies.

The *New York Times* introduced Clark to its readership as "another of the political amateurs" whom Reagan had drafted into government service. The *Times* added that this new "second-in-command" would "revamp" Reagan's administration and help "shape" the direction of state government. The *Times* described Clark as a lawyer/cattle man and former Democrat. Clark's "Democratic mother", reported the *Times*, said her son had moved "so far to the right we can't even discuss politics".[24]

Likewise, the Associated Press said that the "new" Reagan administration might now become more conservative under the influence of the "35-year-old, tall, reserved and usually unsmiling attorney".[25] In the *San Jose Mercury News*, Lou Cannon noted that Clark was a "lanky" rancher-lawyer with a hobby of "horses and kids" who would eagerly help Reagan "turn back the tide of bigness" in government.[26]

Letters of congratulations poured in to Clark. One of the most meaningful was a telegram sent on August 30 from "Gen and Doc Tilley" of Oxnard, who knew the new executive secretary as a little boy. It read: "DEAR BILLIE, OUR CONGRATULATIONS ON YOUR PROMOTION. IT IS DIFFICULT TO BELIEVE [OF] A LITTLE BOY WHO RODE HIS PONY SO MANY MILES TO RECEIVE HIS EDUCATION. NOW LOOK WHERE YOU ARE. LOVE AND GOOD LUCK."

---

[24] Gladwin Hill, "Lawyer Revamps Reagan's Regime". *New York Times*, September 10, 1967.

[25] "Mystery Still Shrouds Battaglia Resignation", *Associated Press*, September 1967. (Note: The exact date was not included on the photocopy of the press clipping at Clark's office.)

[26] Lou Cannon, "Turn Back the Tide of Bigness", *San Jose Mercury News*, August 29, 1967.

Robert Martinez, an old friend from Oxnard, also sent a telegram: "CONGRATULATIONS WISHING YOU THE EVERLASTINGNESS OF A SPIRI-TUAL STRENGTH AND WISDOM FOR CONTINUED POLITICAL SUCCESS."[27]

The Executive Secretary and the Governor

Clark now met with Reagan daily, sometimes hourly, to confer on major issues. It was at this time that Clark coined the phrase and approach "Let Reagan Be Reagan." There had been a rule under Battaglia that the chief of staff always be present when anyone met with the Governor. One of Clark's first acts was to end that restriction, to lift the Battaglia "curtain" around Reagan and allow any cabinet member to meet alone with the Governor.[28] Unlike other Reagan staff, in Sacramento and later in Washington, Clark had full confidence in Reagan. He never thought Reagan needed handlers to guide him.

From the outset, says Clark, he was impressed by Reagan's intelligence, which, he adds, was "very much underestimated". The perception that he was a know-nothing did not bother him. "He'd let it roll by and wink, or give a smile. He had tremendous faith not only in God but in himself and in what he said and stood for." Reagan even used the dummy image to his advantage. "That, 'Golly, gee whiz, oh heck', was, I think, part of his protection; and, at the same time, I think he used it to read into others", Clark explains. "I've always said that he was wiser than his cabinet and staff combined."

Reagan's alleged penchant for occasional "rambling" stories also served a purpose, Clark says. His anecdotes were not directionless digressions, but parables with a message. "They were always related to the point of discussion, and you had to connect the dots. Not everyone picked up on this. Some people thought his mind was wandering, meandering, when in fact it was not at all. If you paid attention, it clicked, and you would realize the point he was making."

---

[27] Clark was so overwhelmed with his new task that he likely never even saw these congratulatory messages. He would have been saddened to learn that they all received the same cursory one-sentence form-letter response: "Thank you for your kind message; I deeply appreciate your good wishes and confidence." Ditto for telegrams sent by Michael Wallace of Oxnard, the Melotts, the Corcorans, A. E. Jewell, and other Oxnard friends.

[28] On the "curtain", see Cannon, Governor Reagan, p. 254.

Clark says that at times, many of us, even Nancy Reagan, failed to see where his stories were leading. He recalls a later trustees' meeting at the Reagan Library. Clark was there, as were the President and First Lady. Reagan began a story that seemed unrelated to the subject at hand, and Clark noticed that Mrs. Reagan's foot was poking the President from under the table—a gesture that said, "Get with it." "In fact," says Clark, "he was right on point—as usual."

Reagan had a "tremendous memory, better than any of ours", Clark continues. "He had an instant recall of previous mini-memos", giving him the ability to keep track of all the details brought forth in meetings. Ed Meese agrees, saying that Reagan probably had a photographic memory.

The Personal Reagan

Starting in Sacramento, Reagan observers state, Clark got closer to Reagan than anyone who knew the man, with the exception of Mrs. Reagan. The two were so close that Reagan biographers such as Lou Cannon, Richard Reeves, and others who worked with both men, say that Reagan regarded Clark as a brother.

"I knew the man intimately", says Clark. "I knew he was a man of faith—faith in himself, faith in God, faith in country." Clark says Reagan reminded him of his father—the greatest compliment Clark can bestow—because of "his integrity and discretion, his vision and good judgment". Like Clark's father, Reagan was a "gentle man".[29]

The relationship was so close that it often did not require verbal communication. "Usually, I knew his thinking, just as I knew my father's thinking", says Clark. "Both my father and Reagan were, surprisingly, men of very few words, and this does surprise people about Reagan. For a man known as the Great Communicator, he didn't need to say much to me, because I understood where he wanted to go, as I did my father.... When my father went into the corral, I knew what he wanted. It was the same with Reagan. I'd be there in a crowd with him and by eye contact I knew what he wanted to do next, if he

---

[29] Clark quoted in an article titled, "Shandon's Clark recalls work on Reagan team", written by reporter Cynthia Neff for the local paper *The Tribune* (photocopy in Clark's files contains no date or full citation).

wanted to move on or whatever. I don't like the term 'body language', but there was a certain chemistry I had with him, like I had with my dad."

Clark and Reagan not only thought alike but also shared some of the same physical characteristics. Both had dark hair and were fairly tall, roughly 6 feet 2 inches and 180 pounds. If the Governor spilled coffee on his jacket, Clark could toss him his.

Both were westerners at heart. Reagan's son Michael says the two men built their relationship "[in] the dirt, in the dust, around horses". He adds, "They were good friends, yes, but they were more than that; they were ranchers." [30] Reagan's personal secretary Helene von Damm says that of all the relationships that Ronald Reagan had, he was probably most comfortable with Bill Clark: "The westernness, the horses. They had so many similarities. Also, Bill didn't crowd him, didn't pressure him on decisions, didn't push him, didn't talk him to death." [31]

Throughout their political careers, both men were accused of being inexperienced, undereducated, overly simple, and even unintelligent. But neither of them seemed to allow these criticisms to get under his skin. They each possessed an easy grace in the face of criticism, a modesty that forbade them from taking themselves too seriously. "There was no false pride there at all—pure humility", Clark says of Reagan. His fame from the movies, television, and then as Governor of California did not go to his head.

One day in the late 1960s, Michael Deaver, whom Clark hired as his deputy chief of staff, was with Governor Reagan at the Waldorf-Astoria Hotel in New York City. Reagan was in town to give a speech, and earlier that morning had called Deaver to suggest a walk. After ten minutes of strolling busy sidewalks, a middle-aged man approached with a grin: "Hey, I know you from television, and you're the best. You're Ray Milland!" Reagan smiled as the man thrust a pen and paper at him for an autograph, recalled Deaver, and unflinchingly signed it—"Ray Milland." The autograph seeker left happy. Reagan moved on as if nothing untoward had happened. [32]

---

[30] Interview with Michael Reagan, May 9, 2005.

[31] Interview with Helen Von Damm, November 21, 2005.

[32] Michael Deaver, *A Different Drummer: My Thirty Years with Ronald Reagan* (New York: HarperCollins, 2001), p. 157.

Clark remembers a similar incident. One day a giggly bobby-soxer rushed toward the former actor, shouting, "Ronald, Ronald—can I have your autograph?" Reagan happily obliged. Without looking at the signature, the young woman said, "Thank you, Mr. Coleman." Reagan merely chuckled and continued on his way.[33]

As a young man under the tutelage of his grandfather, father, and extended family, Clark learned and in turn taught his own children the virtues and the importance of obeying the law, no matter what your station in life. A perfect opportunity presented itself one day in the fall of 1968. Clark was driving his wife and their five children back to Sacramento after attending a Stanford football game. They left the game early and needed to make good time on the road so Clark could attend an important meeting. He was apparently tailgating the car in front of him, or so he was told after being pulled over by a highway patrol car.

The officer immediately recognized Clark as a man he had seen on the news the night before: "that guy who works for the governor". The children, meanwhile, were wide-eyed, noses pressed to the windows, watching their father's every move. Clark explained to the officer that he was rushing to Sacramento for a meeting. "Well, you're in a hurry and need to go", said the officer, dismissing him. "Not in such a hurry that you can't write me a ticket", Clark replied. "See those faces in the back window!" The patrolman walked back to his vehicle and began to write. He returned, handed the slip of paper to the miscreant with a warning scrawled across the form: "Be careful—and Good Luck!"

Reagan recognized the difficulty of finding time for family in the life of politics. Whenever he caught his staff working as he was heading for home, he would open the door long enough to say, "All right, everybody, it's time to go home to your spouses and families!" Regardless, staff meetings with Clark often went on into the night. A "family first" approach to one's work was not always possible with the demands of Clark's position, but one of the compensating benefits of the amount of time Clark spent serving the Governor was the closeness of the Clark and Reagan families. The Clark children frequently went to Reagan's home to swim. One day, they arrived only to learn that a

---

[33] Interview with Bill Clark, July 30, 2005.

schedule conflict meant that young Ron was not there. Not a problem—the Governor swam with them, joining them in a vigorous game of "Marco Polo".[34]

Another dimension of Reagan that added to the depth of his relationship with Clark was the practice of his faith. Clark and Reagan prayed together, and sometimes Clark caught Reagan unawares praying alone. During one of Reagan's first trips out of state as governor, on a TWA flight to Baltimore's Friendship Airport, Clark got word from the captain, "Tell your Governor that Martin Luther King, Jr. has just been shot." He informed the Governor, and Reagan grew silent. Clark walked away and when he turned back to look at Reagan, he saw his head bowed, his lips moving in silent prayer.[35] Reagan frequently borrowed a line attributed to Lincoln, who said that he was often driven to his knees by the "overwhelming conviction" that he had nowhere else to go.

The Chief of Staff Grind and the Nancy Account

Clark, too, turned to prayer for help with his arduous duties, but as a reminder to do so with discretion, he asked his secretary, Helene von Damm, to type up Matthew 6:5–8, and he kept it in his desk drawer: "And when you pray, you must not be like the hypocrites ... go into your room and shut the door and pray to your Father who is in secret."

Clark also relied upon the prayers said by others on his behalf. In times of doubt or difficulty, he was encouraged by the uplifting tone of their notes, some of which he saved over the years, such as this one from his friend Nancy Reynolds: "Dear Bill, I said two more Rosaries—and I think the Man up there is wondering about my credibility gap ... since I don't come around very often. I'm now working on St. Jude—Any other suggestions? God Bless—NCR."

Other forms of encouragement also were gratefully received by Clark. On January 29, 1968, a quiet Reagan supporter, famed cartoonist Charles Schulz, sent him a signed and framed strip of one of his legendary Charlie Brown "Peanuts" cartoons. Eventually it came to hang over the ranch kitchen door.

---

[34] Interview with Linda and Paul Clark, July 30, 2005.
[35] Interview with Clark, August 24, 2001.

One of Clark's priorities in his new job was regular interaction with Nancy Reagan, which began each day at 8:45 A.M. At that time each morning, Ronald Reagan departed the governor's residence for the office, where he arrived, like clockwork, at 9:00 A.M. Once her husband left, Mrs. Reagan phoned Clark. She knew she had fifteen minutes, and typically began the call with, "Oh, Bill, did you read the article about Ronnie in the *LA Times*?" Her concerns, says Clark, were in regard to Reagan's public image and whether or not his message and accomplishments were being correctly reported.

Eye on the clock, she ensured she finished within fifteen minutes, and shortly after the click of the receiver, a grinning Reagan strolled in from the elevator. "He'd be smiling that wonderful cat-bird smile, because he knew she had called", says Clark. "He knew what she was up to, but he always shrugged it off in his good-natured way. He would say: 'Well, she called again, didn't she?'" Reagan, noted Clark, already anticipated the content of the call, since he and his wife had discussed the issue at the breakfast table and had not necessarily agreed on the issue or approach.

Mrs. Reagan's worries did not stop at 9:00 A.M. She called Clark several times a day, sometimes hourly. Clark appreciated Mrs. Reagan's concerns and good counsel even when her position opposed his own. Her judgment was good, he said, and her analyses often keen. Ronald Reagan would not have become either governor or president without Nancy, says Clark, disagreeing with Ed Meese, who said that Ronald Reagan would have become president with or without any of them. "No. He needed us to be good cop/bad cop for him—daily. For instance, he couldn't fire anyone. We had to do that for him", says Clark.

Mrs. Reagan was more vigilant than anyone in protecting her husband from predators and opportunists. Their son Ron has said that while his father trusted everyone, his mother trusted no one.[36] The greatest cause of Mrs. Reagan's anxiety was the constant threat to her husband's life, a cost of statesmanship that would haunt her throughout his political career. The Governor received innumerable death threats, sometimes several per day in the mail. Most of these letters were

---

[36] Ron said this on the PBS documentary on Reagan's presidency. "Reagan", *The American Experience*, television documentary produced by PBS, WGBH-TV Boston, 1998.

shrugged off as "nut mail", Clark says. "There was an old saying that if someone says he is trying to kill you, he's probably the safest guy around." Still, this was a decade that had seen several political assassinations, beginning and ending with the shooting of a Kennedy. When Clark found out that a Cuban communist group might be plotting to kill Reagan,[37] he took the threat seriously and brought it to the attention of Art Van Court, in charge of Reagan's security; Van Court immediately notified the FBI.

Eventually, the phone calls and frequent interventions from Mrs. Reagan became too burdensome for Clark, and he found it necessary to turn over the Nancy Account to someone else. In a fateful move, Clark delegated Mrs. Reagan's concerns to his deputy, Michael Deaver. Clark had discovered Deaver operating the mailroom of the Governor-elect's office and made him his "number-two" man during the transition period after the election. The two worked well together throughout the governor years, says Clark, who found Deaver to be "loyal and hard working, a valued colleague and a much appreciated member of my staff".

Clark Moves On

As 1968 drew to a close, Lieutenant Governor Robert Finch announced he was leaving to join the new Nixon administration in Washington. With that, Reagan came to Clark with an intriguing request: he wanted Bill Clark to become the next lieutenant governor.

A number of top staff lobbied the Governor for the coveted position—a launching pad to a possible governorship. Clark turned down the job. Having already spent two years working long hours for the Governor in Sacramento, he wanted to spend more time with his wife and five children at the ranch.

Normally, when someone declined such an offer, the Governor would move on to someone else. This time, he took the rare step of asking Clark to take a week to think about it and to discuss it with Joan. "That was a crossroads", says Clark. Did he want to run for governor? Could he see himself campaigning? No, he decided that he preferred the behind-the-scene roles of chief administrator, troubleshooter, and

---

[37] See Peter Schweizer, *Reagan's War* (New York: Doubleday, 2002).

trusted advisor. Clark knew he was disappointing Reagan in not accepting the appointment, but he also believed there were others better suited for the job.

Just then, a slot opened for a newly created superior court position in San Luis Obispo County. Reagan asked Clark if he would be interested in taking the post. Clark was, though he had doubts: he did not have a "full, formal legal education", which he considered key to a judicial appointment. He said such positions on the bench were reserved for the "academic minded". On the other hand, Clark had been a lawyer for ten years in a successful practice. His academic qualifications were far from perfect, but they were not completely lacking.

On November 25, 1968, the press office released a statement announcing that Governor Reagan had "reluctantly agreed" to accept the resignation of William P. Clark as his executive secretary, effective January 31. Further, the Governor announced that he would appoint Clark superior court judge in San Luis Obispo County.

> I have long been aware of Bill's desire to return to Paso Robles and the ranch. From the very outset, Bill made it plain that he intended to serve in state government for approximately eight months. At my personal insistence, he graciously agreed to extend his stay in Sacramento. He has contributed much to the success of state government during the past two years. His performance as executive secretary has been outstanding. He is one of the brightest and ablest young men I have ever had the pleasure of knowing. His qualities of leadership and the balanced judgment he has demonstrated in state service will serve in the San Luis Obispo County judiciary exceedingly well. . . .

Clark had been repeatedly described as Ronald Reagan's "No. 1 right-hand man", as "at the side of the governor continually", as a "hard worker, in whom Reagan has great confidence," and "as close to the governor as anyone".[38] He was given a great deal of credit for Reagan's success as governor.

---

[38] See "No Politics! Oh, Brother!", *Tulare Advance-Register*, December 5, 1968; Bob Holt, "Not Everyone's Against Clark", *Ventura County Star-Free Press*, December 4, 1968; "Politics Charge Hits Reagan on Appointment", *Sacramento Bee*, December 1, 1968; and Editorial, "County, Capitol Will Miss Bill Clark, Jr.", *Daily News*, December 3, 1968.

In the *San Jose Mercury News*, Lou Cannon credited Clark with several important accomplishments: He played a "major role" in making important hiring and firing decisions. Also, he and Deaver "showed great skill in shaping some of the unwieldier poverty programs into more manageable and better ones".[39]

As previously noted, a weakness of Reagan was his inability to fire anyone, including those who "made things very difficult", particularly those involved in the Battaglia scandal. Caspar Weinberger further noted: "Bill handled their removal very skillfully and very fairly. . . . This was an important episode that greatly improved the success of the office." Clark "did an excellent job" organizing the governor's office and staff, Weinberger said, and worked well with all of the various interests competing for the Governor's time. He "brought order to the generally chaotic early days of any new administration".

By helping to ensure that Ronald Reagan had a successful governorship, Bill Clark helped ensure that Ronald Reagan would become president. "The Governor was laid out on a bed of linen from the governor's house to the presidency," said Weinberger, "and that was because Bill Clark kept things straight and clean in the Governor's house."[40]

Key to Reagan's bid for the presidency, Weinberger continued, was that his two terms as governor "were viewed as successful and marked by large accomplishments, and Bill Clark had a lot to do with that."[41] As the Governor prepared to run for a second term, he received the approbation of some of the state's top (and most liberal) editorial boards. The *Los Angeles Times* judged Reagan an "accomplished practitioner in the art of government" and a "proven administrator".[42] The *San Francisco Chronicle* stated that Reagan had "saved the state from bankruptcy".[43] *Newsweek* described the Governor as "one of the

---

[39] Lou Cannon, "Reagan Loses Valuable Aide in Clark", *San Jose Mercury-News*, December 1, 1968.

[40] Interview with Cap Weinberger, April 14, 2005.

[41] Ibid.

[42] Quotes cited in Lee Edwards, *Ronald Reagan: A Political Biography* (Houston, TX: Nordland Publishing, 1980), pp. 203, 209.

[43] This quote was used vigorously in Reagan campaign ads at the time. Also see Gary G. Hamilton and Nicole Woolsey Biggart, *Governor Reagan, Governor Brown: A Sociology of Power* (New York: Columbia University Press, 1984), p. 165.

most brilliantly gifted politicians anywhere in the U.S. today."[44] In sum, concluded Weinberger: "I have always thought that Reagan's enormous success as governor, particularly in his first term—the term that propelled him onto the national stage—was in large part due to Bill Clark."[45]

Governor Reagan replaced Clark with Edwin Meese III. The 38-year-old Meese, whom Clark had previously promoted to legal affairs secretary, was Clark's choice. "Five people wanted my job", said Clark. Based on his loyalty, integrity, and discretion, "clearly the right person was Ed."[46] Meese remained with Reagan for the remainder of his gubernatorial years and followed him to the White House.

---

[44] Quotes cited in Edwards, *Ronald Reagan*, pp. 203, 209.

[45] Caspar Weinberger, *In the Arena: A Memoir of the 20th Century* (Washington, DC: Regnery, 2001), pp. 149–52, 161.

[46] Lee Edwards, *To Preserve and Protect: The Life of Edwin Meese III* (Washington, DC: Heritage Foundation, 2005), pp. 15–17.

CHAPTER 5

The California Court

Bill Clark's next stop was the bench. Letters of congratulation flooded in to the judge-to-be, from old friends such as A. E. Jewell, Chief of Police for the city of Oxnard, and Father Tom Behan of the novitiate days. Behan sent a telegram: "ALL HAIL TO JUDGE AND RETURN TO FAMILY WHAT BETTER GIFT FOR THANKSGIVING!" This was the same sentiment expressed by Augustinian Provincial John F. Blethen, who told Bill the appointment would allow more time with his family and to pursue his "love of ranching", but was also a "critical position" for the state of California.

There were also regrets: Glenn Campbell of the Hoover Institution at Stanford regretted that Clark would be leaving Reagan's side. Likewise, Jacqueline Hume, one of the members of the Kitchen Cabinet, congratulated Clark but admitted to being "distressed" at his leaving.

The accolades were countered by political criticism. Clark was to begin the first of his three judgeships on January 13, 1969, but not before considerable uproar. Here a pattern began that continued for the next two decades: from the moment Ronald Reagan appointed Clark to a public position, there would be questions about his qualifications for these high-level jobs.

An editorial in the *Modesto Bee* accused Reagan of hypocrisy in appointing Clark, since Reagan had criticized the previous governor for placing "political hacks and cronies" on the bench.[1]

---

[1] Editorial, "Reagan Fails to Keep His Promises on the Appointment of Judges", *Modesto Bee*, December 6, 1968.

This was a common refrain. Another editorial, entitled "No Politics! Oh, Brother!" howled: "The governor has seen fit to use one of the most honorable public positions for which he holds appointment power to reward one of his political cronies for devoted personal service to his political boss." The editorial called Clark's appointment "a deplorable playing of politics", and called Clark a carpetbagger—a quite unfair criticism of a man who would spend the rest of his life in San Luis Obispo County.[2]

Even the friendly press found reasons to oppose Clark. *The Daily Democrat* of Woodland, California editorialized: "Clark, a lawyer and brilliant man, no doubt is qualified to be a judge. But the trouble is that he isn't a resident of San Luis Obispo County." Instead, said the paper, Clark was registered to vote in Oxnard.

That particular criticism reflected another pattern: Throughout Clark's appointments, the press struggled over the simplest facts regarding his private life. Yes, Clark was registered in Oxnard, but he owned a thousand-acre ranch in San Luis Obispo County, where he was in the process of building his home where he still resides. He told the press from the outset that he and Joan intended to live at the ranch "even if it meant chopping wood for a living".[3]

The *Daily Democrat* registered another common complaint on Clark's appointment: that the Governor had passed up two qualified San Luis Obispo County attorneys who had been approved and endorsed by the local bar.[4] In fact, added the political writer for the *San Francisco Examiner*, Reagan had chosen Clark "without consulting any local committee of the bar".[5]

The San Luis Obispo County Bar Association not only failed to endorse Clark but also overwhelmingly passed a resolution—38 to 9—to censure Governor Reagan for the manner in which he appointed his executive secretary to fill the vacancy. The bar favored the San Luis Obispo lawyer Wickson Woolpert and District Attorney James Powell.[6]

[2] Editorial, "No Politics! Oh, Brother!", *Tulare Advance-Register*, December 5, 1968.
[3] Quoted in "Politics Charge Hits Reagan on Appointment", *Sacramento Bee*, December 1, 1968.
[4] "As We See It: Non Merit Plan", *The Daily Democrat*, December 13, 1968.
[5] Sydney Kossen, "Reagan Can't Find Champion for Program", *San Francisco Examiner*, December 26, 1968.
[6] "Lawyers Vote Censure over Appointment of Superior Judge", *Atascadero News*, December 5, 1968.

This is not to suggest that Clark had no supporters. An editorial from a Ventura County newspaper predicted that residents would "learn to respect Clark the same way we in Ventura County have. We just wish the ranch where he has chosen to live with his wife and children was in Ventura County."[7]

In fact, Clark did receive some support from his new adopted county. The San Luis Obispo County Republican Central Committee unanimously endorsed him,[8] as did the tiny newspaper of Paso Robles, the town that would embrace Clark and for which he would one day do so much. "We will have a new judge, a stalwart young judge, a resident of the Great North County", stated the *Daily Press* in an editorial written by editor and publisher Ben Reddick. "He has many talents that we of this entire county can use. . . . Judge William Clark Jr. comes to serve here as a man of strength. He is needed."

As always with Clark, Ronald Reagan resolutely stuck to his guns. He was undeterred by the criticism, and Bill Clark, for the first time in his life, and ever thereafter, became *Judge* Clark.

* * *

When Richard Nixon heard that fellow Californian Clark was headed to the bench he rued the end of a promising political career. Nixon, the Republican candidate for president, saw Clark and Reagan in Palm Springs: "Bill, you're too young to retire!" asserted Nixon. Reagan immediately fired back: "He is not retiring!"

From January 1969 to August 1971, Clark served the state of California as a judge of the superior court, at the courthouse in San Luis Obispo, only forty miles from Shandon. It appeared that he and the family could now enjoy life back at the ranch, but Reagan continued to promote him. In August 1971, he elevated Clark to the state court of appeal in Los Angeles.

Two years later, Reagan tapped Bill Clark again, this time appointing him Associate Justice to the seven-member California Supreme Court, considered the most progressive bench in the country.

---

[7] Editorial, "County, Capitol Will Miss Bill Clark Jr.", *Daily News*, December 3, 1968.
[8] "Neutral Committee Backs Clark", *San Luis Obispo Telegram-Tribune*, December 10, 1968.

With each new Clark nomination, his qualifications, capabilities and knowledge were questioned, even ridiculed by the activist liberal wing of the state bar.

Confirmation for the California Supreme Court

Despite a confirmation process that was trying for Clark and his friends, Justice Robert Kane and Justice Mildred Lillie, on March 3, 1973, the California Commission on Judicial Appointments voted 2 to 1 to confirm Clark to the State Supreme Court. Attorney General Evelle Younger, a Republican who later ran for governor, voted for Clark, as did Senior Appellate Justice Parker Wood, the only one of the three who had worked with Clark; he and Clark had an unusually warm relationship. Wood respected him, even though they frequently reached opposing results in their judicial opinions. Supreme Court Chief Justice Don R. Wright, a Reagan appointee in 1970, voted against his confirmation; he said he did not consider Clark qualified by education or training.

What Wright did not acknowledge, but must have known, was that fifteen of the forty-three who had served on the California Supreme Court that century had not graduated from law school (this was also true for ten of the forty-four on the U.S. Supreme Court).[9] Like Clark, many of them could not afford law school. More than one observer noted that Wright's criteria would have barred many excellent justices from the court. All along, Wright had been expected to vote against Clark. Wright had been a great disappointment to Reagan, the start of a line of disappointing court picks by Reagan throughout his career. Wright had told Reagan that he favored capital punishment, information that he volunteered, without being asked, only to later lead the fight to ban the death penalty in the state. It was a sign of Reagan's jovial nature that he did not show public anger when Wright, in one of his first statements upon becoming chief justice, said he would set out to prove that he was not Ronald Reagan's "Archie Bunker". The liberal California bench and bar applauded.

Lou Cannon called Clark's two-month confirmation process a "distant early warning" of Reagan's later nomination of Robert Bork to the U.S. Supreme Court. Left-wing groups such as the National

---

[9] Cannon, *Governor Reagan*, p. 382.

Lawyers Guild and National Organization for Women organized against Clark. Ronald Reagan sent a gift to help him through the rough and tumble of the confirmation hearings. The crystal desk piece is engraved "Illegitimus Non Tatum Carborrundum"; that is, "Don't let the bastards wear you down!" signed, "To Bill, from Ron." [10]

Publicly, Reagan was even stronger in his support of his friend, taking the unprecedented step of appearing at Clark's swearing-in ceremony. The Governor's appearance was especially unusual as the ceremony was scheduled for the small courthouse in San Luis Obispo, rather than the traditional venue at the Supreme Court in San Francisco. After flying in unexpectedly, Reagan delivered this impromptu statement:

> Well, I imagine it would be redundant of me to say, Your Honors, ladies and gentlemen present, what a happy day this is for me. In having this present position for the last several years, there are many responsibilities; none of them have I taken more seriously than the responsibility with regard to my choosing of members of the judiciary. Very early in doing that, I thought perhaps some words of Cicero might be a helpful guide to me in addition to the advice and the counsel that I sought from those who were learned in the law. Cicero said: "The great affairs of life are not performed by physical strength or activity or nimbleness of body, but by deliberation, character, and expression of opinion."
>
> I have known Bill Clark from the time that I began holding office, had really only met him prior to that time, but I saw him in the hurly burly of state politics; I saw him when there was great strain and increased activity, and I observed always that ability to remain calm, to use good judgment. I saw the great sense of fairness that he always exhibited, and I should say, perhaps, that in making these various selections, I have also learned that he who would have nothing to do with thorns should never attempt to gather flowers. And I then took the opportunity to appoint Bill to the bench. I saw him there, and I saw the record that he achieved in that; and I happen to believe when someone asks me, "What are you the most proud of—" as an interviewer did just as recently as yesterday "—in all

---

[10] This is, in fact, a bastard Latin. The correct *form*—although this is a modern and humorous invention—would be "illigitimatis non carborundum", which uses the atypical construction of a dative of agency.—ED.

your time in government?" I think that ranking very high among whatever things I might give or offer as something in which I take pride, it will be the appointment of Bill Clark to the bench and now the appointment to this, the highest court in our state.

Thomas Jefferson—I did not overlook the facts with regard to his judicial record in making this appointment; I didn't overlook the fact that he was also a rancher. I spent most of my early life either on plowed ground or close to it and within sight of it, and I recall that Thomas Jefferson said:

"If you state a moral case to a plowman and a professor, the farmer will decide it as well and often better because he has not been led astray by any artificial rules."

Therefore, I can only say that I am going to quit talking because I want to get on with the purpose that has brought us here and see that moment fulfilled. I have the highest expectations, the greatest of trust and confidence and the greatest of respect and affection for the man who will here take the oath of office to the State Supreme Court.

Clark would spend the next eight years meeting Reagan's expectations.

The Rulings of Justice Clark

Justice Clark took the oath of office on March 23, 1973. Of course, he was not about to give up the ranch. He commuted from Shandon to the courthouses in Los Angeles, San Francisco, and Sacramento— distances of, respectively, 188 miles, 220 miles, and 246 miles. How did he do it? By Cessna 206 to San Francisco and Sacramento (weather permitting), taking off from the dirt driveway-turned-landing-strip on his ranch. He drove to Los Angeles, leaving at 3:00 A.M. on Monday morning to beat the traffic before rush hour—a three-hour commute before construction of the I-5 freeway. He would stay in one of the three cities from Monday to Wednesday before returning home to do his writing.

He endured the travel and absence from home to live on the ranch and provide stability for his family. The ranch was close enough to San Luis Obispo to satisfy Joan, who accepted the remoteness and isolation of the ranch. All of the children were doing well, with four of them enrolled at Cal Poly in San Luis Obispo.

Son Colin fondly recalls watching his dad unwind from the court on weekends as Bill surveyed the ranch either by pickup or on horseback, up and down the hills, with his kids and their dog, Lucy, in tow. The ranch was a welcome respite for the Judge.

Each time he stepped down from his old Cessna on his way to the courthouse, Clark walked right into a divide: In 1973, the California Supreme Court was split philosophically with Justices Tobriner, Mosk, and Sullivan considered judicial liberals and Justices Burke and McComb, conservative jurists. Chief Justice Donald Wright usually aligned himself with the liberal wing. The philosophical rift deepened after the 1977 appointment of Rose Bird as Chief Justice by Governor Jerry Brown, and continued throughout Clark's tenure.

Justice Clark participated in thousands of decisions on the California Supreme Court. He wrote many majority opinions, but often wrote dissents countering the activist majority. In time, a great many of these dissenting opinions became law. His first opinion was *Vaughn v. State Bar*, July 16, 1973; the last was *Vista Verde Farms v. Agricultural Labor Relations Board*, March 20, 1981.[11] The opinions cover 1,092 pages—"a lot of work", notes Clark, adding that twenty percent of one's time as a Supreme Court Justice is exciting, while eighty percent is routine— "much like flying".

The Rose Bird court was anything but routine or boring. Looking to shield its liberal-activist rulings from review (and possible reversal) by the U.S. Supreme Court, the liberal jurists purported to rely on the independent state grounds of the California Constitution, rather than the U.S. Constitution. This was considered clever, given that a state supreme court is usually the last word on the meaning of the state's constitution. Bird herself was a vigorous practitioner of the strategy when it assisted reaching her desired result. Justice Clark decried this subterfuge in a series of clearly written dissenting opinions, most notably *People v. Hannon* (1977) 19 Cal.3d 588, and also (in layman's language) in a speech in Los Angeles on April 4, 1977.

The philosophical split was most obvious in the area of criminal law. Clark believed that judges should interpret and enforce the law as written by the legislature, rather than as rewritten by themselves—the

---

[11] The last printed in the volume is *Vista Verde*, but the last decision Clark wrote was *People v. Harris*.

model of a strict constructionist who practiced judicial restraint. Over and over again, this put Clark in the minority, with Justice Frank Richardson the one judge most often concurring with Clark's opinions.

As he was so often in the minority, Clark felt compelled to write solid, succinct dissents to obtain the recognition of the working bar and academia. He wrote more opinions than any other member of the court during his term, dissenting against the activist majority. Yet, he also had his surprising share of majority opinions as well, occasionally swaying the others to accept his conservative positions.

The Death Penalty: People v. Robert Alton Harris and People v. Teron

A particularly noted opinion written by Justice Clark was *People v. Robert Alton Harris* (1981) 28 Cal.3d 935. Harris was executed in 1992, eleven years after Justice Clark wrote his 4-3 majority opinion affirming the conviction and death sentence, the first California execution in twenty-five years.

One legal observer said the Harris trial "was about as close to perfection as trials get. Everyone—the trial judge, the prosecutor, and the defense attorney—did their jobs beautifully." [12] A common error in a capital trial is overreaching by the prosecutor, who, though he can make a case with unassailable evidence, might nonetheless introduce evidence undermining the case on appeal. The prosecutor in this trial did not make this mistake. Still, a flawless job by the prosecutor, pointing to clear guilt, and leading to a death penalty conviction, might not matter to judges committed to finding any pretext to overturn a death-penalty sentence. Clark's staff waited in curious anticipation: What reason for reversal would the liberals on the court seize upon this time?

Predictably, the committed majority circulated internal memos that purported to find the usual errors. One by one, however, Clark and his staff, Dan McGovern in particular, countered their arguments. Finally, Justice Tobriner uncharacteristically broke ranks with his colleagues on the left, writing a brief separate opinion agreeing with Justice Clark that Harris had been given a fair trial.

---

[12] John Murphy, research attorney for Clark from 1975–1977; later, General Counsel, Veterans Administration, Washington, DC.

Rose Bird never once voted to uphold a death penalty conviction. A good sense of the death penalty jurisprudence of the Bird court is found in Justice Tobriner's majority opinion and Justice Clark's dissenting opinion in *People v. Teron* (1979) 23 Cal.3d 103. In his dissent in *Teron*, Justice Clark made the following observation:

> In order to faithfully implement the intent of the Legislature in this case, we must remind ourselves of the evil to be remedied by a death penalty statute. There is no better way of doing so than by review of the facts of this case.

FACTS

In 1975, in Anaheim, defendant brutally murdered Earl Reed for $1.75. Reed choked on his own blood after defendant first beat and then smothered him. When defendant went to Reed's room that night he intended, by his own admission, to rob Reed and then murder him "just so I could get away with" the robbery. Defendant had, he admitted, no other motive for killing Reed.

In 1977, prior to defendant's trial for the Reed murder, defendant was convicted of two other murders in Michigan. One of his Michigan victims was Norma Maxham, a 75-year-old woman from whom he rented a room. When Mrs. Maxham asked defendant to move out of the room he beat her until she was unconscious, tore off her clothes, bound her with electrical cord and hanged her by the neck. After waiting until he was certain of his victim's death, defendant left the house to buy pizza and beer. He returned to the room and, in the presence of the still hanging corpse, ate the pizza, drank the beer, took a shower and watched a football game on television.

While in jail in Michigan awaiting trial for the Maxham murder, defendant hanged a fellow inmate.

Defendant admits having committed at least two other murders, but states he has no idea of the total number of persons he has killed. He explains his incomplete recall by comparing the act of murder to drinking a cup of coffee. A month from now, defendant notes, one is not likely to remember having drunk a cup of coffee today.

Defendant claims he can easily make a knife while in jail, and will knife a guard if given the opportunity. Nothing the prison officials can do will deter him, defendant insists. If released from jail, defendant intends to return to his "everyday type of life."

This is the person the majority free from the gas chamber—modifying his sentence to life imprisonment with possibility of parole—by imputing to the Legislature the intention not to have the 1977 death penalty statute [which provided for life without possibility of parole, as an alternative to the previously mandatory death penalty] apply retroactively.

A review of the recent history of death penalty legislation in California reveals the utter absurdity of the majority's conclusion. (*People v. Teron, supra,* 23 Cal. 3d 103, 121–23.)

Clark had essentially argued that the state was failing to protect its citizenry from this out-of-control, determined killer, leaving no option but execution. So long as the California court was allowing a possibility for Reed to strike yet again, the state was not protecting its citizens. The majority of the court voted against Clark's conclusion.

Too bad Clark never saw the reaction to his opinions at the district attorney's office in Alameda County. One person who did was Lois Haight, a tough prosecutor and deputy district attorney of crime-ridden Alameda County, a future U.S. assistant attorney general, and later California judge herself. One morning each week the staff at the district attorney's office sat around a big table to read the latest court decisions. This was a "very disheartening" process for her and her fellow prosecutors, says Haight, because of the Bird court's numerous decisions that went against victims, police, and law-abiding citizens. "But then," recalls Haight, "we would come to Judge Clark's dissent, read it, and then we would all cheer! We would yell out, 'Oh, thank God for Judge Clark!'" She remembers how agonizing these legal losses were for all of them, including Clark, whom she says was treated "viciously and vindictively" by Rose Bird, but, in turn, "never came down to her level, and was always kind to her". And though they were legal losses, Haight viewed the Clark dissents as moral victories—"they were right; Judge Clark did what was right." [13]

---

[13] Interview with Judge Lois Haight Herrington, August 7, 2006.

Other Notable Decisions

John Murphy, an aide close to Justice Clark, says that a hallmark of Clark's decisions was his "constant effort" to protect individual constitutional rights from government encroachment. Clark often put himself in the position of the property owner.

Consider, for instance, his first majority decision as a Supreme Court justice, *San Diego Coast Regional Com. v. See the See, Limited* (1973) 9 Cal.3d 888. In this case, a developer had obtained a city permit to demolish an old building and construct a condominium before the enactment of the Coastal Zone Conservation Act of 1972, which created a California Coastal Commission. The Commission tried to block the developer from completing construction of the condominium by retroactively applying the 1972 act. Clark saw this as unjust, and ruled in favor of the developer.

In another case, *United Farm Workers of America v. Superior Court* (1975) 14 Cal.3d 902, the court majority held that labor organizers and picketers had the right to enter an agricultural grower's private property to conduct union activities. Justice Clark dissented: this was private property, not public property.

Clark also held for property owners in a number of eminent domain cases, such as *County of San Diego v. Miller* (1975) 13 Cal.3d 684, where he wrote for a unanimous court, and *Agins v. City of Tiburon* (1979) 24 Cal.3d 266 and *HFH, Ltd v. Superior Court* (1975) 15 Cal.3d 508, where he wrote forceful dissenting opinions arguing that property owners should be compensated when government action essentially destroyed the value of their land.

In many other areas Clark issued important decisions. In the area of tort law, Clark sought in his highly acclaimed dissent in *Tarasoff v. Regents of the University of California* (1976) 17 Cal.3d 425 to protect the providers of medical care to the mentally ill by not subjecting them to liability for being unable to predict who may be dangerous in the future.

The Tanner/Bird-Clark Controversy

Justice Clark's respect for the role of the legislature and the doctrine of separation-of-powers was at the center of one of the most controversial incidents of his Supreme Court tenure. In 1975, the California assembly enacted a statute, Penal Code section 1203.06, which declared that probation shall not be granted to a criminal defendant who used a firearm during certain felonies, including robbery.

Harold Tanner was convicted of robbing a convenience store with a firearm. The subsequent case became the subject of two highly publicized decisions by the California Supreme Court. The issue involved more than the specific case of Tanner, questioning whether the legislature had the power to pass such a restrictive law refusing probation to any criminal defendant using a firearm while committing a felony. More specifically, could the court overrule the legislature on this issue? Clark sided with the legislative intent; the liberal jurists backed the trial court's defiance of the legislative mandate.

When the court first decided the matter in December 1978, Justice Tobriner wrote a plurality opinion, joined by Justices Mosk and Newman. Chief Justice Rose Bird concurred with the plurality's holding. Justice Clark authored a strong dissenting opinion emphasizing that the law's statutory language left no ambiguity over what the state legislature had intended: If you use a gun, said Clark, you go to prison. The courts, said Clark, were obligated to enforce the law as written (*People v. Tanner* [1978] 151 Cal.Rptr. 299).

The court's majority decision provoked a firestorm. In response, the court granted a rehearing to reconsider its earlier holding. Governor Jerry Brown and Attorney General George Deukmejian got involved, as did the press. The *San Francisco Examiner* published sharp editorials critical of the court. In response, the court granted rehearing.

This time, Justice Clark wrote the reversed 4-3 majority opinion in *Tanner*, Justice Mosk now having joined him (*People v. Tanner* [1979] 24 Cal.3d 514). The opinion held that the mandatory language of Penal Code section 1203.06 was indeed mandatory, and the courts must obey it.

As fully chronicled in the book *Judging Judges: The Investigation of Rose Bird and the California Supreme Court*, by Preble Stolz, there was much more surrounding the decisions in the *Tanner* case than the legal opinions themselves.[14] The first *Tanner* decision was filed and made public on December 22, 1978. The year 1978 was a general election

---

[14] Preble Stolz, *Judging Judges: The Investigation of Rose Bird and the California Supreme Court* (New York: The Free Press, 1981).

period in California, with Chief Justice Rose Bird on the November ballot. An intense campaign against Bird had been underway that fall, primarily on the grounds that she was too soft on crime.

On the morning of the election, the *Los Angeles Times* ran a front-page story stating that the controversial *Tanner* decision had been ready for filing but had been held back. The implication of the story was that the filing of the decision had been delayed for political purposes—to help progressive Rose Bird win reelection. The *Times* said its story was confirmed by two members of the Supreme Court, whose identities were not revealed. Speculation was that the two justices were Clark and Stanley Mosk.

Though a committed liberal, Mosk was close to Clark. They came to agreement on a number of cases. They became such close friends that Mosk later offered an extraordinary gesture to this man on the opposite side of the political spectrum: If Clark in the mid-1980s desired to return to the court after serving as Reagan's secretary of the interior, Mosk would resign and give him his seat, a very gracious offer that Clark graciously declined.

Clark would one day deliver a eulogy at Mosk's funeral. The last surviving member of that court, Clark brought many of the gathered to tears when he informed them of how he and Mosk had first met—not on the court in the 1970s, but, instead in the winter of 1940 during the school field trip to Sacramento arranged by Bernice. Clark never forgot the gracious tour guide, who happened to be executive secretary to the governor of California, a position that Clark would hold twenty-seven years later. The guide and executive secretary was a young lawyer named Stanley Mosk.

"My father liked Bill Clark very much", says Mosk's son Richard, an associate justice for the State of California Court of Appeal in Los Angeles. "He admired the way Judge Clark treated janitors and others around the court—he knew their names and about them and always inquired about their families. My father, like Bill Clark, got along with everyone—it was a key to his success." [15] Both had the capability as well as the disposition to look beyond political differences.

In 1978, Bird felt her suspicions about Clark and fellow liberal Mosk, whom many had expected to be named chief justice by Governor

---

[15] Interviews with Richard M. Mosk, January 24 and 25, 2006.

Jerry Brown (Brown instead appointed Bird) were justified, and she requested that the Commission on Judicial Performance, the entity that reviews allegations of judicial impropriety, investigate the matter of the leak. The Commission scheduled an investigation that included public proceedings at which a number of justices, including Bird and Clark, were to be subject to cross-examination.

Before he was to testify, Justice Mosk initiated a lawsuit to have the Commission proceedings closed to the public. A special Court of Appeal agreed and ordered the proceedings closed. Ultimately, the Commission announced that its investigation was terminated and that "no formal charges will be filed against any Supreme Court justice."

Morris, McGovern, and Murphy

The four aides closest to Judge Clark in this period were Maury Koblick, Dick Morris, Dan McGovern, and John Murphy, as well as his "great secretary" Betsy Wong.

Maury Koblick and Betsy Wong had worked with Clark's very liberal predecessor, Justice Ray Peters. Clark's relationship with Koblick provides a fine example of the Judge's ability to work with those with whom he disagreed politically or philosophically. Koblick became a research attorney for Clark, continuing in the capacity for which he had served Peters. Koblick gave Clark seven years of faithful service as a "brilliant" aide and generally "good-natured" man.

Dick Morris had been chief of staff to Chief Justice Don Wright, the judge who voted against Clark. Morris was widely considered the best of all the law clerks on the large court staff. The clerks for the various justices were sometimes petty. For instance, none of Wright's staff would speak to Clark's staff during his first months on the court. Morris, however, was an exception.

When Rose Bird replaced Chief Justice Wright, she wanted Morris as her chief of staff, knowing he was a fine manager and scholar. Before she had the chance to approach him, Morris strode down the hall, knocked on Clark's door and said, "Your Honor, if there is ever a vacancy on your staff, would you consider me?" Clark replied, "I have an opening right now."

Bird failed to get her man. Morris' reasoning was simple: his conservative view of the law was closer to Clark's than to that of any other member of the court. The Morris shocker rippled through the building. It also added credibility to Clark and his work.

Clark and Morris got along terrifically. Morris had served on a PT boat in World War II, a factor that brought him closer to Clark on foreign policy as well. Clark called Morris a "very humble man with common sense", which was also Morris' view of Clark.

When Clark was called off the court by Reagan to go to Washington in 1981, Morris asked if he could come along. "Of course", said Clark. Morris worked for Clark first at the State Department, then at the NSC, and then at Interior—all the way through Clark's Washington experience. It was a sad day for Clark when Morris died. His burial at Arlington was attended by Clark and the old staff.

Also clerking for Clark were Dan McGovern and John Murphy.

McGovern, a graduate of UCLA law school, had worked as a criminal appellate attorney in Los Angeles for the California Attorney General's Office. He interviewed with Clark when the Supreme Court sat in Los Angeles for oral argument. McGovern knew Clark's reputation as a conservative, and took pains to make it clear that he was more liberal than Clark on most social issues, but was "moderately conservative" on criminal issues. He stressed he was not a Republican. Clark told McGovern he felt party affiliation should not be a consideration in the position of research attorney. "Clark has always seemed to me to be remarkably nonpartisan for a man involved in party politics", says McGovern.[16]

McGovern found that to be true even in Washington: Like Morris, he followed Clark to the nation's capital to work with him at the State Department.

McGovern found that while Clark "is *intelligent*, he is not an *intellectual*." This distinction is important, says McGovern, because many appellate judges fancy themselves as intellectuals—as law professor types. Clark rarely asked questions during oral arguments, says McGovern, and though he was not privy to them, McGovern suspects that Clark did not participate much in the "thrust-and-parry" at the justices' private conferences. He said that Clark's interest was never celestial ruminations but, rather, the bottom line, whether a proposed decision would make sense in the real world, as the facts and law stood, not as the

---

[16] All quoted material from McGovern is taken from an August 26, 2005 interview.

judges wished them to be. Says McGovern: "He was impatient with justices who got so caught up in the legal arguments that they would follow them to senseless conclusions. In a word, what Clark had was *judgment.*"

McGovern also saw in Clark a quality that had been evident to the Reagan gubernatorial staff and was later manifest when he ran the NSC: "The judge was also a very good *manager.* You might think this is a gift he would have had little opportunity to exercise on the court. However, one of the principal responsibilities of a justice on the California Supreme Court is managing his staff, for none of the justices has the time to write his own opinions, much less conduct the underlying research."

McGovern added an important insight on Clark: "Some justices are remarkably staff-driven. That is to say, the position such a judge will adopt on a case is likely to be determined by the accident of which member of his staff is assigned to work on it.... Clark was not like that at all. I felt free to debate him vigorously on an issue I cared about, but I was never under the delusion that I would be able to talk him into something he didn't believe." McGovern said: "Clark has core beliefs. They coincided with Reagan's. Clark's special gift was in managing others to achieve that common vision."

He points to two other Clark qualities he noticed right away on the California court: Clark, says McGovern, is "humble and laconic". He cites an anecdote as an illustration. Not long after McGovern started working for the Judge, his mother-in-law visited from Kansas. He wanted to introduce her to Clark, but was concerned she would be too shy to enjoy the encounter. It was not a problem, said McGovern: "Clark seemed more shy than she was; she was entirely charmed by him."

One day McGovern and another court staffer, Jerry Kane, discussed a question that fascinated both of them: How did Clark, they asked, "who is so unassuming and who really did seem to have no ambition beyond being a family man and rancher", rise to a judicial position coveted by so many? Jerry Kane came up with the "Helluva Nice Guy Theory": Nice guys sometimes *do* finish first. As a corollary to the "Helluva Nice Guy Theory", they speculated that Reagan advanced Clark's career so much because, in part, Clark was the one person who did not use Reagan to advance himself.

McGovern says that while it is "probably true" that no one who has really gotten to know the Judge dislikes him, Clark made some enemies because of political disagreement. "Because most of us assign bad motives to people we disagree with on issues we care about," says McGovern, "Clark was during his tenure on the Supreme Court intensely disliked by many people who did not know him."

McGovern points to the "open hostility" to Clark's appointment to the Supreme Court by the staff of then-Chief Justice Donald Wright. "I know that when I joined Clark's staff, many of Wright's people made a point of snubbing me", said McGovern. "And it didn't get better when Wright was succeeded by Rose Bird, even though Clark, as I recall, went out of his way to be cordial to her because her own appointment was met with criticism." Another snubbing was even ruder: When McGovern and Morris left the court to join Clark in Washington, a farewell luncheon was given for them. "I wasn't much of a draw," said McGovern, "but Dick had been with the court for years, long before Clark joined it, and he was much loved." Still, Bird's staff boycotted the luncheon. McGovern and Clark never suffered from such animosities; they looked beyond political differences each day merely by working with one another.

On the other hand, says McGovern, court employees with no political axe to grind—the bailiffs, the folks in the clerk's office—were very fond of the Judge. Because Clark spent a couple of days each week working from the ranch, he spent long hours at his desk when he was in San Francisco; hence, he would be in his office when the night janitor came by. "The janitor would have been invisible to most," averred McGovern, "but Clark and he became dear friends. The Judge treated people with dignity."

He says that Clark always tried to give each of his "many friends and acquaintances" their "moment in the sun". He had Clark's Christmas parties for staff and externs in mind. Each semester Justice Clark had three to five law students working for him as externs, and they and all the former externs were invited to each Christmas party. Thus, each year the party in his chambers grew larger, spilling out into the hall. Clark catered it himself, serving beef from his ranch. "As the former externs had become lawyers, you can imagine that some of them were quite pushy in seeing to it that they got face-time with the Judge", said McGovern. "I noticed that Clark would keep his eye on the shyer of the former externs, and during the course of the evening he would take each one of them out into the hall for a quiet chat, asking them about themselves. It meant the world to them."

Clark aide John Murphy has similar observations.[17] He worked for the Judge from 1975 to 1977 as a research attorney. When they first met in 1974, Clark stressed to Murphy the importance of ascertaining the law and applying it as objectively as possible, with full respect to the system of government and the proper role of all three branches.

He taught Murphy that the law is a "great tool of justice that balances and checks the darker passions of mankind. The law must be applied equally to all, not just used as a tool to force an ideology upon others". The law is developed through a process of history, experience, and balance, and must embody basic values that transcend the moment.

Like Morris and McGovern, Murphy, too, followed Clark to Washington, though there he worked not for Clark but as general counsel at the Veterans Administration.

Murphy says that one particular conversation he had with Clark in Washington has stuck with him throughout his life in public service. Clark reminded him that the word "power" is nothing more than a synonym for the word "responsibility"—a responsibility to serve the American people to the utmost of one's ability. In that same conversation, he told Murphy never to give in to the temptation to compromise basic principles and values for personal or short-term gain because, in the final analysis, "what will really matter is what we did for others, not what we gained for ourselves.... There are matters more important than ourselves and our personal interests."

Activities Beyond Justice Clark's Chambers

During this period, as would happen much more often in the 1980s, Clark's name was suggested for a number of jobs in Washington. An article in the *Wall Street Journal* listed him as one of two front-runners to succeed Cap Weinberger as chairman of the Federal Trade Commission. Clark told the *Ventura County Free Press* that this was "mere speculation. I have not applied for the job. I am very happy doing what I'm doing. While I will continue to assist the administration in

---

[17] All quoted material from Murphy is taken from a March 17, 2005 interview.

Sacramento and Washington when I can in my spare time, I do not intend to seek other employment."[18] Clark was in fact offered the chairmanship of the FTC by the Nixon White House, but turned it down.

Another such report at the time, run in an article by Lou Cannon in the *San Jose Mercury News*, was clipped by Superior Court Judge John S. McInerny, who sent it to Clark hoping to persuade him not to leave the court.[19] "You're a glutton for punishment if you go to D.C.!!" he wrote in a June 19 handwritten note. In response, Clark told McInerny: "I have neither plan nor desire for anything east of Shandon!"[20]

Reagan's Emissary

Although no longer Reagan's aide in Sacramento, Justice Clark remained in close contact with the Governor, always available for the call of duty. Reagan delivered a gem, an assignment he knew Clark would appreciate: It was June 1974, and one of Clark's heroes, József Cardinal Mindszenty, had been invited to the University of Santa Clara to accept an honorary degree in recognition of his "courage and ... heroic perseverance in the cause of freedom and justice". Reagan asked Clark to host Mindszenty.

It was not that simple, however. Mindszenty abruptly canceled his plans to accept the degree. The trouble began when the University of Santa Clara named Congressman Don Edwards (D-CA), a pro-abortion politician, to the Board of Regents in September 1973. This was a period right after the U.S. Supreme Court passed *Roe v. Wade*. Edwards' appointment was a concern to pro-life groups, to Cardinal Mindszenty, and to the Mindszenty Foundation in St. Louis.

Soon, there were letter-writing campaigns and threats of picketers from both sides for the June 8 graduation ceremonies at Santa Clara. As the potential confrontation gathered strength, Mindszenty bowed

---

[18] "Judge Clark Seen Choice for FTC Post", *Ventura County Star-Free Press*. Note: The article copy in Clark's files contains no date, though the month and year are clearly July 1970.

[19] Lou Cannon, "California Judge May Head FTC", *San Jose Mercury News*, June 16, 1970.

[20] Clark replied in a letter dated June 22, 1970.

out, canceling his appearance. The Hungarian gave no specific reason. He sent a telegram to university president Father Thomas D. Terry, in which he said only, "I respectfully decline an honorary degree from your university and shall not be present on your campus." [21]

Mindszenty did not, however, cancel his June 5–10 trip to San Francisco as the guest of Archbishop Joseph T. McGucken. And Governor Reagan, for one, was pleased that the Cardinal was still coming to his state.

The Hungarian experience, especially the disastrous uprising of 1956, was carved indelibly into Reagan's consciousness. Earlier as governor, in a Veterans' Day speech in Albany, Oregon, Reagan professed that he could still hear the "echoes" of those Hungarians who in October 1956 had cried out: "People of the civilized world, in the name of liberty and solidarity, we are asking your help.... Listen to our cry." [22] Now, one of them, their spiritual leader, was in California, and Reagan was ready to help in any way he could.

For the task, Ronald Reagan dispatched the one man he knew would not let him down. As he would so many times in the years to come, he called upon Clark, even though Clark was no longer working for him.

Pope Paul VI pursued a policy of accommodation with Russian communism, in the hope of not offending communist regimes and earning from them even harsher treatment of the Church.

In 1971 he asked Mindszenty to depart his beloved country, as did President Nixon. The Cardinal had always refused to leave Hungary until the communists reversed his conviction. Now, however, he obeyed the Pope. He left Hungary in September 1971 and settled in Austria.

Further, in 1974, the year his memoirs were published, Pope Paul VI stripped Mindszenty of his position as primate of Hungary, a gesture intended to improve Vatican relations with Hungary and the rest of the Soviet Bloc.

Clark was very upset with Rome and Washington for their mistreatment of Mindszenty: "They did not recognize the heroism of his life. He was a martyr who had somehow slipped through the cracks."

---

[21] See "Cardinal Refuses Honorary Degree from Santa Clara U.", *Catholic Herald*, June 7, 1974.

[22] Governor Ronald Reagan, "Veterans Day Address at North Albany Junior High School", Albany, Oregon, November 11, 1967.

In June 1974, by contrast, Reagan wanted to ensure that Mindszenty was treated warmly in sunny California. Thus, he sent Judge Bill Clark to San Francisco to officially receive him. Clark did just that, and spent three hours with the Cardinal. It was a warm up: A decade later Reagan would be tapping Clark to meet with Pope John Paul II.

"[Mindszenty] had heard that there were going to be pickets [at Santa Clara University]. So, he said he wouldn't go", Clark says. "He didn't want to walk through the line. He was an old man by then, too old to fight." The two men met, talked, spent precious time together—no lunch or meal.

Within a year of his visit with Clark, Mindszenty died at age 83, in Austria, on May 6, 1975. The communists rejected his body's return to its homeland. Bill Clark has never forgotten him and prayed at his grave in Mariazell, a Marian pilgrimage site in the Austrian Alps. After the collapse of the communist regime in Hungary, the body of the exiled Cardinal was allowed burial in his beloved country.

The Forever-Unqualified Man

As the decade of the 1970s wound down, there was some speculation that Bill Clark might be moving from one Supreme Court to another, a cause for Clark once again to come under fire.

In a September 1980 piece in the *New York Times* entitled, "A Reagan Supreme Court", journalist Jack Greenberg reported that Governor Reagan had had the audacity to appoint to the state's Supreme Court "William P. Clark Jr., whose philosophy was satisfactory but who had never completed law school, who had failed the bar exam, and whose subsequent legal career was undistinguished."[23]

A month later, Howell Raines stepped up at the *New York Times* to note that in an October 14 speech, candidate Reagan had hailed the commissions he created in California to remove politics from the appointment of judges. But how could that be? Raines informed The *Times* readership of the obviously contradictory case of Bill Clark.[24]

---

[23] Jack Greenberg, "A Reagan Supreme Court", *New York Times*, September 15, 1980.
[24] Howell Raines, "Reagan, In Speeches, Doesn't Let the Facts Spoil a Good Anecdote", *New York Times*, October 19, 1980.

The fact that Clark had spent ten years writing highly respected opinions for the appellate and supreme courts of the nation's largest state evidently failed to rectify press perception that he lacked qualification for judicial office.

For Bill Clark, the past was prologue, a taste of more criticism to come. And although he treasured his twelve years on the bench, never for a moment would he entertain the thought of another court or another judicial post.

CHAPTER 6

Mr. Clark Goes to Washington

In February 1980, on Lincoln's birthday, Judge Clark picked up the phone and heard a familiar voice: it was an anxious Nancy Reagan. She asked Clark if he could come right away to Rancho del Cielo, the Reagan ranch in the Santa Ynez Mountains. The Reagan presidential campaign was in crisis.

Campaign manager John Sears, a moderate Republican, who at one point told Ronald Reagan to abandon his pro-life position for political expediency, had been asked to leave. They needed a new chief of staff for the campaign and they needed one fast. The Reagans called on their indispensable man and met with him alone on their mountaintop for several hours into the night. They asked Clark: would he take over as chief of staff? Mrs. Reagan personally appealed to him to leave the Supreme Court for the campaign.[1]

Recalling the evening when the three sat before an open fire, with a plate of cold cuts set before them, Clark described how he and the Reagans talked through the issue to the conclusion that it would not be in the state's best interest for Clark to leave the Supreme Court just yet.

Clark was needed where he was. The balance on the California Supreme Court was precarious; conservatives could not afford to lose the Clark voice, a fact Reagan himself came to recognize as the evening progressed.

Clark told the Reagans he would serve if needed, though he hoped to direct them to another choice. They considered several names. Mrs.

---

[1] For an added reference, see: Steven R. Weisman, "Nancy Reagan's Role Grows", *New York Times*, November 11, 1984.

Reagan balanced a legal pad on her knees and took notes. "She jotted down the names, the points—one, two, three, four." They kept returning to the name of William J. Casey, based on his background and experience—political and governmental.[2]

It was decided that Clark would call Bill Casey. "I called him at his home on Long Island, got him out of bed", says Clark. "And grumpy old Bill said, 'Let me think about it. I'll get back to you tomorrow.'" Clark drove back to his ranch late that night along the Coastal Highway. The next day, Casey agreed to take the position.

The campaign thrived under Casey's direction. In November, Ronald Reagan defeated the incumbent President, Jimmy Carter, winning 44 of 50 states and taking the electoral college 489 to 49—a landslide.

Bill Clark may not have rescued the campaign by himself, but he played a pivotal role in helping to select and recruit the captain who steered the ship in the right direction. It was probably this particular incident that *National Review* had in mind when it credited Clark with "a key role in reviving Reagan's 1980 GOP primary campaign"—one of the core reasons cited by the conservative magazine in naming Clark one of America's most significant and "unsung" conservatives.[3]

* * *

There were other Clark family members who played a part in the Reagan presidential campaign. Bill's son Colin got more involved than anyone, serving on the traveling campaign staff.

Colin was close to the Reagans, having known them growing up. He remembers Mrs. Reagan taking him and the younger Ron to the movie theater to watch "Planet of the Apes". During the scene where Charlton Heston's bare backside is visible to the audience, Mrs. Reagan gasped at the unusual sight of her old Hollywood friend, "Oh, my goodness. Chuck is naked!" The audience heard her and had a good laugh.[4]

---

[2] Clark does not recall who came up with the name first, or if Casey was the suggestion of one particular person. Lou Cannon reports that Nancy came up with Casey's name. See: Cannon, *Governor Reagan*, p. 466.

[3] "Unsung Conservatives", p. 33.

[4] Interview with Colin Clark, June 25, 2006.

Throughout the 1980 campaign, Colin was present for every Reagan speech and stop. In New York City in November 1979, when the Governor formally announced his candidacy, the Secret Service misplaced Mrs. Reagan's jewelry/makeup bag. This was no small matter. When she got it back, she took it directly to Colin and said, "Colin, you take care of this. From now on, this is your responsibility." As for Mr. Reagan, "he was as charming one-on-one as he was in public", says Colin. "He was always interested in you, in your life and what you were doing." [5]

Colin found ways to add some fun to the long, wearisome days on the campaign trail. He inherited his father's penchant for practical jokes— "an integral part of being a Clark, it seems", says his wife, Linda.

The Secret Service agents assigned to Reagan had a "good luck monkey", a stuffed animal named Bobo, which, when activated, clapped his cymbals and sang "On the Road Again" by Willie Nelson. Each time the plane took off, BoBo did his thing, with the tune playing over the intercom. One day, Colin and Mark Hatfield, Jr. kidnapped Bobo and sent a ransom note to the Secret Service along with a Xerox copy of Bobo. The rhyming ransom note, written by Colin, was signed by the Bobo Liberation Army, a reference to the Symbionese Liberation Army, Patty Hearst's captors. The Secret Service knew Colin was the culprit but could not find Bobo anywhere. The reason was that Colin had enlisted the assistance of Governor Reagan, who hid Bobo in his suitcase.

Mr. X

It was assumed that Bill Clark, who was so close to Reagan and had worked with him so well in Sacramento, would be tapped for a top spot in the new administration. Public whispers of Clark being appointed to this or that position started with a November 8, 1980, *New York Times* piece reporting that Clark was a leading candidate for attorney general, a job that went instead to Clark friend William French Smith, who had requested the position.[6] Clark had been asked to consider

---

[5] Ibid.

[6] Hedrick Smith, "Reagan seeks to emphasize role of Cabinet Members as Advisers", *New York Times*, November 8, 1980, Section 1; Page 1.

the post by the appointments committee, as well for the positions of CIA director and secretary of agriculture. In each case, he declined.[7] There was one slot, however, that remained unfilled.

The presidential-transition group created an organizational chart listing all the cabinet members, sub-secretaries, and various appointed positions. Each line had a preferred name or list of options. One spot, however, the deputy secretary of state position, was filled with an "X", placed there by Reagan himself, without comment or explanation. This was to be Ronald Reagan's man at State—a pick the President-elect held close to his vest.

No one knew the name of this enigmatic "X", who was most assuredly not *the* Mr. X, the famous diplomat George Kennan, a major Reagan critic. It became a resident parlor game among the politicos to take guesses. Who was this man? X turned out to be Clark—another riddle, and another series of puzzling questions ensued. Why Bill Clark as deputy secretary of state? Clark was a sure bet for chief of staff or attorney general or any of a number of other high-level posts. But why the number-two job at the State Department?

The answer was provided by Representative Bob Lagomarsino (R-CA), the Governor's congressman: Ronald Reagan needed an "America desk" at the State Department. To Reagan, State frequently seemed more concerned with the interests of America's friends and neighbors than America itself. Moreover, Secretary of State designate Al Haig was an unknown quantity to Ronald Reagan. Who could Reagan count on? One person came to mind: Bill Clark.

Clark had warned Reagan that his foreign-policy credentials were slim, as Reagan knew. "I told him, 'I know nothing about foreign policy or foreign affairs' ", says Clark. "He turned to me and said, 'Bill, that's exactly why I want you there. I have all the "experts" I need.' "

Clark's candidacy for the State post appeared in newspapers on January 2, 1981, roughly three weeks before the inaugural. The California Supreme Court justice confirmed to the *San Francisco Examiner* that he had indeed been asked to become deputy secretary of state, but had not decided if he would take the job. As one of two remaining Reagan appointees on the state's high court, Clark told the *Examiner* he was concerned

---

[7] Clark said this in his February 2, 1981 testimony before the Senate Foreign Relations Committee.

his departure would give Democratic Governor Edmund G. Brown Jr. the opportunity to replace him with a judicial liberal.[8]

It was during this period Clark began to receive his first heavy dose of national press coverage, which means he began suffering the media's constant inaccuracies in reporting on his record. In a January 3 story, the *Washington Post* incorrectly reported that Clark had "flunked out" of Stanford—the start of a continuing line of misrepresentations regarding Clark's academic record.[9]

January 20, 1981: The Inaugural

Ronald Reagan would not let Bill Clark get away easily. He liked having Clark around. Dan McGovern, Clark's aide from the California court, reports that when the President-elect and the Judge flew into Andrews Air Force Base after the election, Reagan said to Clark, "I think we should keep horses tied to a tree out here, in case we need to make a quick getaway." [10] Yet, there was much more to the relationship than a friendship.

Clark had unwittingly created a problem for himself: He had proven to Reagan, unintentionally, that he was indispensable. So, Reagan wanted him in Washington. He needed his loyal aide in a place that demanded loyalty.

This was made clear shortly before Reagan was about to be sworn in as president. Clark's son Colin and Colin's fiancée, Linda, were both there. It was on that day Colin and Linda announced to Bill and Joan that they had just gotten engaged. It was a day of more than one new beginning for the Clarks to celebrate.

Linda was impressed that Bill and Joan were seated in the box behind the Reagans, along with former presidents, senators and congressmen, and Republican actors such as Bob Hope and Jimmy Stewart.

When the Reagans first arrived, Linda recalls, the President-elect and his wife entered the platform on the other side of the velvet cord from the Clarks and began shaking hands with dignitaries. When Reagan spotted

---

[8] See Cass Peterson, "Transition Notes", *Washington Post*, January 3, 1981, A6; and Steven Weisman, "Reagan Bids Aides . . . ," *New York Times*, January 9, 1981.

[9] Peterson, "Transition Notes".

[10] Interview with Dan McGovern, April 1, 2005.

Bill Clark, she continued, he went over to him on the other side of the cord and engaged Clark in a "pretty intense, low-voiced" conversation.

Ronald Reagan had spoken frequently during the 1980s of how he wanted people on his team who did not want to be in Washington, who had to be cajoled into the job. It was a classic conservative message: the Founders' notion of the citizen-politician, who like the Roman statesman Cincinnatus responds to the call of duty, reluctantly leaves his farm for a few years of government service, and then happily returns home where he continues his duties to faith, family, and community. As far as Reagan was concerned, Bill Clark embodied this ideal of the public servant.

The New Deputy Secretary of State

On January 23, 1981 came the announcement from the White House: President Reagan had nominated William P. Clark as the nation's number-two man at Foggy Bottom.

A profile of Clark appeared in the next day's *Washington Post*, written by a new staffer at the *Post*, a former Sacramento beat reporter by the name of Lou Cannon. In a feature article entitled " 'Just Plain Bill' Is a Law-and-Order Type Who Makes Things Go", Cannon stated: "Back on the ranch in San Luis Obispo County, Calif., he is just plain Bill, a gangling, unassuming neighbor who likes to ride and swap jokes with fellow ranchers. . . . But in the inner circles of those who have been with Ronald Reagan since Day 1, William P. Clark will be remembered best as the chief of staff who came aboard in 1967 when the governor's office was in shambles and made it run smoothly." Cannon added some prophetic wisdom: "Wherever he has gone, Clark has been controversial at first but has wound up making friends in unexpected quarters."

Cannon also addressed the immediate cause for concern: Clark's lack of foreign-policy experience in one of the top foreign-policy posts in the world. "But Clark's administrative talents are well-demonstrated, and he expects to get a lot of help in the State Department", wrote Cannon, who in turn quoted Clark as saying: "I'm surrounded by expertise in every area. I expect to take full advantage of that expertise." [11]

---

[11] Lou Cannon, " 'Just Plain Bill' Is a Law-and-Order Type Who Makes Things Go", *Washington Post*, January 24, 1981, A6.

The other report in the *Washington Post* that day—by Robert Kaiser—had a different theme, focusing on those behind Clark's nomination. It noted another reason for Reagan's reliance on Clark at State: Certain members of the new President's inner circle, especially White House counselor Edwin Meese III, thought the new President needed a "totally loyal friend" at the State Department "to keep an eye" on Secretary of State Al Haig. Later Haig announced his "enthusiastic endorsement" for the selection of Clark, whom Haig called a "superb choice", partially ending press speculation that Haig had reservations.

Kaiser also reported that Clark, whose education Democrats were already questioning, "had to withdraw from Loyola, an evening law school, because of poor grades." [12] Already, the *Washington Post* had Clark flunking out of Stanford, then flunking out of law school, and then flunking the bar.

The Interrogation of Bill Clark

Clark's appointment required Senate confirmation. His confirmation hearings before the Senate Foreign Relations Committee convened on Monday, February 2, at 10:02 A.M., in room 4221 of the Dirksen Senate Office Building, with Chairman Charles H. Percy (R-IL) presiding. [13] Percy's opening statement noted that the deputy secretary of state is the second highest ranking official in the State Department. The deputy secretary functions as the secretary's principal advisor and, in the secretary's absence, serves as acting secretary of state.

A Republican, Percy was on Clark's side. In his pitch for the rancher, Percy informed his colleagues that in 1966 Clark had put aside his law practice to help the Governor in Sacramento and gained a reputation as "a man of outstanding organizational and administrative abilities, a man who could get the job done and done well". Percy said that he had personally telephoned the new Secretary of Defense Weinberger, who called Clark "A superb manager and tremendous asset to Governor

---

[12] Robert G. Kaiser, "Haig Enthusiastic After Californian Gets Job at State; Old Friend of Reagan Appointed", *Washington Post*, January 24, 1981, A1.

[13] The following dialogue is from the Hearings before the Committee on Foreign Relations; United States Senate; Ninety-Seventh Congress; First Session on Nomination of Justice William Patrick Clark, of California, to be Deputy Secretary of State; February 2 and 3, 1981; U.S. Government Printing Office, Washington: 1981.

Reagan during his first term of office." Weinberger, said Percy, attributed "a major part of the success of that administration to the administrative abilities and capacities of Justice Clark". While in Sacramento, said Percy, Clark was widely regarded as "an efficient and hardworking public servant, who could be counted on to deal with important government matters without buckling under the pressure. Certainly, these qualities are essential for a deputy secretary of state."

After Percy, Senator Sam Hayakawa (R-CA) also offered a ringing endorsement of Clark. Then, before the questioning from the other senators began, Clark provided his statement. He began:

> First, I wish you to know that I am here because the President has asked me to take this position. While I have in no way sought this or any other post, the urgency of the President's request weighed heavily in my determination to accept his call. It was in response to this, his seventh call to duty that I appear before you....
>
> I bring to this committee and to the administration, if confirmed, no formal training in foreign policy. I fully recognize that I must devote myself to accelerated study of substantive issues within the framework of past experience. I have begun that learning process. This being my first major experience in the field of foreign affairs, I view its responsibility with the deepest seriousness, all the more so because I believe we have reached an intersection in history when enormous stakes rest on our ability to conduct a successful foreign policy....
>
> I would not have accepted the President's call if I did not feel I could serve my country well in this position.

Clark acknowledged his limitations, adding that his formal education had become the subject of "some curiosity", and quipped that his youngest son Paul asked if it would be necessary for the Judge to return to school. He answered, "Paul, that may be determined by what happens today." Clark conceded to the senators: "I would like to come to you with some degrees, but I do not."

Of the Democrats who questioned Clark, the most memorable was Senator Joe Biden (D-DE): "I, for one, think it admirable the way in which you have conducted yourself in getting to and through school", began Biden. "I have a great deal of admiration for you."

Biden then proceeded to pillory Clark, asking him a series of specific questions that he assumed the Judge would not be able to answer.

The *Washington Post* published excerpts of this expression of Biden's "admiration" in its opinion section, under the title "The Interrogation of Justice Clark".[14]

BIDEN: "I sincerely hope you can answer these questions.... Let me begin with southern Africa—not South Africa, but southern Africa, such as Namibia, Zimbabwe, Swaziland, Mozambique, Angola and so on.... Can you tell me who is the Prime Minister of South Africa?"

CLARK: "No, sir, I cannot."

BIDEN: "Can you tell me who the Prime Minister of Zimbabwe is?"

CLARK: "It would be a guess."

BIDEN: "Can you tell me what the major bilateral issues are between the United States and Brazil at this point?"

CLARK: "I am unaware of the priorities. But from my general reading, I think one concern regarding Brazil is definitely balance-of-payments problems, the economy. I will stand corrected, I am sure, from all kinds of expertise when I get back to the State Department, but I believe Brazil is No. 1 in debt at the moment on the international scene."

BIDEN: "I really don't like doing this, Justice Clark, but I don't know how else to get at the point. What are the countries in Europe, in NATO, that are most reluctant to go along with theater nuclear force modernization? From what countries do we have the greatest difficulty getting cooperation in the placement of long-range nuclear weapons on European soil?"

CLARK: "I am not in a position, as you already have suggested, Senator, to categorize them from the standpoint of acceptance on the one hand and resistance on the other."

BIDEN: "Well, then, let's talk about England for a moment. England is a long-standing and staunch ally and is going through some difficult

---

[14] The piece ran in the *Post's* "Outlook" section on February 25, 1981.

times. Can you tell us, just from accounts in the newspaper, what is happening in the British Labor Party these days?"

CLARK: "I don't think I can tell you with specificity what is happening in the British Labor Party these days."

BIDEN: "I really apologize, Mr. Justice. I know you are on the spot, and I don't know how else I can do my job. This is one of the most distasteful question-and-answer periods in which I have participated. And, by the way, no one but me, not my staff, suggested that I use this approach.... But this issue with regard to you, Justice, in my opinion, is not whether or not you are bright. I think you are a bright man.... I have incredible regard for you. I really mean that."

Biden finished the grilling by announcing that he would not be supporting the nomination. Clark responded, "I respect that position, Senator. I just have one point to make." Clark then explained that President Reagan did not bring him on board as a policy expert. "Regarding making policy," said Clark, "I have discussed this with both the President and the Secretary. Perhaps I did not make that clear, or maybe you came in a little after my description of what we consider to be the role. My position will not be involved in making policy, but rather in coordinating and implementing in the position as deputy secretary of state."

After Biden's interrogation on country leaders, there was more difficult questioning, especially from Democratic Senator John Glenn (D-OH). Chairman Percy and Senator Nancy Kassebaum (R-KS) intervened to defend him.

Clark hung in there and took his beating. Maybe in the back of his mind he was thinking of his grandfather. As Clark told an aide later, "My grandfather always told me God hates a coward."

After a few hours, Percy thanked Clark for his testimony. The committee adjourned at 3:10 P.M. A vote on Clark was scheduled for Tuesday, February 3, when the committee reconvened at 10:15 A.M.; Clark would not be present.

On Tuesday, there was debate and give-and-take. Most interestingly, Clark received the backing of fellow Californian Alan Cranston, a Democrat and the most liberal member of the committee. "Over recent days", explained Cranston, "I have consulted a wide number of prominent citizens who fulfill quite diverse roles in public and private life in California, including fellow justices of Justice Clark on the State Supreme Court, Democrats and Republicans. I have received both positive and negative statements about the nominee.... I have concluded", said Cranston, "that he is a fast learner when he wants to be and that he is a sound administrator." The feisty Cranston added: "He is able to get right to the heart of an issue", and "he can take a problem and boil it down to its essence."

Senator Jesse Helms (R-NC), the most conservative member of the committee, approved of Clark, seeing him as a refreshing change: "We have had too much pretentiousness in Washington, D.C., from people who pretend to know everything", said Helms. "As for the State Department, maybe it would be a pretty good thing to have somebody down there who knows he does not know it all, who has an open mind, and who is willing to look and listen." Helms called Clark "a good American" who "is dedicated to this country".

The most thoughtful defense of Clark came from Senator Percy:

> Now, this is not a Cabinet post, but a sub-Cabinet position. He was asked to take off his robes, where he was making $82,000 a year, and to accept $60,000.[15] This is a $22,000 a year pay cut. And then he comes before the Senate committee just after he has seen what General Haig went through. With my full support, every member of this committee subjected General Haig to one of the toughest, certainly the longest, hearings in the history of the Senate Foreign Relations Committee.
>
> Now we all have had a chance to talk with Justice Clark, and on a one-on-one basis there is no one better. I came away exhilarated from our meeting together. I felt that he was a man with whom I could deal, who had leveled with me, who was honest with me about his lack of experience in foreign policy, and who gave me his judgments and his opinions.

Chairman Percy introduced a point that had been ignored in press coverage of the Clark hearings:

---

[15] Clark would be taking a substantial pay cut in his new job. He had received $82,000 as a California Supreme Court justice, and would make $62,662 in his new post.

I would turn to one section of the testimony yesterday when I asked Justice Clark if he was familiar with the Murphy Commission Report. He said he was. The Murphy Commission Report of 1975 addressed the management of the State Department and was a most distinguished commission. . . .

The Murphy Commission Report came to the conclusion that a major part of the State Department's institutional problems was due to the lack of a senior official who, in a sense, managed the store. We all know that an organization functions best when it knows where it is going and has someone to guide the running of it. The recommendation of the Murphy Commission was that the deputy secretary be charged with the responsibility of being the inside man, while the Secretary would focus on external problems. I asked Justice Clark:

"In your opinion, is that recommendation a worthy one and would it be one of your principal responsibilities, then, to see that the department itself functions effectively, efficiently, and smoothly and is responsive to the requirements of the Secretary and the President? Justice Clark [responded]: 'My answer is yes, Senator.' "

Now that is right to the point. It covers the scope of his job and what he intends to do and it covers exactly what the President of the United States wants him to do. . . . That is the kind of man that the Murphy Commission concluded was needed at a very high level within the State Department.

Chairman Percy had everyone's attention. He was correct: Bill Clark was the perfect answer to the concerns of the Murphy Commission. In the end, the committee voted 10 to 4 to confirm Clark. The nays were Biden, Glenn, Paul Sarbanes (D-MD), and Christopher Dodd (D-CT). Alan Cranston was the only Democrat to support the nomination.

In spite of his confirmation, the damage to Clark was done. "Clark embarrassed both himself and the administration", Reagan Press Secretary Larry Speakes said later.[16] As for the man who set him up, after his interrogation of Clark, Biden casually pulled him aside in the hallway and said, "Hey, Judge, no hard feelings. . . . And don't worry: I didn't know the answers to those questions either." [17]

---

[16] Larry Speakes, *Speaking Out* (New York: Scribner, 1988), p. 269.
[17] This is Clark's recollection.

The Aftermath of the Hearings

Joe Biden may have been "sorry, Judge, really", but the fact was that he had so humiliated Clark that the Judge became the laughing stock of the world. The press lampooned him with headlines such as, "A Truly Open Mind" (*Newsweek*, February 16, 1981), "Next Question: A Clean Slate for State" (*Time*, February 16, 1981), and "Boning up at the State Department" (*U.S. News and World Report*, February 16, 1981).

Time magazine introduced Clark to the American public in this way: "He dropped out of Stanford University with poor grades. He flunked out of Loyola University Law School.... Now Reagan has named William P. Clark Jr., 49, Deputy Secretary of State, even though the appointee admits that his only firsthand experience for the job 'was 72 hours in Santiago' in 1967."[18]

Foreign papers called him a "nitwit" and the "Don't Know Man". The London *Daily Mirror* editorialized: "America's allies in Europe—Europe, Mr. Clark, you must have heard of it—will hope he is never in charge at a time of crisis."

The feeding frenzy was on. Reporting on Clark's answers to certain foreign-policy questions shifted to rampant personal inaccuracies, mostly focused on the Judge's alleged lack of intelligence: He was every newspaper's flunkie—having allegedly flunked out of law school and even Stanford.[19] Ironically, the same journalists that chided Clark for not knowing basic facts themselves got the basic facts wrong in reporting on Clark.

The Soviets reported on Clark's confirmation hearings. TASS, the official Soviet news agency, stated: "In the course of the committee's hearing it became clear that Clark is not competent." TASS repeated the examples that Biden had elicited. "Still," added TASS incredulously, "members of the committee supported Clark's nomination to such a responsible post.... But for all practical purposes he knows hardly anything about foreign policy and, as he admitted in Congress, does not know how he is going to fill in this gap."[20]

---

[18] "Next Question", *Time*, February 16, 1981.

[19] See Peterson, "Transition Notes"; and Robert G. Kaiser, "Haig Enthusiastic After Californian Gets Job at State", *Washington Post*, January 24, 1981.

[20] Moscow TASS, statement released in English 1535 GMT, February 4, 1981. Statement was republished by FBIS as "Senate Committee Approves Clark Appointment", February 5, 1981, pp. A9–10.

From the east coast to Siberia, the media had crowned their dunce, and somehow Clark was able to joke about it. On February 6, he appeared at a birthday party for Reagan. A reporter shouted out, "Mr. Clark, what are you giving President Reagan for his birthday?"

"That's a surprise", the new deputy secretary answered. Another reporter could not resist a jab: "Mr. Clark, who's the prime minister of Zimbabwe?" Clark replied: "That's a surprise, too."[21]

Clark's family, however, found it hard to chuckle. Eldest son Pete, a gruff, no-nonsense man, who wears flannel shirts, Wrangler jeans, and a Western hat, was twenty-three-years old at the time, and was bothered by the treatment of the man he so admired. "You take it personally", says Pete. "My siblings and I have always been extremely proud of him and his success."[22]

Colin Clark took it hard, too. He was there in the hearing room, and absorbed each Biden jab like a punch to the stomach. "I was absolutely fried, furious," says Colin. "[Senator] Nancy Kassebaum saw how upset I was."[23]

Bill Clark was aware that his family was hurt. "I wasn't bothered by the treatment," he maintains, "but my dad and my kids were.[24] My only concern was embarrassing my president and my family. I regarded it as something of a ritual you have to go through."[25]

The ritual ended on February 24, when Clark's appointment came before the full Senate, which approved his nomination by a vote of 70 to 24. Some key Democrats, such as minority leader Robert C. Byrd (D-WV), voted against him. The twenty-four nays constituted the

---

[21] Donnie Radcliffe and Elisabeth Bumiller, "Birthday Bonanza", *Washington Post*, February 7, 1981, C1.

[22] Interview with Pete Clark, July 15, 2005.

[23] Interview with Colin Clark, June 25, 2006.

[24] As was cousin Pat, at the time completing a graduate program in Ireland. Defense written to *The Irish Times*, Feb. 10, 1981, included: "The candour of his remark regarding his foreign policy experience being 'limited to 72 hours in Santiago' is lost upon his detractors (we won't mention the humour). They prefer to be 'embarrassed' to such an extent that they do not note Mr. Clark's further remarks: 'I'm surrounded by expertise ... I expect to take full advantage of that expertise.' ... Admittedly, I am biased in favour of Mr. Clark. I believe him to be a man of integrity and outstanding ability. As an individual, I can afford my bias. A first-rate newspaper, as I believe yours to be, cannot."

[25] Clark quoted by Bernard Gwertzman, "For Haig Deputy, on the Job Training", *New York Times*, March 13, 1981, p. A3.

largest number of no votes cast against any Reagan appointee for the first administration.[26]

* * *

During those first weeks in 1981, journalists did not know that Mr. Clark was suffering physically. He was grappling with a very early onset of Parkinson's disease, but at that time Clark had no definitive diagnosis. His symptoms were tentatively diagnosed as multiple sclerosis in 1973, then, as Lyme disease in the mid-1980s, before finally being confirmed as Parkinson's in 2006.

When Pete married his sweetheart Elena in August 1980, Clark wore a huge bandage over his head, which photographers airbrushed from the wedding pictures. The reason for the bandage: doctors had done a brain biopsy in search of the elusive ailment.

The severity of Clark's illness was such that his specialists at Stanford advised him in 1981 not to take the job at State. The stress, they told him, would only exacerbate the symptoms. Moreover, even before the onset of Parkinson's, Clark in 1979 was being treated for arthritis with a new experimental treatment.

All of this was the start of health problems that would plague Clark for the rest of his life. However, Clark does not use his health as an excuse for his poor performance at his confirmation hearings. Quite the contrary, he readily blames his ignorance. For example, about the "72 hours in Santiago" line, Clark says, "They thought I was kidding, but I wasn't. That's all I knew." [27]

---

[26] See Laurence I. Barrett, *Gambling with History: Ronald Reagan in the White House* (New York: Doubleday, 1983), p. 331.

[27] In 1967, at the Governor's request, Clark flew to Santiago to check on a Great Society program being sponsored by California and Chile. He found the program had been corrupted and was "untenable", recommending it be canceled, which promptly happened upon his recommendation to Reagan.

CHAPTER 7

The America Desk

Deputy Secretary of State William P. Clark rolled up his sleeves and got to work. He was now the number-two man at State, second only to Secretary Al Haig, the former four-star general who had flamboyantly informed the press that he was Ronald Reagan's "vicar" of foreign policy.

Clark recalls his first meeting with Haig. Like all their subsequent meetings, it was cordial. It began, as did so many introductions to Al Haig, with a bang. "I'll tell you what your job is", the General informed Clark. "You, Bill, are going to run the building. I'm going to run the world."

Clark indeed proceeded to run the building. During their first week together, Clark asked his boss when he planned to hold a staff meeting. With his eye on the world rather than on the conference room, Haig shrugged: "If you think we should have staff meetings, let's do it, and you run them." So, Clark ran them—on a daily basis. At these meetings Clark surrounded himself with experts, roughly twenty upper-level officials and their staffs, and required each of them to "attenuate" his issue. "I loved staff meetings", says the administratively inclined Clark. "We tried to have thirty-minute meetings where I would go around the table and let everyone have a say, not unlike our staff meetings in the Sacramento days." Everyone left the meetings briefed on the important matters of the day and equipped with clear directions for actions to be taken.

Clark thought it was odd that Haig, a former NATO supreme commander, neither enjoyed nor required staff meetings. Still, when Haig was in his office across the hall from the conference room, Clark typ-ically dropped by and asked him to join the gathering, encouraging Haig to make an appearance to verify that the general was "in com-mand". Haig always smiled, and sometimes came along, though he let Clark run the meetings. He brought his trademark cigarettes, usually leaving the table early. Clark appreciates the deference and respect he received from Haig. "We worked wonderfully together", says Clark. "Before long, we were addressing each other, when alone, as 'Uncle Al' and 'Uncle Bill.'"

Haig's door was always open to Clark. He saw Clark as his bridge to the White House and to President Reagan, and requested that Clark attend all his high-level meetings, no matter how sensitive. "That's unusual for a Cabinet member", says Clark. Moreover, Haig delegated many additional tasks to the deputy secretary, especially as they became overwhelming in number and substance. "From the outset," adds Clark, "the problems began piling up to the point where there was far more on Al's desk than he could handle. When something new came in that needed immediate attention, I'd say, 'Al, do you want me to take that one?' and he invariably would answer, 'Bill, would you do that for me?'"[1] Clark would then delegate the issue to the appropriate under- or assistant secretary.

An example of the many projects Haig delegated to Clark was the coordination of policy pertaining to the upcoming Law of the Sea conference. After quickly discovering that the acting head of the delegation, George H. Aldrich, had not been following Reagan policy, Clark acted decisively. He dismissed Aldrich only forty-eight hours before the conference was scheduled to resume at the United Nations.

Most senior staff in the Reagan White House did not like Al Haig. A typical appraisal was provided by Richard Pipes, the Harvard Sovi-etologist who served on the Reagan National Security Council (NSC): "Although I have said that he liked everyone, I believe Reagan from the outset did not like Alexander Haig", wrote Pipes. "Haig's aggres-sive bearing, his mocking expression, his superior airs visibly annoyed Reagan." At NSC meetings, "Haig would roll his eyes to express scorn

---

[1]John M. Goshko, "Clark, After a Shaky Start Has Gained Respect at State; Clark has Gained Respect, Serves as a Bugger for Haig", *Washington Post*, December 14, 1981, A1.

for the foreign policy pronouncements of various people around the table, as if imploring heaven to witness his suffering." [2]

Pipes' take on Haig was the common assessment; yet, Clark did not share it.

"He was very kind, very gracious", says Clark of Haig. "I got along with him well. He included me in every breakfast, every meeting, with one exception. . . ." Clark notes that the one exception was Haig's regular, weekly meeting with reporter Bob Woodward, the *Washington Post* journalist who along with Carl Bernstein cracked the Watergate story and brought down a president. Many observers believed that Haig was the infamous secret source, Deep Throat. Clark's relationship with Haig was such that he once asked Haig if he was Deep Throat. Haig said nothing, and merely grinned at Clark, apparently enjoying the common misperception. [3]

Haig had some early critical advice for Clark: Find an excellent secretary. In his first day on the job, Clark was given a book, three inches thick, filled with the names of secretaries. At the top was Jacqueline Hill. Clark called her first. She had worked at State since 1961, including for Henry Kissinger. During Hill's interview with the judge, Clark first asked, "So, what was it like working for Henry Kissinger?" When she responded, "I'm sorry, sir, but I can't go into that," Clark immediately intervened: "Perfect. You're hired."

Both laughed. There were no more questions. Clark found Hill to be an extremely reliable secretary. She remained with him as his executive assistant and loyal friend throughout his career in Washington, beginning at State, continuing at the Department of the Interior—and on into his subsequent law practice.

Winning Hearts and Minds

Almost immediately Deputy Secretary Clark began winning over his critics, as is evident in a March 13, 1981, *New York Times* article by Bernard Gwertzman, one of the first reporters to take the new man at State seriously.

---

[2] Richard Pipes, *Vixi: Memoirs of a Non-Belonger* (New Haven, CT: Yale University Press, 2003), p. 168.

[3] Interview with Bill Clark, February 24, 2005.

The article focused on Clark's concerns over the spread of communism in Central America and the Caribbean—America's so-called backyard, or, as Clark put it, America's *"front* yard". Gwertzman noted that the new deputy was now heading the administration's interagency group on El Salvador, where, said Clark, if the anticommunist government did not survive, other countries in the region would be destabilized by communist activity, emanating from there and Cuba. Clark explained that Cuba had a "plan to go on to Honduras, Guatemala, Belize, and then . . . to Mexico itself". When asked by Gwertzman if the Reagan administration feared a "domino effect" in that part of the world, Clark replied, "We do." [4]

While Clark was bullish about stopping communism in Central America, he did not disregard human rights in the region, including in El Salvador, where certain elements in the right-wing government were resisting needed reforms and had ordered a number of political killings. Some reporters credited Clark on this score. *Newsweek*, for instance, later concluded: "The human-rights policy that [Clark] developed involved a more evenhanded condemnation of abuses by right and left-wing governments than many critics expected, and he placed far more emphasis than Haig on having U.S. officials in El Salvador help to locate the killers of two American labor advisers and four church workers." Said one State Department official of Clark: "He was not willing to overlook a violation of law just because our side in El Salvador committed it." [5]

Another group headed by Clark was the State Department's committee dealing with ambassadorial appointments. Every Monday night in his office, he convened a meeting that included Walter J. Stoessel Jr., Under Secretary of State for Political Affairs, and L. Paul Bremer, the executive secretary of the department. They usually spent ten to fifteen minutes discussing each embassy and who should lead it. The next morning, Clark discussed their recommendations at the White House with Mike Deaver, Reagan's deputy chief of staff, the same job for which Clark had hired Deaver back in Sacramento; Richard V. Allen, the national security assistant; and E. Pendleton James, personnel chief. Clark then took the agreed

---

[4] Gwertzman, "For Haig Deputy, on-the-job Training".
[5] "Can Bill Clark Do the Job?", *Newsweek*, January 18, 1982.

upon names to Haig for his approval before they were presented to the President.[6]

It was during this period that Clark became forever known as "Judge" or "The Judge", even though he requested people to call him Bill. "The name seems to have stuck", he says. "Even at State, when I was 'Mr. Secretary', people called me 'Judge.'"

The New Life of Bill and Joan

Bill and Joan moved into a small apartment in Potomac Plaza, across the street from the Watergate complex, close enough to the State Department that Clark could walk to work, which he did no later than 7:00 A.M. The first order of business was to read the overnight cables and intelligence reports, as compiled and delivered by Bremer.

Clark's walks to the office were terminated when he was notified he had appeared atop Moammar Kaddafi's hit list. It was Oliver North, at the National Security Council, who informed Clark that he could no longer walk to work because he was "being watched" during his walks.[7] At that point, Clark was ordered to start using the limousine and driver that had been assigned to him.

The Washington scene was a very different life for the couple. Joan adapted well. She was respected for her cultural background, education, and ability to deal with difficult people and situations with aplomb and charm.

As Bill toiled at the office for fifteen-hour stretches at a time, Joan discovered worthwhile endeavors of her own. She took a crash course in Spanish at the Foreign Service Language School and served as a docent at State. Given her love and knowledge of classical music, she was given the task of managing the President's box at the Kennedy Center, a role she greatly enjoyed. She accompanied her husband on a number of international trips, and she was there for advice when called upon. When Bill once said in defense of Nancy and Ronald Reagan, "Any man who doesn't consult his wife on important issues can't have a very good marriage", he had his own relationship with Joan in mind.

---

[6] Gwertzman, "For Haig Deputy, on-the-job Training".

[7] Interview with Ollie North, July 21, 2006. This was learned by North through the secret service and intercepts.

"It's the No. 2 Men"

A March 1981 piece in *U.S. News & World Report*, entitled "It's the No. 2 Men Who Really Run Government", described the role being fulfilled by Bill Clark. "Nobody voted for them and they are rarely found in the spotlight, but decisions made every day by top deputies in the Reagan administration will go a long way in shaping the nation's future.... Behind closed doors in offices scattered across the nation's capital sit a handful of men, little known and seldom seen, who wield vast powers over the lives of all Americans." These men, said the article, are "the No. 2s", the under secretaries or deputy directors "who hold the real control over day-to-day operations of Washington's sprawling bureaucracy". While cameras focus on secretaries of departments "as they glide around in their limousines to cabinet meetings and congressional hearings", it is "their top assistants left back at the office who often run the show." [8] Bill Clark was not only among those profiled, he was the chief reason for the article.

The piece called Clark, "A Man with Connections", as well as "a man of clean-cut good looks and easy manner". The article quoted Clark as saying: "It has often been said that the most brilliantly conceived foreign policy will not succeed without the most thorough attention to execution. The enormous skill of our dedicated Foreign Service professionals will be wasted if the department is not administered efficiently." That was Clark's task, noted the newsweekly.

Another article on Clark that month appeared in the *Washington Post*, noting that an area Clark intended to administer effectively was Ronald Reagan's Latin America policy. Throughout that March, the issue of communism in Central America continued to intensify, as it would through Reagan's eight years as president. Clark said the administration's "most urgent objective" was to stop the flow of weapons to Salvadoran guerrillas by going to "the source".[9]

On March 18, Secretary of State Haig publicly accused the Soviet leadership of supporting "terrorism" in Central America and trying to establish a beachhead in the region. Two weeks later, on April 1, the

---

[8] "It's the No.2 Men Who Really Run Government", *U.S. News & World Report*, March 2, 1981, p. 36.

[9] Karen DeYoung, "El Salvador: Where Reagan Draws the Line; Reagan 'Sends a Message to Moscow' via El Salvador", *Washington Post*, March 9, 1981, A1.

Reagan administration suspended $15 million in aid to Nicaragua due to the Sandinista government's support of communist rebels in El Salvador.

It was widely reported that Clark was personally responsible for pushing President Reagan into a stronger stance against communism in Central America, a position for which Reagan became well known. Asked about these reports years later, Clark conceded they were true and that he had to nudge Reagan, not because the President was weak on communism or failed to perceive the seriousness of the threat but because of the intensity of the internal opposition Reagan faced, particularly from his own State Department. Clark was fulfilling Reagan's goal of having an America desk inside State.

Clark said State generally was "inordinately" focused on America's relationship with Western Europe—with Paris, London, and Bonn. Clark acknowledged the importance of these alliances, but he was also very concerned with the Western Hemisphere—with Central and South America. "That was the most significant bilateral relationship we had at the moment, and it had been left unattended", he says. "These are our closest neighbors."

When Clark first stressed this point at the State Department, eyebrows were raised. Yet, once this non-expert went through the reasons and made his case, from immigration to the communist threat, no one disagreed.

The French Request to Remove Kaddafi

Another concern of the new administration was situated in North Africa. The French government approached Reagan's team with a plan to assassinate Libyan dictator Moammar Kaddafi, who with Soviet military aid was sending arms and troops to neighboring Chad, a former French colony in the throes of civil war. Alexandre de Marenches, the director of France's external intelligence agency,[10] came to the United States asking for American help to kill Kaddafi during a parade, by

---

[10] SDECE was the *Service de Documentation Extérieure et de Contre-Espionnage*, which was the title of France's external intelligence agency from November 6, 1944 to April 2, 1982, when it was replaced by the *Direction Générale de la Securité Extérieure*, commonly known as the DGSE.

use of an explosive device placed near the reviewing stand.[11] "Our answer", says Clark, "was that we understood their feelings toward the man, but we don't do assassinations."

An executive order existed banning assassinations, first signed by President Gerald Ford and later supported by President Carter. The Reagan administration had no thought or intention of modifying the order.

Ronald Reagan had met with de Marenches before, in Los Angeles on December 16, 1980, during the transition period for the President-elect.[12] The Frenchman was impressed with Reagan, remarking on his "modesty" and lack of "self-importance", and he shared Reagan's view of communism. Indeed, de Marenches warned Reagan about the Soviet Union, which he called "the empire of evil". (He later entitled his memoirs *The Evil Empire*.)[13]

Intelligence sources interviewed for this book confirmed Clark's recollection of de Marenches' request. "He came over to the United States probably in early February 1981", said one source. "His interlocutor was Vice President Bush. The purpose of the visit was to discuss the removal of Kaddafi. He came to try to get us involved operationally in the plan.... He wanted not just our moral or political support but to get us involved in the actual operation."[14]

This same source said that the plan proposed by de Marenches was consistent with French thinking at the time and the concerns and purposes of the Safari Club, the group of countries—France, Egypt, Saudi Arabia, Morocco, and the Shah's Iran—banding together to fight the spread of communism and counter Soviet imperial designs, particularly in Africa. Formed by de Marenches in the mid-1970s, the

---

[11] Clark cannot pinpoint the exact date of the meeting. De Marenches (1921–1995) was head of SDECE from November 6, 1970 to June 12, 1981. Thus, the meeting could not have taken place after June 12, 1981. Moreover, Reagan was sidelined from March 30 through nearly all of April after being shot on March 30 by John Hinckley. De Marenches himself speaks of meeting with Reagan "shortly after he assumed office", which is consistent with Clark's memory that it occurred in the first several weeks. An intelligence source (see below) told us that it was "early February 1981". See Alexandre de Marenches, *The Fourth World War* (New York: William Morrow, 1992), p. 15.

[12] See Morris, *Dutch*, p. 472.

[13] Ibid; and Alexandre de Marenches, *The Evil Empire: the Third World War Now* (London: Sidgwick & Jackson, 1988), p. 188.

[14] Said the source: "I know the fellow who was with de Marenches—the French aide, a high-level individual in French intelligence." This aide was a key source for this information.

group was worried by the unwillingness of the United States to check the Soviets during the post-Watergate, post-Vietnam era, which was marked by a liberal Democratic Congress and a liberal President in Jimmy Carter.[15] The Club sought to fill the power vacuum created by years of American passivity.

De Marenches did not discuss his plot to kill Kaddafi in his 1986 and 1992 books. On the contrary, he noted that Egyptian leader Anwar Sadat had asked de Marenches in 1978 for help in "disposing of [Kaddafi] physically" and that he had declined the request. "The fact is," wrote de Marenches, "I was not in charge of a team of hired assassins."[16]

March 1981: the Attempted Assassination of Ronald Reagan

The Kaddafi assassination was never attempted, whereas another was not only attempted but came close to succeeding.

On March 30, 1981, at 2:25 P.M., as Ronald Reagan was exiting the Washington Hilton after giving a speech, he was met with a barrage of bullets fired from the revolver of John Hinckley, Jr. The President and three other men were wounded, one critically, in the attack. Reagan was whisked away in the presidential limousine, which was diverted to George Washington Hospital after it was discovered that the President had been hit.

Clark was at the State Department when he got word Reagan had been shot. He was with Secretary Haig, who said to him, "I'll go over there," meaning the White House, "and you man the ship here. Bill, stand by. We'll have to get out a proper statement for the benefit of our allies and 'non-friends', assuring them that all is well."

Haig raced to the White House to the center of activity in the Situation Room. He and Clark remained in direct communication by secure phone. According to a widely circulated story, Haig then tried to seize the reins of government. "I'm in charge!" he reportedly declared in the Situation Room at 1600 Pennsylvania Avenue.

Clark says it is unfair to characterize Haig's infamous words as reflecting a desire to take over the presidency and leapfrog the Constitution,

---

[15] According to accounts, the group held its first meeting in Riyadh in 1976.
[16] See de Marenches, The Evil Empire, pp. 138–42. Also his The Fourth World War, pp. 196–97 and 224–25.

which requires the vice president to step into the gap. Vice President Bush was not present at that moment—someone needed to take command, and right away. Haig was simply trying to establish order in the Situation Room, Clark explains, and to make it clear that all was operating smoothly atop the world's largest power. This was, after all, a tense Cold War period, and one did not know how the Soviets might react.

"The place was in great confusion and the vice president was in the air", says Clark. "Al reminded people that as the principal cabinet member he was going to take charge of the meeting, not of the White House. So some of his detractors overplayed the meaning of what he said. . . . What he said was correct—that he heads the national security interest, that he's the primary cabinet member. So, he did take charge in attempting to get a statement written and in trying to calm the others who were present."

Moreover, Haig knew what to do because of his experiences in the Nixon administration. "He had been through a lot in the Nixon years", adds Clark. There had been low periods for Nixon during which Haig effectively served as president. So, on March 30, 1981, Haig knew what to do better than anyone in that room.

Nancy's Response

Nancy Reagan was devastated. Ronald Reagan was her hero, her life. "My life began when I got married", she had often said. "My life began with Ronnie." [17] Now, her husband's life was in grave danger.

Mrs. Reagan shared a private reaction with only a handful of people, including the Reagans' current pastor, the Reverend Louis H. Evans of the National Presbyterian Church in Washington, D.C. "I'm really struggling with a feeling of failed responsibility", she confided to Evans and several intimates. "I usually stand at Ronnie's left side. And that's where he took the bullet." [18]

---

[17] Quoted in Joseph Lewis, *What Makes Reagan Run? A Political Profile* (New York: McGraw-Hill, 1968), p. 46; and Lou Cannon, *Reagan* (New York: Putnam, 1982), p. 141.

[18] Evans remembers the gathering place as a kind of "reception" with a couch and some chairs. He is not sure of the name of the room, but believes it was not part of the White House living quarters.

Bill Clark had always viewed Nancy as Ronald Reagan's protector, and her response appears to underscore the case. Clark was not surprised to learn that Mrs. Reagan had made such a remark. "She would have laid her life down for her friend—for her best friend", he says. "She would have done that for him."

Clark talked with Mrs. Reagan right away. The day after the shooting she and Clark sat together, the two of them, with the head surgeon at George Washington University Hospital who, after operating on the President, gave them a briefing on Reagan's condition. Clark remembers certain details well: "He said the first thing that they look for in an open chest is the color of the lung material, noting that if it's pink, it means non-smoker, and the probability of much higher healing, much faster. If the lung material is gray or dark, it suggests heavy smoker and they have greater concern, greater work to do. They were relieved to see that his lung was a pinkish color. I remember that well."

Reagan's wound "was far graver than was reported at the time", Clark adds. Nonetheless, Reagan survived, and his recovery was quick, especially for a 70-year-old. Reagan told Clark and others that he believed God had spared his life for a special purpose, for something related to the grand struggle against Soviet communism. He was convinced that what had happened to him was not merely physical, but also spiritual. Reagan was transformed by the attack, which fueled his feeling of divine purpose over the next eight years.

His sense of being saved for a purpose was affirmed by several prominent Catholics. On April 17, Good Friday, he received face-to-face counsel from New York's Terence Cardinal Cooke, a man with whom Reagan became close. "The hand of God was upon you", Cooke told Reagan, who grew very serious. "I know", he replied. "I have decided that whatever time I have left is for Him." [19] In June, President and Mrs. Reagan had a private meal with Mother Teresa, who told him that after the shooting she had stayed up for two straight nights praying "very hard" for him to live. She then looked at Reagan and said pointedly: "You have suffered the passion of the cross and have received grace. There is a purpose to this. . . . This has happened to you at this time because your country and the

---

[19] See Paul Kengor, *God and Ronald Reagan*, p. 200.

world need you." The Great Communicator was speechless, as was his wife, who broke into tears.[20]

One year later, Ronald Reagan would have an equally powerful encounter with Pope John Paul II at the Vatican, but not before the Pontiff experienced an attempt on his own life.

May 1981: the Attempted Assassination of Pope John Paul II

On May 13, 1981, Mehmet Ali Agca shot and critically wounded Pope John Paul II in Saint Peter's Square. The Pope lost a great deal of blood, and the complications that followed nearly took the Pontiff's life—facts that were unknown at the time to those outside the operating room,[21] not unlike the situation when the attempt was made on Reagan's life.

Agca's motives for shooting the Pope were more complicated than Hinckley's reasons for shooting Reagan. The "confused young man", as Reagan charitably called Hinckley, claimed to be vying for the attention of actress Jodie Foster. Many suspected, however, that the Pope's assassin had been hired by communists. Clark disallowed himself to speculate.

These commonly held suspicions were hardly unjustified. Communists had tried to kill Eugenio Cardinal Pacelli in Bavaria a few years before he became Pope Pius XII.[22] After World War II, communists launched a malicious disinformation campaign to discredit Pius XII as a Nazi collaborator.[23]

Their fear of the man in Rome increased with the October 1978 election of an even more aggressively anti-communist pope, a Pole named Karol Wojtyła. Poland was one of the few nations within the Soviet empire where Catholicism managed to survive, in spite of the brutally repressive atheistic-communist regime. The Soviets were threatened by the Church reaching into Poland to tap its first non-Italian

---

[20] See Kengor p. 209; and also Dinesh D'Souza, *Ronald Reagan: How an Ordinary Man Became an Extraordinary Leader* (New York: Free Press, 1997).

[21] Pope John Paul II, *Memory and Identity* (New York: Rizzoli, 2005), pp. 160–62.

[22] H. W. Crocker III, *Triumph: The Power and Glory of the Catholic Church* (New York: Three Rivers Press, 2001), p. 403.

[23] See Ronald J. Rychlak, *Hitler, the War, and the Pope* (Our Sunday Visitor Press, 2000), pp. 14–15; and Crocker, *Triumph*, p. 401.

pope in 455 years and first Slavic pope ever.[24] When the native son appeared before millions of Polish people in June 1979 and dramatically told them "Be not afraid", the Soviet leadership was terrified.

Did Agca pull the trigger at the behest of communists? The debate continues to this day.[25] Whatever his motives, the Pope's reaction to the attempt on his life was similar to that of Ronald Reagan when he was shot. Both men sensed God's intervention in their lives and in history; both believed they had been chosen to help fulfill God's purposes in the world.

April to Late May: the Shostakovich Defection

For now, however, Bill Clark had a State Department to manage. After a few months of running the building, in April Clark began a series of concrete actions and policy changes. The first of these was quite unforeseen.

Bill and Joan had retired for the night on April 12, 1981, when the red phone rang. It sat near Joan's side of the bed, due to a short wire. As was her custom, she reached over, grabbed the phone and, without waking, handed it to Bill. "Bilchick! Bilchick!" yelled an excited voice into the receiver. "Help me!"

It was Mstislav Rostropovich, the Russian-born music director of the National Symphony Orchestra in Washington. With Joan's handling of the presidential box at Kennedy Center, she and Bill had become good friends with Rostropovich, who affectionately called Clark "Bilchick", while Clark called him "Slava".

"You know I'll always help you", Clark answered his friend. "What is it?" An anxious Rostropovich explained that Maxim Shostakovich, conductor of the Soviet Radio Symphony Orchestra, and his nineteen-year-old son, the orchestra pianist, had escaped their managers after a

---

[24] See George Weigel, *Witness to Hope* (New York: HarperCollins, 2001), p. 3.

[25] Agca's subsequent remarks were inconsistent. He did, however, say on at least one occasion that communists were behind the plot, specifically Bulgarian intelligence. Others began investigations, grasping the gravity of the allegation. *New York Times* columnist William Safire stated that communist involvement—particularly fingerprints that led all the way to Moscow—would constitute "The Crime of the Century". To cite just one of innumerable examples of suspicions of Bulgaria, see this early account: "A Murky but Intriguing Trail", *Time*, December 27, 1982, p. 25.

performance in West Germany and turned themselves over to the police. They wanted to defect to the United States. Shostakovich was the son of the famous Russian composer Dmitri Shostakovich and regularly appeared on Moscow television. He was a celebrity of national importance in the Soviet Union, as well as an internationally acclaimed musician.

"Bilchick, what should I do next?" asked Rostropovich. Clark sprang into action with a series of phone calls. In a matter of a few hours, he and his staff had arranged for Shostakovich and his son to be moved from a police station near Munich to the U.S. consulate in Frankfurt, where they were sent on their way to freedom.

A week and a half later, Maxim Shostakovich was in Washington, where he mounted the podium at the Kennedy Center to conduct—not an orchestra—but his first American press conference in his first public appearance since he and his son defected to the West. "Both my son and I voluntarily renounce the status of Soviet citizenship", stated the forty-two-year-old conductor, in Russian. "No matter how difficult it was to leave, it would have been even more difficult for me to stay—to witness the innocent spirit of my son being broken and brutalized as it collided with our reality."

Shostakovich's decision to defect had been "ripening" all of his "conscious life", he said. "Our exodus is a profoundly conscious step, a sign of protest ... my spiritual legacy from my never-to-be-forgotten father." He added that he had "unfailingly" chosen to live in the United States because of "the attention the U.S. government pays to the rights of man". Yet, said the conductor, that decision was bittersweet; it was "painful and frightening" because "all those whose lives have touched mine will be harshly punished." Asked if he had tried to defect before, he answered, "There are no *two* attempts." [26]

One month later, on Memorial Day, Maxim Shostakovich led the National Symphony Orchestra on the west lawn of the Capitol with the Stars and Stripes unfurled. [27] It was quite a victory not only for the two Russians, but also for the America desk at the U.S. State Department. The press gave a lot of attention to the Shostakovich

---

[26] Curt Suplee, "Anatomy of a Defection", *Washington Post*, April 24, 1981, F1.

[27] Francis X. Clines, "Maxim Shostakovich Plays Overture to a New Life", *New York Times*, May 26, 1981, A2.

affair. The *Washington Post* reported that Clark had "paved the way" for the defection.[28]

The prestigious new U.S. citizens wanted to thank Clark for his help and asked him what they could do to show their gratitude. Clark thought they had already been through enough and was not expecting anything in return. Then, a thought occurred to him: He asked the Russians if they might consider performing at his and Joan's favorite festival, the San Luis Obispo Mozart Festival held every August. The two Shostakoviches replied that they not only would be pleased to perform, but also would bring along a friend: Maestro Rostropovich.

"They had no idea where San Luis Obispo was", says Clark. "They didn't care where it was. They wanted to do that for us." So, Slava flew to California with his cello and the two Shostakoviches. They stayed at the Clark ranch, where the Russians got a taste of western living. "We had a grand old time", says Clark.

The concert was a huge success for San Luis Obispo. People traveled in from all over the state, from San Francisco to Los Angeles, filling the small concert hall, sitting outside as well as inside. The festival not only netted $20,000, but also went down in musical history as the first place the Shostakoviches and Rostropovich performed together in the United States.[29]

It was fitting that one of Bill Clark's first public accomplishments at the State Department was to help free people from behind the Iron Curtain, a continuation of his Counter Intelligence Corps days in West Germany, when he first helped communist refugees find freedom in the West.

June 1981: South Africa

Clark's first foreign-policy trip—his "maiden voyage", as he puts it—was to South Africa and Zimbabwe. He departed on June 9. He first met with South African Prime Minister P. W. Botha, "the man whose name I didn't know at my confirmation hearing", Clark wryly notes. His next meeting was with the leader of Zimbabwe, Robert Mugabe, another man he could not name for Senator Biden. With subsequent study and briefings, he now knew them well.

---

[28] See Donnie Radcliffe, "Washington Ways", *Washington Post*, March 30, 1982, p. B2.
[29] Radcliffe, "Washington Ways".

Along with Chester Crocker, Assistant Secretary of State for African Affairs, and Elliot Abrams, the Assistant Secretary of State for Africa, Clark went to South Africa to discuss Namibian independence and apartheid. Clark was the highest-ranking U.S. official to visit South Africa since Secretary of State Cyrus Vance traveled there in 1978.[30]

Clark met with Botha twice on June 11 in what the press dubbed "a high-level American effort" to obtain from Botha a commitment to fulfill a previously adopted United Nations plan for bringing about independence and black majority rule in the territory of Namibia, then administered by South Africa. Namibia had been controlled by South Africa since World War I, but a Marxist guerilla group with backing from Libya and Cuba had been fighting a protracted war of independence since the 1960s, prompting U.N. interference. In spite of the U.N., South Africa was unwilling to give up the territory and wanted guarantees for the protection of the white minority living in Namibia before considering a deal with the Reagan administration.

At one point during the intense negotiations Botha lost his temper, and Clark told the prime minister, "Take us to the airport. We have our plane waiting unless you're willing to follow our agenda, which was agreed upon before I got here." Botha was stunned, but Clark held his ground, saying, "It was nice being with you and hopefully we'll meet again some day." He stood up and announced that he and his team were leaving for a scheduled meeting in Paris, where Clark was leading a U.S. delegation.

Clark left the room, and the building. He and his entourage boarded their host's helicopter and headed to the airport via a short stop at the dramatic tip of the continent, where they watched the convergence of the two great oceans in silence. When they got to the tarmac Clark said, "Well, we better get going; it's still daylight." As they walked toward the steps of the plane, a motorcycle messenger skidded up to the group and said, "Come back, we'll follow the agenda as agreed."

Clark's hard-line approach prompted a change of heart in Botha, and talks were restarted at a Capetown hotel.[31] The results were a rare two-hour, one-on-one meeting at which, says Clark, "We effectively

---

[30] Murphy, "Clark, in S. Africa, Sees Botha Twice on Namibia".

[31] Joseph Lelyveld, "Linkage in Africa; News Analysis", *New York Times*, July 15, 1982, A2.

said, 'We are not the Carter administration, whose policy was to berate you in public. We will abhor apartheid, but we will not emphasize it in public, and we will not embarrass you in public as did the prior administration.' " The South Africans appreciated that. It was Reagan's constructive policy, said Clark, that the administration could be more effective by privately reprimanding human-rights violators rather than by publicly shaming them; the latter approach merely embarrassed and infuriated countries like South Africa, which felt they were being used by American politicians looking to score political points with liberals back home.

The two sides, as the *New York Times* noted, reached an agreement that "led South Africa to drop virtually every ... procedural demand and quibble that it had [once demanded] of the Carter Administration".[32] American press accounts judged the trip a notable diplomatic accomplishment by the Clark delegation.

The Soviet press, on the other hand, gave the Clark talks a different spin. On June 13, TASS reported on the trip, repeatedly referring to South Africa as "the racist country", trying to make Clark and the Reagan administration guilty by association. "[M]any observers come to the conclusion that the White House emissaries visited the racist country in order to finalize details of a secret political and military agreement between Washington and Pretoria", said TASS, blasting the "imperialist and reactionary forces" represented by Clark. This, said TASS, was the "focus of talks between William Clark and the racist ringleaders.... All this shows that the Reagan administration's policy towards Africa is an integral part of its generally aggressive efforts aimed at elevating world tension and increasing the danger of war." [33]

Clark knew at the time of his visit to South Africa that the Soviets would be watching his moves closely. They also had interests in the region. Moreover, the approach taken by the Reagan administration toward South Africa might very well signal the approach America would take toward other repressive yet pro-western regimes in Africa and elsewhere.

---

[32] Ibid.

[33] "Reportage on Clark Mission to Southern Africa", statement by *TASS*, June 13, 1981. Published in FBIS, June 15, 1981, p. J1.

Other Duties at the America Desk

Deputy Secretary Clark gave a major policy speech on June 24 to the Austrian Foreign Policy Association in Vienna, attended by a visibly icy Soviet ambassador seated in the front row in an attempt to make Clark as uncomfortable as possible. The address, Clark's first of several in the years ahead, was directed not merely at the Soviets but also at U.S. allies in Western Europe, to gauge how they would react to a strong anti-communist line by the Reagan administration.

Clark candidly offered a stark contrast between the American and Soviet systems. The Berlin Wall, "that ugly barrier to freedom", said Clark, served as "an eloquent demonstration of the character of the Soviet system", which "imprisons rather than frees" and "divides rather than unites". The dictatorship in Moscow pursued "expansionism and aggression", he said, and America would not take a backseat in that struggle. As Clark spoke, the Soviet ambassador hissed. Later he complained to the Austrians, who offered him equal time.

The Soviets were not the only ones piqued by Clark that summer. On July 22, he criticized Prime Minister Menachem Begin after he launched air strikes against southern Lebanon, from where Palestinian forces were attacking civilian settlements in Israel. The city of Beirut was bombed, leaving many Lebanese dead or homeless; Clark told the press that the President felt "disappointment" with Israeli actions. He suggested that Israel's military moves had set back American diplomatic initiatives in the Middle East and made it politically difficult for the Reagan administration to resume deliveries of F-16 fighter-planes pledged to Israel. Secretary of Defense Weinberger agreed that Begin's course "cannot really be described as moderate at this point, and it is essential that there be some moderation." [34]

The next day, certain members of the Reagan administration, in a response making the front page of the *Washington Post*, publicly rebuked Clark and Weinberger for their statements.[35] White House Chief of Staff James A. Baker III told reporters Clark and Weinberger were

---

[34] Charles Mohr, "2 Top U.S. Officials Critical of Begin for Military Acts", *New York Times*, July 23, 1981, A1.

[35] Lou Cannon and Don Oberdorfer, "White House Softens Begin Criticism; White House Softens Criticism of Begin; Weinberger, Clark Rebuked", *Washington Post*, June 24, 1981, A1.

speaking for themselves, not for the administration, when they criticized Begin.[36] This was among the first public disagreements between Clark and Baker.

Though surprised by Clark's candor, Begin seemed to have formed a grudging respect for the deputy secretary. The two carried on a careful but friendly relationship, Clark says. The Israeli government was dependent upon U.S. foreign aid, and each time Begin sat down in the Oval Office, says Clark, he brought with him a "wish list". He had done this with the previous president, Jimmy Carter, who would note which items he could approve and could not approve for Israel, but often Carter's responses were left vague. Begin knew how to turn this lack of clarity to his advantage. When he spoke to the press corps following an Oval Office meeting, he sometimes said that Carter had agreed to more than had been explicitly stipulated, forcing the President to accede to the matters of contention.

State Department veterans had informed Clark of this Begin tactic. Thus, the deputy secretary of state was ready for the maneuver when Begin met for the first time with President Reagan. Before the meeting, Clark warned Begin not to try this tactic with the new administration; doing so could be detrimental to America's security interests. If Begin did so in spite of this warning, Clark warned, he would tell the press that Begin seemed to be "confused". Or, as Clark told Begin, he would "step on his right foot". Begin was taken aback at Clark's frankness but smiled. He said it was clear Clark was also an old lawyer.

Weeks after Begin's visit, Clark met with Egypt's President Anwar Sadat, who shared with Begin the Nobel Peace Prize for signing the Camp David Accords. Sadat's visit to Washington received no media attention, and Clark was Sadat's main host, as Reagan was at Rancho del Cielo and Secretary of State Haig was not available. In fact, Haig, admittedly pro-Israel, was playing golf at the time.

Clark was by no means anti-Israel, he said, but he and Weinberger both thought they had a role to play in "balancing the ship", which seemed to them tilted heavily to the Israel side by Haig, the President, and others. Part of leveling that balance, said Clark, meant remembering that Egypt was the other half of the Camp David Accords, and

---

[36] Ibid.

the second-largest recipient of U.S. foreign aid. It also meant strengthening relationships with other countries in the Middle East. For example, in 1981, Clark was openly supportive of the controversial Reagan
decision to sell AWACs (military reconnaissance planes) to Saudi Arabia, a move that was opposed by Israel but that later paid off in the
U.S. economic war against the Soviet Union.[37]

Clark expressed admiration for Sadat and said they got along very
well. During his visit, Sadat learned that a previously arranged delivery of F-16s to Israel was, by happenstance, to arrive in Tel Aviv the
same day that he was to return to Cairo, carrying messages of American goodwill and assurances to the Egyptian people that America was
their ally. Sadat turned to Clark, with whom he was by then on a
first-name basis, and said, "Bill, is there any way of putting off that
F-16 arrival for a few days?" Sadat did not ask that the shipment be
canceled, only that it be briefly delayed.

Clark tracked down Haig on the golf course. "Al," he said, "this
seems like a very reasonable request to me. The timing is bad. That
[F-16] arrival would undo the good message he's carrying back to
his Egypt." Haig responded: "Nope, nope. It has been scheduled
for some time and we can't disappoint Israel." Clark challenged:
"Well, Al, I disagree, and I think we ought to place this before the
President at the ranch and let him decide." Haig was not pleased; he
knew the President would side with Clark, as he did on most everything. Clark got Reagan on a secure line. The President listened and
sided with the deputy secretary. The shipment was delayed for a
week.

Clark escorted Sadat to the chopper landing from where he began
his journey home. He was the last U.S. official to see Sadat alive, for
not long after his return to Egypt, Sadat was assassinated by radical
Muslims who disapproved of the Camp David Accords and any attempt
to make peace with Israel.

---

[37] Reagan in a news conference, October 1, 1981, stated: "I have proposed this sale
because it significantly enhances our own vital national security interests in the Middle
East. By building confidence in the United States as a reliable security partner, the sale will
greatly improve the chances of our working with Saudi Arabia." Caspar Weinberger, who
also supported the sale, later stated: "One of the reasons we were selling the Saudis those
weapons is because of the hope that lower oil prices would result." (Quoted by Schweizer,
ed., The Fall of the Berlin Wall, p. 44.)

A Vacancy on the U.S. Supreme Court

Just as Clark was becoming an important foreign-policy player, the former California Supreme Court judge received an extraordinary consideration: to return to the Supreme Court, this time, the U.S. Supreme Court, the highest court in the land.

On June 18, 1981, sixty-six-year old U.S. Justice Potter Stewart, a popular swing vote among the court's nine, announced he would be stepping down on July 3, after twenty-three years on the court. The next day, both the *Washington Post* and the *New York Times* placed Bill Clark on a short list of nominees including Ed Meese and then Attorney General William French Smith.[38]

Reagan asked Clark if he wanted to be considered for the vacancy. "Well, it's an honor to be considered," said Clark, "but I've served on the court now for twelve years at three levels. I'm truly enjoying the work I'm doing for you now. I'd rather stay where I am." The President replied, "That's what I thought you'd say, Bill." Reagan pulled a piece of paper from inside his coat pocket and crossed Bill Clark's name off the list.

Tracked down by the *Washington Post*'s Lou Cannon, Clark told the former Sacramento reporter: "I've made it clear I don't want to be considered for the high court." Cannon said Clark did not give a reason other than expressing a desire to return to his California ranch after completing his present job, where, reported Cannon, a "high White House official" said Clark was "badly needed"; he was serving as a crucial "buffer" between White House aides and the "sometimes mercurial" Al Haig.[39]

Cannon noted that administration officials were "looking hard" for a woman to fill the vacancy. Citing an official, he named only one woman as a prospect: 44-year-old White House aide, Elizabeth Dole, wife of Republican Senator Bob Dole. Intelligent, attractive, conservative, and pro-life, Elizabeth Dole did not get the call.

---

[38] Lou Cannon, "Chance to Name Woman; Reagan Given Opportunity to Name Woman Justice; Jockeying Could Be 'Real Headache'", *Washington Post*, June 19, 1981, A1; and Steven R. Weisman, "Stewart Will Quit High Court July 3; Reasons Not Given", *New York Times*, June 19, 1981, A1.

[39] Lou Cannon, "Clark Withdraws as a Court Possibility; State's Clark Withdraws As Possibility for Court", *Washington Post*, June 27, 1981, A1.

Clark knew that Reagan was considering a woman for the seat, and the President enlisted his help to find the right one, asking Clark to interview Sandra Day O'Connor, who was under consideration. Clark and O'Connor spoke for an hour and a half. He reported back to Reagan that O'Connor seemed fine: "qualified, competent, capable". The president made notes on his yellow legal pad. A grinning Reagan said, "Well, Bill, what did you talk about with her?" Clark smiled, "Well, we talked about horses and dogs and cows and kids and life." Reagan chuckled, "That's what I figured." Clark knew that William French Smith was screening O'Connor, and assumed that Smith, as the attorney general, would cover key social and legal issues such as abortion and capital punishment.

On July 7, 1981, President Reagan nominated O'Connor for the U.S. Supreme Court. On September 25, O'Connor became the first woman to be sworn in to the highest court in the land. Expected to be a moderate, O'Connor proved not to be moderate on abortion. She was a crucial swing vote in ensuring that no state laws limiting or regulating abortion in any way would be upheld by the Supreme Court. For this reason, Clark looks on his role in selecting O'Connor with "great regret".

Some question Clark's judgment in passing up the chance to serve on the U.S. Supreme Court. Had he been a U.S. justice, would *Roe v. Wade* have been overturned, might abortion on demand have been reversed? Perhaps, but at the time he briefly considered a position on the high court, he was being called elsewhere—to Ronald Reagan's side in the fight against Soviet communism. There is only so much one man can do, and taking on the Soviets was enough of a task for one lifetime.

The Road Ahead

With his court days now firmly behind him, the Divine Plan for Bill Clark—and his role in the Reagan administration—came into focus. Clarity was provided by two unlikely sources—the media and the State Department.

The same media that had once torpedoed Clark now praised him for his work at State. The fifty-year-old Clark was widely regarded as the most influential and powerful man to occupy the State Department's second-ranking job since George Ball had done so in the 1960s, and not just during the twenty-five times he filled in for Haig as act-ing secretary of state.[40] Profiles of the "quick study" ran in major newsweeklies, with titles like "Clark Comes on Strong at State."[41]

Clark had also won over some of the career civil servants inside the State Department with his disarming, down-to-earth manner. "Every time we've dealt with Clark, we've been impressed", said one senior State official. "If I have a complaint, it's that the Judge ... doesn't do more."[42]

Though a pretty elite group, the State Department staff came to like Clark. One Clark incident rapidly became a legend at Foggy Bot-tom. Joe Bullock, Clark's official driver, mentioned to the Judge that he needed to pick up his own car from a repair shop at some time during the day. He was trying to figure out how to get there in time. Clark told Bullock to take the two of them to the repair shop. Once

---

[40] Similarly, a July 13, 1981 piece in *Newsweek* stated: "More and more, Haig asks his deputy's opinion at policy briefings, which Clark often tries to speed up or cut short so that decisions can be made more quickly. And Clark has added elements of political wis-dom and restraint to State's negotiations with the White House over sensitive ambassado-rial positions." David M. Alpern, "Haig's Guidance Counselor", *Newsweek*, July 13, 1981, p. 29. The piece was so laudatory that Senator Howard Baker (R-TN) took it to the Senate floor as vindication of his support of Clark during the confirmation process, and asked it be printed in its entirety in the Congressional Record. See "Judge William P. Clark's Rave Reviews", *Congressional Record—Senate*, July 8, 1981, pp. S7268–69.

[41] The Walczak piece in *Business Week* stated: "When President Reagan named old friend William P. Clark to be Deputy Secretary of State, Washington insiders were quick to pre-dict that the conservative California jurist would be in over his head.... But after four months spent diligently boning up on foreign policy, Clark is surprising some of his critics and is emerging as a major power at State.... But as he gains confidence Clark is ... making his presence felt on substantive foreign policy issues.... 'Clark and Haig are start-ing to develop a good working relationship because Haig recognizes that Clark was put there to represent the interests of Reagan and the senior staff', says one top White House political aide. 'At State, Clark will play the tough cop, shaking up the bureaucracy.' Clark's unique standing with the President, and Haig's acceptance of it, could foreshadow a role of unprecedented importance for the deputy secretary. In most instances, the No. 2 man at State has been an anonymous figure who focused on routine administrative matters. But with Haig overextended and, to some observers, still showing some debilitating effects of his recent heart surgery, Clark is certain to be called upon to shoulder an increasing share of the policy burden. The areas where Clark is most likely to get involved are those where the Administration is planning radical policy shifts such as U.S.-Soviet relations, arms con-trol, and East-West trade—and in the monitoring of such crisis points as Central America, Southwest Asia, and Poland." Lee Walczak, "Clark Comes on Strong at State", *Business Week*, June 15, 1981, p. 139.

[42] David M. Alpern, "Haig's Guidance Counselor", *Newsweek*, July 13, 1981, p. 29.

they got there, Clark drove the official car back to the State Department himself, an act that not only amazed the State Department motor pool but also endeared him to many State officials and employees.[43]

Most important for Clark was the relationship he had forged with Al Haig. As John Goshko reported in the *Washington Post*, "at least twice Clark was instrumental in diverting Haig from a collision course that could have had disastrous results for the administration's image." Clark stepped in and gently dissuaded Haig from demanding that Ronald Reagan apologize for critical comments about the secretary leaked by White House aides. When Haig "exploded in public anger" at the decision to give control of the government's crisis management machinery to Vice President Bush rather than to himself, Clark sat with the secretary for hours and talked him out of resigning.[44] In gratitude for Clark's intervention, Bush gave the deputy secretary a framed photo of himself and Clark together, with an inscription: "To Bill Clark— Blessed are the peacemakers. With friendship and respect. George Bush."

Yes, the Judge was providing a public service merely by handling Al Haig. Clare Boothe Luce joked with Clark that he should write a book entitled *The Care and Feeding of Al Haig*. "Haig would drive us nuts", said Clark. "He always felt he could do a better job than Ronald Reagan. But I loved the guy anyway."

As the end of 1981 drew near, Bill Clark, in a striking turnabout, was winning hearts and minds. His name now appeared as no less than a potential replacement for Al Haig, or, as reported in the *Washington Post*, as a possible candidate for "an important insider's slot at the White House".[45] Indeed, Ronald Reagan had a major promotion in mind for his old ally from Sacramento.

---

[43] Interview with John Murphy, March 17, 2005.

[44] John M. Goshko, "Clark, After a Shaky Start Has Gained Respect at State; Clark Has Gained Respect, Serves as a Bugger for Haig", *Washington Post*, December 14, 1981, A1.

[45] This *Washington Post* piece, which was tellingly titled, "Clark, After a Shaky Start, Has Gained Respect at State", reported that "Clark's standing within the administration is so high that he frequently is mentioned as a potential successor to his boss, Secretary of State Alexander M. Haig Jr., or as a possible candidate for an important insider's slot at the White House."

CHAPTER 8

Ronald Reagan's National Security Advisor

By the end of 1981, both Bill Clark and the press had become comfortable with his presence and performance at the State Department. Then, on the morning of December 18, Washingtonians opened their *Post* and read that William P. Clark "now appears the most likely choice" as Ronald Reagan's next national security advisor and head of the National Security Council (NSC), the "frontrunner" to replace the embattled Richard V. Allen in the White House.[1]

Former National Security Advisor Henry Kissinger was aware of the news and coincidentally bumped into Bill and Joan shortly after it was made public. He urged Clark to take the job: "Yes, yes, take it!" Kissinger said. "It's the most wonderful job in Washington." He added that it was also the most politically dangerous job because, unlike the situation of the secretary of state, there is no safety net of staff to fall back on when work reaches overload proportions. Staff is purposely kept small, small as in "lean and mean", says Clark, "so that it can move quickly in fulfilling its mission for the President."[2]

For some time, the handwriting had been on the wall for Dick Allen, under whom foreign-policy coordination and articulation had come to a halt, by reason of the refusal of Haig and Allen to

---

[1] Martin Schram, "Reagan Declines to Say if Allen Will Retain Job, Even if Cleared", *Washington Post*, December 19, 1981.
[2] Interview with Bill Clark, February 1, 2007.

communicate.[3] "It was a difficult situation", says Clark. "The national security advisor and secretary of state would not speak, when in fact they must, sometimes hourly. This left a void, and that void was essentially filled by Weinberger and Haig who went their own respective ways on matters of defense and foreign policy during the first year of the Reagan administration."

Clark, a man of known integrity with a track record of working well with Secretary Haig, was Reagan's top choice to replace Allen. Clark liked and respected Allen. In his February 1981 testimony before the Senate Foreign Relations Committee, he had referred to Allen as "engaging and brilliant".

The New Year began auspiciously for Clark. On the front page of the January 1, 1982, *Washington Post* was this top story: "Allen's Job Expected to Go to Clark". The article reported that President Reagan intended not only to make Clark his next national security advisor but also to increase greatly the power that went with the position.[4] Clark was moving into a crucial post, one about to receive a major makeover.

Fittingly, the two stories and photo to the right of the Clark headline concerned the Solidarity movement in Poland, now under siege by the Moscow-controlled government that had recently imposed martial law and jailed hundreds of anti-communist activists. Clark and Reagan saw that supporting Solidarity was key to unraveling the Soviet empire, a strategy the two men would pursue with Clark at the helm of the NSC.

Previously, there had been "no single focal point" in the White House for contact with top officials of the State Department, the Defense Department, and the Central Intelligence Agency. "The person who is the national security advisor must have direct access to the president", said one senior official. "And just as important, he must have the perception of direct access in the eyes of State, Defense and the CIA."[5]

---

[3] Sol W. Sanders, "A new Reagan foreign policy for 1982", *Business Week*, December 28, 1981.

[4] John M. Goshko and Martin Schram, "Allen's Job Expected to Go to Clark", *Washington Post*, January 1, 1982.

[5] Ibid.

As the *Washington Post* noted, this new understanding of the position of national security advisor represented an "about-face". Previously, the Reagan White House had attempted to avoid the concentration of power in the hands of the national security advisor.[6] In order to limit his authority, the advisor had been subordinate to Meese, who along with Mike Deaver and Jim Baker constituted the "troika", as it was called by Washington insiders, that formed Reagan's "chief of staff".

There had been a good reason to rein in the national security advisor. In the two prior administrations, there had been serious tensions between former advisors Zbigniew Brzezinski (under President Carter) and Henry Kissinger (under Presidents Ford and Nixon) and their respective secretaries of state. Yet, it turned out that even with the changes made by the Reagan administration, the friction between State and NSC remained. Worse, the conflicts were accompanied by a new problem: a lack of policy process.

Under the revised system, prompted by Reagan and written by Meese with the input of Clark and others, National Security Advisor Clark would have direct and immediate access to President Reagan and direct operational responsibility. Clark would deal directly with Secretary of State Haig, Defense Secretary Weinberger, and CIA Director Casey. The job was tailor made: no one got along better with all four men than did Bill Clark.

In fact, Clark got along so well with Haig that many administration officials were reluctant to see him pulled away from State. Yet, the President's top advisors thought Clark could expand his mediating role at State into "an even wider sphere" from inside the White House.[7] Haig agreed, saying he was pleased to have his friend there.

On January 4, 1982, upon returning from a lengthy meeting with close political advisors in Palm Springs, California, Reagan formally announced that Allen was resigning and would be replaced by Clark.[8] Clark was now Assistant to the President for National Security Affairs,

---

[6] Ibid.

[7] Ibid.

[8] John M. Goshko, "President Agrees to Replace Allen in Security Post; Reagan Agrees to Plan to Replace Allen, Upgrade Advisor Job", *Washington Post*, January 3, 1982.

more commonly called National Security Advisor, which is not abbreviated "NSA" because these are the well-known initials for the National Security Agency in Fort Meade, Maryland.

The statement released by White House Press Secretary Larry Speakes stated:

> In consultation with the members of the National Security Council, Mr. Clark in his new role will be responsible for the development, coordination, and implementation of national security policy, as approved by the President. In addition, he will be responsible for providing staff support and for administering the National Security Council. As Assistant to the President for National Security Affairs, Mr. Clark will have a direct reporting relationship to the President. This expanded role for the Assistant to the President for National Security Affairs, as announced today, will implement recommendations made to the President by the Counselor to the President, Edwin Meese III, following a review of the national security process.

Immediately after the announcement, Clark held a press conference. The first question he faced predictably concerned his qualifications: "Do you feel ... you are now fully equipped to handle the job of national security advisor?" Clark's answer: "Yes, sir."

Press Reaction

Though some commentators expressed doubts about Clark's qualifications, much of the press saw him as well suited for the task based upon his performance at State. *Time* noted that the choice of Clark was "met with general approval in Washington", adding that Clark was a "down-home quick study" whose colleagues at State had come to "trust" him as a "clear thinker who had a gift for calming his sometimes tempestuous boss".[9] His temperament made him "ideal for the job in ways that Allen was most troublesome".[10]

Hedrick Smith reported in the *New York Times* that Clark was a mediator who could "smooth over differences, speed the process and bring people together", a "tall, slender, boyish-looking Californian"

---

[9] Ed Magnuson and Laurence I. Barnett, "Nation", *Time*, January 18, 1982.
[10] "Allen Exit", *Time*, January 11, 1982.

who possessed "a winning modesty and a willingness to listen that is unusual for a high government official".[11]

Clark acknowledged that he lacked the "intellectual credentials" of predecessors such as McGeorge Bundy, Walt Rostow, and Henry Kissinger, noted *Newsweek*, but, argued the weekly, "he has demonstrated a solid, pragmatic approach that may yet serve Reagan well."[12] Even James "Scotty" Reston, a fierce critic of the administration who considered Reagan a buffoon, was complimentary, saying "Mr. Clark is a sensible, intelligent and likeable man who enjoys both Mr. Reagan's confidence and the gift of compromising the differences within the President's staff and Cabinet."[13]

Equally surprising, Mary McGrory, the liberals' liberal, mustered praise for Clark: "He looks like a Norman Rockwell version of a judge. All, with the possible exception of Rose Elizabeth Bird, who served with him on the California Supreme Court, attest to his niceness.... His gifts as a conciliator are widely praised." McGrory judged that Clark had in the last year "received an extraordinary press, based primarily on his feat of having housebroken the wayward secretary of state", who, "under Clark's tutelage, has learned to behave like a team player". She noted that Clark and Reagan were soul mates: "Ideologically, they are twins.... Like Reagan, he regards conflict in terms of good versus evil."[14]

National Review joined in the praise for Clark, calling him a "gifted administrator, a man of captivating friendliness who can disagree without rancor", but the magazine also underscored a crucial point missed by the liberal press: "If some of Richard Allen's enemies, particularly in the media, had it in for him because he is a hard-liner on the Soviet Union, they will derive small comfort from Clark's appointment."[15]

The Russians were discomfited by Clark's new position and with his additional authority. Clark's earlier top appointment to the State Department had "amazed" people, noted TASS, as Clark "had

---

[11] Hedrick Smith, "Allen Quits Security Post; Reagan Hails His 'Integrity'; Haig's Deputy Is Successor", *New York Times*, January 5, 1982.

[12] "Can Bill Clark Do the Job?", *Newsweek*, January 18, 1982.

[13] James Reston, "From Allen to Clark to What?", *New York Times*, January 6, 1982.

[14] Mary McGrory, "What Clark Is Not: A Careerist, an Academic, and Ideologue; NICE", *Washington Post*, January 12, 1982.

[15] Editorial, "Allen to Clark", *National Review*, January 22, 1982.

admitted himself that his foreign policy experience was equal to zero". Now, said TASS, the incompetent Clark had been appointed to an even higher post! The Soviets backed up their assessment by quoting the French, who, according to TASS, had concluded Clark served as indisputable proof that the appointment of officials to top posts in the Reagan administration was based not on qualifications but on a unique combination of "primitive anti-communism" and "total ignorance". The French newspaper *Le Monde* had it right, continued TASS, when noting that this "rise of an ignoramus" had happened not by merit but merely because he was the president's personal friend.[16]

The New National Security Advisor

Bill Clark quickly learned that his new job ran seven days a week at all hours; he was constantly on call to receive information, which he promptly relayed to the President, often awakening Reagan in the middle of the night.

Each evening it was lights out for Clark at 9:00 P.M., a habit he had started as a child. He was up and ready to go by 3:00 or 4:00 A.M. In those early hours of the morning, L. Paul Bremer III (later appointed by President George W. Bush to direct reconstruction projects in Iraq after the 2003 invasion) sifted through the 4,500 in-bound communications per day to screen out the most important material for Clark, who, in turn, selected top priority items to discuss in meetings with his staff and later with the President in his daily briefing at 9:30.

Once at the office, at 7:00 A.M. Clark met with NSC staffers Bud McFarlane, John Poindexter, and Tom Reed. When Clark walked into the Oval Office at 9:30 A.M. to report to the President, one of the three men usually accompanied him at his invitation. These three, said a profile in *U.S. News & World Report*, had become "names to be reckoned with", so much so that along with Clark they were referred to as a "Mini-State Department" in the basement of the White House.[17]

---

[16] TASS statement in English released on January 6, 1982, published by FBIS as "Reaction to Clark Security Appointment Noted", January 18, 1982, p. A5.

[17] "A Mini-State Department at the White House", *U.S. News & World Report*, July 26, 1982.

In those morning briefings of the President, Vice President Bush was usually present, if available, as were Meese and Baker, with Deaver occasionally dropping in. After that, the day was just beginning, and usually did not end until Clark arrived home at about 8:00 P.M., with little left of the day to spend with Joan. Kissinger had been right about the demands of the job.

Clark was given free rein to shape the NSC staff. One of his first moves was to appoint three conservatives as outside consultants: his old friend Tom Reed, who in the 1970s had left Governor Reagan's office to become Secretary of the Air Force; William F. Buckley Jr., noted author and founder of *National Review* magazine; and his long-time friend Clare Boothe Luce.

After ten somewhat reclusive years following the death of her husband, Clare accepted Clark's request to serve as an unpaid advisor to the National Security Council, but Reagan had more in mind for her. In 1981 he appointed Luce to the President's Foreign Intelligence Advisory Board. She moved from her home in Honolulu to an apartment in the Watergate complex near Bill and Joan. Clark says that Reagan "loved Clare". Indeed, he would later award her the Presidential Medal of Freedom.

There were other new hires by Clark: For his deputy, he chose Robert C. "Bud" McFarlane, a counselor at the State Department and one of Haig's closest advisors. He named two State Department aides as NSC assistants: Jeremiah O'Leary, a former White House correspondent for the *Washington Star*, and Dick Morris, the clerk who had signed up with the Judge upon his appointment to the California Supreme Court in 1973.[18] Another key person Clark included was John Poindexter, a navy admiral who preferred life at sea to politics.

Clark hired a number of bright and promising twenty- to thirty-year olds, some of whom had worked with him on the courts: Sven Kraemer, Roger Robinson, Paula Dobriansky, Ken deGraffenreid, John Lenczowski, Regina Borchard and Henry Nau.[19] From the National Security Council, many went on to higher posts of trust and confidence.

---

[18] Steven R. Weisman, "A Haig Confidant Gets Post at White House", *New York Times*, January 21, 1982.

[19] Clark described Lenczowski as a "brilliant man, good man. State and the liberals on our staff disliked him intensely. I liked him very much."

Thirty-one-year-old Roger W. Robinson, Jr., joined the Reagan team in March 1982, three months into Clark's tenure. He became senior director of international economic affairs at the NSC, where he ran the bulk of U.S. international economic policy involving foreign policy and security dimensions. Says Robinson of the task facing Clark, Reagan, the NSC, and himself: "[The] goal was to stress out the Soviet economy, particularly its hard currency cash flow, and fully exploit its rigidities, to engage Moscow on every front—through our military build up, the war of ideas and the battleground of the Third World. It was a systematic assault on the Soviet Union in virtually every category of activity." [20] Clark was assembling for Reagan a team committed to winning the Cold War, particularly through the use of Robinson's financial strategy.

Clark also brought along his secretary, Jacque Hill, who describes Clark's collaborative approach with his staff. "He always said that all of us worked *with* him, not *for* him", she says. Hill enjoyed watching the surprise in the eyes of the new hires when from the first Clark "acknowledged their knowledge", treated all of them equally, asking for their expertise and input. She observes that Clark "got the most" out of those who worked for him. [21]

David Laux, a China expert at the CIA who had worked at the U.S. embassy in Beijing, was hired by Clark to help formulate policy regarding Asia. Laux was one of more than forty specialists on Clark's staff, and he was immediately impressed by the way Clark made use of his experts. "He was humble but asked penetrating questions", says Laux. "It was clear that he was a man of wisdom and experienced in judging men. I instinctively liked him."

Laux still laughs at one memory. When Clark summoned him to discuss a pressing concern on China, Laux noticed him squirming and grimacing. He asked the Judge what was wrong, and Clark explained that his back was bothering him, the result of a few old horse injuries. Laux did daily exercises to strengthen his back muscles, due to compression fractures to his spine from an early hang-gliding accident and his days as a marine and a boxer. Clark asked him to demonstrate, so Laux got down on the floor and demonstrated. Clark knew a few

---

[20] Interviews with Roger Robinson, June 6 and 8, 2005.
[21] Interview with Jacque Hill, May 9, 2005.

exercises himself: "Let me show you the ones I do", he offered. As both men did their stretches on the floor, secretary Jacque Hill escorted a delegation of distinguished but confused visitors into the room.[22]

Laux was influenced by Clark in a way he did not anticipate. A former altar boy who once considered the priesthood, Laux had drifted away from the Catholic Church and had become an agnostic. In 1984, he accepted an invitation to the National Prayer Breakfast, after which he joined a weekly White House prayer group. Eventually he began attending services and a weekly Bible study at the National Presbyterian Church. "Bill saw me go through this whole process and it made us closer friends", says Laux, adding that he sought out Clark's advice on spiritual matters. "I have a huge respect for this man, who has been a profound influence in my life." [23]

According to Laux, Clark's daily morning meetings with the NSC section chiefs, as well as his meetings with staff each Friday, resulted in a motivated and productive team. "It also resulted in a National Security Advisor and President being very well briefed on world developments", he says.

Each staff member was asked to bring to the weekly meeting a one-page summary of events in his respective area. Clark would read the summaries and pass them on to Reagan, who would study them over the weekend. Monday morning would find the reports, complete with presidential notations in the margins, back in the hands of the author.

Clark's collaborative approach "gave every staff member a tremendous sense of being relevant and being listened to and appreciated". Like Hill, Laux says, "You felt you were working *with* [Clark], not *for* him. As a result, the loyalty of the NSC staff to Clark, and by extension to Reagan, was 'remarkable'." He adds, "I have never seen such loyalty by a staff to their leader as existed on Bill Clark's NSC." [24]

Even more extraordinary than Clark's teamwork was his practice of taking his experts to his meetings with the President, to "give the President a few words" on the issue at hand. It is known that other

---

[22] Interview with David Laux, May 16, 2005.

[23] Ibid.

[24] Ibid.

national security advisors preferred to brief the President on their own.[25]

Clark could make visible use of his staff without feeling any threat to his own position, explains John Poindexter, because he was confident of Reagan's friendship and trust. Clark was "personally secure enough to know where he wasn't an expert and where to rely on assistants to fill in his gaps in knowledge".[26]

Clark's practice of asking NSC specialists to join him in briefing the President was deeply appreciated by all of them, including Richard Pipes. The Harvard Sovietologist had been brought to the NSC in 1981 by Dick Allen as part of a two-year leave from his academic post. Pipes felt that his work, under the previous national security advisor, had been carried in to the President without acknowledgment that Pipes had prepared it. That was not at all the case with Clark, whose motto was captured in a plaque sitting on Reagan's office desk since Sacramento days: Never take credit for something that you can pass on to someone else.

Within two months of Clark's arrival, Pipes was asked to brief the President and from then on did so fairly frequently. Also, Clark put the names of Pipes and other specialists on the memos he prepared for the President. "As long as Allen was security advisor," Pipes says, "I was not permitted in Reagan's presence."

Pipes adds that he was very fond of Clark. "He was not especially knowledgeable on the subject of foreign policy, but I found that, like Reagan, he had very good judgment. And what was very important was that he was very close to Reagan."[27] Also, Clark "was not a politician; he told the truth as he saw it."[28]

As he had with the mini-memos in Sacramento, Clark was careful to provide the President with all sides of an argument, usually in one- to three-page memos. "Bill was always fair and tried his best to be an 'honest broker' in presenting the Defense, State, and Intelligence views and recommendations to the President", recalls Poindexter. Clark's "only objective", he says, was to ensure that

[25] Ibid.

[26] Interview with John Poindexter, October 25, 2005.

[27] Interview with Richard Pipes, September 27, 2005.

[28] Interview with Richard Pipes, November 2, 2005.

Reagan's policies were "given a chance, not corrupted, and always implemented".[29]

The Western White House

An important task of Clark's security team was preparing a program of readiness, including a plan for continuity of government outside of Washington, in the event of nuclear attack. They created a "crisis management center" at the NSC, a group on hand to react instantly to a foreign crisis.

Not until after Reagan died, did Clark talk about the security problems he had to grapple with each time the President stayed at his Rancho del Cielo in the Santa Ynez Mountains. Reagan's visits to Rancho del Cielo were so frequent that the location became known as the Western White House;[30] during his presidency he spent a total of one year's worth of time there. Unbeknownst to the nearby Santa Barbara residents enjoying the beautiful climate and beaches, each time Reagan visited the ranch, Soviet nuclear subs were poised at sea ready to strike the mountainside if so commanded.

"That was part of the Cold War game", says Clark, shrugging off the weight of the threat he felt at the time.[31] He staffed a "situation room"—some called it the War Room—in the Biltmore Hotel in the nearby town of Montecito; this became the nerve center, the primary means of communication between the White House and the Reagan Ranch. "Remember," explains Clark, "this was the height of the Cold War, the Brezhnev period, and direct and immediate communication with Washington and beyond was critical."

Communication among the President and his people was of utmost importance given the issues confronting the administration. For example, it has been stated over the years that some within the Reagan administration, Al Haig in particular, considered it in the West's best interest to blockade Cuba. On this point, Clark provides some clarification: He confirms that Haig did request that the U.S. Navy at least

---

[29] Interview with John Poindexter, October 25, 2005.

[30] For the record, Reagan, according to Clark, did not like the term "Western White House", but said, "There is only one White House."

[31] See Chuck Schultz, "Former aide recounts close calls handled by 'Western White House'", *Santa Barbara County News*, February 7, 2005.

consider the feasibility of encircling Cuba with ships—a full blockade. Jim Baker, on the other hand, thought that a blockade could lead to open conflict and was strongly opposed to it.[32]

Clark adds another significant piece of information on Cuba: Ambassador Vernon Walters visited Castro a number of times while Clark was at the NSC. These were secret one-on-one talks and were ordered by the secretary of state. On one such occasion, Haig dispatched Walters to Havana without informing the President.[33] Clark learned about the trip when Walters was already on his way. He reached Walters at the Miami airport and called him back. Upon Walters' return, the ambassador met in the Oval Office with the President. "We discussed the trip and its importance", says Clark. "Ronald Reagan approved its scope, but made clear that he should always be informed of these matters in advance."

The Haig-Walters incident was symptomatic of Clark's view of his role on behalf of the President—"to remind all who was boss". For instance, he occasionally spoke up at Baker staff meetings and asked the question some senior staff did not want to hear: "Has anyone bothered to ask the President about this?" This caused an annoyed silence from some, but Clark felt it necessary to let the President be the president—and commander-in-chief.

Meese, Baker, and Deaver

Many of the NSC staff shared Reagan's political philosophy and appreciated Clark's respect for Ronald Reagan. Jim Baker and Mike Deaver, on the other hand, treated the President "rather like a grandfather whom one humors but does not take very seriously", observed Pipes.[34]

Clark's appointment to the NSC had been backed by the two of them, Baker and Deaver, who attempted to use this support to request help in a move against Ed Meese. Deaver and Baker preferred that Meese move to a position outside the White House. They suggested to Clark that the old Kissinger northwest corner, now Meese's office,

---

[32] Clark did not record the date of the incident, but believes it happened between January and June 1982.

[33] Here again, Clark, who did not take notes, recalls the incident as occurring between January and June 1982.

[34] Pipes, *Vixi*, p. 176.

should rightfully be his as national security advisor. Clark disagreed; Baker and Deaver countered with suggesting that the issue be laid before the President. Clark had no objection to meeting with the President, but made it clear that he had no desire to move into the "coveted" corner office and would state as much. No meeting was ever scheduled. Clark's falling out with Deaver and Baker thus began on that first day. It was a foreshadowing of what was to come.

A Top Priority: Unauthorized Disclosures

From the beginning, the Reagan administration had suffered from frequent unauthorized release of sensitive national security information to the press by anonymous sources inside the White House. The purpose of the leaks was to control the President. By feeding information to the public via the media, men inside the White House could bring external pressure upon Reagan to abandon or stay clear of policies they did not support.

On January 12, 1982, Reagan publicly stated that leaks of national security material had become "a problem of major proportions within the U.S. government". He ordered immediate enforcement of existing law on communication between government officials and the media. He sharply warned that "all legal methods" would be used to investigate anyone releasing classified information and that steps would be taken to stop such conduct in the future. The White House then issued a statement declaring the actions necessary to stem a "virtual hemorrhage of leaks in the national security area which the president believes have hampered formulation of foreign and defense policy".[35]

On that day, in response to recommendations made by his new national security advisor, Reagan signed directives requiring that "all contacts with any elements of the news media" relating to security or intelligence matters must have the advance approval of a certain "senior official".[36] Bill Clark was that senior official. Reagan had placed Clark at State because he needed an "America desk" at Foggy Bottom. Now, he needed one in the White House as well.

---

[35] Michael Getler, "Reagan Orders Crackdown on Leaks", *Washington Post*, January 13, 1982, p. A1.
[36] Ibid.

The press was outraged. A front-page *Washington Post* article claimed that the rights of the press were being violated, that restrictions on information were not needed, and that the President failed to provide examples of damaging leaks.[37]

There were plenty of examples. As recently as the previous month, Reagan's decision to sell fighter aircraft to Taiwan was leaked; the Chinese, who adamantly opposed the sale of any military equipment to Taiwan, were furious when they learned about the decision in the newspapers. In addition, the *Washington Post* had recently reported (from leaked information) that Soviet MiG-23 fighters had been clandestinely delivered to Cuba in packed crates. After the article was published, according to Reagan officials, the crates disappeared; they were camouflaged or smuggled out of Cuba.[38]

Most troubling, someone disclosed information about secret U.S. military operations in Lebanon, specifically, covert details regarding a trip to Lebanon by Bud McFarlane, Clark's deputy at the NSC. Clark and others were convinced that this leak endangered McFarlane's life.

The new security measures were not intended to punish the media, Clark explained. "The press has been doing its job—collecting information—better than the government has been doing its job—protecting national security information."[39] No one in the Reagan White House blamed the press for the leak problem, he said. The fault lay with the informers inside the administration, whose motives Clark struggled to understand.

It was fitting that on February 2, the day the White House released Clark's official memorandum to Reagan on the "Protection of Classified National Security Council and Intelligence Information", an *unidentified* White House official told the *New York Times* that David Gergen, the assistant to the president for communications, had "expressed misgivings" over the policy. This was not a surprise; Gergen was widely

---

[37] Ibid.

[38] Steven R. Weisman, "Reagan Issues New Rules on Classified Documents", *New York Times*, February 3, 1982, p. A19.

[39] Michael Getler, "Reagan Orders Crackdown on Leaks", *Washington Post*, January 13, 1982, p. A1.

suspected of being one of the biggest leakers in all Washington, along with Jim Baker.[40]

Baker was enraged when he learned of the new policy, according to a piece by Francis X. Clines in the *New York Times*. "I'll be goddamned!" shouted Baker from the back of his limo when he "suddenly discovered that his then rival in the Reagan inner sanctum, William Clark", had obtained the President's signature on an order that could involve lie detector tests and possible criminal charges against those unlawfully disclosing classified information. He immediately ordered his driver to turn around; he was headed for a "showdown" in the Oval Office.[41]

Why did Baker get so upset? John Lofton offered an answer in the *Washington Times*, citing a May 1982 article in the *Texas Monthly*: "Above all, he [Baker] leaks things to the press. Many regular correspondents are agreed that Mr. Baker is the most adroit leaker in the White House."[42]

So, then, asked Lofton, rhetorically, why was Baker fuming when he learned that leaks would be investigated by, as Reagan put it, "all legal methods"? Because, said, Lofton: "Jim Baker, who is also a lawyer, knew an administrative Bill of Attainder when he saw one coming down the pike."

The press became obsessed with the issue. Over the next several weeks, the *Washington Post* alone ran at least ten stories on Clark and the new policy. Could this be Watergate all over again? Were the Nixon "plumbers" just around the corner? That question was in fact posed to Reagan in a press conference. In response, the President did the right thing: he openly laughed. In one press conference, he was asked four times if he and Clark planned to use lie detectors on suspected leakers.[43]

Though Reagan avoided discussing the issue of lie detectors, Clark says that the unauthorized disclosure of classified information had gotten so bad—and was at times a crime—that Reagan did consider employing a polygraph. On more than one occasion, staff saw Reagan hit his desk in frustration and demand: "This [the leaking] has got to stop!"

---

[40] "Draft of Order on Press Disclosures is Studied by the White House", *New York Times*, February 2, 1982, p. D23.

[41] Francis X. Clines, "James Baker: Calling Reagan's Re-Election Moves", *New York Times*, May 20, 1984.

[42] John Lofton, "Mum's Not Word with Jim Baker", *Washington Times*, June 1, 1984, p. A4.

[43] Reagan, "The President's News Conference", January 19, 1982.

It did not stop. A lengthy criminal investigation to identify the source of the Lebanon-McFarlane leak came up empty-handed. Amazingly, the *New York Times* story on the investigation was itself the product of unnamed sources. "By several accounts," reported Steven Weisman, "the investigation has raised tensions and suspicions at the White House and created enormous controversy over its advisability. Several administration officials, asking not to be identified, deplored it." It looked as though the leakers might be leaking information on the investigation of leaking information.

The only official who agreed to be quoted by name in the *Times* story, said Weisman, was Ed Meese. Weisman added that "another official" said that Bill Clark had suspected that Jim Baker, "or someone associated with him", had given out the information. "Still another official", wrote Weisman, said that Clark had "overreacted" and created needless internal suspicions.[44]

Clark had merely done what his President asked, and what he and Reagan felt that national security and the law demanded. This did not gain him the graces of Gergen and Baker.

Clark viewed unauthorized disclosures as a sign of poor character and judgment. Says John Poindexter: "I don't know of a single time that Bill leaked anything to the media, and I doubt he ever did."[45] It angered Clark that members of the White House staff would employ this backhanded maneuver to undermine decisions with which they disagreed. They did not have the courage to disagree with the President in the open, for fear of losing their positions, and they could not concede a loss when their points of view had not won the day with Ronald Reagan. Their solution was to go behind the President's back to promote their own agendas over that of presidential policy.

Rave Reviews

In spite of the negative press generated by Clark's classified information policy, within a couple of months the national security advisor was receiving favorable coverage. A March 1982 piece in *Newsweek*

---

[44] Steven R. Weisman, "2-Month Old Inquiry by F.B.I. Fails to Find Source of Disclosure", *New York Times*, November 24, 1983, p. B13.

[45] Interview with John Poindexter, October 25, 2005.

titled "Clark Cracks NSC Whip", stated that after "a year in disarray" under Dick Allen, the NSC was "quietly being restored to the lofty status" it had enjoyed under Kissinger and Brzezinski. Since his appointment, said *Newsweek*, Clark had "virtually disappeared from public view", but was "very visible where it counts—inside the White House, where his early efforts are getting the highest marks". The magazine quoted one senior Reagan aide: "'Wonderful!' is the word I would use to characterize having him in the White House. He's doing what badly needs to be done: bringing foreign policy into the White House where you don't have Haig and Weinberger making it on the road and then telling us what the decisions are." [46]

Newsweek claimed that Clark had "reprimanded his old boss", Al Haig, as well as Secretary of Defense Weinberger, for their public spats and "informed them" that policy decisions were the President's prerogative and that "the path to the Oval Office is through him." Clark was a national security advisor who could "speak for the President, bang heads and pull chains", exulted a White House aide.[47]

Despite some grumbling, said *Newsweek*, Haig and Weinberger appeared to be reconciled to the new system, "an acceptance helped along by the eight to ten daily conversations with each of them that Clark manages to fit into his fifteen-hour day". Added *Newsweek*: "The most significant blessing has come from the President himself, who reportedly commented favorably on all the NSC-originated changes, then inquired quizzically of an aide, 'Why hasn't this been done before?'" [48]

Other articles were similarly laudatory. An April piece in *U.S. News and World Report*, entitled, "New Force in Reagan's Foreign Policy", said nearly the same: "The President's security advisor is concentrating power in the White House and cracking the whip over Weinberger and Haig. Reagan has been drawn by Clark into a greatly expanded role in managing foreign policy, an area that the President tended to shun during his first year in office." Moreover, all major public statements issued by State, the Pentagon, or the CIA now had to be cleared in advance by the White House. Presidential decisions

---

[46] Mark Starr, "Clark Cracks NSC Whip", *Newsweek*, March 13, 1982.
[47] Ibid.
[48] Ibid.

that in the past were conveyed verbally had to be formalized into signed orders to ensure quick implementation without delay or confusion.[49]

Clark's achievements were all the more remarkable, said the *Washington Post*, because he was "the most inexperienced person in foreign policy and security matters to hold the key job at the president's elbow in two decades". The "paradox" about "The Judge", said an official, is that "now we have an advisor who is fair, has great common sense, has a close relationship with the president, and is a perfect adjudicator." [50]

Clark's influence with Reagan was such that even individuals who had Reagan's respect and ear often leaned on Clark to ensure a certain message got to the President. This was evident in a handwritten August 6, 1982, memo from the desk of the director of the CIA. "Bill—This is the subject I wanted to get to the boss on", wrote Bill Casey. "Will you see that he gets this on his way to California when he'll have a chance to ponder without the distractions of the White House[?] I'll be in touch. Bill Casey." The letter to Reagan that Casey attached laid out four top political concerns: the Middle East, the economy, crime, and the ever-expanding federal government. The former 1980 campaign chief believed these matters were seriously weakening "our ability to complete what we came here to do".[51] Even someone as close to Reagan as Bill Casey went through Bill Clark to get the President's attention.[52]

Clark and the Ex-Presidents

Another Clark practice that further reflected Reagan's trust was his monthly briefings with the surviving ex-Presidents—Richard Nixon, Gerald Ford, and Jimmy Carter. There had been some previous

---

[49] Robert A. Kittle, "New Force in Reagan's Foreign Policy", *U.S. News and World Report*, April 12, 1982.

[50] Michael Getler, "Clark Curbs Administration Turf Struggles", *Washington Post*, May 17, 1982.

[51] The memo lay in a box in Clark's house for over twenty years, marked only with an annotation in the upper right corner that reads "save".

[52] This was in part due to Casey's personality. He simply felt more comfortable going through Clark. "Bill, I've got something for the President", he would call Clark to say. Clark recalls: "He'd always want me to present whatever he had, whether with or without him. He seemed to have this reluctance to meet with the President personally. Bill was kind of a loner. He flew alone."

communication between the White House and the ex-Presidents, but it had been infrequent and sporadic. The regular briefings were Clark's idea, and Reagan embraced the program right away. For their part, the ex-Presidents knew, as did many in the current administration, that Clark had Reagan's respect and ear, and that their concerns and suggestions would make it to the President.

Clark usually briefed the ex-Presidents in person, jetting to their homes. It was clear to Clark that they deeply appreciated these meetings. Each of the three men had left his presidency in defeat, yet all had healthy minds and a feeling that they still had something to contribute, particularly Nixon and Carter.

Nixon's passion was foreign policy, and by 1982 he was trying to reinvent himself as the nation's premier elder statesman on foreign affairs. His contact with Clark came as a great blessing at a needed time. These meetings were warm, even touching, says Clark. The scheduled hour with Nixon quickly became three hours, he adds. Back at the White House, Reagan was always interested in what his fellow Californian had to say.

Clark usually met with Nixon in New Jersey, "at his home in the woods", though sometimes they met in Palm Springs. Nixon was so eager to meet with Clark that he often walked right up to the Jet Star door to greet him. "He couldn't wait to get into the issues", says Clark of Nixon. "Couldn't wait."

Clark found the Nixon home quiet and lonely. Nixon had once told his aide Monica Crowley that most people picture famous individuals always surrounded by friends and associates. That was not the case, said Nixon, who was often alone, with only his wife, Pat, at his side.

Nixon met with Clark in his favorite room, just off the living room, where he had an open fire glowing. He always insisted that Clark sit in his "good luck" chair, offering him a Bourbon and water. They spoke to one another with ease, Clark says. When he opened his briefing book to get to business, Nixon lit up. "He'd pick up the issue I introduced and then run with it", Clark said, "and then dominate the discussion."

Nixon, naturally, was particularly keen on the East-West relationship, but also on the Middle East. Clark became the "briefee" rather than the briefer. Judge Clark was always a good listener, and that was what Nixon craved at this period in his life.

Clark says Nixon was the finest mind he ever encountered in foreign policy, not an atypical assessment of the former President. "He was far more insightful, probing, profound than the best I knew in foreign policy, including Henry Kissinger", says Clark. "He would sometimes direct: 'Now, you tell Ron he has to fire that person!'"

Clark's meetings with President Ford were not as interesting or memorable, as Ford was more interested in the economy and domestic issues than foreign affairs.

Unlike his meeting with the two Republicans, Clark's first engagement with Carter was not so chummy. In 1980, the Georgia Democrat had lost reelection to Reagan in a landslide, watching Clark's friend take 44 of 50 states. He was bitter over the loss, blaming the Reagan people and even the electorate, from whom he felt a strong rejection, as did his wife, Rosalynn.

When Clark knocked on the door for that initial get-together in Plains, Rosalynn met him at the door. She was reserved, barely extending her hand. Clark explains: "She was known to be bitter over the [1980] campaign as well, over the people in the Reagan campaign, whom she felt had treated her husband unfairly." As Carter and Clark sat down to talk, Clark noticed Rosalynn standing in the shadows of the adjoining kitchen, interested, as always, in whatever concerned her husband.

Carter was cool at first, but as the two men conversed they gradually struck a rapport, as Clark did with nearly everyone he met. Bill Clark was likable, period. Ronald Reagan was well aware of his top hand's likable personality—surely a factor in his accepting Clark's proposal to initiate these sensitive encounters.

By the second or third briefing, Clark and Carter had become "close friends". Like Nixon, Carter was attuned to foreign affairs, particularly the Arab-Israeli peace process. He and Clark discussed the progress made between Israel and Egypt after the Camp David Accords that Carter had brokered—his greatest achievement. "He was enormously proud of that accomplishment," says Clark, "and justifiably so." Carter's response to the meetings—it was "gratifying" to have Clark keep him abreast of the security issues facing the administration.[53]

---

[53] William E. Farrell and Warren Weaver Jr., "Birds of a Feather", *New York Times*, February 23, 1984.

Clark conceived of these private briefings with the ex-Presidents as a courtesy to them, but he also realized their insights could prove beneficial to American foreign policy. Clark's information gathering at these meetings was in keeping with his view of his role as national security advisor: Present the President with as much information and as many helpful viewpoints as possible.

Testing Reagan in Managua

When Clark first arrived at the NSC, he was on the alert for instances in which the Soviets would try to test Reagan. The historians on Clark's staff warned him about this possibility, since the Soviets were known for challenging new presidents. When Clark asked his staff where they suspected that test might occur, they were not sure, though they figured Berlin might provide the opportunity.

The test of Reagan in Berlin never transpired, but Clark and his crew considered that events underway in Managua, Nicaragua, might well provide the anticipated challenge; Reagan thought so as well.

In the spring of 1982, the Reagan team received reports that the Soviets were behind the construction of a large new airfield west of Managua. The size of the airfield and its runway suggested two things: First, it was being constructed for use by military planes, not for the purported boost in tourism. Secondly, the Nicaraguans did not have the financial resources to lay out a landing strip of that size. The runway was large enough to handle large military transports and bombers, as well as revetments for fighter aircraft. "This was for Soviet MiGs", says Clark, "and certainly not for Pan-Am airlines."

The runway might be the test, and Reagan knew it. Clark remembers that the President grew angry then serious in the Oval Office the morning he received the information during Clark's regular briefing. He turned to Secretary of State Haig and told him: "You tell [Ambassador Anatoly] Dobrynin that if they [the Soviets] move MiGs into that new lengthened airfield in Managua, we'll take them [the MiGs] out within twenty-four hours." Haig delivered the message. "We wanted them to know that we meant business", said Clark. Ultimately, the Soviets backed down from building the airfield—and from testing Reagan in Managua.

Reagan and Clark were ridiculed by the left as paranoid for their fear of communism spreading throughout Central and Latin America. To cite just one of numerous examples of how Reagan and Clark were later vindicated in their concern over Nicaragua, Sandinista leader Moises Hassan gave an important interview to the *Miami Herald* in July 1999, in which he confirmed the Sandinistas' expansionary aims.[54] "The Sandinista leadership thought they could be the Che Guevaras of all Latin America, from Mexico to Antarctica", said Hassan. "The domino theory wasn't so crazy."

He confirmed that the Sandinistas had a commitment for MiGs from the Soviet Union. He learned of the MiG plan in 1982, when he was minister of construction and the Sandinistas began building a base for the jet fighters at Punta Huete, a remote site near Lake Managua. The Sandinista leader reported that the site included a ten-thousand-foot concrete runway, the longest in all of Central America. This runway was capable of handling any military aircraft in the Soviet fleet. "It was top secret", revealed Hassan nearly twenty years later. "We even had a code name, Panchito, so we could talk about it without the CIA hearing. But somehow the Americans found out."

Another key figure, Alejandro Bendana, secretary general of foreign affairs in the Sandinista government, added that Nicaraguan pilots were sent to Bulgaria, where they were trained to fly the MiGs. However, the Soviets eventually backed out, said Bendana, even after the site was finished.

Ronald Reagan's bold threat to the Russians clearly had an impact. Yet, there were many daring actions to come. Reagan now had his top hand at the NSC, and the Judge and his team were ready to join the President in an all-out assault on Soviet communism.

---

[54] Glenn Garvin, "We Shipped Weapons, Sandinistas Say", *Miami Herald*, July 18, 1999.

CHAPTER 9

Laying the Foundation for Cold War Victory

With American national security interests scattered throughout the world, there were many urgent issues calling for the national security advisor's attention, but the most important of Clark's activities were those he undertook to win the Cold War with the Soviet Union, a goal of Reagan's since his earliest days in Sacramento. Clark notes, "Fast forwarding from the Sacramento 1960s to the Washington 1980s, it was up to us as his cabinet and staff to convert the President's early vision into underlying policy, policy into strategy, strategy into tactics, and on to implementation and ultimate success." [1] As the manager of Reagan's foreign and national security policy, Bill Clark played the leading role in prosecuting the Cold War. He "did more than any other individual to help the President change the course of history and put an end to an empire that was, indeed, the embodiment of evil", [2] said NSC staffer Norman Bailey.

The Partners

Along with Ronald Reagan, Clark, like his father and grandfather before him, went after the bad guys. He and Reagan were perceived by many

---

[1] William P. Clark, "President Reagan and the Wall", Address to the Council of National Policy, San Francisco, California, March 2000, pp. 3–5.

[2] Norman A. Bailey, *The Strategic Plan That Won the Cold War: National Security Decision Directive 75* (McLean, VA: The Potomac Foundation, 1999), p. i.

as lawmen in hot pursuit of political bandits, winning by wits rather than firearms. Clark brought into the White House his grandfather's U.S. marshal badge and Colt .45, which were encased in a glass box and hung near a 1967 photo of Reagan, his father, and himself on horseback. He continued to wear his Truman/LBJ-style stockman's hat, western boots, and signature suits, always dark, always three-piece.

In the high-stakes area of national security, Clark's unique relationship with Ronald Reagan proved invaluable. Roger Robinson spoke of a near telepathy between the two men, an unspoken almost subliminal understanding, a seamlessness in their thinking existing since the gubernatorial days. The communication between them, spoken and unspoken, offered a tremendous working advantage to Clark, as Reagan handed him the steering wheel of his foreign policy. The confidence and trust that the President placed in his national security advisor was the intangible secret weapon in the new American offensive against the Soviets.

Many in the White House saw firsthand the special relationship between Clark and Reagan. David Laux noticed right away that Clark's impact on Reagan "was huge", and that he was "almost certainly President Reagan's most trusted adviser." [3] Tom Reed agreed that Clark was "utterly essential" to Reagan, especially to his Cold War strategy. "Clark was absolutely key to that." [4] The longest serving member of the Reagan cabinet, Secretary of Defense Cap Weinberger, said Clark was Reagan's closest friend in the White House. "Ronald Reagan knew him better than anyone who worked for him going back to the governor years, based on the trust, loyalty, and relationship they had built."

Reagan knew he could count on Clark's dedication to him and to their shared vision of America's place in the world. Clark was an "honest broker" among the various administration agencies and departments advancing differing recommendations, says Ed Meese. He "viewed himself as an extension of the President", rather than as the world's smartest man. "He saw to it that the President's objectives were met and directives were carried out." [5]

[3] Interview with David Laux, May 16, 2005.
[4] Interview with Tom Reed, April 6, 2005.
[5] Interview with Ed Meese, June 7, 2005.

Taking the Gloves Off

The President spent his first year in office trying to get the "domestic house in order", says Clark, the economy being his chief priority. At the end of 1981, Reagan kicked the foundation and felt that the bricks were now solidly in place. According to Clark, Reagan then called his foreign-policy staff into the Oval Office and said, "Gentlemen, our concentration has been on domestic matters this year, and I want to roll the sleeves up now and get to foreign policy, defense, and intelligence." [6]

Clark says the sleeves were up the first week of January 1982—the week he was appointed national security advisor. It was then, says Clark, "at the President's direction", that the administration began "the study of the overall Soviet situation and what our existing relations were and what they should be". These study directives developed into "decision directives".

According to Clark, Reagan's "strategy to accelerate the demise of the Soviet Union" consisted of five pillars: "economic, political, military, ideological, and moral". Among these, Clark says the "less well understood" part of the strategy was the "economic dimension" [7]— for which Clark was point man. Steven Weisman of the *New York Times* called Clark the administration's "biggest proponent of putting economic pressure on the Soviet Union". [8]

When Clark was asked directly if the administration had initiated economic warfare against the Soviets, he did what Ronald Reagan did when confronted with the question: He avoided or flat-out denied it, knowing that in the interests of national security, he could not be forthcoming.[9] He would not publicly admit the White House had declared war—even economic war—against the Soviet Union until years later, when he could afford to be candid. In March 2000 he spoke openly about the economic war, citing a personal encounter he had in 1982 with the Soviet ambassador at a diplomatic function.

---

[6] Clark in Peter Schweizer, ed., *Fall of the Berlin Wall* (Stanford, CA: Hoover Institution Press, 2000), p. 69.

[7] Bailey, *The Strategic Plan That Won the Cold War*, p. ii.

[8] Weisman, "The Influence of William Clark", p. 17.

[9] "Reagan's Foreign Policy—His No. 1 Aide Speaks Out", *U.S. News & World Report*, May 9, 1983.

"[Anatoly] Dobrynin whispered to me, 'You have declared war on us, economic war.' Yes, we had." [10]

Clark and Reagan had intended to "roll back" the Soviet Union through a strategy aimed at "changing the Soviet system from within", he explains. They aimed at further destabilizing the already weak Russian economy by tightening export controls, restricting high technology transfers, and accelerating arms competition. All of this would expose the Soviet system "for what it was", [11] an economic failure.

Ed Meese noted that in order to devise and implement such a multi-layered economic approach, Reagan depended upon Clark's "strategic mind", which brought a sense of "discipline" to the White House national-security process and to the formulation of foreign policy. [12] He developed a "systematic process", says Meese, for the way in which the Reagan White House would deal with the communists.

Helene von Damm, who was hired by Clark in the Sacramento days and became Reagan's secretary in Washington, was impressed with Clark's administration of the NSC. "Bill was always even tempered and even keeled", she says. "He always got the job done—extremely hardworking, very straightforward. If there was a challenge, he would go right after it." He was "tough" but "never mean", and "also shrewd. . . . He could plan things very well." [13]

The Directives That Won the Cold War

Under Clark's direction, the most consequential National Security Decision Directives (NSDDs) of the Reagan administration were completed, a direct result of Clark's commitment to launching a series of studies laying out the direction of America's national-security policy. These official policy documents enunciated the formal strategy and plan of operation to undermine Soviet communism. NSDDs 2 through 120—which the Clark team wrote—"created the national security policy" of the Reagan administration. [14]

---

[10] Clark, "President Reagan and the Wall".
[11] Ibid.
[12] Ed Meese, interview.
[13] Helene von Damm, interview.
[14] Clark in Schweizer, ed., *Fall of the Berlin Wall*, p. 69.

One of the more important directives, NSDD-32, was written by Tom Reed and signed by Reagan on May 20, 1982. Now referred to by Reed as "The Plan to Prevail",[15] the classified directive stated the following objective: "To contain and reverse the expansion of Soviet control and military presence throughout the world ... to contain and reverse the expansion of Soviet influence worldwide".

The thinking behind the directive was explained the following day in a speech at Georgetown's Center for Strategic and International Studies (CSIS). The speech was drafted by Tom Reed and revised and delivered by Bill Clark. "We must force our principal adversary, the Soviet Union, to bear the brunt of its economic shortcomings", Clark said.

The Georgetown speech unveiled the cornerstone of a "new strategy" by the United States, reported the *New York Times'* Richard Halloran. The strategy enunciated by Clark "made official a theme that several administration officials have hinted at, that of exploiting Soviet economic weaknesses".[16]

Initially, the *Washington Post* missed the point of Clark's address and focused instead on his statements about the MX missile and the defense budget. On June 15, however, the *Post's* Michael Getler reported on the economic strategy of the administration in an article entitled, "Economic Leverage on Moscow Sought".[17]

Other than the *Times* and the *Post*, there was little coverage of Clark's revealing speech, and the lack of media attention was noticed at the NSC. In a May 28 memo sent to Clark by staff member Bob Sims, entitled simply "Judge's Speech", Sims noted that "major columnists ... have not dealt with the Strategy speech."[18] It was clear to Sims and other members of the NSC staff that the media had missed the central point of the address.

The gravity of Clark's words at Georgetown was not lost upon the Soviets, who made use of their government-controlled press to shoot a few more arrows at the Reagan administration. An article by

---

[15] Thomas C. Reed, *At the Abyss* (New York: Ballantine Books, 2004), p. 235.

[16] Richard Halloran, "Reagan Aide Tells of New Strategy on Soviet Threat", *New York Times*, May 22, 1982, p. A1.

[17] Michael Getler, "Economic Leverage on Moscow Sought", *Washington Post*, June 15, 1982.

[18] The May 28, 1982 memo from Bob Sims to Clark is contained in Clark's files.

Aleksey Petrov in *Pravda* said that Clark's speech gave priority to the "cult of the fist", rather than to curtailing the arms race. His "bellicose appeals" represented the "worst specimen of anti-Soviet demagogy" and was "calumny of the lowest kind", a "manifestation of extreme adventurism and militarism." [19]

TASS agreed. "The decision to establish the world domination of U.S. imperialism through blackmail, aggression, armed piracy and threats unleashing a nuclear war is the essence and trend of the U.S. new military-political strategy," wrote TASS, "the elaboration of which was recently completed by the Ronald Reagan administration. The main provisions of that comprehensive militarist program were set out by William Clark ... in his yesterday's speech." [20]

As Richard Pipes noted in a memo to Clark, the "most interesting feature" of the TASS article was that it failed to acknowledge two key points in the address: "that it is our purpose to have the Soviet Union bear the consequences of its economic mismanagement and that we want to turn Soviet energies from expansion to internal reform". The omission of these points, with the Soviets instead exaggerating the military component of the new strategy, demonstrated "how extremely sensitive the Soviet leadership is to this argument"—that the communist economy cannot deliver basic goods and services. "It ought to be hammered home time and again until the message gets through to the Soviet people." [21]

On May 29, 1982, the Reagan administration released a five-year defense guidance report, which Pentagon officials called the "first complete defense guidance of this Administration". The next day the *New York Times* reported that the 125-page unpublished document would "form the basis" for the administration's budget requests for the next five years and was a "basic source" for NSDD-32, which, the *Times* observed, was now "the foundation" of the administration's overall approach to the

---

[19] This four-page analysis appears to have come from the American consul in Leningrad. Dated May 29, 1982, it is titled, "Petrov Article Questions U.S. Commitment on Arms Control", and is held in Clark's files.

[20] TASS analysis, titled, "Whence the Threat to Peace", May 22, 1982, published as "Clark Speech on 'New' U.S. Strategy Viewed", in *Foreign Broadcast Information Service*, FBIS, May 25, 1982, p. A1.

[21] May 27, 1982 NSC memo from Pipes to Clark, titled "Your Georgetown Speech", held in Clark's files.

Soviets.[22] "As a peacetime complement to military strategy, the guidance document asserts that the United States and its allies should, in effect, declare economic and technical war on the Soviet Union."[23]

The *Times* did some solid reporting in a September piece, entitled "After Détente, the Goal Is to Prevail", informing its readers that whereas Presidents Truman through Johnson sought to contain the Soviet Union, and Nixon, Ford, and Carter sought détente, President Reagan was determined to push "Russian influence back inside the borders of the Soviet Union", and "to loosen Russian controls over Eastern Europe". Tom Reed was quoted in the report: "We believe the free world can prevail." The article continued: "The theme of prevailing runs through the Pentagon's Defense Guidance, a five-year strategic plan, and through a strategic review ordered by the President's national security advisor, William P. Clark."[24]

More NSDDs

It was widely reported that Clark had "taken charge of the foreign policy machinery of the administration". According to White House communications director David Gergen, "Clark has more and more taken the reins of foreign policy."[25] Many inferred from such reports that Clark had usurped the President's role, but Clark never took control from the President; rather, he helped his President take the reins that were rightfully his by law as commander-in-chief. He wanted Reagan to do what he was elected to do, to fulfill the national defense duties given to him by the Constitution and the citizens of the United States. It just so happened that Reagan's foreign affairs agenda matched perfectly with that of Bill Clark.

That agenda called for many more policy directives, specifically 48, 54, 66, and 75, aimed at liberating Eastern and Central Europe from Soviet domination. Probably the most important of these directives was 75, written by Richard Pipes, assisted by Roger Robinson, and

---

[22] Richard Halloran, "Pentagon Draws Up First Strategy for Fighting a Long Nuclear War", *New York Times*, May 30, 1982, p. A1.

[23] Ibid.

[24] "After Détente, the Goal Is to Prevail", *New York Times*, September 23, 1982.

[25] Hedrick Smith, "Clark Emerges as a Maker of Policy", *New York Times*, May 31, 1982.

signed by Reagan on January 17, 1983. NSDD-75 underscored two key U.S. tasks: first, "To contain and over time reverse Soviet expansionism. . . . This will remain the primary focus of U.S. policy toward the USSR"; and second, "To promote, within the narrow limits available to us, the process of change in the Soviet Union toward a more pluralistic political and economic system in which the power of the privileged ruling elite is gradually reduced." The State Department actually fought to remove this language—historic words that set forth the goal of winning the Cold War.[26]

The Soviets clearly understood the intentions of the administration. "Directive 75 speaks of changing the Soviet Union's domestic policy", stated a Russian newspaper. In other words, "the powers that be in Washington are threatening the course of world history, neither more nor less."[27] It was due to Reagan's and Clark's insistence that Pipes' prophetic language remained in the text.[28]

Clark explains the necessity of promoting change from within the Soviet system. "It made little sense to resist Soviet aggression if our policies strengthened the regime internally", he says. Above all, "our plan was to avoid subsidizing the Soviet economy." He and Reagan wanted to undercut the Soviet system, not bolster it. Clark saw war with the Soviet Union as "inevitable unless we changed the Soviet system from within".[29]

The Reagan Team and the Vatican

Both Clark and Reagan believed that Poland was the key to breaking the Soviet grip on Eastern and Central Europe.[30] Poland was "the

---

[26] Pipes discussion with Paul Kengor, September 27, 2005, in Grove City, Pennsylvania.

[27] G. Dadyants, "Pipes Threatens History", *Sotsialisticheskaya Industriya*, March 26, 1983, p. 3, published as "New Directive on USSR Trade 'Threatens History'", in *Foreign Broadcast Information Service*, March 29, 1983, pp. A6–7.

[28] Interview with Richard Pipes, September 27, 2005.

[29] James P. Lucier, "Eight Years That Shook the World", *Insight*, March 22, 1999.

[30] This is seen in a number of sources. Among them, William P. Clark confirmed this fact with the author. We can also view Reagan's early understanding of the importance of the Pope to communism in Poland in a June 29, 1979 radio broadcast. Located in "Ronald Reagan: Pre-Presidential Papers: Selected Radio Broadcasts, 1975–1979", October 31, 1978 to October 1979, Box 4, RRL; and Skinner, Anderson, and Anderson, *Reagan, In His Own Hand*, p. 176. Also: Reagan, *An American Life*, pp. 301–3; and Reagan, "Address at Commencement Exercises at Eureka College", Eureka, Illinois, May 9, 1982.

hub of the Soviet empire—of the seven adjoining countries, second in priority only to Russia itself", Clark said, calling Poland "the geopolitical lynchpin of Soviet rule in Central Europe".[31] If a crack in the Iron Curtain could begin in Poland, perhaps the entire bloc could be split. But what could prompt this rupture? Was there any hope that Poland could begin the break-up of the Soviet bloc?

Hope materialized with two forces rising up in Poland simultaneously in the 1970s: Lech Walesa and his Solidarity movement and a cardinal from Krakow named Karol Wojtyła, who became the first non-Italian pope in 455 years and the first Slavic pope ever. Clark and Reagan both saw the timing of these events as nothing short of providential.

The first and most significant meeting between President Reagan and Pope John Paul II took place on June 7, 1982, six months into Clark's tenure at the NSC. The two shared many common experiences and beliefs. Both Reagan and John Paul II had been actors as young men, and both first became involved in global politics by confronting Nazis before Bolsheviks. With fascism defeated, they turned their attention to communism. Each man was also committed to protecting the sanctity of human life and viewed widespread abortion as one of the great tragedies of their time.

The Polish Pontiff perceived in Reagan a Protestant who was friendly to Catholicism. Reagan's father had been a Catholic. The President respected his father's faith and counted many Catholics among his intimates and staff.

Clark arrived in Rome ahead of Reagan to help lay the groundwork for the historic meeting. He consulted with a number of Vatican officials, and before the President arrived, Clark conferred with the Pontiff for a couple of hours, the first of several discussions they would have in the years ahead. The topics ranged from "politics to business, always returning to the spiritual—he wouldn't let you out of reach of the spiritual", says Clark.

Clark remembers the media crush as Reagan's arrival drew near. The White House press corps was there, and among the reporters was

---

[31] "The Pope and the President, A Key Adviser Reflects on the Reagan Administration", a profile/interview with Bill Clark, published in *Catholic World Report*, November 1999, pp. 54–55.

columnist Mary McGrory. She was stuck behind a rope, corralled with the rest of the reporters who were all bucking like broncos to burst free. McGrory saw Clark and asked for his help in finding a more advantageous spot. "Just tell them you're my wife, Mary", Clark deadpanned. McGrory took Clark's advice and was shown to a seat reserved for Joan. When the real Joan Clark arrived, "I had some explaining to do", Clark says. Mike Deaver was sent to remove McGrory from Mrs. Clark's seat.

When President Reagan arrived, he and Pope John Paul II sat facing one another in a room at the Vatican Library, where they talked for almost an hour. They discussed the assassination attempts against them the previous year, as well as their shared sense of purpose; both believed they had survived the attacks, which occurred six weeks apart, because God had saved them for a special mission—a special role in the divine plan of life—relating to communism's collapse in the Soviet bloc.[32]

Archbishop Pio Laghi, apostolic delegate to Washington, said that Reagan told the Pope: "Look how the evil forces were put in our way and how Providence intervened." Clark added that each man referred to his survival as "miraculous". In regard to the fate of the Soviet empire, says Clark, both believed that "right or correctness would ultimately prevail in the Divine Plan" and that "atheistic communism lived a lie that, when fully understood, must ultimately fail."[33]

Following the meeting, the two men agreed to aid Poland's Solidarity trade union, hoping it could be a wedge to splinter Eastern Europe. Clark said that this shared vision needed to be translated into an "underlying policy" and "strategy to defeat Soviet aggression and oppression".[34] That implementation was Clark's job.

Back in Washington, a close relationship developed between Clark, Casey, and Pio Laghi. Clark and Casey met many times with the papal nuncio to share intelligence and brief him on the administration's position on certain issues. "Casey and I dropped into his [Laghi's]

---

[32] Carl Bernstein, "The Holy Alliance", *Time*, February 24, 1992, pp. 28 and 30. Reagan expressed his shock on the assassination attempt—and offered his prayers—in a May 13, 1981 cable to the Pope. The cable is filed in ES, NSC, HSF: Records, Vatican: Pope John Paul II, RRL, Box 41, Folder "Cables 1 of 2".

[33] "The Pope and the President", pp. 54–55; and Bernstein, "The Holy Alliance", pp. 28–30.

[34] Ibid.

residence early mornings during critical times to gather his comments and counsel", says Clark. "We'd have breakfast and coffee and discuss what was being done in Poland."[35] The coffee was cappuccino, real Italian cappuccino. When either Clark or Casey thought it was time to touch base with Laghi and the Vatican, one would call the other and ask, "Would you like to have some cappuccino?"

The link to Laghi was known only by "a core group" that included Ed Meese. Clark and Casey "would brief Laghi on items the Reagan team thought the Pope should know and on matters of mutual interest", Meese said, "Laghi, in turn, would do the same from his end."[36] This correspondence was coordinated by a handful of officials, outside of State Department channels.[37] Even today, the existing records remain classified.[38]

The Clark–Casey tandem proved to be a formidable weapon against the Soviet Union. "I think that they together orchestrated a lot of what happened in Poland and the Soviet Union", says Owen Smith, Bill Casey's son-in-law.[39] There were at least six occasions when Laghi came to the White House to meet with Clark or Reagan or both regarding Poland. Each time, Laghi entered through the southwest gate to avoid the press.[40] Casey, Ambassador Walters, and U.S. Ambassador to Rome Bill Wilson provided briefings at the Vatican. Casey and Ambassador Walters went to the Vatican alternately, with Walters traveling more frequently than Casey, says Smith. "They made a lot more visits there than records indicate", he adds, "and very often met with the Holy Father privately."[41]

---

[35] See Bernstein, "The Holy Alliance".

[36] Ed Meese, himself a longtime Reagan confidant, says that Clark's "link" to the Vatican, particularly the Laghi connection, was guarded information known by certain people in the White House, though generally not known throughout the administration. Interview with Ed Meese, June 7, 2005.

[37] Clark's deputy, Bud McFarlane, said that these discussions were handled completely outside of normal State Department channels. McFarlane knew that Clark and Casey were meeting with Laghi, and that Laghi had seen the President, but says that he was personally unaware of the substance of the discussions. See: Bernstein, "The Holy Alliance," pp. 28–35.

[38] Examples of the secrecy are seen in fully redacted documents at the Reagan Library, located in ES, NSC, HSF: Records, Vatican: Pope John Paul II, RRL, Box 41, Folders "Cables 1 of 2" and "Cables 2 of 2".

[39] Interview with Owen Smith, December 30, 2005.

[40] See Bernstein, "The Holy Alliance".

[41] Interview with Owen Smith, December 30, 2005.

The substance of these meetings with the Pope, notes Clark, typically included Poland and Central America. Reagan had an insatiable appetite for information on Poland, Clark says. Often Reagan's first question at the daily briefing would be, "What's happening in Poland this morning?" Clark made certain the President always had an answer.

Clark and Laghi found that they shared other interests besides Poland, and the two men established both a professional and personal relationship. Joan occasionally reserved the President's box at the Kennedy Center for the papal nuncio. She sometimes accompanied Laghi to concerts, which the Vatican representative seemed to enjoy very much.

The Ash Heap of History

After the first meeting between the President and the Pope at the Vatican, Reagan and Clark flew to London, where on June 8 the President gave what is now considered one of his greatest speeches: the Westminster Address, which predicted "a great revolutionary crisis" in "the home of Marxism-Leninism, the Soviet Union".

Reagan described "a plan and a hope for the long term—the march of freedom and democracy which will leave Marxism-Leninism on the ash heap of history". Moreover, said the President, "the ultimate determinant in the struggle now going on for the world will not be bombs and rockets, but a test of wills and ideas—a trial of spiritual resolve". He called for "a crusade for freedom".

Many consider the Westminster address Reagan's finest speech. Though speechwriter Tony Dolan prepared the initial draft, Reagan edited and rewrote parts of the speech.[42] He, along with Clark, fought those from the White House and the State Department who wanted to delete the features that made the speech so memorable.

"Bill played a central role in making the Westminster Address possible", says Peter Robinson, the Reagan speechwriter who wrote the

---

[42] An early draft of the speech, which is probably the first draft, was dated May 19. Written by Dolan, it was overhauled by Reagan. The May 19 draft was twenty-four pages long. Twenty-seven entire paragraphs were removed by Reagan. These were complete paragraphs, in addition to dozens of sentences and hundreds of words the President slashed. Likewise, he made numerous additions. On this, see: Paul Kengor, *The Crusader: Ronald Reagan and the Fall of Communism* (New York: Regan Books, 2006), pp. 140–43. The May 19 draft is located at the Reagan Library in PHF, PS, RRL, Box 5, Folder 83.

historic Berlin Wall address. "He worked with Tony Dolan and others to preserve the really important language, which others kept trying to cut."[43] Here again, Clark was in the role of ensuring that Reagan's wishes were carried out. Yet, he did more in this particular speech than preserve the President's intentions.

Dolan's initial draft invoked Winston Churchill's historic "Westminster" address, delivered four decades earlier at Westminster College in Fulton, Missouri. The English prime minister had famously declared that an "Iron Curtain" had descended across the European continent, "from Stettin on the Baltic to Trieste on the Adriatic". Dolan's text had Reagan repeating the phrase, until Bill Clark checked a map.

Clark noticed that the bottom part of Churchill's Iron Curtain, Trieste to the south, included Yugoslavia, Marshall Tito's maverick state that, although socialist, had distanced itself from the Soviet Union. Clark did not want his President to pull a Gerald Ford or Dean Acheson and mistakenly name Yugoslavia as a member of the Evil Empire; the Soviets already had enough satellites. Clark thus handwrote a plain order onto the text: "Avoid lumping Yugoslavia in with the Soviet bloc."[44]

For that matter, the region of Trieste seemed almost to include parts of Greece and Austria. Had Churchill been sloppy? Had Harry Truman not spent a few billion dollars stopping such countries from going red? With Clark's edits, the new line read: "From Stettin on the Baltic to Varna on the Black Sea".

There was more, but Clark did not need to consult a map for his other geographical correction. The text stated that during "the dark days" of World War II, Britain, "this place—like an island—was incandescent with courage." Clark wrote in the margin: "It is an island." The text was changed to "this island". Clark also judged that the serious address had "too many jokes". He indicated on the text that the first joke in the introduction was "not funny".

Later, Lou Cannon and others would call the Westminster address Ronald Reagan's most prescient speech, "predictive of the events that

---

[43] Interview with Peter Robinson, March 11, 2005.

[44] The source who first found and underscored these edits was a reporter named Frank Warner who wrote an excellent piece titled, "New Word Order" in the *Allentown Morning Call* on March 5, 2000.

would occur in Eastern Europe".[45] Clark teasingly questioned Reagan on his predictions in this and other speeches: Did the President truly believe that communism would collapse, and, if so, when? "I would kid him", says Clark. "I would ask: 'Okay, if you're so smart, then tell me when it's going to happen!' He would just smile and say, 'You just wait and see. It will happen.'"

June 1982 to October 1982: Economic Warfare and the French

When Clark and Reagan returned to Washington from London, they began tightening the screws on the Soviet Union, looking for the best available means to strangle its economy. They tried to enlist European allies in an effort to halt the construction of a massive, 3,600-mile gas pipeline the Soviets were constructing through Siberia. Reagan wanted to stop the pipeline project which he knew Moscow could not complete without Western assistance. He was often nearly alone in that resolve, with the exception of a handful of advisors, including Bill Clark.

The French formed the strongest line of resistance to Reagan's efforts to undermine the Soviet economy. Desperate for revenue, the French wanted to help the Soviets build the Siberian pipeline. When French President François Mitterrand was asked by the *Washington Post* if he shared the Reagan administration's enthusiasm for economic warfare, the "impish" leader "vigorously" bristled at the very thought.[46]

The pipeline was not the only source of conflict with the French. There were other issues of disagreement, and the French were openly disdainful of Ronald Reagan, not only of his policies but also of him personally, calling him a dummy, the "Hollywood cowboy", and other names. The insults were coming from the highest levels of the French government, from Foreign Minister Claude Cheysson and President Mitterrand himself.

The name calling was reflective of the general French attitude toward the administration, Clark thought, but Jeane Kirkpatrick told him, "Oh, Bill, don't worry. The French treat each other that way."

---

[45] Cannon, *Role of a Lifetime*, pp. 272–74.

[46] Jim Hoagland, "France Refuses to Wage Economic War on Soviets", *Washington Post*, June 15, 1982.

Nevertheless, neither he nor Reagan could take the insults lightly, not because they offended Reagan, but because the two men thought a public rift between France and America was hurting the Western alliance. Also, the insults were being served up in Africa regarding U.S. policy toward Namibia and South Africa, an issue Clark had worked on as deputy secretary of state. Clark and Reagan thought France's behavior was hurting the administration's efforts to bring peace to the region.

The Reagan administration repeatedly asked the French government to refrain from mocking the American leadership in public, but to no avail. The French continued the drubbing for months. Finally, Reagan dispatched his "fireman" to put out the fire. On October 27, 1982, Mr. Clark was on his way to Paris for a face-to-face meeting with Mitterrand. He met with the French President for two hours at the Élysée Palace, bringing Evan Galbraith, the U.S. Ambassador to France, who took notes and prepared a memorandum of the conversation. Also present were Jacques Attali, Mitterrand's personal advisor, and an interpreter.

The French socialist leader defended his outspoken criticism of the Reagan administration by arguing that the Americans were guilty of "hegemony" and of violating the sovereignty of other nations, such as France and the Soviet Union. Whether Mitterrand knew it or not, he was speaking the Moscow line.[47] He said Reagan should scrap his plan to stop the pipeline.

Clark responded by saying that neither Reagan's principles nor his personality would allow him to desist from his economic strategy against the Soviet Union.[48] He informed Mitterrand Reagan was not going to tolerate French efforts to hinder him and that they should either come around to the American position or the White House would consider canceling the U.S. nuclear agreement with France. Or, as Ambassador Galbraith put it more diplomatically in his memorandum, Clark noted that "problems have occurred", and "it may be necessary to review some of our policies as they relate to France."

---

[47] One can find this exact objection particularly in TASS press releases at the time and in the pages of *Pravda* and *Izvestia*.

[48] The best early source on this was Laurence Barrett. See: Barrett, *Gambling with History*, p. 301.

Yes, Clark had used the word "review"—twice, but this seemingly harmless word was the equivalent of a verbal hand grenade. France was under the U.S. nuclear umbrella, meaning that America had long pledged to retaliate against any nation launching missiles against France. France was in no position to defend itself against a nuclear attack, or even nuclear blackmail, and needed this American guarantee. Moreover, France needed continued U.S. technical assistance for its own developing nuclear program. To lose this American support would be disastrous.

Clark raised other issues with Mitterrand. When he brought up Latin America, Mitterrand, according to Galbraith, "reacted dramatically, saying that he had more or less forgotten about this region because they had greater concerns elsewhere, and implied that the United States was obsessed with the region". Of course, Clark and Reagan were obsessed with the region, for reasons they felt were entirely defensible.

Clark proceeded to make the case for U.S. concern over Latin America. When he told Mitterrand that Cuba had received about $1 billion worth of Soviet military equipment since January—comprising about four hundred thousand tons, the largest shipments ever—Mitterrand acted surprised. When Clark mentioned that he had learned that Fidel Castro might be visiting France in coming weeks, en route to Sweden, Mitterrand said there was no immediate plan for such a visit.

Clark was not finished: He laid out the extensive "subversive" activity not only in Cuba but also in Costa Rica, El Salvador, Honduras, Nicaragua, and Panama, and offered to provide a lengthy briefing on these activities to members of the French government. He also pointed to the suppression of the Church in some of these countries. "President Mitterrand was slightly sarcastic at this point," recorded Galbraith, "stating we [the United States] will only be deemed right when a tragic development takes place in Central America." It was not clear to Clark what Mitterrand meant by this.

The Frenchman confessed that his leftist countrymen had certain sympathies for "revolutionary groups". Nonetheless, he did concede that U.S. policy toward Cuba, while "wrong", might "as time goes on . . . be proven right". This was progress, Clark thought.

When Clark broached the Africa issue, including the name calling that had been directed at Reagan by French officials, Mitterrand, in the words of Galbraith "appeared dumb-founded. He professed not knowing what we were talking about even though he himself had made such remarks while in Africa this month." Clark told Mitterrand that his comments had been immediately reported by major U.S. newspapers such as the *New York Times* and *Washington Post*. He said the administration "found it offensive to be criticized unreasonably in public by our friends and contrary to the way in which we do things". Clark said that if such statements continued, the White House would have no alternative but to respond to them publicly. Mitterrand defended the remarks by claiming that Ambassador Kirkpatrick had made some unflattering comments that had bothered the French. When Clark pressed for specifics, noting that Kirkpatrick was the administration's leading Francophile, and one not likely to make petulant comments about the French, Mitterrand smilingly dismissed the matter as a peripheral issue. He ended by granting that all sides, including the French, should make an effort to tone down their rhetoric.

With respect to Soviet domination of the Poles, Mitterrand stated "fairly vigorously" that "nothing can happen in Poland. The very nature of the communist movement will not allow anything to happen. If necessary, they will act brutally but it is impossible for them to allow the society to become liberal." No, concluded Mitterrand, Poland was doomed to decades of continued communist rule. Reagan and the Pope should leave it alone. They should take the French approach.

As for the Siberian pipeline, Mitterrand said the Reagan administration was wasting its time economically pressuring the Soviets. He was certain that, with or without a pipeline, communism was not about to collapse, whether in the Soviet Union or Poland.

In contrast, Reagan was so certain that economic warfare would weaken the Soviets, Clark said, that on the pipeline he had committed to a course that would deprive the U.S. economy of about $500 million in revenue for 1982 alone, during the middle of a recession, damaging him politically.

Mitterrand ended the meeting with "a statement of goodwill", noted Galbraith, complimenting Clark for being a "good adviser and effective advocate" for his President and saying he wished Clark were a member of his own staff. He also thanked Clark for the "frank and serious" discussion and said he would think through the statements he had made. Clark suggested that any "additional comment" should be exchanged directly between the two leaders.

"All in all," reported Galbraith, "Mitterrand put on quite a performance. Several times he played innocent.... He sprinkled in some intended humor, smiling often.... He was conciliatory and generous in his attitude to Mr. Clark, whose presentation obviously impressed Mitterrand."

Upon exiting, Clark and Galbraith successfully avoided the press—as they had done during their entrance. Two phone calls were made to the U.S. Embassy in Paris, asking about the two men walking in and out of the Élysée. The media officer at the embassy responded (truthfully) that he did not know the identity of the two Americans.[49]

The Departure of Al Haig

Secretary of State Al Haig became increasingly concerned about the protests of the French and other U.S. allies over Reagan's economic strategy. The former NATO commander did not want to pursue an anti-Soviet policy that punished NATO members who continued to do business with Russia. Reagan's attempt to stop the Siberian pipeline, therefore, was strongly opposed by Haig and the State Department.

Many expected Bill Clark's collegial relationship with Al Haig to change once he left Foggy Bottom for the post of national security advisor. Haig, after all, had clashed with Richard Allen, and with most everyone else. According to Clark, however, the two continued to work well together. "Here again, at the NSC, I got along with him fine", says Clark, though he added Haig and he had some differences of opinion on certain issues.

Contemporaneous accounts reveal that about two months after Clark joined the NSC, Haig began complaining that Reagan was leaving him out of critical policy decisions. A handwritten note from Clark to Haig on White House letterhead, dated March 27, 1982, reveals that the secretary thought that his relationship with President Reagan was deteriorating:

---

[49] This, too, was reported in Galbraith's memo.

Al:

Today you expressed several points that concern me:
1. the President "lacks trust and confidence" in you—
2. the President has "backed away from his commitment to the PRC"—
3. the President has "made a grave mistake on his MX decision"—
4. the President has failed to follow your advice on Salvador—

Al, if you truly believe all the above, we have a problem—

Bill

This was signature Bill Clark: terse, reserved, and representative of Reagan and his interests.

Clark recalls one of many conversations he had with Haig during this period. "Why does the President allow me to twist in the wind?" Haig asked Clark. Clark insisted this was not the case, offering as proof the log of daily phone calls made by President Reagan to the secretary of state between April 30 and May 2, 1982. Haig was not only being kept informed, Clark argued, but being kept informed directly by the President himself on a daily basis. In addition, the secretary of state had direct access to the President at Cabinet meetings and security briefings.

Haig was not reassured. The fact was the Reagan administration had a problem with him, and he had a problem with the administration. It was only a matter of time before there would be a parting of ways.

During the June 1982 economic summit at Versailles, the conflict over the Siberian pipeline intensified, and both Clark and Haig lost their tempers. The *New York Times* reported that Clark and Haig "confronted each other several times in several days in what aides described as 'shouting matches' on several issues". The *Times* noted that while this was typical of Haig, it was unusual for Clark, whose hallmark was "mellowness and reserve".[50]

Haig behaved in an "offensive manner", as Richard Pipes put it, even to the point of insulting Nancy Reagan—a big mistake for anyone wishing to remain in the good graces of the President. "Clark returned from Versailles furious with [Haig]",[51] he said.

---

[50] "Haig-Clark Feud Emerging over Foreign Policy", *New York Times*, June 22, 1982.
[51] Pipes, *Vixi*, p. 182.

As for Haig, he returned insisting he would not remain a part of the Reagan administration unless he was the sole spokesman for administration foreign policy. "I'm either going to run foreign policy or quit", he announced to White House aides on the plane.[52] What particularly needled the secretary of state was Bill Clark's ascendancy in foreign policy, which, said one aide, was "torturing Haig".[53]

Yet, the true problem for Haig was not Clark's ascendancy but the President's ascendancy, says Clark, adding that he was merely ensuring that *Reagan's* policies were enacted, not *Haig's*. Clark saw that Haig and his State Department were not committed to Reagan's policy of putting the economic clamp on the Soviets and pushing Western allies to do the same.

Over the next two weeks, the pipeline issue came to a head. At a Friday, June 18, 1982, Cabinet meeting, the NSC put forth its options to the President for dealing with the Soviet pipeline. The council favored the "Clark option", sometimes dubbed the "hard-line option", endorsed not only by Clark, but also by Weinberger. It penalized European firms cooperating with the Soviets in constructing the pipeline. The bulk of Reagan's Cabinet pressed him to abandon the Clark option, and the State Department offered a counter-proposal.[54]

At the end of a heated discussion, everyone listened in hushed anticipation as Reagan spoke up: "Well, they can have their damned pipeline", he said, pausing to hear the relief exhaling from many around the table. Then, Reagan hit the table with his fist and finished his sentence: "But not with American equipment and not with American technology!" He stood and left the room, as some expressions of pleasure transformed into looks of dismay. Judge Clark then declared, "We have a Presidential decision!" Those who had sided with the State Department "were crestfallen", says Roger Robinson. "Those were Reagan's last words at the meeting. And I will never forget them."[55]

---

[52] Lou Cannon, "A Long Series of Conflicts Culminates in Decision to Accept Resignation", *Washington Post*, June 26, 1982.

[53] "Haig's Quick Shifts Had Reagan Aides Looking at Ceiling", *Washington Post*, June 26, 1982.

[54] Alexander Haig, *Caveat* (New York: Scribner, 1984), p. 312; and Cannon, *Role of a Lifetime*, p. 169.

[55] Interviews with Roger Robinson on June 6 and 8, 2005.

Al Haig was not present at the meeting. He was in New York, meeting with Soviet foreign minister Andrei Gromyko. Undersecretary Lawrence Eagleburger represented State and offered the Haig alternative to the Clark option. When Haig learned what had happened in his absence, he was furious. He believed Clark scheduled the meeting on that particular day because the secretary of state was out of town. "Absolutely not!" Clark says. "It was a regularly scheduled meeting."

When Haig returned a few days later, a small briefing session was held in the Situation Room with Haig and Clark both in attendance. Secretary of Labor William Brock, who had just returned from Western Europe, was there as well. During the session, Brock was debriefed on the Western European reaction to Reagan's June 18 pipeline decision. He described being "lambasted, savaged" by the Western Europeans.

Already incensed, Haig was now purple with rage. Veins protruded from his neck and forehead. He pointed at Clark and raised his voice, accusing Clark of sandbagging him, of waiting until he left for New York to call the meeting. "You did this!" Haig yelled at Clark. That was one of Haig's biggest mistakes; Clark, of all the President's men, could not be treated that way. He responded by calmly asking all staff to collect their notes and leave the room.[56]

"Bill was the President's closest associate and valued friend", says Robinson, "Al was talking to the alter ego of the President of the United States—on matters of national security and much more, the same organism." Shouting at Clark, adds Robinson, "was a defining moment for Al Haig. It was very dramatic—the kind of thing that history rarely records." [57]

There was more sealing Haig's fate. Robinson received reports that Secretary Haig had suggested to "certain counterparts" in Western Europe that he might be able to bring Reagan around to their point of view on lifting pipeline sanctions. More pointedly, information was circulating that Haig was providing these types of assurances to senior Western European officials without the President's knowledge or approval. Robinson was very troubled with the information and

---

[56] Ibid.
[57] Ibid.

took the rare step of requesting a private meeting with his boss—Bill Clark.[58]

Clark read Robsinson's report, reading glasses resting down near the end of his nose. It took him a couple of minutes. His face showed no emotion, no expression. After he finished, he stood silent for another minute or two. He then looked at Robinson, who also remained standing, and said, "What do you think?" Robinson, who had only been at the NSC for a few months, replied: "I think the secretary of state may have become a national-security issue in and of himself."

Robinson raised constitutional concerns, pondering if Haig, according to the statements, was exceeding his mandate as secretary of state. It seemed, said Robinson, that Haig was telling European foreign ministers or heads of state that, effectively, *he* would take care of issue X, Y, or Z; that was the President's job, not the duty of the secretary of state. Clark replied simply, "I agree."

Clark had once been a Haig fan, said a White House aide, but a rift between the two men developed when Clark "began to force Al to accept that it would be the president's policies, not Al's. Al just simply wouldn't buy it."[59] Said one senior State Department official: "Haig knew Clark was someone he couldn't beat, and he felt that policy was drifting in ways he couldn't control."[60]

On Friday, June 25, 1982, after a working lunch of the NSC had just adjourned in the Cabinet Room of the White House, President Reagan said to Secretary of State Haig, "Al, may I see you for a moment?" Haig then learned that his latest offer to resign, made the day before, had been accepted by the President.[61]

Haig had offered to resign before, a common gesture by top administration officials during difficult times, though presidents usually refuse the offer. This time, however, Reagan accepted Haig's resignation. "No one tried to talk Al out of resigning this time", said one administration official. "No one wanted to."

[58] Ibid.

[59] Steven R. Weisman, "Reagan and Aides Meet with Shultz to Review Policy", *New York Times*, June 27, 1982.

[60] John M. Goshko, "Haig Resigns at State; Shultz is Named", *Washington Post*, June 26, 1982.

[61] Steven R. Weisman, "Reagan and Aides Meet with Shultz to Review Policy", *New York Times*, June 27, 1982.

The secretary of state had managed to engage in a confrontation "with every major member of the administration". First he considered the three chief members of the White House staff—Baker, Deaver, and Meese—to be "ignorant", noted the *Washington Post*. Then over at the Pentagon, "Weinberger drove him up the wall", just as "the White House drove him up the wall." Now, Bill Clark disappointed him.[62] Apparently, the entire administration was off course, except for Al Haig.

Though the falling out with Clark was the ultimate cause of Haig's departure from the administration, it would be unjust to blame Clark for the outcome. Clark was the only person left who still had any patience for the man—but even Bill Clark's patience had its limits. As Clark's press assistant, Jeremiah O'Leary, told it, Clark was "the last to give up" on the contentious Haig, "and the general was not fired by Reagan until Clark finally had enough."[63]

O'Leary estimated that the last straw might have come when Haig demanded an airplane with windows for a flight to London, which, said O'Leary, probably tipped Clark over the edge. "I was in the hotel room in Jamaica for nearly an hour during this harangue by Haig on the phone", recalls O'Leary, "and it was the only time I ever heard Clark swear."[64] This was on top of the occasional "bruised feelings" that Haig displayed whenever he thought that he did not receive his "proper place" in receiving lines and motorcades. Haig did not "suffer" in silence,[65] wrote the *New York Times*.

Clark remembers the airplane incident: Haig "hated planes without windows", he says. Knowing this, Jim Baker arranged for a plane without them for the general. "Baker did it out of spite because he knew Al would go ballistic", says Clark with a grin, acknowledging the absurdity of the continual White House infighting.

The Next Secretary of State

Before Haig was gone, Clark and Reagan had privately discussed his successor. In Clark's mind, the choice came down to two men: George

[62] Cannon, "A Long Series of Conflicts".

[63] "Haig-Clark Feud Emerging over Foreign Policy", *New York Times*, June 22, 1982.

[64] Jeremiah O'Leary, "Judge William P. Clark—An Appreciation", *Washington Times*, October 24, 1983.

[65] "Haig-Clark Feud Emerging over Foreign Policy", *New York Times*.

Shultz and Henry Kissinger. He wrote a brief, half-page assessment of both men, intended for the President's eyes only, which he handed (unsigned and undated) to Reagan.

On White House letterhead, Clark listed the pros and cons of the two candidates without offering a personal vote. On Shultz, he wrote: "Extremely well respected among industrialized democracies of Europe and Japan", and, "good team player". For the cons, Clark judged that Shultz was "not familiar with [the] ongoing crisis in the Middle East", and that, "Someone in the State Department above the Under Secretary level has to know something about the Middle East. If Haig leaves, no one will." As for Kissinger, Clark called the former secretary of state and national security advisor one of "the best" minds in the world on foreign affairs, and said that he was "good on current crises issues", and "could pick up Middle East diplomacy and give it the leadership it needs to avoid becoming a catastrophic failure". Kissinger's negatives included the fact that he was, "[h]istorically, not a good team player—although better than Haig."

President Nixon and Kissinger had pursued détente with the Soviet Union, a policy of accommodation that Reagan and Clark strongly rejected. Reagan therefore was at times uneasy about advice from Kissinger, though he and Clark both perceived that Kissinger had moved closer to their position.

Clark says he and Kissinger "were pretty close, even though we differed ... on policy toward the Soviets". His friendship with Kissinger was not generally known by either the press corps or official Washington. Many inside the Beltway viewed Kissinger as egotistical and difficult to get along with, but Clark "found a lot of humility in the man, contrary to the common perception of him".

Rather than viewing Kissinger as a threat or as a man whose boots he could never fill, Clark saw him as a resource, and often called him for advice. Kissinger reciprocated, frequently phoning Clark. When Clark found himself in a quandary, he could count on Kissinger to help him out, usually with a sage story about the dark days. "He reminded me of what he went through over Vietnam", says Clark. "He told me not to give in to the left, because they would only demand more."

Despite his relationship with Kissinger, Clark privately leaned toward Shultz as Haig's successor. Reagan agreed, and George P. Shultz was chosen to be his second (and longest serving) secretary of state. He was named to succeed Haig the very day Haig resigned.

The new secretary of state was optimistic about his ability to get along with the national security advisor. In his confirmation hearings, Shultz told the Senate that he anticipated no discord with Clark and expected that the two together would serve the President "cooperatively and loyally". "The relationship", Shultz told the senators, "will be one of teamwork."[66] An analysis in *U.S. News & World Report*, aptly titled, "Foreign Policy: One More Try", captured the spirit of optimism, noting that both Shultz and Clark were "honest brokers" and Shultz, unlike Haig, would "argue his case quietly, and if the decision goes against him, he will accept it and implement the policy without a fuss."[67]

July 1982: NSDD-48

By the time Haig left the White House in late June, several Cabinet members and many others in the administration were opposing Reagan's economic strategy against the Soviet Union. These officials wanted arms control, but they had no interest in action intended to undermine the Soviet economy if it might result in estranging America's European allies. Agreeing with the ruling elites in most of Western Europe, explains Roger Robinson, these officials believed that the Soviet Union was invincible and "a permanent part of the geopolitical landscape that would be there for generations to come".[68]

Clark knew something must be done about the opposition; if not, the Reagan administration, like previous administrations, would accept as given the captivity of millions of people throughout Eastern and Central Europe. Reagan, Clark, Casey, Weinberger, Kirkpatrick, and Meese were in agreement; they needed to fight the Cold War to win.

In order to win, Clark recognized that he and his staff needed to wrap their "arms around the inter-agency process".[69] "If you don't control the policy *process*," explains Robinson, "you'll be end-runned

---

[66] Murrey Marder, "Shultz Says He and Security Chief Clark Anticipate No Discord", *Washington Post*, July 21, 1982.

[67] "Foreign Policy: One More Try", *U.S. News & World Report*, July 26, 1982.

[68] Roger Robinson, interviews.

[69] Ibid.

and ultimately wiped out [by those who oppose the president's policies]. There are too many opportunities for prima donnas and major policy players to eviscerate presidential decision-making and erode presidential policy—if you don't effectively discipline the policy process."

Someone or something needed to take command and steer overall Reagan Soviet policy in the direction Clark and the President desired. To this end, Clark and his staff created the Senior Interdepartmental Group-International Economic Policy (SIG-IEP), a Cabinet-level body that, though chaired by the secretary of the treasury, reported through the national security advisor to the president. The purpose of the group was to make sure that when it came to economic policy related to the Soviet Union and their satellites, national security would trump American and European commercial interests.

Haig went out in late June, and SIG-IEP went up in July. "That was it", says Robinson. "That was when Bill Clark established utter primacy over East-West economic decision-making and over international economic policy with foreign policy and national security implications. . . . It was then", continues Robinson, "that the lights of accommodation went out in Western Europe." Policy control by Clark meant that Western Europeans, and those in the Reagan administration who sympathized with them, would not succeed in stopping Reagan's and Clark's campaign against the Kremlin.

After Clark was no longer at the National Security Council, SIG-IEP was dismantled by the efforts of James Baker and Richard Darman. When Robinson, who was the group's executive secretary, married and left Washington for a ten-day honeymoon in Jamaica, Baker and Darman leaned hard on Bud McFarlane, then national security advisor, to break up SIG-IEP. When Robinson returned, his interagency group was defunct,[70] but by then, so was the Soviet economy.

Fall 1982: The MX, the Nuclear Freeze, and the Bishops

As fall approached, the Reagan administration pursued the MX missile, an integral part of Reagan's platform of peace through strength and a weapon the Kremlin had been trying to thwart with the help of

---

[70] Ibid.

the global left. The MX became a front-and-center issue for Reagan, and for Bill Clark.

Research and development of the MX started before Reagan became President. Designed to carry multiple warheads with stunning accuracy, the missile was to be deployed in mobile launchers. By the time Reagan became President, however, the effectiveness of mobile launchers was being questioned, and many Democrats in Congress wanted to scrap the program.

Reagan came up with an alternate deployment method. His multibillion-dollar plan called for placing one hundred MX missiles in underground silos, where they would be protected with thickly reinforced concrete and steel from incoming enemy missiles. The President promised Congress that he would lay out a final plan by December 1. As the *Washington Post* noted, the President's decision would be "heavily influenced" by two men in particular, Secretary of Defense Cap Weinberger and Bill Clark.[71]

The three men wished to devise a name for the MX, a name that would encapsulate policy as well as performance. The Colt .45 once carried by Bill's grandfather as U.S. Marshal and now hanging on the national security advisor's office wall in the White House basement was often discussed by Clark and Reagan. In the Old West, the gun was known as "the Peacemaker", an ideal name, suggested Clark, for the MX missile, the purpose of which, after all, was peace through strength.

Ronald Reagan enthusiastically embraced the idea of naming the missile in honor of Marshal Bob's gun; however, he decided to tweak the name a bit, changing it to the less aggressive "Peacekeeper". Clark called his old friend Cap Weinberger and told him: "The president wants to name your new pistol the Peacekeeper."

On November 22, in a speech to the nation, Reagan announced his decision to deploy one hundred MX missiles. Two weeks later, on December 7, Congress voted to reject funding. The Reagan team, however, would not give up without a fight. They began an all-out campaign on behalf of the weapon, with Clark being one of the central players.

---

[71] Michael Getler, "Science Adviser Confident About MX Plan", *Washington Post*, September 9, 1982.

As the Reagan administration intensified its efforts, so did the opposition. An anti-nuclear weapons movement rose up around the country and the world, denouncing not only the MX, but also other Reagan defense programs, including the Pershing II missile and the B-1 bomber. The "nuclear freeze" movement, which was supported by the Soviets, favored "freezing" the number of nuclear weapons in the world by not manufacturing new ones. Massive protests throughout America and Western Europe, including a crowd of close to one million in New York City's Central Park,[72] stunned the Reagan administration.

The freezers included celebrities and vocal leftist groups, such as the Communist Party, Greenpeace, and Physicians for Social Responsibility. The National Conference of Catholic Bishops (NCCB), which prepared a pastoral letter condemning nuclear war as immoral, particularly a first nuclear strike, favored a freeze on nuclear weapons.

Clark assumed a special role with the bishops. He was in contact with Joseph Cardinal Bernardin and other prelates. His letters to Bernardin were lengthy, including one seven-pages long, part of a package that contained letters from State Department veterans Eugene Rostow, Lawrence Eagleburger, and Defense Secretary Weinberger. These letters were polite; their point was to clear up misunderstandings and factual mistakes. The conclusions of the NCCB, Clark believed, were based on mistaken assumptions.

Bishop Raymond Lucker, for example, complained to the press that the Reagan administration was pushing an arms buildup rather than seeking disarmament.[73] His statement revealed "a common misunderstanding of the Reagan administration's policy", Clark says. Yes, the administration favored an arms buildup, but for the *purpose* of achieving disarmament. An arms buildup was needed to bring the Soviets to the negotiating table in the first place. After all, the Soviets were not about to cut missiles without the United States giving up something in return.

Weinberger adds: "Ultimately, we all felt that you could and should get arms control and other agreements with [the Soviets], but that

---

[72] Estimates on crowd size vary from 500 thousand to 1 million on June 12, 1982.

[73] Marjorie Hyer, "U.S. Bishops Firm on Pastoral Letter", *Washington Post*, November 18, 1982.

Ranger Bob Clark and bride Alice at Castaic, California, 1905

Three-year-old ranch hand, ready to saddle up

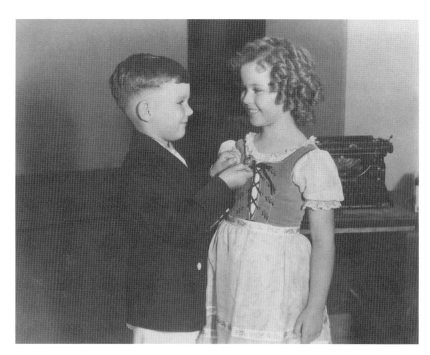

Billy Clark deputizing Shirley Temple, 1935

William P. Clark, Deputy Secretary of State and Shirley Temple Black, Foreign Affairs Officer, 1981

Billy Clark conferring with Tom Mix, 1938

Billy Clark on Macaroni, ZX Ranch, 1949

The first Clark plane during construction, 1945

Off to town in the Navy SNJ

*Transporting Cap Weinberger to the ranch in the Korean War "Bird Dog",
July 18, 1993*

Entrance road/runway/landing strip at Clark Ranch

Special Agent Clark meets old friend and classmate James D. "Bub"
McCormick, also stationed in Germany

Johanna "Joan" Brauner, the future Mrs. Clark

Army Counter Intelligence Corps residence and office in Mannheim

Governor Ronald Reagan's first Rancheros ride, May 1967

Close friends from Villanova days and fellow Rancheros: left–right: Charlie Doud, future Presidente of Rancheros; Bill Clark; Pete Dailey, Ambassador to Ireland; John Gavin, Ambassador to Mexico, May 6, 1983

Three generations of Clarks leading 700 riders on the annual Rancheros Visitadores trail ride through the Santa Ynez Valley; left to right: Bill Sr., Bill Jr., and Pete, late 1980s

Bill Sr.'s last Rancheros ride, Bill Jr. driving Clark Company coach, May 1991

Enjoying life: dinner at Clark residence in Oxnard, pre-campaign 1966

Nancy Reagan and Bill Clark, State of the State address, January 1967

Associate Justice Clark extends official welcome from Governor Reagan to Jozsef Cardinal Mindszenty. Mindszenty's host, Archbishop McGucken, stands to the right, June 1974.

Joan and Bill attending White House formal event, 1981

State's Deputy Secretary in discussion with former Secretary of State and National Security Advisor Kissinger, April 1981

Egypt's President Anwar Sadat and Bill Clark, Acting Secretary of State, saying their goodbyes in summer of 1981, little suspecting Sadat was heading home to assassination four days later. The assassination was carried out by radical Muslims objecting to the Camp David Accords.

To Bill Clark —
Blessed are the peacemakers.
With friendship & respect
George Bush

*Vice President George H. W. Bush and Deputy Secretary Clark,
July 21, 1981*

*Acting Secretary of
State Clark holds a
briefing urging 1,500
Americans—mostly oil
company employees—
to return home
voluntarily from Libya,
December 10, 1981.*

Peter Dailey, later U.S. Ambassador to Ireland; Ireland's Taoiseach (Prime Minister) Garret FitzGerald; Deputy Secretary of State Bill Clark in Ireland. Fitzgerald was hosting his first state dinner, held in honor of Joan and Bill Clark, December 1981. It was also Clark's first diplomatic mission abroad.

Walking from State Department to the White House and greater responsibilities, December 1981

National Security Advisor Clark and Secretary of State Haig receive Egypt's President Mubarak at Diplomatic Entrance to the White House, February 4, 1982

Good friends with opposite views, March 12, 1982

Clark, Reagan, and Haig rounding the corner at the White House, March 25, 1982

Joan Clark meets Holy Father John Paul II in Rome, June 1982

Jim Buckley, Bill, and Cap Weinberger discussing "The Radios", July 1982

Prime Minister Indira Gandhi, President Reagan, and National Security Advisor Clark bettering relations between India and the U.S., July 1982

A serious moment inside ... Clark, Bush, and Reagan, August 1982

A relaxing moment outside ...

Ambassador and Mrs. Chai Zemin meet with National Security Advisor and Mrs. William Clark, September 1982. Chai Zemin later became President of the People's Republic of China.

Discussing special mission with Donald Rumsfeld, October 13, 1982

Clark briefs President Reagan and former President Ford on National Security issues while Counselor Ed Meese takes notes, October 25, 1982.

National Security Advisor Clark greets U.S. ally Chancellor Helmut Kohl, November 15, 1982

Clark carving California ranch beef for NSC staff Christmas dinner at Blair House, Friday, December 17, 1982: left to right: Secretary of Defense Caspar Weinberger; Judge Clark; executive assistants to Reagan and Clark: Helene von Damm and Jacque Hill; President Reagan

The best of friends stand by the President: U.S. Representative to the U.N. Jeane Kirkpatrick and National Security Advisor Bill Clark, Spring 1983

Quietly awaiting Prime Minister Thatcher's arrival for Williamsburg summit, May 28, 1983

To and from on Air Force One

Cover of
Time *Magazine,*
August 8, 1983

Secretary of the Department of Interior William P. Clark

Interior Secretary Clark addresses group at Templehof Airport, Berlin, May 11, 1984. The President had requested Clark lead the delegation to the celebration recognizing the 35th anniversary of the end of the Soviet blockade of the city.

Peace Talk. Clark and Saddam Hussein in Baghdad, January 1986.

"Best Wishes to Judge Bill Clark, my South Georgia hunting partner, Jimmy Carter, 3/84"

With Father Joseph Fessio, S.J., and Molana and Philipa, daughters of Amadeus

Clark and Amadeus beginning their 6:00 A.M. constitutional through Rock Creek Park and up Capitol Mall during Clark's days at Interior

Bernice holding King Louis, and Bill Sr. petting Cissy, in their Camarillo home, December 1986

Chapel Hill

Bruce Haley

could only happen once we rebuilt our defense and bargained from a position of strength." [74]

The approach seemed simple and straightforward to the Reagan team. Nevertheless, Lucker's assessment of the administration was shared by many clerics in America. Mary McGrory had it right when she imagined a conversation in the White House Situation Room: "Where is Cardinal Spellman now that we need him?" [75]

The White House did not have the late Cardinal Spellman, nor the late Bishop Sheen, but Clark knew another famous Catholic anti-communist: Clare Boothe Luce, to whom he and Reagan turned for assistance in dealing with the bishops. "Clare was there at the core of the team", says Clark. "She was enormously helpful."

Other Catholic intellectuals, such as Michael Novak at the American Enterprise Institute, also challenged the freeze arguments of the bishops. The debate between the bishops and their staffs on one hand and the Reagan administration and anti-communist Catholics on the other became big news. The full text of the Reagan administration's formal letter to the bishops, signed by Bill Clark, was reprinted in many newspapers, including the November 17 *New York Times*.

The secular media, which normally objects to the infusion of faith into politics, were, for the most part, behind the bishops and welcomed them into the public square with open arms. Similarly, though priests were not permitted to appear on Soviet television, nor even in Soviet hospitals, the disarmament cause of the American bishops was warmly reported by Pravda.

To be sure, many American Catholics supported Reagan and questioned their bishops on defense matters. One such person was a Catholic priest from Chicago named John Kmech, a former prisoner of a Siberian concentration camp. "I know how deceitful the Soviet government is", Kmech wrote to the President on December 10, 1982. "They propose peace to the world while they build-up their war machinery." He typed uppercase letters for emphasis: "DO NOT BELIEVE THEM! DO NOT TRUST THEM!!" Kmech continued:

---

[74] Interview with Cap Weinberger, April 14, 2005.

[75] Mary McGrory, "Reagan Having a Tough Time Riding Herd on the Shepherds", *Washington Post*, November 18, 1982.

"I back you 100%, and I apologize for the silly ramblings of the American bishops. . . . Forgive them for they know not what they do."

Reagan wrote back to Kmech: "I can't tell you how much your letter . . . meant to me and how grateful I am. . . . If only more people and, yes, if the Bishops could hear and heed the words of someone like yourself who knows firsthand the Godless tyranny of Soviet totalitarianism." Kmech was just one of a number of priests who wrote to Reagan pledging support, convinced that the bishops were wrong.[76]

Winning the MX

The President also received mail from the opposition. For example, some elementary-school teachers organized a letter-writing campaign, in which their students told the President he was a bad man for "favoring" nuclear war. "President Reagan, you have been totally irresponsible!" wrote a sixth-grade girl at Wellesley Middle School in Massachusetts. "Are you trying to ruin the world by bombs? Who cares if Russia keeps making bombs[;] they'll stop if we make the first move." A sixth-grade boy wrote: "Mr. Reagan, how would you like it if the world blew up and you were the only person left on earth!" Another boy lectured the President: "Don't give me that excuse that the Russians have more nuclear bombs than us, you can't use that excuse forever. I mean someday the public will find out that we have more nuclear bombs than the Russians do and they'll burn you at the stake."

Clark was constantly making phone calls and writing letters to congressmen, pundits, and heads of non-profit organizations, trying to win support for the President's MX plan. He helped develop a list of talking points for phoning senators, as well as a general legislative strategy. The correspondence from the period was intense, and must have been a factor in exhausting Clark. Recalling the episode, Clark took a breath, "The MX—boy, that was a dog fight."

The protests from the nuclear freezers continued unabated throughout the world, and the movement had great success in maligning and mischaracterizing Reagan as a warmonger. Yet, there was some

---

[76] For example, another was Rev. Stephen Majoros of Toledo, Ohio, who wrote a February 4, 1983 letter.

positive news for the administration: Eventually the bishops adjusted their position on the development, production, and deployment of new weapons systems, calling for a "curb" rather than a "halt". This modified language appeared in the third draft of the letter, which, at 150 pages, was one-third longer than the second version and was released on April 5, 1983.

Clark was credited with making a difference. Asked by the *New York Times* whether objections by Reagan officials had an impact on the third draft, Cardinal Bernardin cited a specific quotation from a Clark letter, which emphasized that Reagan nuclear policy was guided by "compelling moral considerations", including, among other things, not permitting the targeting of population centers. Bernardin conceded that the bishops had "misunderstood" the administration's position and that Clark's letter had "clarified" Reagan policy for the third draft of their pastoral letter, which the cardinal said was "more flexible".[77]

When the final pastoral letter was released, the *New York Times* headline read: "Bishops Rethink the Unthinkable".[78] The State Department agreed that the letter had been rethought and "substantially improved". Clark publicly commended the "important and reasonable contribution" of the bishops to the public debate on nuclear weapons. However, "the bishops had to retract some of their statements because they had them wrong", Clark said. "They simply had their facts incorrect."

Despite the intense and mostly unflagging opposition, the Reagan administration persevered in its pursuit of the MX. On May 25, 1983, Congress approved funding for a modified version of the MX missile program by a vote of 59 to 39 in the Senate. It was a big victory for Bill Clark and his President.

Public Diplomacy

The MX controversy taught Bill Clark the importance of combating the Soviet propaganda machine. Clark and Reagan were convinced

---

[77] Kenneth A. Briggs, "Bishops' Letter on Nuclear Arms is revised to 'More Flexible' View", *New York Times*, April 6, 1983.

[78] "Bishops Rethink the Unthinkable", *New York Times*, April 10, 1983.

that if the White House could do a better job of informing people about the issues, it would be better able to influence public opinion regarding key aspects of the Reagan national security agenda, including the peace-through-strength approach to arms negotiations and the efforts to halt the spread of communism in Central America. It was "definitely Bill's idea" to focus public relations efforts on building support at home, says Ed Meese, particularly for policies dealing with the Soviet Union and Central America.[79]

In January 1983, Clark spearheaded an effort to hone the administration's "public diplomacy". The President appointed him to head a Cabinet-level committee including Weinberger, Shultz, and Peter McPherson, administrator of the Agency for International Development. Clark asked Charles Wick and Gil Robinson of the United States Information Agency (USIA) to help him with the work of the new committee. "Clark called me one day and asked, 'How do we calm down public opinion?'" Robinson says. "'We need help in getting the word out on the Pershings, on Nicaragua, on Afghanistan.' He told me he was calling on behalf of Ronald Reagan and himself; both wanted to do this."[80]

Clark also called upon his old Villanova teammate Peter Dailey, now Ambassador to Ireland (he had been Reagan's campaign advertising manager in 1980), to help win backing for U.S. efforts to place Pershing II intermediate-range nuclear missiles in Western Europe, which in the spring of 1983 would be an even tougher task than getting domestic funding for the MX. The Soviets were planning another "peace offensive", and the nuclear freezers apparently believed that the Kremlin was made up of peaceniks, whereas Reagan, along with Weinberger and Clark, wanted to blow up the world.

The thinking behind Reagan's Pershing II plan was as follows: The Soviets already had 580 SS missiles deployed throughout Eastern Europe. These were intermediate-range missiles in range of targets in Western Europe and Asia. According to Reagan's plan, if the Soviet Union did not remove those missiles, the United States would deploy 572 intermediate-range missiles of its own in Western Europe. As an alternative plan, Reagan's "zero–zero option" called for both the United States and the Soviet Union to reduce these missiles to zero.

---

[79] Interview with Ed Meese, June 7, 2005.
[80] Interview with Gil Robinson, May 27, 2005.

The Soviets characterized the Reagan administration as a nuclear-missile-craving belligerent, and the nuclear-freezers eagerly joined the chorus. Throughout 1983 massive anti-American demonstrations were staged in Western European capitals, and support even for the zero–zero plan eroded.

Nonetheless, the administration was able to convince Western European leaders, particularly Britain's Margaret Thatcher and West Germany's Helmut Kohl, to accept the deployment of Pershing IIs on their soil—a deployment that eventually led to the Intermediate-range Nuclear Forces (INF) Treaty in December 1987. Through INF Reagan achieved his zero-zero reduction with Mikhail Gorbachev. It was the greatest of all nuclear-weapons treaties, the first and only treaty to abolish completely an entire class of nuclear weapons.

"Everything we did was about telling the truth", says Gil Robinson. "It was what today has been called a 'No-Spin Zone.'" Yet, Clark's public relations team did more than work to convince skeptical Western Europeans of the sincerity of Reagan's calls for arms control. The unprecedented $65 million "public diplomacy" campaign also financed scholarships and "institutes for democracy" in the West—as Reagan had promised in his June 1982 Westminster address in London.[81]

March 8, 1983: "Evil Empire"

Despite the smoke screen of Soviet propaganda, Clark and Reagan knew this much about the Soviet Union: Since its founding in 1917, the USSR had grown increasingly merciless and oppressive. On March 8, 1983, in a bold example of public diplomacy, Ronald Reagan said just that, dubbing the Soviet Union an "Evil Empire".

Clark says that Reagan was "incredibly careful with such bellicose language" and "did not at all" shoot from the hip. When he used tough words, they were for "a preconceived purpose and never for an *ad hominem* attack".

Reagan's words had their impact; they were greeted with joy inside Soviet prison camps and captive nations, but met with outrage and

---

[81] Lou Cannon, "U.S. to Fund 'Democracy' Institutes", *Washington Post*, January 21, 1983.

denial at the Kremlin and among the American left.[82] Garry Wills spoke of a Russian girl who wanted to know why Ronald Reagan considered her "irredeemably evil".[83] Surely Wills knew that Reagan considered the Soviet *system* evil, not the Soviet people, for whom he felt only sympathy as victims of that cruel regime. Reagan saw Russians as a wonderful people, with deep religious roots, who had suffered terribly at the hands of communist oppressors.

Before the U.S.-USSR Summit in Geneva, Reagan had said: "[W]e are all God's children. The clerk and the king and the Communist were made in His image. We all have souls." He urged a group of American and Soviet exchange students to understand that "we're all God's children." He said, "I pray that the hand of the Lord will be on the Soviet people." [84]

In his Evil Empire speech, Reagan requested that fellow Christians join him in his prayers for Russia. "[L]et us pray for the salvation of all of those who live in that totalitarian darkness—pray they will discover the joy of knowing God." [85]

Reagan and Clark were fond of a prayer that both felt typified their role in regard to communist peoples and nations, and the difference they hoped to make from the White House: It was a prayer attributed to Saint Francis of Assisi, the following excerpt of which was particularly meaningful to Reagan and Clark:

Lord, make me an instrument of your peace. . . .
Where there is doubt, let me sow faith.
Where there is despair, let me sow hope.
Where there is darkness, let me sow light.[86]

Reagan saw himself as sowing freedom—including religious freedom—in communist countries, as did his national security advisor and top hand, Bill Clark.

---

[82] See Kengor, *God and Ronald Reagan*, pp. 254–57.

[83] See Garry Wills, "Faith and the Hopefuls", *Sojourners*, March 1988, p. 15.

[84] For references, see Kengor, *God and Ronald Reagan*, p. 277.

[85] The text copy at the Reagan Library reveals that Reagan himself penciled that line into the speech.

[86] Clark, "President Reagan and the Wall", p. 10. Clark says the prayer is called the Universal Peace Prayer of Saint Francis.

March 23, 1983: SDI

On March 23, 1983, two weeks after the Evil Empire speech, in a nationally televised address that surprised most of his own administration, Ronald Reagan announced his Strategic Defense Initiative (SDI), his vision for a space-based, missile-defense system capable of targeting and intercepting Soviet nuclear missiles. Four days before the speech, only Bill Clark, Bud McFarlane, John Poindexter, and science advisor George Keyworth knew what was coming.[87] Even Edward Teller, the father of the hydrogen bomb, who had talked with Reagan about the concept of missile defense as early as 1967, said he was "completely surprised" by the announcement, albeit pleasantly surprised.[88]

The secrecy was necessary because of the problem with unauthorized disclosures. Clark had managed to keep the project secret for quite some time. Among their early discussions, the most crucial meeting came in December 1982 with Reagan, Clark, and the Joint Chiefs of Staff. Reagan posed the "what if" question to the military brass, asking what if America moved away from reliance on offensive deterrence to, instead, reliance on missile defense?

Reagan's remarks that day were jarring. It was not every day that the President of the United States floated the notion of flipping U.S. nuclear doctrine on its head. To be certain they heard the President correctly, one member of the joint chiefs, Admiral James Watkins, immediately followed the meeting with a telephone call to Clark: "Did we just get instructions to take a hard look at missile defense?" Clark

---

[87] On this, Ed Meese is especially informative. See: Meese, *With Reagan*, pp. 101–16. George Keyworth said that on the Saturday before the speech that Wednesday evening, "the only people who were knowledgeable, the only people who knew what was going on", were Reagan, McFarlane, Poindexter, Clark, and himself. That was it. Only those five. "A day or so later [Ray Pollock was] involved." Closer to the time of the speech, Gil Rye also became involved. Rye wasn't involved until the time came to write the necessary messages to various embassies. He confirmed that "it is true that not many people in the Defense Department had any idea that the President was going to make the speech." He said Cap Weinberger and Richard Perle were both in Portugal for a NATO conference. "They knew something was happening," said Keyworth, "but only on Sunday or Monday." "It was most definitely a surprise", summed Keyworth. Source: Keyworth interviewed by Baucom, September 28, 1987, RRL, OHT, Folder 37, Box 8, pp. 27–29.

[88] Interview with Edward Teller, July 15, 2003. Also see transcript of Edward Teller interviewed by Donald Baucom, July 6, 1987, RRL, OHT, Folder 35, Box 8, pp. 7–9.

answered: "Yes." [89] The joint chiefs now had their marching orders, as did the NSC.

Like Reagan, Clark was uncomfortable with the doctrine of MAD—Mutual Assured Destruction, based upon thousands of nuclear weapons aimed at population centers: The existence of such weapons, assumed MAD, would ensure that neither side would launch them and unleash nuclear Armageddon. Thus, all of those missiles with nuclear warheads were considered a "stabilizing" force.

Reagan did not like this theory, and neither did Clark. "Bill understood the president's complete reluctance even to consider the nuclear option", said Secretary Weinberger, whose Department of Defense would take charge of the new defensive initiative. "Bill was strongly supportive of a strategic missile defense that destroyed missiles in the air. He and Ronald Reagan understood that it took only eighteen minutes for the first of those missiles to arrive, and they were not at all comfortable with that." [90]

Other meetings were held on the issue, again with very limited invitations, including a February 11 discussion with Reagan, Clark, Weinberger, McFarlane, and the Joint Chiefs of Staff. [91]

Once the secret was revealed in the March 23 speech, Clark's past work to keep the initiative silent angered some in the administration who had been kept ignorant. Predictably, they began complaining to the press. A week after Reagan announced the initiative, the *New York Times* ran a piece entitled, "Now, Talk of New Strains Among the Top Aides". The article noted the rifts that had opened between Baker, Deaver, and Clark, noting that Clark was "now ascendant as the foreign policy formulator at the White House". [92]

The story was filled with quotes from unnamed Reagan "officials" who complained that Clark had withheld from them "many details" of the SDI proposal, which, reported the *Times*, following the lead of Senator Ted Kennedy (D-MA), was "Mr. Reagan's answer to the film 'Star Wars.'" Several White House aides complained that they had

[89] Edwards, *To Preserve and Protect: The Life of Edwin Meese III*, pp. 61–62.

[90] Interview with Cap Weinberger, April 14, 2005.

[91] See McFarlane's memoirs, *Special Trust*, pp. 229–30.

[92] Steven R. Weisman, "Now, Talk of New Strains Among the Top Aides", *New York Times*, March 31, 1983.

received their "first look at the key proposal" only hours before the speech and consequently were unprepared to inform Congress of the President's intentions. The implication was that Clark was an obstacle to the performance of their duty.

The *Times* played up this angle: Clark was not so much protecting the President's ideas and ability to advance national security, but rather was keeping crucial information from a Congress that had a constitutional right to be informed. "Mr. Clark's practice of keeping information from others had become annoying to both Mr. Baker and Mr. Deaver", the *Times* continued. "The two [Baker and Deaver] were also said to feel strongly that Mr. Clark 'isn't getting material to the president in a timely manner,' according to a senior official."

The assertion angered Clark who, more than any other of Reagan's advisors, made it his mission to get the material to the President. The *Times* piece made it clear that certain people in the administration now, more than ever, had Clark in their crosshairs.

Clark did not keep *everyone* in the dark on SDI. Those who could be trusted to keep secrets were told. For instance, he informed Secretary of State Shultz, but as late as reasonably possible. Keyworth recalled briefing Shultz during a Monday meeting in the Oval Office before the Wednesday evening speech. Shultz responded by calling Keyworth a "lunatic", and did so in front of Reagan. He insisted SDI would never work and "was the idea of a blooming madman".[93] Shultz did not then know that SDI was entirely Reagan's idea.

Shultz was not the only official opposed to SDI. Richard Perle, in particular, was against it. He telephoned George Keyworth and told him to fall on his sword, to confront the President and tell him he had no alternative but to publicly oppose the new idea—*anything* to get the President not to give the speech.[94]

Keyworth said that even Reagan stalwart Fred Ikle was "violently opposed" to SDI.[95] So was Bud McFarlane. If *these* men were against SDI, where could Reagan find any support at all? The answer was Bill Clark, and his backing was fundamental to the initiative's success.

---

[93] Keyworth interviewed by Baucom, September 28, 1987, RRL, OHT, Folder 37, Box 8, p. 25.

[94] Ibid, pp. 25–26 and 35.

[95] Ibid.

The night before the speech was scheduled to be given, recalls Clark, "My deputy, McFarlane, handed me his draft and said, 'Bill, can you talk him [Reagan] out of doing this?' 'No way', I said. . . . No one supported him on this announcement but a few of us." So, McFarlane had done his duty, Clark says. "[He] helped put the words together, as instructed, for that speech. As a military officer, he saluted and drafted for us. Then he came to me almost in tears to say, 'You've got to talk the President out of giving this. It's not ready and violates certain treaties.'" [96] Clark asked McFarlane to reduce his concerns and those of others to a short memo.

Only a half-page in length, the memo was entitled, "DoD Staff Reservations About Your Initiative in the Speech". Signed by Clark, it informed Reagan of the "very strong views of DoD Staff against [the] speech". Particularly upset were Richard Perle and Ron Lehman who, the memo states, had expressed "their most extreme concern at the uproar which the initiative will cause", especially in Europe. In Lehman's words, reported Clark, the speech "will create a furor from which we will never recover".

The Clark-McFarlane memo recommended that Reagan follow up on the concerns of Lehman and Perle by soliciting the assessment of Weinberger and General Vessey, Chairman of the Joint Chiefs of Staff. Clark's handwritten notes at the bottom of the memo state that he did not send the memo to Reagan but instead briefed him in person on the content of the memo the same day.[97]

So, here again, Clark was providing his President with the reaction of all sides to the latest major initiative, including a side that Clark and Reagan did not endorse.

In spite of the serious objections from men he respected, Reagan wanted to proceed with the announcement of the initiative. So, Clark made sure that Reagan did, and further saw to it that the President's wishes were carried out after the speech. SDI was extremely important to Reagan; it was his favorite project, entirely his baby. Cap Weinberger, Ed Meese, and others later credited Clark with ensuring that the President's initiative was carried through.

---

[96] Clark, "President Reagan and the Wall", pp. 8–9.
[97] Draft is contained in Clark's personal files.

Peter Dailey, Clark's teammate, joins Weinberger and Meese in this regard, and underscores a key point on Clark's contribution: "SDI changed the whole balance of political and military thinking in the world", says Dailey. "And Bill drove that policy through. Nobody appreciates or even knows that." Dailey continues: "Ronald Reagan said, 'There has to be another way', meaning a better way than Mutual Assured Destruction.... He had the vision to see that. In response, Bill said, 'The President wants another way, and we need to see he gets it. We'll make it happen, Mr. President.'"

Dailey explains the difference between proposing a policy and implementing one: "You must understand that it's one thing in Washington for a president to have an idea; it's quite another thing to get that idea through. Bill got it [Reagan's vision for SDI] through. He helped drive the decision through the bureaucracy. That was no easy task." [98]

Harry Truman once predicted that his successor in the White House, Dwight Eisenhower, would come to the Oval Office and order, " 'Do this, do that'—and nothing will happen!" Said Truman: "Poor Ike. It won't be anything like the Army!" Reagan was fortunate that he had Bill Clark to get his initiatives off the drawing table, especially in the case of SDI.

Clark steered SDI through intense resistance and ridicule both inside and outside the administration. Opposition came from journalists, academics, scientists, and statesmen, at home and abroad. "I guess I have never seen such opposition to anything", George Keyworth said. "But [Reagan] was absolutely committed." [99] So was Bill Clark.

It is impossible to present all that Clark did as national security advisor—from pushing free-market economic initiatives for Central America, such as the Caribbean Basin Initiative, an early precursor to NAFTA, through to his staunch support of Radio Martí and Radio Free Europe, the latter headquartered in Munich, and successfully led by Jim Buckley, brother of William F. Buckley.

Yet, it is widely agreed, by sources from Edmund Morris to Strobe Talbott, that SDI was the single most powerful tool in bringing the Soviets to the negotiating table, just as Reagan and Clark believed it

---

[98] Interview with Peter Dailey, January 17, 2006.
[99] Keyworth interviewed by Baucom, pp. 25–26, 35.

would, thereby helping end the Cold War.[100] The Soviets have admitted as much: Genrikh Trofimenko, the director of the prestigious Institute for U.S.A. and Canada Studies of the Russian Academy of Sciences, states that "ninety-nine percent of all Russians believe that Reagan won the Cold War because of [his] insistence on SDI".[101]

SDI—The Star Wars initiative, "the idea of a blooming madman"— the vision of a space-based missile defense system that brought the Soviets to the bargaining table—received more derisive press than any other initiative introduced during Bill Clark's years as national security advisor. A significant action that escaped the notice of the press, however, occurred in a part of the world much closer to home, the part of the world Bill Clark calls America's front yard.

---

[100] This is a fact admitted by sources as varied as Lou Cannon, Edmund Morris, George Shultz, Strobe Talbott, John Lewis Gaddis, Raymond Garthoff (to a degree), and top level Soviets such as Eduard Shevardnadze, Alexander Bessmyrtnykh, Vladimir Lukhim, and Genrikh Trofimenko, listed in Kengor, *The Crusader.*

[101] Trofimenko speaking at 1993 Hofstra University conference on the Reagan presidency, published in Eric J. Schmertz et al., eds., *President Reagan and the World* (Westport, CN: Greenwood Press, 1997), p. 138.

CHAPTER 10

Protecting America's Front Yard

In April 1983, Bill Clark alone knew that he would soon be leaving the National Security Council. In that same month, Clark spearheaded an operation notable for both its historical achievement and the secrecy with which it was handled. Only a handful of administration officials were aware of the operation, an important Cold War intervention that saved a South American country from going communist and becoming a strategic asset of the Soviet Union. Clark's close relationship with Reagan helped to make the intervention both possible and successful. That very relationship, however, was causing destructive division in the White House, accelerating Clark's decision to move on, to head back to the ranch.

Only recently, more than twenty years after the fact, have some of the participants in this highly sensitive operation chosen to speak about it. Those participants took almost no notes and kept few written records of their involvement. The covert operation was named Operation Giminich after a prized horse given to President Reagan by the president of Brazil, a country that would play a central role in the effort that is best remembered simply as "Suriname".[1]

Before the invasion of Grenada, the downing of flight KAL 007, and the killing of 241 Marines by a suicide bomber in Beirut, the small South American nation of Suriname received top priority among

---

[1]This chapter is the product of repeated interviews with the participants in this operation. It went through multiple drafts, each time receiving the carefully approved (and incorporated) input of each participant.

the principals in the Reagan National Security Council. An intervention in the country was seen as crucial to stemming the global advance of Soviet communism and keeping Moscow out of America's front yard. Though unrecorded in histories of the time, the struggle for Suriname was a significant contest in the Cold War.

Slightly larger than the state of Georgia, Suriname is a country of 440,000 located in northern South America on the Atlantic Ocean between Guyana (to the west) and French Guiana (to the east), with Brazil sharing its southern border. After Columbus had sighted the coastline in 1498, various colonial powers claimed the area before the Dutch started settling it in 1616. The Dutch brought in African slaves as field hands for the coffee and sugar plantations, and Suriname became a Dutch colony in 1667. Asian workers began arriving after the abolition of slavery in the late nineteenth century. From the legacy of imported labor, the majority of the population is East Indian or Javanese; one-third are Creole. The descendants of runaway black slaves make up ten percent of the population. Many religions are practiced in Suriname: Hinduism, Islam, Dutch Reformed Protestantism, Roman Catholicism, and Judaism.

Suriname gained full independence from Holland on November 25, 1975. Democratic political forces had been taking shape within the country, and by the time of independence there were enough people favoring a parliamentary system for such a government to be formed. While much of Latin America was moving toward socialist dictatorship, Suriname was one of the few countries taking a different course. By 1977, a prime minister had been chosen and subsequently re-elected.

However, on February 25, 1980, a coup led by Desi Bouterse overthrew the elected government. Bouterse appeared to be looking to Grenada and its Marxist prime minister, Maurice Bishop, as a model.[2] At Bishop's suggestion, Bouterse accepted Fidel Castro's overtures and welcomed a Cuban ambassador to the capital, Paramaribo, in 1982. Landing at an airport that had been constructed by the Allies in World War II, Cuban aircraft were making regular flights to Suriname bringing Cuban assistance and advisors. Eventually Castro's security personnel began training and serving as Bouterse's bodyguards, while

---

[2] Jack Anderson and Dale Van Atta, "Suriname Becoming Another Cuba", *Washington Post*, December 2, 1985, p. C17.

Surinamese officials flew to Cuba for instruction.[3] It was only a matter of time before Bouterse implemented the Fidel Castro methods of governing.

Many of Suriname's citizens were unhappy with the sudden disappearance of their young democracy. Voices throughout the country and in the Netherlands criticized the new regime. In response, in December 1982, Bouterse ordered the arrest and execution of fifteen prominent opposition leaders; among them were union officials, physicians, journalists, and attorneys.

The United States and the Netherlands reacted to the executions by suspending economic relations with the Bouterse regime, a terrible blow to Suriname's economy. The Netherlands had been providing $100 million annually in foreign aid, which the small nation depended upon. The country also relied upon American interests in its bauxite mines, first tapped after World War I when the U.S. firm ALCOA started excavating bauxite deposits in the eastern region of the country. During World War II, more than seventy-five percent of U.S. bauxite imports came from Suriname.[4]

The American and Dutch economic sanctions turned Bouterse even more to Havana, and the Reagan National Security Council took notice. In a memorandum to President Reagan, Clark wrote, "Cuba, in its role as a Soviet pawn, is rapidly increasing its influence with the Suriname government." He informed Reagan that five agreements "covering a wide variety of fields" had been signed between Cuba and Suriname beginning in 1982. "Apparently," continued the memo, "the Cubans believe they will be tilling fertile soil and that their prospects are good for Cubanizing Surinamese society."[5]

Cuban ambassador Oswaldo Cardenas, a senior intelligence officer who met frequently with Maurice Bishop and Michael Manley of

---

[3] Ibid.

[4] Data from the U.S. State Department's country profile of Suriname.

[5] "Memorandum for the President, Subject: Operation Giminich", from William P. Clark, Assistant to the President for National Security Affairs. Clark says that the memo was drafted by CIA staff officer Al Sapia-Bosch. Note: My copy of this three-page, double-spaced memo is a draft that lists the dates "April 18 or 25, 1983" at the top. This is not the date in which the draft was delivered to Reagan. The draft is a summary of what happened through August 1983. I am not in possession of the final draft. Nonetheless, the document is extremely helpful in providing information on the effort.

Jamaica, had become a close advisor to Bouterse, Clark reported. Cardenas, averred Clark, was probably influential in persuading Bouterse to travel secretly to Cuba in May 1982. That visit, relayed to Clark by American intelligence, was highlighted by a "long session" with Fidel Castro, who asked Bouterse to work against the spread of U.S. influence in the Caribbean.[6]

U.S. intelligence also discovered that a Soviet embassy had been designated for Suriname.[7] The Kremlin had selected a building for the embassy and had plans to seek full diplomatic representation. The Soviets were negotiating an arrangement with Bouterse that included various forms of assistance, such as doctors, teachers, advisors, and military equipment. Karl Hubenthal, an American missionary in Suriname, recalls the genuine concern among some of the citizenry over the encroachments of the Soviets. "People were fearful that the country would become a Soviet satellite."[8]

There was another important player in the mix: Moammar Kaddafi. U.S. intelligence found that Libya had packed three transport planes with arms and communications equipment for Suriname, just as preparations were being made for the opening of the Soviet embassy. Libya's participation raised the stakes, says Clark. "We were in a foot race", he adds. "That's another reason why we had to move so quickly. Time was of the essence."

Suriname's Strategic Implications

The fate of Suriname was important to the national security of the United States. With its nearly 240 miles of coastline along the Atlantic, Suriname could become another Cuba, which the Soviets used to stage their maritime surveillance aircraft, employed to track U.S. submarines carrying nuclear missiles. American subs hid in the south and mid-Atlantic within launching distance of the Soviet Union. In trying to locate the subs, Soviet aircraft had a limited range from their bases in Cuba, a major source of frustration for the Soviet military. Yet, if the Kremlin could secure a foothold in Suriname, its

---

[6] Ibid.
[7] See Reed, *At the Abyss*, p. 271.
[8] Interview with Karl Hubenthal, September 9, 2005.

problem of reaching the mid-Atlantic could be resolved. The Soviet Union could greatly enhance its surveillance capability.

Clark reported to Reagan that the focus of his concern over Suriname was that the Cubans, and through them the Soviets, would establish a base on the northern tip of South America. Such an outcome would give the Russians greater ability not only to gather intelligence, but also to control influence over shipping in the area. "Because of Suriname's strategic location," he wrote, "the Cubans and Soviets would have the potential to control the Southern Caribbean and endanger shipping lanes", including those used for the transit of crucial commodities, such as petroleum from Venezuela, to U.S. ports on the Gulf Coast. Clark warned Reagan and the NSC principals that Cuba and the Soviet Union were moving to secure an outpost to spread their political and military might throughout the western hemisphere.[9]

In 1982–1983 some in the Reagan administration were concerned about the possibility of the Cold War becoming a hot war. Clark had studied the work of Harvard Sovietologist Richard Pipes, who in the 1970s examined possible war scenarios for the U.S. government. According to Pipes, the Soviet leadership was confident it could win a war with the United States through both conventional and nuclear superiority. Clark found Pipes convincing, to the consternation of some in the White House who feared that any talk of war could provoke the Russians and panic the public. Clark, however, considered it his duty to inform the President of any appropriate measures that could keep America prepared for possible all-out war.

The anxiety over a possible war with Russia was heightened by Soviet and Cuban activities aimed at expanding communism in the western hemisphere. In the 1970s, when Peru's military overturned its constitutional government, the United States suspended relations, prompting Peru's new junta to turn to the Soviets for military assistance, which included weapons and officer training. The Soviets were also providing aircraft, tanks, and artillery to Nicaragua, where a large airfield was being constructed west of Managua with a runway adequate for large military transports and bombers, as well as revetments for fighter aircraft. The Sandinista government in Managua, bolstered by a large Cuban presence, was flexing its new military muscle to

---

[9] William P. Clark, "Memorandum for the President, Subject: Operation Giminich".

impress El Salvador and Honduras to the north and defenseless Costa Rica to the south. It was already supporting the communist guerillas attempting to take over El Salvador. The Reagan administration did not want Suriname added to the growing list of Soviet assets.

Beyond Cold War strategic considerations, there were also fears within the Reagan NSC that U.S. citizens in Suriname, primarily those connected to the embassy and ALCOA, could be taken hostage by the increasingly bellicose regime. As one Pentagon source said: "We had ascertained that Bouterse had the ability and possibly the intention to seize some or all of them [U.S. citizens], and we could have a hostage situation there." [10] America was especially sensitive to this concern: Only four years earlier during the Carter administration, 52 Americans were taken hostage and held for 444 days in Iran.

Reagan's Team Responds

Once the Reagan team decided that they needed to turn back the Soviet-Cuban presence in Suriname, Clark and his staff considered courses of action that for the most part had been developed by the CIA. The agency had been examining options for several months in consultation with various departments of the government.

Concurrently, the CIA had undertaken an effort to build up an alternative Surinamese government, which was being formed in exile chiefly in the Netherlands and was led by a highly respected Surinamese physician named Dr. Henk Chin A Sen. The plan being developed by the CIA called for the exile group to enter Suriname immediately behind a paramilitary force, in order to be ready to take over the government once Bouterse was ousted.

The primary target of the assault by this paramilitary force was a fortified compound near a beach in Paramaribo, which held Bouterse and his followers. There were two possible attack scenarios: one was an assault from the sea, by which troops would storm the beach and take the compound; the other was to take the World War II era airfield. The concern with the second plan was that it involved a much longer travel distance to the capital and the compound, and the success of an attack required surprise.

---

[10] Interview with (Ret.) Gen. Paul Gorman, September 15, 2005.

It was concluded that the airfield had to be taken in order to insert the government-in-exile and to prevent its use by Bouterse as an escape route or by Cuban troops should the conflict be prolonged. Still, the negative remained: the long drive from the airfield to the compound left open the possibility of ambushes, destroyed bridges, and other means of counterattack. In the end, it was recommended that both scenarios should be employed—the airfield would be taken and the paramilitary force would *also* take the beach.

The composition of the force to be used needed to be determined. There was no question among the planners that there had to be at least a small contingent of armed Surinamese drawn from the exile community. Finding the candidates was not easy because the Surinamese are a peaceful people, generally not prone to violence; nevertheless, a group was eventually identified for training.

The Surinamese force required the addition of more troops. The planners looked elsewhere in South America: the Venezuelan intelligence service had a commando unit of about one thousand men. Initial discussions indicated that the Venezuelans would make this unit available for the assault on the airfield and the subsequent thrust up the road to the compound. Within several weeks, however, the Venezuelans reneged. The possibility of using Hondurans was discussed, but no conclusion was reached.

Sources say that it was Duane "Dewey" Clarridge, the chief of the CIA's Latin American Division in the Directorate of Operations and Bill Casey's "right arm" for Latin America, who came up with the idea of using South Koreans—a suggestion met by mirth and wonderment inside the agency. Yet, Clarridge's suggestion was not without merit: he argued that the South Koreans had a large fishing fleet operating off northern South America, which occasionally sailed into Paramaribo to replenish supplies. Also, the South Korean government was very friendly with the United States, and the Korean Marine Corps was tough and well-trained. Clarridge proposed that two companies of South Korean Marines be transferred at sea to the South Korean fishing fleet, where they would be concealed. The fleet would make a routine stop in Paramaribo and, once darkness settled, would undertake the assault on the compound. For support, the CIA dispatched paramilitary officers undercover to Paramaribo to reconnoiter compound headquarters, an adjacent garrison, the airfield, and the road to Paramaribo.

The plan did not envisage the use of U.S. military personnel, but would be supported by a few CIA experts and would have American backing financially and politically. The Department of Defense was, however, drawing up a contingency plan for the evacuation of U.S. citizens from the embassy in Paramaribo and from the ALCOA plant.

Clark carefully considered the operation recommended by the CIA. He described it to Reagan and regularly updated the President on the plan as it progressed: The plan, the national security advisor told the President, was to move into Suriname with a paramilitary force and "carry out a rapid operation to seize the Surinamese military head-quarters [the compound], the military garrison, and the international airport and to remove Bouterse".[11]

Here was the embodiment of what political analyst Charles Krau-thammer had once famously dubbed "the Reagan Doctrine": the United States would provide support to surrogate, indigenous forces, short of employing American troops. Under no circumstances would U.S. soldiers be sent in.

In keeping with the NSC process, Secretaries Weinberger and Shultz were fully (and separately) briefed on the CIA's proposed plan. Shultz, in his briefing, said almost nothing, but did not openly object to the plan. However, those present for the briefing sensed from Shultz's silence that he rejected a paramilitary solution. Moreover, Clark himself was not ready to recommend the CIA proposal to President Reagan.

Learning of Shultz's attitude at the briefing (Clark was not present), Clark's mind raced back to a phone call he had received from former President Richard Nixon a few months earlier. When Nixon was informed that his former secretary of labor had been named to replace Al Haig as Reagan's secretary of state, Nixon telephoned Clark from New York: "Judge, tell Ron there's one problem I want to warn him about with George Shultz: When things go bad, he'll say that he had not been briefed or informed." NSC and State Department sources acknowledge that Shultz was routinely briefed and at times was even "over-informed" of all NSC interagency matters, usually by Clark him-self. Indeed, Clark conferred with Shultz several times daily.

For some time, Clark and Reagan had been considering an alter-native to the CIA plan. The alternative plan called for Clark to visit

---

[11] William P. Clark, "Memorandum for the President, Subject: Operation Giminich".

the leaders of Suriname's neighbors, Venezuela and Brazil, and attempt to persuade *them* to take the lead in solving the Suriname problem. One course was to request that Venezuela and Brazil "mount a joint force to deal with the issue"—a joint military operation to enter Suriname and remove Bouterse.[12] The United States would support this plan politically and financially but not militarily. Another course was to ask them to "purchase" Bouterse by offering him aid.[13] Either way, the hope was that the Venezuelans and Brazilians could be encouraged to clean up their own neighborhood rather than face some form of U.S. military intervention.

There is an essential component to Clark looking to Brazil for possible cooperation, one that underscores the importance of personal diplomacy in foreign policy: Clark was confident of Brazil's assistance, certain that the president of Brazil, General João Baptista Figueiredo, would do his best for Ronald Reagan based on the excellent rapport established between the two men. Five months earlier, in December, when Reagan and Clark met with Figueiredo in Brasilia, they set aside their formal talking points and chatted about life, and horses. The three rode together, and Reagan made the mistake of admiring one particular horse—Giminich—a gesture which, in that part of the world, is understood by the host as an opportunity to offer a gift. Soon after, the horse was shipped thousands of miles to the United States as a gift to the American President from the Brazilian President. Clark had not forgotten that gesture. He had also recalled that the two men discussed the menace of Soviet expansionism in the area.

Both Clark and Reagan placed great stock in personal diplomacy. As Ronald Reagan said later, "Personal relations matter more in international politics than the historians would have us believe. Of course, nations will follow their overriding interest on the great issues regardless, but there are many important occasions when the trust built up over several years of contacts makes a real difference to how things turn out."[14] Indeed, says Clark, in his conversations with leaders,

---

[12] Ibid.

[13] For the record, Reagan and Clark never contemplated assassinating Bouterse, a non-option for a number of reasons.

[14] Ronald Reagan, "Margaret Thatcher and the Revival of the West", *National Review*, May 19, 1989.

Ronald Reagan came across as charming and honest. Reagan frequently created longtime friendships from a one-time meeting, as was the case with the prime ministers of Britain, Canada, Japan, India, and Australia, and later with Mikhail Gorbachev and others. Reagan also made a good and lasting first impression with the President of Brazil, and Clark suspected that the friendship between the two men might now pay dividends in the Suriname mission.

Reagan and Clark knew they had to keep their planning completely secret, even within the White House. There were those in the administration who might divulge the information to the press. Said one NSC member of these sources: "Had they known [of the mission], it would've been in the *Washington Post*."

The plan was in danger of being exposed at the final White House meeting on the operation between Reagan, Clark, and members of the National Security Planning Group (NSPG). Don Regan, then secretary of the treasury, entered the Oval Office as Clark and his team were briefing Reagan on the final plan. Clark and the others grew quiet. Secretary Regan sensed from the sudden silence that something was afoot. The President made a snap judgment: he decided not to keep the information from Regan. He told the secretary about the diplomatic mission, but asked him for secrecy. Regan kept his word. Operation Giminich was about to become the best kept secret in Washington.

After these White House meetings, the CIA's deputy director John McMahon told Dewey Clarridge to report to Clark in the Situation Room for a meeting on the Suriname situation. Clarridge would be taking a trip with Bill Clark, an urgent weekend flight to Venezuela and Brazil.

The Trip

Clark arranged to fly to South America in a nondescript Air Force plane, but Ronald Reagan insisted he use the presidential jet, which Reagan believed would reinforce Clark's authority to his hosts. The aircraft was loaded late at night inside the hangar at Andrews Air Force Base outside Washington. To conceal further the true nature of the mission, Clark brought along his wife, giving the appearance of going on a routine diplomatic trip.

In addition to Bill and Joan Clark, those making the trip included Dewey Clarridge; Vice Admiral John Poindexter, a member of the NSC staff and future national security advisor; Walt Raymond, an NSC staff member and former CIA officer; Al Sapia-Bosch, another NSC representative and a former Latin America specialist from the CIA; and Lieutenant General Paul Gorman, Assistant to the Chairman of the Joint Chiefs of Staff. Gorman was slated for promotion in May to command U.S. SOUTHCOM in Panama, joint headquarters responsible for Central and South America. Gorman was also the principal liaison between the Joint Chiefs of Staff and the NSC, State Department, and the CIA, and regularly attended NSC meetings. The State Department would be represented by the respective ambassadors at the two destinations.

The group first landed in Caracas, Venezuela, to meet with the president of the country. The plane touched down at nightfall and was parked out of sight, "in the weeds someplace", as one member of the group remembered vaguely. The delegation headed to a hotel and joined up with William Luers, U.S. Ambassador to Venezuela. From there, Clark and Luers left for the office of President Herrera Campins.

At a private meeting with only Luers and Campins, Clark shared intelligence on the Soviet-Cuba-Suriname connection. This was a "Castro operation directed out of Havana", he told Campins. The goal was to draw a line from Havana to Paramaribo as a "choke point" against the United States. Clark described Soviet interests in the area. "A Soviet presence there [in Suriname] is completely unacceptable", he told Campins.

In seeking to enlist Venezuela's support, Clark reminded the President that the United States was the single largest buyer of Venezuelan petroleum, and a good friend. He played the friendship aspect to the hilt. Nonetheless, Campins turned Clark down; Venezuela would not partake in any kind of an operation against Suriname, the Soviet Union, or Cuba.

Venezuela's reluctance stemmed in part from previous damaging leaks from Washington, specifically regarding covert Venezuelan assistance to the government of El Salvador, which was fighting the FMLN[15] communist guerrillas. The Salvadoran regime had received negative

---

[15] Farabundo Martí para la Liberación Nacional.

press because of brutal tactics employed by certain elements in the military. At the same time, the regime was successfully thwarting communist rebels who, if they came to power, would likely be even more vicious and certainly more destabilizing to Latin America. Venezuela's cautious, secretive assistance had been leaked to the press by certain Democrats in Congress who hoped to torpedo Reagan's Central America policy. As Clark later noted, "Our reputation for maintaining promised confidentiality had been gravely damaged by this and similar incidents of premature disclosure."

Clark tried to assure Venezuela (and Brazil) that the United States could preserve the confidentiality of this mission. Venezuela, however, was not reassured. Campins feared the media reaction if it were revealed that his nation had participated in moves against Suriname.[16]

The next morning the group met at Luers' residence to fine-tune their briefings, which would next be given to the Brazilians. The group flew on to Brasilia, where they were welcomed by Langhorne "Tony" Motley, an ex–Air Force officer who was U.S. Ambassador to Brazil. Motley was born and raised in Brazil, he spoke fluent Portuguese and was very close to the Brazilian President and many other top officials from the executive branch and legislature. "Motley was important to this meeting", said one member of the delegation. "I can't stress that enough. He knew these guys really well."

When Clark's group arrived, Motley was hosting a delegation from the U.S. Department of Commerce at his residence, and the Clark visit had to be concealed from them. Consequently, Motley and his wife prudently shuffled the Clark team around while entertaining the delegation from Commerce. "It was quite a performance", recalls one member with a laugh.

Clark, Clarridge, Gorman, and Motley met with the Brazilian leadership, with Motley doing the interpreting. The briefings took place at the Granja do Torto, the small bungalow Brazilian President Figueiredo preferred over the presidential palace. Joining Figueiredo was General Octavio Medeiros, chief of Brazil's intelligence service, and General Danilo Venturini, the national security advisor to Figueiredo.[17]

---

[16] William P. Clark, "Memorandum for the President, Subject: Operation Giminich".

[17] There was a fourth Brazilian present, whose name today escapes the U.S. participants.

Clark began by extending Reagan's personal greetings and gratitude for the hospitality shown to him in Brasilia five months earlier, with special reference to their horseback riding. Figueiredo responded by acknowledging his fondness for Reagan and asked that Clark convey his warmest regards. Clark and his team then made their presentation to seek Brazil's assistance. Clark gave basically the same presentation to Figueiredo that he had made to Campins in Venezuela, again reiterating that a Soviet presence in Suriname should not be tolerated. He made clear President Reagan's strong desire that something be done about Soviet plans to expand into the region. He had Figueiredo's attention, especially when he referred to the mission as Operation Giminich, which heartened the Brazilian President. Clarridge briefed the Brazilians on the situation in Suriname and its broader strategic implications, with special focus on the ramifications of a Soviet military base.

Next came General Gorman's briefing.[18] Gorman had put together what he later called "a *representation* of an operations plan to deal with a situation like that in Suriname". He presented "crude but believable sketches" of U.S. military capabilities on a map that resembled Suriname. He portrayed a situation in which U.S. citizens were at risk of being taken hostage by a brutal dictator, and said that America was "prepared to do whatever is necessary to protect those American civilians". Gorman displayed military symbols for drop zones and an amphibious landing, plus "operational arrows" surrounding a town. Such maneuvers could be carried out by U.S. forces from bases in the United States, Panama, and from U.S. ships in the Atlantic fleet.

His was not, says Gorman, a "real plan" in the sense that it bore any resemblance to an actual U.S. operations plan. However, his briefing was a "realistic representation" of American capabilities, "based on one possibility, not a plan" to invade Suriname with U.S. forces from Panama. "We never actually told anyone in that room that we were going to use military force", says Clark. "We never said we were going to activate war plans."

Gorman remarked to his Brazilian hosts that the U.S. military was intimately familiar with the large airfield in Suriname constructed during World War II to ferry U.S. aircraft to North Africa. He calculated

---

[18] The information that follows is taken from an interview with Gorman on September 15, 2005, plus subsequent communication on other occasions.

that it could be used to land a lot of large aircraft "in a helluva hurry". That landing strip, Gorman told his hosts, was "still strategically and operationally significant in that region". A U.S. Airborne division could be landed there. As Clark notes today, "You can draw all kinds of inferences from a drop zone." The Brazilians immediately did.

The primary goal of his "representation", explained Gorman, was to persuade the Brazilians to take care of the Bouterse problem on their own, to make it unnecessary for the United States to organize and orchestrate a major deployment. "It would be far better for them to do this", said Gorman. "For heaven's sake, why would they not want to? This was a very unstable situation on their border." The politically shaky Brazilian leadership could not afford this kind of chaos to its north.

The Reagan message was unmistakable: If Brazil did not intervene, the U.S. military might be forced to. President Figueiredo appeared to understand, and later stated to Clark that he did not want to disappoint his "good friend" President Reagan.

This, however, was not the complete story. Clark did not show all of his cards. The reality was that the United States would not take direct military action. Privately, Reagan and Clark determined beforehand not to carry out an invasion with U.S. troops; they wanted to avoid such an operation at all costs, consistent with Reagan doctrine.[19]

Clark admits that though the briefings were certainly not a bluff, "there was some 'stretch' in the plan—to get them [Brazil] alerted and moving." Reagan and Clark hoped that the image of U.S. troops parachuting into Suriname for whatever reason, including being part of an evacuation force, would persuade the Brazilians to take care of business in their own neighborhood, without the intervention of the United States. President Reagan, in his last Oval Office briefing before the team left for Venezuela that night, admonished that "we must guard against reinforcing the Latin American contention that we are the overbearing colossus to the north."

Brazil's brass was taken aback at the specter of U.S. forces crashing into South America. As one member of Clark's group put it: "The Brazilians' consternation was manifest. They would've preferred to ignore the problem. But the presentations clearly made it impossible to ignore."

---

[19] See Reed, *At the Abyss*, pp. 271–72.

Participants recall Figueiredo's reaction; he was obviously nervous and concerned.[20]

The Brazilians excused themselves to the kitchen, where they convened privately. They returned forty-five minutes later with their response. President Figueiredo agreed that his country would take action. He would not necessarily field an invasion force. He did not want a military operation, either Brazilian or American. Yet, he and his colleagues also dreaded a Soviet presence next door. They would do something, they told Clark—they would keep it within the family; they would keep it local. In turn, Clark expressed his President's gratitude and promised to maintain strict confidentiality concerning the meetings, the plans, and the commitment—which explains why this story has not been written before this time.

As Clark reported back to Reagan, the Brazilians agreed "to cooperate and undertake a policy to diffuse the Cuban and Soviet threat". Specifically, wrote Clark in his memo to Reagan, the Brazilians would offer Bouterse "extensive assistance and cooperation in economic development, trade, education, technical assistance and military aid."[21] Their on-the-spot estimate, cooked up in the kitchen that day, was $25 million. For Suriname, Brazilian aid would be more attractive than Cuban aid, since Cuba was dependent on Russia. The support Fidel had promised to Bouterse had been slow in coming, making a Brazilian offer even more enticing.

To make the deal with Bouterse, Brazil's leaders crafted a "carrot and stick" approach, Clark says. They dispatched to Paramaribo one of their best ambassadors, Luis Philippe Lampreia, who later became Brazil's foreign minister, to offer the aid package. Then, only days later, Brazil deployed a military unit on its northern border. One pair of investigative reporters claimed that "literally under the gun", Bouterse agreed to decrease the Cuban presence in his country in return for a multi-million-dollar aid deal with Brazil.[22]

---

[20] Ibid.

[21] William P. Clark, "Memorandum for the President, Subject: Operation Giminich".

[22] Anderson and Van Atta reported that the aid totaled $300 million. The CIA contact on the deal insists that the $300 million figure is inaccurate, and that the aid package was always $25 million.

According to U.S. intelligence, in August 1983, only four months after Brazil's intervention, Cuban Ambassador Cardenas reported to Havana that there had been a noticeable decline in Suriname's relations with Cuba and the Soviet Union since the opening of a dialogue between Suriname and Brazil. National Security Advisor Clark offered his assessment in a memo to President Reagan: "Your policy was a distinct diplomatic and personal success. Not a shot was fired! Cuban influence was severely reduced." [23]

The Rocky Road Ahead

Clark was not surprised when he was criticized for his activities related to Operation Giminich by some members of the administration. Jim Baker, who controlled scheduling for Air Force One and Two, became angry when he found out that Clark had taken off for South America in the presidential jet without his approval, even though the plane had been ordered by the President himself. When Clark returned to Andrews Air Force Base, a staff member asked him: "My gosh, what have you done to Baker and Gergen?" Apparently, both men were quite unhappy with the perceived unauthorized nature of Clark's trip. If to spare their feelings, however, Clark had informed them in advance of Operation Giminich, there would have been an unacceptable chance that the trip could have been leaked or even jettisoned. "Sorry," answered Clark, "but it was a matter of national security. It was in the national interest that we did what we did at the President's request, including his order for secrecy."

Jim Baker did not see it that way. According to one source, Baker informed Leslie Stahl, at CBS's *Evening News with Dan Rather*, that Clark in an unauthorized excursion had created further division between the NSC and other senior staff. Baker did not tell Stahl about the Suriname endeavor because it was unknown to him. Operation Giminich remained a secret for the life of the Reagan administration and beyond.

Neither Bullet Nor Inch

No matter the personal political fallout, the Suriname operation was an example of attempted communist and Soviet expansion being blocked

---

[23] William P. Clark, "Memorandum for the President, Subject: Operation Giminich".

from a politically and strategically important outpost in the western hemisphere. Like his father and his grandfather, Bill Clark had kept the bad guys at bay without a shot being fired.

Another operation in the region later that year did make use of an invasion scheme similar to the one drawn up for Suriname. On October 13, 1983, the Marxist leader of Grenada, Maurice Bishop, was killed in a coup led by members of the communist party and Grenadian army who were acting with the support of Cuba and Russia. Bishop had just returned from Washington, where he had met with Clark. There is some conjecture that this visit might have precipitated his assassination.

The power grab gave America both a reason and an opportunity to push the Cubans and the Soviets out of Grenada and diminish their influence in the Caribbean. Though these strategic considerations were important, also a source of concern was the safety of one thousand students, most of whom were American, at the medical school on the island.

At the request of the Organization of Eastern Caribbean States and the governor general of Grenada, the Reagan administration sent troops on October 25, 1983, about a week after Clark had resigned from the National Security Council. American forces met with resistance from both Grenadian and Cuban military personnel, but, within a month, the island was under U.S. control. By mid-December the Marxist leadership had been replaced with a pro-western, constitutional government and American troops had returned home.

Thus two communist takeovers in Latin America were prevented in 1983 by the Reagan administration. Reagan's team would also keep Marxism out of El Salvador and undermine it in Nicaragua, where the Sandinistas stood for election and were defeated in 1990. Ronald Reagan had repeatedly said that he was committed to ceding "not one inch" of territory to communism anywhere, least of all in America's front yard. Near the end of his administration, on August 15, 1988, he could declare that in the 2,765 days of his administration "not one inch of ground has fallen to the communists." He pointed to Grenada, but he did not mention Suriname;[24] yet, the action there offered

---

[24] Reagan, "Remarks at the Republican National Convention", New Orleans, Louisiana, August 15, 1988. He updated the tally in an October 1, 1988 speech at Georgetown.

another stark contrast to the record of prior administrations: From 1974 to 1979, the Soviets had added, according to slightly varying accounts, ten or eleven nations to their list of client states.[25]

In the 1970s, Ronald Reagan often cited data from Freedom House marking the total number of free and unfree nations in the world. In 1980, the year before his presidency began, there were 56 democracies in the world. In 1990, the year after he left, there were 76. Those figures continued an upward trajectory, rising to 91 in 1991, 99 in 1992, 108 in 1993, and 114 in 1994. Overall, this was a doubling since the Reagan administration began. By 1994, sixty percent of the world's countries were democracies. By comparison, in the mid-1970s, the figure was less than thirty percent.[26] Among these new ventures in freedom: 88 percent of Latin American and Caribbean nations are democracies, as are 92 percent of South American nations. This world-wide explosion of freedom is one of the great stories in the history of humanity, and surely one of the grandest developments of recent years.

Some credit for this worldwide explosion of freedom must be laid at the doorstep of the Reagan administration, with Bill Clark at the helm of the NSC.

---

[25] Reagan NSC member Constantine Menges says that between 1975 and 1980, eleven new "pro-Soviet regimes" were established. Tom Henriksen of the Hoover Institution says that from 1974–1979 the Soviets "incorporated ten countries into their orbit". Source: Constantine C. Menges speaking at 1993 Hofstra University conference on the Reagan presidency, published in Schmertz, *President Reagan and the World*, pp. 29–30; and Thomas Henriksen, "The lessons of Afghanistan", *Washington Times*, December 29, 1999.

[26] This data was provided by Freedom House staff, April 8, 2002.

CHAPTER 11

Policy for the Pacific Rim

During Bill Clark's tenure as national security advisor, U.S. policies in Asia were substantially improved and balanced, says David Laux, China hand for the NSC, and later Chairman of the American Institute in Taiwan, *de facto* U.S. "Embassy" in dealings with Taiwan. Clark agrees. "Some of the most successful of our foreign affairs policies", says Clark, "were those implemented by the East Asia team at the NSC, and their counterparts at the Departments of State and Defense, substantially because of their ability to work in harmony. The whole operation was a model of how to coordinate policy formulation and implementation." Many credit the improvement in U.S. relations in East Asia to the efficiency and dependability of the team, led by senior NSC staff member Gaston Sigur, U.S. expert on Japan.[1]

Japan's Rising Sun

The overriding priority of President Reagan's foreign policy in Asia was the U.S. alliance with Japan. NSC's Gaston Sigur, special assistant

---

[1] Sigur was a legend among Asia hands during the Reagan Administration. A product of the Army language school's Japanese program in World War II, he later earned his Ph.D. at the University of Michigan in Japanese Studies. He served in Afghanistan and elsewhere along with his eleven years in Japan. Following his stint at the NSC he was appointed Assistant Secretary of State for East Asian Affairs. Gifted with an enormous sense of humor and great common sense, he was a natural leader, highly respected by his colleagues at the NSC and State and Defense. He began teaching at George Washington University in 1972, and the university named its Center for Asian Affairs, established in 1991, after him. Sigur taught there until his untimely death in 1995.

to the President for Asian affairs, was particularly valuable in nurturing and strengthening that relationship, says Laux. Sigur, during his eleven years of service in Japan, had become a good personal friend of Yasuhiro Nakasone—which in turn, led to the warm personal relationship between President Reagan and Nakasone, Prime Minister of Japan from 1982 to 1987. The leadership styles were similar; the two exchanged frequent phone calls and messages. The "Ron-Yasu" friendship bolstered U.S. trade agreements with the dynamic Japanese economy, and strengthened the vital defense relationship between Japan and the United States, of great importance to both countries.

In 1982, Japan's economy surpassed that of the USSR, an amazing accomplishment, continues Laux, given that the USSR was roughly two hundred times larger than Japan in area, had two and one half times as many people, and many, many more natural resources. Japan had virtually no natural resources other than the brains, energy, and ingenuity of its people, and a democratic form of government.

The strengthened relationship provided an important advantage to U.S. foreign policy making: the U.S. and Japanese economies together provided tremendous economic clout in dealing with problems of all sizes, not just with developing nations in Asia, but throughout the world. "Neither we, nor Japan, nor anyone else gave this accomplishment the praise and attention it deserved in the Cold War", says Laux. But President Reagan, Bill Clark, and Cap Weinberger understood its importance. This solid underpinning provided the rock-like foundation on which Reagan's overall Asia policy was based.

"Balancing" the Two Chinas

The other priority, and substantially more complex problem, was to improve U.S. relations with mainland China without weakening support for Taiwan—to promote greater balance in our relations with Beijing and Taipei.

When the Chinese Communists, with weapons and assistance from the Soviets, overran mainland China in 1949–1950, General Chiang Kai-Shek, with troops, government functionaries, refugees and families totaling some two million people, fled across the ninety-mile Taiwan Strait to Taiwan (Formosa), declaring Taipei the capital of the Republic of China in exile. Taiwan and its six million people had been returned to China five years earlier, in 1945, after fifty years of occupation by Japan. The Republic of China claimed to be the legitimate government of the mainland Chinese and hoped for the day when the United States would assist them in returning.

With the outbreak of the war in Korea in June 1950, the United States had the 7th fleet patrol the Taiwan Strait to protect Taiwan against any invasion attempt by Chinese Communist forces. The U.S. continued to recognize and support the Republic of China on Taiwan through the 1950s and 1960s, with mainland China the renegade.

In 1971, the United Nations granted the seat "Nationalist" China had held, for the twenty-one years it had been in exile, to Communist-ruled Beijing, ousting the Republic altogether. Reagan, then Governor of California, wrote directly to President and Madame Chiang Kai-Shek, whom the Reagans knew personally: "Mrs. Reagan and I want you to know how deeply shocked and disappointed we were by the completely immoral action of the U.N. General Assembly." [2]

In that same year, National Security Advisor Kissinger made a secret trip to China to pave the way for improved relations and a visit by President Richard Nixon. In 1972, Nixon made his famous trip to China and, as part of a strategic effort to widen the split that had developed between China and the USSR, began the process of improving U.S. relations with China. The "Shanghai Communiqué" of February 1972 was signed, in which both sides pledged to work toward the normalization of relations. "Representational offices" were established in Beijing and Washington in May 1971, but the arrangement stopped short of establishing formal diplomatic relations.

During the Carter administration, the United States joined the herd of nations switching diplomatic recognition from Taiwan to mainland China—effective January 1, 1979. With formal diplomatic relations with the Republic of China government on Taiwan being severed, a private organization, the American Institute in Taiwan (AIT) was established and placed under contract to the State Department to manage the relationship. Taiwan established a similar counterpart organization

---

[2] Reagan wrote a June 12, 1979 letter to a friend saying that he supported a "bettering of relations with mainland China." However, he felt that "the dumping of a long time friend and ally, the Republic of China on Taiwan", was unforgivable. Reagan letter to Lorraine and Elwood Wagner, June 12, 1979, YAF collection.

entitled the Coordination Council for North American Affairs (CCNAA).

Congress, worried that the Carter government had gone too far, passed a unique bill entitled the Taiwan Relations Act in April 1979, which laid out, as a matter of law, the terms under which U.S. relations with Taiwan would be conducted. The Act incorporated the American Institute in Taiwan as the instrument for conducting these relations.

Ronald Reagan's sympathies through all this were almost entirely with Taiwan. He felt Carter's recognition of the People's Republic of China was premature, and frequently described Taiwan as a "lighthouse" off the coast of China, showing the people of China a better way of life, with far more freedom and economic prosperity than the communist system allowed. Moreover, Reagan feared that favoring China over Taiwan would allow the balance of power in Asia to tip too far toward China, thereby threatening the security of America's non-communist allies in the region.

In case anyone were in doubt on where Reagan's sympathies lay in regard to the two Chinas, he made his position absolutely clear in his campaign for the presidency in 1980. "There will be no more Taiwans", he declared to one audience. "There will be no more betrayals of friends by the United States!" [3] However, Reagan well understood the overall dynamics of the Cold War and the strategic importance of taking advantage of the Sino-Soviet split by continuing to give incentives to China to separate further from the USSR.

Once elected, the new President took early steps to alleviate Chinese concerns. Soon after his inauguration, in March 1981, Reagan sent a personal message to China's Deng Xiaoping through former President Ford, stating he wished to improve U.S. relations with China. This was followed by similar messages carried by Secretary of State Al Haig in the spring, then Vice President Bush in June 1981. Bush had headed the U.S. liaison office in Beijing in earlier years and was liked and highly regarded in China. However, no real response to these overtures was received.

The mainland Chinese had decided to play hardball with the new administration. At the North South Economic Summit held in Cancun, Mexico, in October 1981, the Chinese delivered a bilateral

---

[3] Quoted by Barrett, *Gambling with History*, pp. 206–7.

message to the United States: they were not going to send any Chinese officials of the rank of Vice Minister or above to the United States nor allow U.S. officials Assistant Secretary level or above to visit China until the question of U.S. arms sales to Taiwan was defined.[4] Discussions on nuclear matters, technology transfer, and other matters were also halted. Thus began ten months of tough negotiations, ending with the Taiwan Arms Sales Agreement of August 17, 1982, a genuine compromise on both sides.

The United States agreed to limit the sale of arms to Taiwan to amounts sold in the past, and to diminish them over time (with no length of time specified) in return for China's promise of a peaceful policy toward Taiwan. Deng Xiaoping said privately to Ambassador Hummel in Beijing that the reduction in arms sales "didn't mean by only a dollar per year".[5] The United States informed Deng that the U.S. wouldn't "nickel and dime" China on ordinary troop movements in Fujian Province, but that any significant arms buildup opposite Taiwan would be regarded as a breach of the agreement; in such circumstances the United States would provide Taiwan what it needed to defend itself.[6]

President Reagan, when he approved this agreement, personally dictated a side letter for the record, stating that if China deviated from a peaceful policy and began to station troops or advanced weapons opposite Taiwan, the U.S. would provide Taiwan whatever weapons it would need to defend itself under such circumstances. This letter was kept in Clark's personal safe at the NSC.

President Reagan and Clark privately briefed congressional leaders on these negotiations and the resultant agreement and assured them that if the military balance in the Taiwan Strait changed because of China's development of new sophisticated weapons or acquisition of them from other sources, the President was prepared to make any adjustment necessary to make certain there continued to be a balance of power in the Taiwan Strait.

---

[4] The meeting was attended by President Reagan and Secretary of State Al Haig. Premier Zao Ziyang and Vice Premier and Foreign Minister Huang Hua represented China. Source: David Laux.

[5] An Arthur Hummel memo recording Deng's words, as recalled by David Laux, February 19, 2007.

[6] "Nickel and dime" terminology from Laux, February 19, 2007.

Clark also made a point of being especially cordial to Taiwan's representational office—the Coordination Council for North American Affairs—which Taiwan representatives jokingly referred to as the "Chevy Chase National Athletic Association". He made a point of dropping by Taiwan's celebrations recognizing their national day, and met privately with representatives to pay his respects. He also accepted occasional dinner invitations to private dinners with Fred Chien, head of CCNAA, at Twin Oaks, the magnificent old mansion in northwest Washington, D.C., used by the Taiwan representative for "social" but not "official" functions—personal diplomacy, at which Clark excelled, again at work. Clark also approved the sale of certain defense technologies and systems within the parameters of the Taiwan Arms Sales Agreement.

Clark assigned David Laux to establish private personal liaisons with C. J. Chen, Deputy of Taiwan's representative office on the one hand, and with Ji Chaozhu at the Chinese Embassy on the other, to discuss and "solve" difficult and sensitive problems between the respective governments. These channels proved very useful in dealing creatively with certain difficult and sensitive issues.[7]

Meanwhile, the Sales Agreement initiated a period of great improvement in U.S.-China relations, with Clark playing a key role in planning an exchange of high-level visitors between the two countries. Secretary of State George Shultz went to China in February 1982; the President's Science Advisor, George Keyworth, followed shortly after; Secretary of Commerce Malcolm Baldrige made the trip in May. The U.S. government also increased the level of technologies it would allow American companies to export to China.

"Perhaps one of the best measures of the success of President Reagan's policy toward China and Taiwan during Bill Clark's tenure as national security advisor was that it did not become an 'issue' during the 1984 presidential election campaign", says Laux. Indeed, the relationship

---

[7] Both C. J. Chen and Ji Chaozhu had distinguished careers following their Washington, D.C. assignments. C. J. Chen held several senior positions in Taiwan, including Minister of Foreign Affairs, and was also their top representative in Washington, D.C. Ji Chaozhu was Ambassador to Fiji, and Ambassador to the United Kingdom, and later Under Secretary of the United Nations. In his own autobiography he mentions the "walks on the Connecticut Avenue Bridge" with David Laux in working out solutions to some of our bilateral problems.

between the United States and China, no longer the "Sleeping Giant", continued to improve after Clark's move to the Department of Interior, with Chinese Premier Zhao Ziyang's visit to the U.S. in January 1984; President Reagan's visit to China in May 1984; and Chinese President Li Hsien-nien's visit to the United States in July 1985. And it all started on Bill Clark's watch at the NSC.

Other Nations on the Pacific Rim

During Clark's time at the NSC, the "four economic tigers" of Asia—South Korea, Taiwan, Hong Kong, and Singapore—continued their march toward economic stability accomplished through a combination of democracy or "guided" democracy, and free enterprise—or, put another way, the absence of total dictatorship and state-planned economies. The contrast with their own economy had a psychologically therapeutic impact on China's Deng Xiaoping. Clark and his Asia staff were convinced this was the reason Deng Xiaoping elevated Zhao Ziyang into the job of Premier in 1980, following Zhao's four-year governorship of Szechuan Province. Zhao had turned his province from a rice-deficit province into a rice-surplus province, using private incentives and rewards for results above and beyond state rice production quotas. Deng wanted Zhao to do the same thing on a national basis. Thus began the transformation of China throughout the past twenty-five years, turning it into the world's third-largest economy with prospects of becoming the world's largest.

South Korea focused on the development of its economic sector, with the protection of an American military presence, leading it to its increasingly vibrant and powerful hi-tech economy. Meanwhile, North Korea's focus on its military and neglect of economic development has made it an economic disaster area—sustained largely by economic aid from China, the USSR and, more recently, South Korea.

The ANZUS (Australia, New Zealand, United States) organization, established during the Truman administration, continued strong during Clark's tenure, with meetings being rotated annually between the three countries. ANZUS was basically a three-way defense pact, requiring participating nations to cooperate on defense matters in the Pacific Rim area.

While there were occasional rough spots—Australia wished to strengthen ties to mainland China while the U.S. was committed to protecting Taiwan—U.S. and Australia remained strong, thanks to, as Laux put it, "shared values, a congruence of strategic interests, as well as a proud history of defense cooperation".

The U.S. had stewardship over the United Nations Trusteeship of the Pacific Island nations of the Marshall Islands, the Federated States of Micronesia, and Palau, which had been held by the Japanese until the end of World War II. Clark saw to it that the U.S. moved toward the establishment of independence for these three small and unique nations—both while he was at the NSC and then at Interior.

Of the Southeast Asia nations—the Philippines, Indonesia, Vietnam, Cambodia, Laos, Thailand, Burma, Malaysia, and Singapore— the major problem during Bill Clark's tenure was the unique issue of large numbers of American servicemen still "missing in action" (POW-MIA's) from the Vietnam War.[8] Clark took close personal interest in this issue and remains a supporter of the cause. Ann Mills Griffiths, Executive Director, National League of Families of American Prisoners and Missing in Southeast Asia—an active, vibrant organization, says Clark—has visited Chapel Hill. Ann's brother, Lieutenant Commander Jim Mills, disappeared while on a low-level bombing mission September 21, 1966.

The Secret to Successful Policy Making

Policy making and implementation for the Pacific Rim worked, simply because the team followed the formula set by Clark for the entire NSC: simple but effective mechanisms were put in place to coordinate policy and make certain that all key players were singing from the same sheet of music. As a specific example, Laux cites the case of the East Asia team: Bill Brown, Deputy Assistant Secretary at State; Jim Kelly, Deputy Assistant Secretary at Defense; and Laux, met every Wednesday for lunch (in addition to communicating frequently each

---

[8] Southeast Asia was the staff responsibility of Dick Childress on the NSC staff during and after Bill Clark's stint as National Security Advisor. Childress did an able job with some difficult problems, most notably with the POW-MIA matters with Vietnam, and with the troubles in the Philippines.

day)—to discuss every issue in U.S. relations with both China and Taiwan. Additionally, every two months this group met with Gaston Sigur, Special Assistant to the President for Asia on the NSC; Paul Wolfowitz, Assistant Secretary of State for East Asia; and Rich Armitage, then Assistant Secretary of Defense for International Affairs. With this kind of close coordination, nothing fell through the cracks.

"The arrangement had my enthusiastic blessing", says Clark. "When you work together, anything is possible. If you're squabbling with each other, nothing gets done."

CHAPTER 12

Clark's Final Months at the NSC

In the months prior to Clark's departure from the National Security
Council, it was widely reported that the NSC was now "the hub of
activity" at the White House, thanks to Clark's leadership, and that
certain areas of U.S. policy, for example, Central America, "bear the
stamp" of Clark.[1]

Unlike the previous two high-profile national security advisors, Kissinger and Brzezinski, the press acknowledged that Clark represented a
"rather remarkable shift" in improving the way business was conducted around the White House and in managing the nation's security. Unlike Kissinger and Brzezinski, said one former White House
aide, Clark did not think he "knew it all"; and yet, as the *Washington
Post* noted, Clark somehow carried this humility along with unprecedented access to the President.[2] Clark had developed into possibly
the most powerful national security advisor in history.

The post of national security advisor began with the National Security Act of 1947. In his fulfillment of the role, Henry Kissinger is
often considered first in prominence and influence, with Zbigniew
Brzezinski running a distant second. Yet, as Roger Robinson notes,
Clark was more powerful than Kissinger because of his unique rapport
with an exceptionally powerful president—a president who had an
enormous impact on world events.

---

[1] John M. Goshko and Lou Cannon, "White House Moves to Toughen Latin Policy",
Washington Post, May 28, 1983.

[2] See Michael Getler, "For NSC Staff, It's Heady to be the Hub of Activity", *Washington Post*, May 16, 1983.

In comparing the Clark-Reagan relationship with that of other national security advisors and presidents, Robinson maintains: "Bill Clark and Ronald Reagan communicated implicitly, wordlessly, as one mind—that's the difference. They seemed to be one organism, one strand of DNA." Kissinger and Brzezinski, on the other hand, did not have a kindred relationship with their respective presidents. Ford and Kissinger were two completely different individuals, and Ford was not a powerful President.[3] Like Ford, Carter was not perceived as a strong President; and, Carter's national security advisor, Brzezinski, was thwarted and frustrated by Carter's siding with Secretary of State Cyrus Vance, Brzezinski's polar opposite, especially on Cold War matters. Even the Kissinger-Nixon relationship had its limits: Kissinger was very much treated as Nixon's employee, his subordinate; he and Nixon never had the personal relationship Clark and Reagan enjoyed. Robinson states unequivocally: "As a *pair*, in particular, it's difficult to equal Ronald Reagan and Bill Clark."[4] This closeness continued to be evident in a number of notable policy matters that occurred during the summer of 1983.

In keeping with the President's commitment to cut missile arsenals—a dedication to which Clark (like Reagan) was not credited while in office—Clark was selected in August to head the Senior Arms Control Policy Group, a new interagency committee given the task of developing a strategy to achieve arms-control negotiations with the Soviet Union. He was a natural pick, having already been advising Reagan on nuclear arms, as is evident in two memos he wrote to Reagan.

In a memo dated July 9, Clark examined four subject areas: U.S.-Soviet relations, the Middle East, Central America, and the Pacific Basin. His point in raising these "cosmic matters", wrote Clark, was to emphasize that "we don't have a lot of time remaining; . . . to make an effort on all of them, we need to use our talent better." After assessing this big picture, Clark attended to the pressing "business at hand". He attached two papers for Reagan—a short analysis of a letter recently received from Soviet General Secretary Yuri Andropov and a suggested response drafted by Clark. However Reagan decided to

---

[3] Interviews with Roger Robinson, June 6 and 8, 2005.
[4] Ibid.

respond, wrote Clark, his response to Andropov should be in long-hand, which "has made a deep impression on the Soviets in the past". Reagan proceeded to do just that.

In another critical memo to Reagan, written on August 5 and entitled "Summitry", Clark laid out U.S. objectives in any summit with the Soviet Union, particularly in regard to arms control, but also regarding human rights, "regional" issues, and "bilateral" issues. The memo analyzed the potential impact of new U.S. missile deployments in Europe—INF/Pershing II—before concluding with advice for Reagan on public diplomacy and a negotiating schedule. Most importantly, it warned that any summit with the Soviets must make real progress on substantive issues and not be held merely for pageantry or polls.

The Irish Connection

While at the NSC, Clark continued to manage short stays in the land his Clerken and Lynch forebears fled in the Famine years. He had grown to love Ireland during his early days at State and throughout the years used it as a personal "refueling" stop on journeys to or from one hot spot or another, some of those hot spots being in Ireland itself. One of his favored pastimes: sailing a thirty-one-foot sloop single-handed in the frigid waters of the Irish Sea, in spite of the weather.

Clark's first official assignment in regard to Ireland was a touchy one, given to him in his first months at State. The Reverend Ian Paisley, fiery founder of the Democratic Unionist Party in Northern Ireland and violently opposed to concessions to Catholics, wished to come to the United States to campaign and had applied for a visa. When the request hit the news, a number of death threats against the Orangeman were received by the State Department. Al Haig prudently handed off the request to his deputy who came up with this unique disposition: the United States could not grant a visa to the Reverend Mr. Paisley, as the United States could not assure his safety and security in this country.

Clark made his position on the Irish question clear in an interview on Radio Telefís Éireann's *Today Tonight* program in 1981, stating, "It is the hope and prayer of all Americans that Ireland will be united." [5]

---

[5] As quoted by Andrew J. Wilson, *Irish America and the Ulster Conflict: 1968–1995*, Blackstaff House: Belfast, Northern Ireland, 1995, p. 244.

The remainder of his years of quiet work—with Irish Ambassador to the United States Seán Donlon, the Irish diplomatic corps and others—will remain unrecorded in this work with one exception: His intervention following Prime Minister Margaret Thatcher's "Chequers" speech, in which the Iron Lady managed to offend possibly not only the entire population of the Republic of Ireland, but the seventy million Irish descendants of the famine diaspora around the globe.

In Thatcher's defense, it must be stated that IRA activities in Northern Ireland and London short-circuited any sympathy she had for Ireland's Troubles. Ireland's Taoiseach (Prime Minister) Charles Haughey's grudging support during the Falklands War she considered an "unforgivable betrayal", reinforcing her "natural antipathy toward the Irish".[6] But December 1982 brought in a new Taoiseach, Garret FitzGerald, as moderate as Haughey was fiercely nationalistic. There was great hope for the Anglo-Irish summit to be held at Thatcher's retreat, Chequers, even though Thatcher herself had narrowly escaped death with the IRA bombing of the Brighton Hotel during a Conservative Party Conference the previous month.[7] Discussions would center on a tentative Anglo-Irish Agreement in which the Republic of Ireland proposed to amend its constitutional claim to sovereignty over Northern Ireland if, in exchange, Britain would agree to a formal political role for Dublin in Ulster's affairs. None came to pass.

In her press conference following the summit, Margaret Thatcher opened with forty-five minutes of praise for the negotiations—but then, when questioned about the three political options advanced for the proposed agreement, she could not contain her anger, responding with her "now-infamous 'Out, Out, Out'" remarks. The *Irish Times* reported Thatcher to be "as offhand and patronizing as she is callous and imperious". FitzGerald himself was reported to have described Thatcher's response as "gratuitously offensive".[8]

A political solution for the Troubles in Northern Ireland now seemed beyond the pale of possibility. The constitutional nationalists determined

---

[6] Chris Ogden, *Maggie: The Portrait of a Woman in Power* (New York: Simon and Schuster, 1990), pp. 221 and 189.

[7] Five were killed in that bombing and thirty-four injured, including two of Thatcher's senior advisors.

[8] Andrew Wilson, *Irish America and the Ulster Conflict: 1968–1995*, p. 243.

to make another appeal for support to President Reagan, who had in the past declined any involvement in reaching a solution for Ulster, yet urged "that part of the world to seek reconciliation".[9] Reagan's help was deemed the essential component to affect compromise. He was an acknowledged ideological and political soul mate of Thatcher, as was his top hand Bill Clark.

Former Ambassador Seán Donlon reached his good friend, Bill Clark, with an urgent plea. President Reagan and Prime Minister Thatcher were scheduled to meet at Camp David on December 22, 1984 to discuss ramifications of the Strategic Defense Initiative. Would Clark use his influence with the President to persuade him to discuss the situation in Ireland and, perhaps, to enlist his support for the constitutional nationalist cause? Yes, he would; yes, he did. Any discussion of Ireland between the two had the benediction of tradition; Reagan had long depended on Clark to keep him informed regarding what was happening in Ireland—not only politically, but anything of interest in the "auld country". Reagan was well aware of Clark's position. He had more than once urged Reagan to suggest to Prime Minister Thatcher that London treat her counterpart in Dublin with greater dignity.

In the following January, the White House admitted that the President and the Prime Minister "exchanged views on Northern Ireland" and that the President "stressed the need for progress and the need for all parties concerned to take steps which will contribute to a peaceful resolution".[10] Reagan encouraged Thatcher to make new proposals to the Irish government before her return to Washington in February. Eventually, Reagan offered American financial support in the event of an agreed-upon political initiative.

According to Andrew Wilson, Seán Donlon and Garret FitzGerald both believe that "William Clark's intervention was the crucial factor in persuading Reagan to discuss Irish affairs. Against specific advice from the State Department [under George Shultz] the president raised the issue.... American pressure played a 'decisive role in persuading

---

[9] Statement of the Presidents: The Reagan Administration, March 17, 1983. Source: Andrew Wilson, p. 241.

[10] Letter from the U.S. Department of State to Mario Biaggi, January 17, 1985. Source: Andrew Wilson, p. 244.

Thatcher to modify her position which eventually resulted in a new Anglo-Irish package offering an institutionalized role for the Irish government in the administration of Northern Ireland'." [11]

Following this breakthrough, continued intervention by Clark and others on both sides of the American political spectrum helped to bring about an "historic, reconciliatory and transforming moment in British-Irish history". [12] Ultimately, on March 26, 2007, traditional adversaries Ian Paisley, Democratic Unionist Party, and Gerry Adams, Sinn Féin, agreed to commit to forming a power-sharing executive for the government of Northern Ireland.

This was the first time in history that Protestant evangelist Paisley, for whom Clark had been unable to assure safety in his first months at state, agreed to negotiate directly with Roman Catholic Adams. British Secretary of State Peter Hain agreed to relinquish governing power to a coalition led by these "polar opposites of provincial politics", [13] with every hope it would put an end to "centuries of discord, conflict, hurt and tragedy", [14] in Northern Ireland. On May 8, 2007, it came to pass as anticipated: the long-polarized parties joined forces to form a localized government for Northern Ireland.

Diplomatic Recognition of the Vatican

Another of Clark's unrecorded activities at this time involved his effective support of President Reagan's desire for diplomatic recognition of the Vatican. The United States had only a special presidential representative to the Vatican, William Wilson, who had a small staff of five at an office outside of Vatican City. In contrast, over one hundred other nations had ambassadors to the Vatican.

Though Reagan expressed his intention to establish formal ties with the Vatican "and make them an ally" [15] early in his presidency, for the first two years of his administration, this desire generated almost no

---

[11] Garret FitzGerald interview with Andrew Wilson, December 1990; Seán Donlon, "Bringing Irish and Diplomatic and Political Pressure to Bear on Washington", *Irish Times*, January 25, 1986, as quoted by Wilson, p. 245.

[12] *Irish Times*, March 27, 2007, Front Page.

[13] Shawn Pogatchnik, Associated Press, March 27, 2007.

[14] Gerry Adams as quoted by Pogatchnik.

[15] Bernstein, "The Holy Alliance," p. 31.

steam inside the White House. By mid-July 1983, however, a majority of the members of the House Foreign Affairs Committee, discreetly backed by Clark and others on Reagan's team, introduced legislation repealing an 1867 law that banned the use of federal funds to maintain an ambassador to the Holy See.[16]

A number of internal White House memos were circulated to put wind behind the sails of the effort. An August 11 memo from Clark to Jim Baker noted that the State Department saw "some foreign policy advantages to formal diplomatic relations", which was a more positive view on the issue than that previously held at State.

In November, Congress passed the repeal, allowing the President to establish diplomatic relations with the Vatican for the first time in U.S. history. While Clark played a pivotal role in the outcome, there were others who had supported the initiative, he says, including William Wilson, Reagan's personal representative to the Vatican and Frank Shakespeare, former Director of the USIA and Ambassador to Portugal. Following passage of the repeal, Wilson served as the first U.S. Ambassador and Minister Plenipotentiary to the Holy See, followed by Frank Shakespeare.

Opposition to official recognition of the Vatican came mostly from Protestant Christians. The President received a number of letters listing objections, including some from Evangelicals invoking the argument for separation of church and state. Clark adds that despite these objections during consideration of the issue, there was surprisingly little reaction once recognition was formally extended, perhaps because of the trust many Evangelicals placed in Reagan.

The Kissinger Commission

Also in July 1983, Clark formed a presidential bipartisan commission on Central America with Henry Kissinger as chairman. The Kissinger Commission dedicated the next six months to a thorough examination of U.S. and Central American bilateral interests, with an emphasis on social issues.

---

[16] The legislation would not only officially recognize Pope John Paul II as a major world statesman in the eyes of the United States, it would also help to end (at least symbolically) decades of "anti-papist" sentiment, a motivating factor in the creation of the initial 1867 Congressional law.

Some Democratic legislators, as well as the National Conference of Catholic Bishops (NCCB), criticized the group. Senator Robert Byrd (D-WV) called it a "smoke screen for the administration to get its way" on Central America and contended that the White House had already made the commission's final decisions. Said Archbishop John R. Roach of St. Paul-Minneapolis, on behalf of the NCCB: "U.S. policy toward Nicaragua presently has the effect of deepening the internal crises in the country and escalating the dangers of war in the region." [17]

Clark and Reagan did not see it that way; rather, they were looking to bring freedom to communist Nicaragua. Neither did the press, which widely credited Clark for "energizing the system" when it came to Central America policy, and for at least striving to find some kind of a bipartisan consensus. [18]

Perhaps the most interesting memento from this episode was a September 22, 1983 personal letter from Kissinger to Clark. Kissinger was preparing to visit Central America to conduct his commission work, and he understood there was a "minimal chance" that he might be captured by "guerrillas or terrorists" in the region. "In that unlikely event I hereby request that no negotiation for my release be conducted except, of course, a formal request for an unconditional end of my captivity", he instructed Clark. "If any letter or other communication from me requests any concessions whatsoever you should assume it was made under duress against my better judgment." He signed it, "With high regard, Henry A. Kissinger."

August 1983: Time and the New York Times

In the otherwise positive press that Clark received for his work with the Kissinger Commission, there was the suggestion that he alone was directing foreign policy, to the exclusion of Shultz and Baker. Moreover, he was portrayed as an anti-communist hardliner who was perhaps pulling Reagan too far to the right.

---

[17] Fred Hiatt, "Democrats in Congress Question Latin Commission", *Washington Post*, July 23, 1983.

[18] Lou Cannon, "President's Strong Man Stretches South", *Washington Post*, August 3, 1983.

Fueling the perception that Clark was exercising undue influence over the President were two August 1983 cover stories in two of the nation's most influential publications—*Time* and one week later, the *New York Times* magazine.

Maureen Dowd, then a reporter, not yet a famous columnist, wrote the piece for *Time*. "An apolitical man, Clark is clearly driven more by his devotion to the president than by personal ambition", she wrote. He was "the second most powerful man in the White House", and thus, by extension, one of the most powerful men in the world—a long way from the woods of Red Bluff.[19]

Steven R. Weisman of the *New York Times* added that no one could equal Clark's influence with Reagan. Despite his lackluster education, reported Weisman, Clark had shown he was "ideally suited" for his current job, and "no one" could match Reagan's confidence in him. "He has more access to the president than anyone else at the White House, and no one is more devoted to letting Mr. Reagan act on his instincts."

Weisman's article defended Clark against the charge that he lacked depth. It quoted Cap Weinberger, who stated that it was "a mistaken, basically rather bigoted sort of notion" that because Clark did not have certain academic credentials or previous professional experience he was not qualified to work in foreign policy. An unnamed aide stated further: "Bill Clark has the right view of history and America's role in the world. You don't need a lifetime of incestuous, elitist thinking about foreign policy to know who America's friends are and who aren't."

Weisman also quoted Clark: "I've never felt inhibited by a lack of background, because I feel the process is really no different here from what it was on the court. It's human experience, human nature, try-ing to determine credibility of sources ... on where lies the truth. And once you feel confident that you have the truth on a set of facts, it's not difficult to make a recommendation."

As Weisman further noted, nearly one hundred NSDDs had been written since Clark took the helm—an astonishing figure. This alone sufficed to show that Clark's background had hardly led to a dearth of productivity.

---

[19] Dowd, "The Man with the President's Ear".

For personal insights on Clark, Weisman turned to Jeane Kirkpatrick, who said that the Judge "fulfills the stereotype of the strong, silent type. He's decent, upright, honest, forthright and serious." She said that while it had been said that Ronald Reagan looked upon some of his employees as sons, he viewed Clark as a brother.

Weisman's final words concluding his article were these: "The president's future seems more tied to Mr. Clark than ever." [20] Both his and Dowd's articles made clear that Bill Clark was Reagan's most trusted, influential aide, and, whether Clark intended it or not, extremely powerful.

Both the Weisman and Dowd articles were generally complimentary profiles of a humble national security advisor, the interesting family from which he came, and his remarkable relationship with the President of the United States. It is hard to imagine that they could have done anything but help Clark.

Yet, rather than signaling to Clark that he had at last earned the respect of the establishment, the *Time* and *New York Times* pieces convinced him that his time was running out. Al Haig had warned him, "Once you've made the cover of a major newsweekly, your legs come off." Any major article that even implied a certain advisor had achieved primacy in foreign policy was not necessarily helpful to the subject. Clark recalls heading home to his apartment, walking inside, and telling his wife, "Joan, let's pack."

Baker, Shultz, Deaver, and, most significantly, Nancy Reagan were piqued by the publicity. The *Time* feature provoked Secretary of State George Shultz[21] because it relegated him to secondary status, mentioning him in a sidebar titled "Disappearing Act at Foggy Bottom". More damaging to Clark's relationships with Baker, Deaver, and Mrs. Reagan was the affirmation that Clark enabled Reagan to follow his conservative instincts, which worried the First Lady and those on the President's staff who wanted the President to maintain his popularity by moderating his approach.

The Dowd and Weisman articles generated numerous follow-up pieces, some agreeing with their assessments; others, not. Reagan was not listening to nuanced thinkers, to level-headed people like Baker

---

[20] Steven R. Weisman, "The Influence of William Clark", *New York Times Magazine*, August 14, 1983.

[21] George P. Shultz, *Turmoil and Triumph* (New York: Scribners, 1993), p. 317.

and Deaver, but instead to strident anti-communists, wrote Mary McGrory in her July 26 column. "Reagan is listening to other drummers: to such fanatically anti-Soviet counselors as national security affairs advisor William P. Clark and U.S. Ambassador Jeane J. Kirkpatrick." In her August 7 column, she stated that Clark "believes the Soviets are to blame for everything, perhaps even the August humidity. Ms. Kirkpatrick is similarly obsessed." [22]

The August 15 *Washington Post* ran an article titled "Shultz No Longer Perceived as Driving Force in Foreign Policy". This piece expressed the concern that Shultz had been steamrolled by the "get-tough approach advocated by Clark and other hard-line presidential advisers". [23]

Reagan and Clark were neither surprised nor bothered by critics like McGrory and the editors of the *Post*, whose political philosophy was at odds with their own. However, when Deaver and Mrs. Reagan—especially Mrs. Reagan—read negative assessments of the President, his policies, and his choice of advisors, they reacted with alarm.

As for George Shultz, though Bill Clark did not know it at the time, and would not until Shultz published his memoirs years later, he had come to see Clark as his enemy—this after four days of press stories trumpeting "Clark victorious over Shultz and State". He too viewed Clark as dangerously more hard-line on communism than Ronald Reagan, but perhaps more importantly, he saw him as a rival.

In his memoirs Shultz relates how he used the media's image of Clark to turn Nancy Reagan against him. On July 29 Nancy Reagan called Shultz about the *Time* feature on Clark. "She was furious. She thought Clark ought to be fired. I could tell she was very upset. . . . Clark did not have the president's best interests at heart, she said. I told her that I felt Clark was just 'in over his head.'"

Shultz figured that Clark's departure was now "only a matter of time". While he knew, he wrote, that "Ronald Reagan, with his soft heart, would never fire Clark"—implying that Reagan wanted Clark to go—he also believed that "at some point, Nancy would prevail upon him to act in his own interest."

---

[22] Mary McGrory, "Avoiding Latin War", and "Hot Spell Suspicions", *Washington Post*, July 26 and August 7, 1983.

[23] John M. Goshko and Michael Getler, "Shultz No Longer Perceived as Driving Force in Foreign Policy", *Washington Post*, August 15, 1983.

On August 4, "an angry" Shultz held a "showdown meeting" with Ronald Reagan in the Oval Office in light of "the waning influence of the administration's senior diplomat", reported Don Oberdorfer in the *Washington Post*.[24] The meeting, said Oberdorfer, quickly followed the *Time* piece (August 1) and then, an August 3 article by Lou Cannon in the *Washington Post*, which reported that Clark had emerged as the dominant figure in Central America policy. That evening, NBC correspondent Marvin Kalb reported that "senior administration officials" felt that Shultz might exit the administration out of frustration and unhappiness.

More Clark and Shultz

Clark considered Shultz a faithful friend and colleague, and was fond of him and his wife, O'Bie. A framed photo of Bill and Joan, along with Cap, Shultz, and O'Bie, hangs in the hallway of Clark's home, with this glowing inscription to Clark from Shultz: "With my admiration for the sustained high quality of your public service and for your strength of character and my thanks for all your help and your friendship."

Thus, Clark reacted to Shultz's charges against him in his memoirs—which portray Clark as a hindrance to sound foreign policy, as well as other unfounded attacks, both personal and professional—with shock. He was so surprised that he even questioned whether Shultz wrote his own autobiography; and, if he did not write it, whether he reviewed it before it was published.

Many of Clark's former colleagues rallied behind him. Weinberger was particularly angered, and baffled, by Shultz's personal attacks on Clark. Former members of the NSC staff considered a point-by-point rebuttal, and raised the notion more than once. Clark told them no.

Family

The two years as Governor Reagan's chief of staff had been taxing, robbing Clark of precious time with his young family. The two years as President Reagan's national security advisor had been utterly draining.

---

[24] Don Oberdorfer, "'Disgrace'; Shultz's Roar on Policy-Making Got Results", *Washington Post*, October 23, 1983.

Even though all of the children were grown and out of the house, with the youngest, Paul, now twenty years old and a U.S. Marine, and the oldest, Monica, twenty-seven, Bill's time with Joan was extremely limited, and his parents were growing older in Camarillo, a long way from Washington, D.C.

As Bill Sr.'s Parkinson's progressed, Bernice's financial anxieties returned to haunt her. Bill Jr. did his best to assuage his mother's concerns and to alleviate his parents' financial burdens, in one instance responding to a telephone call with a handwritten note: "Your statements were pretty disheartening—and, I believe, inaccurate. Throughout childhood I listened to a lot of discussion and some grief over not having enough money to meet the family needs/desires. . . . I believe you spend far too much time fretting about such things. . . . You certainly know we are not ever going to let you down. Love, Billy." [25]

One way Clark could combine his duties to both family and country was by visiting his parents whenever his national security job took him to his situation room at the Biltmore Hotel in Montecito. During one of Clark's visits to his parents, afforded by Reagan's visit to the Western White House, the phone rang as the three were sitting down to dinner. Bernice answered: "I'm sorry, he's eating his supper", then hung up the phone. "Who was it?" Bill asked. "The White House", Bernice answered. "Now finish your supper." [26]

A special time for Clark and his father occurred in 1983, when the two made a swing together through the northern part of California near Redding and Red Bluff, to look over the ranch where they had lived decades earlier. They decided to make a surprise visit to one of the few Clark friends from those days—few because of the great distances between neighbors. They dropped in on the Govers.

Clark had been a childhood classmate of Dan Gover and Doug Fleming—the three used to climb a cinder cone together. Fleming, now an artist, remembers Clark as "a lovable, kind, quiet and gentlemanly fellow from the time he was ten years old".

Clark saw Gover, stopped the car, and walked over to him. "I thought [he] was someone just looking for directions", said Gover. Instead, Clark held out his hand and said, "Hi. I'm Bill Clark. Remember me?"

---

[25] The letter was written and dated, August 11, 1983.
[26] A favorite family story. PCD.

Yes, he did. He had been reading about his old comrade in the newspapers. In spite of his important position, Clark was as easy to be with as when they were kids together. "It just wasn't a big deal [to him]", said Gover. "Clark is probably among the most powerful men in the world, really, but he doesn't make you feel at all uncomfortable. He's a good man." [27]

Bill's dad agreed with that assessment of his son, and made that clear one day during these final weeks of his son's service at the NSC. Some three thousand miles away, William Pettit Clark, "Bill Sr.", was being honored at the Ventura County Fairgrounds. Now a seventy-six-year-old ex-rancher, ex-rider, and ex-police chief suffering from cancer and Parkinson's, the senior Clark walked very slowly, with the help of friends, through the livestock pavilion named in his honor. It was a fitting tribute not only to William Pettit's service to the county but to the fair as well, an association that began when he collected tickets at the gate as a kid.

Dressed in the usual Western garb and leaning on a carved, wooden cane, he spoke of past fairs and said he was honored that the community had christened a William P. Clark Pavilion which, he said, came as a "great surprise". He also spoke of his famous son—whom he called a "sidetracked" rancher who remained a "pretty good buckaroo"—and noted that the boy frequently telephoned his parents, though they were never sure of his location. "He called from Rome the other night", said Mr. Clark. "We thought he was some-place else. ... I started a conversation with him, and then the phone would ring. He has a lot of phones!" [28] And he added that he was impressed with his son's accomplishments: "Oh, I'm pretty proud of him." [29]

September 1983: KAL 007

In Clark's final days at NSC, his life progressed as usual as illustrated by the following TelCon conversation with Oleg Sokolov, Chargé at

---

[27] John Crowe, "Clark's Ties to Cottonwood Renewed", *Record Searchlight* (Redding, CA), October 19, 1983.

[28] Phil Pattee, "Honored Ex-Rancher", *Oxnard Press*, October 5, 1983.

[29] Ibid. It is interesting to note that today, Bill Jr., at the same age, suffers from the same disease, and carries the same carved cane.

the Soviet embassy. Sokolov was the "special channel", or designated embassy officer, to pass messages to Clark.

SOKOLOV: Hello, Judge Clark?

CLARK: Yes.

SOKOLOV: I am Sokolov, Chargé of the Embassy.... I have something to tell you in confidence. I have received instructions to personally deliver to you a sealed envelope—a letter from Andropov to President Reagan. I should receive the envelope by tonight—around 7:00 or 8:00 P.M. It is being flown by our diplomatic pouch. I know you have a long schedule, so I thought I would tell you in advance. If I receive it early enough today or perhaps it might come later, could I or should I telephone you again and bring it to you because I have instructions to speedily do that and personally to you?

CLARK: That is acceptable and you estimate that it will be between 7:00 and 8:00 P.M.?

SOKOLOV: Yes, but might be later with all of the plane delay possibilities. We do try to handle very carefully. Might be slightly later.

CLARK: If I have to leave the office before 7:00—I do have an engagement—I will probably have to leave at 7:30. I will call you on the same line and tell you where I will be and you could meet me at that position if you wish.

SOKOLOV: Good. I feel from my instructions they would like to have it done as early as possible so I could tell them the letter has been handed to you.

CLARK: I assure you only the President will be apprised of this message and this conversation.

SOKOLOV: This is important.

CLARK: Only the President will know of the message that you will deliver to me.

SOKOLOV: Very good. I will expect a call from you around that time.

CLARK: If I don't hear from you on this line that you have it [earlier] I will phone you personally giving you my later location. It will be within city limits.

SOKOLOV: Very good. Thank you, Mr. Clark.[30]

This was typical of the tasks that Clark dealt with as national security advisor. Not so typical was an event that happened not long after this exchange.

On September 1, 1983, a South Korean airliner, flight 007, took off from New York City en route to Seoul. It held 269 passengers, including 61 Americans. The computer on the plane's automated guidance system was apparently set incorrectly, allowing it to stray into Soviet airspace. Soviet fighter planes stalked KAL 007 before blasting it out of the sky, killing everyone on board.

The President was at his Rancho del Cielo when he received the news from Clark, who called him from the Biltmore Hotel situation room. "I told him Bill Casey just relayed an unsubstantiated report that the Soviets may have shot down an airliner, possibly Korean", says Clark. "Bill," Reagan responded, "let's pray it's not true."[31] Then he added, "If it is, let's be careful not to overreact to this. We have too much going on with the Soviets in arms control. We must not derail our progress. We cannot derail our negotiations." He summed up: "Bill, if it's confirmed, we've got to protect against overreaction."[32]

Clark was not able to confirm the details for the President until 7:10 A.M. the next morning.[33] Then, Clark remembers, the President wanted all of his advisors to gather so that he could hear opinions and recommendations of all the principals in the NSC before deciding on a course of action. "Bill," he said, "round table it."

It was often assumed that Reagan, the hard-liner, wanted to condemn the Soviets at each and every opportunity. To be sure, he was

---

[30] The exact date of the conversation was August 4, 1983.

[31] Edmund Morris, *Dutch*, p. 492; and Clark, "President Reagan and the Wall", p. 11.

[32] The last quote is cited in Hedrick Smith, "Reagan's Crucial Year", *New York Times*, October 16, 1983.

[33] David Hoffman, "Airliner, Lebanon Crises Cut Short President's Stay in California", *Washington Post*, September 1, 1983.

angry. Yet, he reacted in a much more statesman-like manner than his detractors would ever have expected.

Weinberger and Shultz, who often disagreed, wanted to hit the Soviets hard over KAL 007. "Shultz, Weinberger, Kirkpatrick, and Casey all recommended he be fairly harsh", says Clark. "Every one of the principals recommended a tougher response than the President was comfortable with. Again, he did not want to derail the progress we had worked so hard to achieve with the Soviets. He wanted to cut missile arsenals, on both sides."

Reagan decided on a good-cop/bad-cop strategy. He would express a continued willingness to negotiate with the Soviets, while Clark applied pressure; thus, the task went to Clark to level harsh words against the Soviets. In a speech on September 15 to the Air Force Association, Clark accused the Soviets of "mass murder" and a "twisted mentality" in shooting down the airliner. "The sickening display of Soviet barbarism in the Korean Air Lines massacre shocked all of us", Clark said. "But at the same time, this dramatically brutal act must be deemed consistent with the behavior of a Soviet government that continues to terrorize and murder the Afghan people, using chemical weapons on Afghan villages; a Soviet government that sponsors the repression of the entire Polish nation." The White House press office distributed a text of the speech to demonstrate that it expressed administration policy.[34]

September was the last full month of Bill Clark's tenure as national security advisor. KAL 007 would be his final foreign-policy crisis.

October 1983: Clark resigns from the NSC

On October 13, 1983, Ronald Reagan hit Washington with a bombshell when he announced that William P. Clark was resigning his position as national security advisor and was being nominated for the post of secretary of the Interior. The announcement made all the front pages.[35] Speculation began immediately.

---

[34] Lou Cannon, "Clark Accuses Soviets of 'Mass Murder'", *Washington Post*, September 15, 1983.

[35] To cite one example, see: "Clark Appointment Catches State Department Unawares", *Washington Post*, October 14, 1983.

Baker and Deaver were "delighted" with the change at the NSC, according to anonymous sources.[36] Clark's unusual day or night access to Reagan, from the outset, was said to have "shook" Baker and Deaver, who lost their exclusive control of the President's schedule and communication following Clark's appointment. Clark was often told that Baker and Deaver and their associates—particularly David Gergen and Dick Darman—began many inner-staff meetings by asking, "How can we roll Clark today?"

Clark generally took it in stride. After all, he had the President's confidence and support. He took it personally, however, when the Baker team went after certain "ideologues" they did not like.

One such person was Faith Whittlesey, a conservative on Baker's own staff who served as Ambassador to Switzerland. Clark and others believe that the bad press Whittlesey received was the product of a campaign of leaks carefully planted by the Baker people. Clark felt it necessary to defend "this good lady". He complained to Baker once or twice about the smear campaign. Nothing happened. As it continued, he felt compelled to raise the issue in front of the president, with Baker present. Clark said, "Jim, someone on your staff is brutalizing Faith in the media, and she has done nothing to deserve this." Clark's staff concluded that Gergen was the guilty party. Reagan took notice, and sternly ordered Baker: "I want this to stop."

After they left Reagan's office, Baker could not contain his anger and later called Clark. "It was the only time Baker lost his temper with me", says Clark. Prior to this moment, Clark and Baker seemed to have an understanding that they were going down parallel lines; they respected their differences and generally did not openly clash—until this incident.

The "unauthorized disclosures"—as the lawyerly Clark carefully calls the leaks—had been a source of irritation from the beginning, but the reason for them was the deeper component to the Clark-Baker division. Clark agreed with Reagan on all of the important issues, respected him, and trusted his political instincts. Baker, on the other hand, in the estimation of Clark and others, distrusted the "let Reagan be Reagan" approach to White House policy making. Clark

---

[36] Steven R. Weisman, "Among the Staff, the Mood Is Testy", *New York Times*, November 28, 1983.

is among those who believe that Baker never gave Reagan the respect he deserved.

Clark is also of the opinion that his problems with Baker spilled over to his onetime excellent relationships with Mike Deaver and Nancy Reagan, which had deteriorated since the gubernatorial years. "Baker tried to convince her [Nancy] that Cap and I were too aggressive with the Soviets," says Clark, "that we were too hard-line, that our conservative postures could start World War III, that we were irresponsible for convincing the President to double the defense budget." On the World War III charge, Clark once retorted: "Tell them upstairs that if they would read their intelligence traffic, they would know that we have been in World War III for some time."

Mrs. Reagan and Deaver had convinced themselves that Ronald Reagan would somehow be celebrated by the establishment press and perhaps even the Nobel Committee as the "peace president". As an indicator of the degree to which this thinking was naive, Reagan ultimately put an end to the Cold War (by adopting nearly every policy the Baker group counseled against), prompted the dismantling of the Berlin Wall, breached the Iron Curtain, bankrupted the USSR, and negotiated the greatest arms cuts in all history, but received no credit as the peace president. Instead, the Nobel Peace Prize went to Gorbachev, who repeatedly claimed he was against taking down the wall and to this day states that the Soviet breakup was a "tragic mistake".[37]

"Mike Deaver was not so much interested in the substance of foreign affairs", explains Clark. "He would drift in and out of various NSC meetings. He might take a position on something based on how it had been written in the *Washington Post* that morning, or to be written tomorrow. But, in a way, that was his job and he did it very well."

The distancing from Nancy was troubling to Clark. In 1970, Mrs. Reagan had wept openly when Clark left the gubernatorial staff; ten years later, in 1980, she had urged him to rescue her husband's bid for the presidency. Now, in 1983, she wanted him gone from his national security position. In 1970 and 1980, she had felt that Clark's presence

---

[37] See Michael Cox, "Beyond the Cold War in Europe: A Review Article", *Soviet Studies*, 44, no. 6, December 1992, pp. 1099–103.

was good—very good—for her husband. Now, she concluded that Clark's presence was harming him.

Nancy Reagan is always best understood as her husband's supreme protector. He was always first, even above herself. Also, Mrs. Reagan was one for whom ideological conservatism, including anti-communism, or any ideological commitment of any stripe, for that matter, was not an animating force. She had one constituency: Ronald Reagan.[38] Clark always respected, in fact lauded, Mrs. Reagan's total commitment to her husband.

"I think it's quite clear as to the reason why all the Californians, except Mike Deaver, fell out of favor with Nancy", says Helene von Damm, who knew the Reagans well in both California and Washington as principal secretary to the Governor and the President. "The Californians, like Ronald Reagan, shared a conservative philosophy, a mission, and goals to meet, even if the press was bad in response. They accepted the bad press without retreating. Mrs. Reagan did not have a solid philosophy and was not driven by a mission. A Republican, yes, but not one with a mission." She adds, "She was concerned only with her husband's place in history. That was her worry, and, I guess, her only mission, and she was very sensitive to bad press. And when the press suggested Bill Clark was in charge, as in the *Time* piece, that was it as far as Mrs. Reagan was concerned."

The Californians who fell out of favor, including Clark, Lyn Nofziger, Ed Meese, and Cap Weinberger, were all principled conservatives who were convinced of the correctness of Ronald Reagan's approach and strategy. Among them, one person who was more candid about the splits, and not worried about offending people, was Lyn Nofziger.

"Ronald Reagan's greatest failure was trusting people he should not have trusted", said Nofziger. "Ronald Reagan always thought if people worked for him, they would be loyal to him, but there were people who were more loyal to themselves than to Ronald Reagan."[39]

---

[38] Quoted in Joseph Lewis, *What Makes Reagan Run? A Political Profile* (New York: McGraw-Hill Book Co., 1968), p. 46; and Lou Cannon, *Reagan* (NY: Putnam, 1982), p. 141.

[39] Ralph Z. Hallow, "A Not-so-mellow Skeptic Sees a GOP with No Focus", *Washington Times*, November 28, 2005.

The senior staff, summed up Lyn Nofziger, was split "into two parties: the Reagan people and the Baker people". While Nofziger had his "ups and downs" with Mrs. Reagan and Deaver, he saw the third member of the troika as the primary problem. Of Baker, Nofziger summarized: "He's a guy who's arrogant, who thought he knew better than the President. I don't think he's an honorable man." [40]

The sentiment was classic no-nonsense Nofziger. When the Nofziger quote was read to Clark, he chuckled and said: "Some of us would not be so frank in our assessment."

The Baker people not only cheered Clark's resignation but also favored replacing him with none other than Jim Baker. Deaver, too, was excited by Clark's exit: he would replace Baker as the new Reagan chief of staff.

Baker and Deaver arranged a press conference for 3:00 P.M. on October 14, the day following the announcement of Clark's resignation, to announce their new positions. Reagan had agreed to the plan; he was tired of the bickering and wanted to get the thing over and done with. [41] The two men were stopped in their tracks, however, by what the Times called a "counterattack" mounted by Meese, Weinberger, Casey, and Kirkpatrick. The Times was unaware of Clark's own role in preventing Baker from becoming his replacement.

When Reagan informed Clark of his decision to make Baker his next national security advisor, Clark paused. He reminded Reagan that this was a major appointment and, as was his custom, he should round-table it. Reagan did not want to hear this, though he usually round-tabled major decisions. Reagan wanted to move on, but Clark convinced him to talk the situation over with the "principals". [42] So Reagan summoned them—Clark, Meese, Casey, and Weinberger—into Clark's small office to discuss the issue. They were all certain of one thing: no Baker atop the NSC.

Bill Casey was particularly adamant. His reason for disapproving of Baker was on the minds of everyone in that room, namely, that Baker was the biggest leaker in town and thus would never command the trust of the national-security community. Casey was courageous

---

[40] Ibid.

[41] Reagan, An American Life, p. 448.

[42] Edmund Morris put it this way: "Clark, who kept a Colt .45 on permanent display over his desk, lost no time in rounding up a posse.... Reagan found himself corralled in Clark's office." See Morris, Dutch, p. 499.

enough—as always—to make the point clearly and directly to the President.

Reagan changed his mind. "I decided to reverse myself and scrap the change", he said later.[43] He chose Clark's lackluster but non-controversial deputy, Bud McFarlane, to be the next national security advisor.

The Baker and Deaver press conference was canceled—a day that began with such promise for the pair had ended in disappointment. Baker "took it well", said Reagan, but Deaver was "pretty upset". Reagan did not like conflict, and wrote in his diary: "It was an unhappy day all around."[44]

Why Did Clark Leave?

The shell-shocked press scrambled to ascertain why Bill Clark was resigning. In a front-page story in the *Washington Post*, Lou Cannon wrote that Clark was worn out from the persistent bickering, the eighteen-hour days, the cables in the middle of the night, the time away from his family, and the lack of attention to his ranch.

Most importantly—and this was not reported to the extent it should have been, by Cannon or anyone else—Clark concluded that the mounting tensions within the White House were hurting rather than helping the President. He felt that those attempting to undercut him at every opportunity were undercutting Reagan's well-defined policies and that undermining was not going to stop. Clark told Reagan that he had become a lightning rod, adversely affecting the very national security policy they had worked so hard to create and implement. Could he stay and fight? Never one to promote himself, Clark was not about to launch an internal battle or an external public relations campaign in his own defense.

And yet, there was more to his decision to leave: Clark believed not in "term limits", but in "term fulfillment", and he felt that by the end of 1982 he had "pretty much fulfilled" his obligations at the NSC. This was a point on which his NSC staff—as loyal to him as he was to Reagan—did not agree. David Laux remembers when Clark made the announcement of his resignation to his staff at the regular Friday evening staff meeting: "Everyone was shocked; tears came to the eyes of

---

[43] Reagan, *An American Life*, p. 448.
[44] Ibid.

a number of the staff members. One woman, an officer detailed from the Defense Intelligence Agency to the NSC intelligence staff, stood up, and with tears streaming down her face, said, 'Judge, you can't do this! The President needs you; we need you; you're the ideal man for this job. Please reconsider; please don't go.' Several others wrote letters urging him to reconsider." Nonetheless, Clark resolved that the "train was back on the tracks" and that he and his NSC staff could now turn over a "well-oiled machine" to the President.

Reagan said he was moving Clark out of the NSC at Clark's request.[45] Some thought the President was merely covering for his old friend, helping Clark to save face. Yet, Reagan's explanation did not change after he left the presidency. He wrote in his memoirs that after two long years, Clark "asked to be relieved of his post, and agreed to take on the slower-paced job of secretary of the interior; he was fatigued and wanted a change".[46]

The seeds for the move had been sown in December 1982, when Clark first told Reagan he wanted to go home. He was already fed up with fighting Baker and Deaver, and after one of his and Reagan's many "philosophical discussions" about returning to private life on the ranch, Clark offered his resignation. This was not the same as when Al Haig offered to resign with no intent or desire to step down; Clark was in earnest. Reagan was surprised, and upset. He immediately called Ed Meese and Helene von Damm to ask their advice.

"Bill, this is the first time I've ever rejected a resignation", Reagan responded. "In time there may be something else." [47] He put Clark's resignation letter in his top drawer.

Then, in October 1983, the top spot at Interior opened up, and it was perfect—not too intense but yet another area where Reagan needed a troubleshooter and trusted ally to turn a mess around. He said to Clark: "I want you to consider going to Interior to place some oil on [Secretary] Jim Watt's water—to calm the waves." Clark took the assignment.

Clark's press assistant Jeremiah O'Leary, in a contemporaneous account, conceded that Clark was "deeply unhappy" over the internal

---

[45] New York Times, October 23, 1983.

[46] Reagan, An American Life, p. 448.

[47] Lou Cannon, "Overtaxed, Clark Sought Interior Post", Washington Post, October 15, 1983.

strife at the White House, "but his total adherence to Reagan's well-being and policies would not permit him to leave ... without Reagan's acquiescence, ... in accordance with his own code of loyalty." [48]

George Shultz sent Clark a warm goodbye note, dated October 17, in which he expressed to Clark his "warm personal regards", his "thanks", his "appreciation" for Clark's "many contributions to the country's foreign policy", and for his "extraordinary efforts to make the process of formulation and execution of foreign policy work well". He told Clark he looked forward to sitting next to him at Cabinet meetings once Clark shifted to Interior. It had been high praise when Shultz told the *New York Times* a few weeks earlier that Clark was "very effective" in an "extremely tough job".[49]

Celebrating in Moscow

The Soviet leadership was thrilled with Clark's departure. "Most connoisseurs of the Washington political cuisine", said *Pravda*, without naming names, "agree that bellicose adventurist Clark has brought nothing but disgrace to the White House." U.S.-Soviet relations might improve with the removal of this man who "looked at the world through a Colt barrel", the paper added.

In the same article, *Pravda* did exactly what Clark in September had predicted the Soviet government would do: The newspaper claimed that KAL 007 was a U.S. "espionage flight over Soviet territory". When Clark had suggested the Soviets might make such a claim, he was not taken seriously by the White House moderates. Yet, Moscow not only accused Washington of using KAL 007 to spy on them, but also asserted that it was Bill Clark who gave the order for the passenger plane to carry out the espionage mission. "After the failure of that provocation", added Pravda, Clark had the audacity to lead the "anti-Soviet hullabaloo" that condemned the Kremlin's behavior in the incident.[50]

---

[48] Jeremiah O'Leary, "Judge William P. Clark—an appreciation", *Washington Times*, October 24, 1983.

[49] Weisman, "The Influence of William Clark", p. 20; the note, dated October 17, 1983, is in Clark's files.

[50] Cited in: "Soviets Call Clark a Scapegoat" and "Soviets-Clark", United Press International, October 15, 1983.

Clark's Troops Rally

Of course, many in the White House interpreted the Soviets' glee over Clark's departure from the NSC as a significant indicator he needed to stay. One group that did not take Clark's resignation happily was that tight-knit core he had assembled at the NSC.

The morning they heard the news, Roger Robinson, John Lenczowski, Sven Kraemer, and Ken deGraffenreid composed letters trying to convince Clark to stay. These letters were heartfelt, personal, and candid, pleading with Clark to reconsider, predicting nothing short of catastrophe if he left.

"It has been an honor for which I have not always been worthy to have worked for you", wrote Ken deGraffenreid to Clark. "I must express to you my deepest concern about what this move may mean for the fate of our country. The hour is late for the United States in this century of totalitarian challenges." He predicted: "Many of us have struggled for this President as we have, and have tried to help you in this struggle, because we believed that when all was said and done Ronald Reagan and Bill Clark understood that we were at this profoundly moral junction in the life of our country." DeGraffenreid urged Clark to reconsider and "tell the President that he needs you most where you are now."

DeGraffenreid typed his letter on October 14, as did Sven Kraemer. Kraemer's letter had a similar theme and tone of desperation: "For the sake of our President and the country, I urge you and the President to reconsider.... I know I am speaking for much of your NSC staff, and am surely joining others elsewhere, in this urgent plea."

Kraemer laid out over a half-dozen examples of crises he had seen in his previous twenty years in government, which included twelve years on the NSC staffs of four other presidents. He feared that disaster could come to the Reagan NSC without Clark at the helm. He worried about "ethical" lapses that could occur without Clark in control. The stakes were too high for Clark to leave, said Kraemer. "I urge you and the President to reconsider the fateful step you have contemplated.... It will be the most important dissent of your life", he told the Judge. "Please stay.... You will continue to have our support and our prayers and will be serving our President and our country in a cause that transcends us all."

On Saturday morning, October 15, Clark got two more lengthy letters. One was a four-page handwritten letter from Roger Robinson, which
began: "Bill: As you know, I have never written a personal letter to you
before." He cautioned that "this country is in the throes of one of the
most perilous periods in its history", and was sure that no successor could
do the job that Clark had done. "[Y]ou have emerged in my mind as
one of the truly great figures of our time", he wrote in closing.

John Lenczowski's letter, also dated October 15, featured more specific concerns than any of the others. He began by saying that when
he heard of Clark's resignation, first from a friend, "I literally thought
he was joking ... [the] decision came as a great shock." He told
Clark he was being inundated with phone calls and letters, particularly from "Reaganauts", saying they were "flabbergasted", and that
the decision was "completely illogical", "madness", a "catastrophe".

Lenczowski said the decision was "a grave mistake", "disastrous"
for the country and its national security, in more ways than he said he
could describe. Clark's exit was a "critical loss" for the President's
ability to make the best decisions. He noted that Clark was "the one
person" who protected Reagan and ensured that he succeeded in fulfilling the mandate that swept him into office.

Lenczowski, a Polish American, was especially worried about Clark
being replaced by the "powerful forces advocating 'détente', accomo-
dationism, 'trade-with-the-Soviets-no-matter-what', self-censorship and
retreat", and which would "gain a virtual monopoly in presenting
foreign policy options to the President".

The NSC staffer rued a dreadful image: the pragmatists arranging a
photo-op of Reagan and Andropov shaking hands over a phony deal
that did nothing but advance Soviet self-interests—"a photo whose
effects will be that ninety percent of the words of truth about Soviet
communism uttered by the President as well as his entire career will
be flushed down the tubes".

John Lenczowski concluded with this appeal to Clark: "You once
told me that we were put in our jobs by an act of Providence. I believe
that. But I don't think that the President's decision to transfer you was
a decision inspired by the same Providence. Too much is at stake for
you to walk away from this job."

The letters deeply affected Clark, he says, yet he felt his task as
national security advisor had been achieved, that he had done all that

he was brought in to do, particularly given the restraints and limitations he faced.

* * *

Despite the grief, Bill Clark had no regrets about his time in the West Wing; as he states: "I would do it again a hundred times over." [51] Reagan was appreciative. He wrote Clark a personal letter on November 7 in which he told him that "few in government" had done more than he had done to maintain a posture of strength and security for the country. He told Clark that he had demonstrated "an acute sense" of the realities and difficulties of world politics. "You have been there time and again, ready to serve, and I've always valued your counsel", wrote Reagan. "All of us owe you a great debt of gratitude. Thanks for being there, as you always are." [52]

The peace through strength plan was in place and ready to prompt five summits over the next four years, with the indispensable assistance of men such as Cap Weinberger. SDI was unleashed, as was aid to Solidarity in Poland and to freedom fighters in Afghanistan and Nicaragua. More, a relationship with a diplomatically recognized Vatican was thriving, the USSR was denounced as an "Evil Empire" headed to the "ash-heap of history", communism had been halted in spots like Suriname, and a strategy to liberate Eastern and Central Europe and reform the USSR was formalized with a number of bold NSDDs. The crucial developments that occurred in the second Reagan term had roots in what Ronald Reagan and Bill Clark discussed in the Sacramento days and implemented in the first term. As he, his President, and his staff realized, the foundation for a Cold War victory had been laid, and the course had been set.

---

[51] Clark, "Alumni Spotlight / Q&A", *Vista Magazine*, p. 19.
[52] The November 7, 1983 letter on White House letterhead is held by Clark in his files.

CHAPTER 13

Troubleshooting Again

Clark at Interior

Bill Clark's resignation from the National Security Council was not the only surprise President Reagan gave the country on October 13, 1983. Reagan's nomination of Clark to replace the controversial James Watt at the Department of the Interior was equally unexpected. *Newsweek* called it "Reagan's October Surprise".[1] *U.S. News & World Report* noted that the idea to appoint Clark was the President's alone, discussed with no advisor but Clark.[2]

Jim Baker and Mike Deaver had compiled their own list of preferred candidates for the Interior post, which they quietly shared with preferred media sources.[3] Indeed, Reagan "senior aides" had been suggesting to reporters that Representative Manuel Lujan (R-NM) would be getting Watt's job.[4]

---

[1] "Reagan's October Surprise: He Stuns Aides—and the Nation—by Naming NSC Chief William Clark to the Interior", *Newsweek*, October 24, 1983.

[2] *U.S. News & World Report*, reflecting the collective media's low opinion of Reagan as a puppet on a string manipulated by his staff, claimed that, "The sudden choice of William Clark as the new Interior Secretary shows a side of Ronald Reagan rarely displayed so openly before: That he is capable of making major decisions with scant advice from his aides." The news magazine correctly reported that the idea to hire Clark was "the President's alone, and he discussed it with no advisors but Clark until a day before his choice was made public. The secrecy underscored the bond between Reagan and Clark." Robert A. Kittle, "Why Reagan Turned to Clark", *U.S. News & World Report*, October 24, 1983, p. 23.

[3] Steven R. Weisman, "Clark's Move to Interior Makes External Waves", *New York Times*, October 16, 1983, p. 1.

[4] Kittle, "Why Reagan Turned to Clark".

James Watt had become a major political problem, especially as Reagan's re-election campaign was commencing. He often made colorful and at times outright offensive remarks. At the moment, Watt was under fire for the recent comment that a coal advisory board was made up of "a black ... a woman, two Jews, and a cripple".[5]

Asked why Reagan decided to replace Watt with Clark in such a sudden and dramatic fashion, Press Secretary Larry Speakes said, "The President decided he wanted to do it and he did it." Another reason, noted by UPI, was that Reagan wanted to make the announcement before word was leaked by "senior aides" hoping to sink the idea before it was official.[6]

It did not take long before the media began to question Clark's qualifications for this latest post. At his next press conference, Reagan was asked by CNN's Dean Reynolds: "Mr. President, your recent nomination of Judge Clark as Interior Secretary shocked just about everybody but yourself and Judge Clark, I think. I wonder, sir, if you can tell us what qualifications he has for that Interior Department post?" The contingent of reporters filled the room with chuckles, but Reagan calmly and confidently praised his friend: Clark was "a very able and fine administrator" with a "great" and "personal ... interest and knowledge in this field." "I believe he will do a fine job", said the President, adding: "He is a God-fearing Westerner, a fourth-generation rancher, a person I trust, and I think he will be a great secretary of the Interior."[7]

Perhaps Bill Casey put it best: the President knew that Bill Clark liked ranches, so he put him in charge of the busiest ranch in the world.

* * *

The Department of Interior might have seemed like a step down for a man who had been a global political player; but as Mike Feinsilber of the Associated Press noted, Clark was about to assume his third sensitive assignment in as many years.[8]

---

[5] Ira R. Allen, "Clark Cools Watt Style", United Press International, October 15, 1983.

[6] "Watt-Surprise", United Press International, October 14, 1983.

[7] Ronald Reagan, "The President's News Conference", October 19, 1983.

[8] Mike Feinsilber, "Appointee Has Reagan's Trust", Denver Post, October 14, 1983.

Reagan and Clark's reasons for the move were best described by Lyn Nofziger, who said that Reagan had once again turned to his "troubleshooter" to smooth out a rough spot in his administration. "As Interior secretary, Clark will operate differently than his predecessor James Watt", wrote Lyn Nofziger in an op-ed piece for the *Washington Times*. "He is lower-keyed. He is more careful in his approach and in his words. While he does not back away from a fight, he does not daily gird his loins and go joyfully to do battle with the infidel." Nofziger added that Clark would "seek to work with the critics of the president's policies whenever possible, rather than confront them. He will not make as compelling news copy as Watt nor will he be such a good direct-mail fundraiser for the environmentalist groups, who used Watt as a devil to scare innocent environmentalists into contributing to their various causes."

Clark was about to rob the environmentalists, and the Democrats for that matter, of a sizzling arrow in the quiver of objections to Reagan in the 1984 presidential race.[9] How were they going to demonstrate that Reagan is an enemy of the environment, and thereby of the health and well being of all living creatures, with affable and animal loving Bill Clark running the Interior Department? The "environmentalists are going to miss Watt", Nofziger said.

The old salts from Sacramento understood the move. They had seen it many times before, from the first days of the Clark-Reagan relationship. Veteran California reporter Frank Van der Linden echoed Nofziger, stating that Clark was being tapped yet again by Ronald Reagan for his "trouble-shooting" role. Likewise, the *Sacramento Bee* saw that Reagan had called in his "fireman" to put out the "political flames".[10]

Fireman Clark's amiable and conciliatory manner hardly guaranteed that he would be instantly and warmly embraced by the environmentalists. He was, after all, Reagan's man and a Republican. Smith Hempstone rightly predicted in the *Washington Times*: "Clark, like Watt, will

---

[9] Lyn Nofziger, "Clark as Troubleshooter (again)", *Washington Times*, October 19, 1983, p. C1.

[10] Frank Van der Linden, "Clark and Richardson: Trouble-shooting Team Brings Legal Talents to Interior Department", *Sacramento Union*, August 12, 1984, p. B6. The *Sacramento Bee* piece ran on October 14, 1983.

be branded an environmental antichrist by the self-anointed cardinals of the Sierra Club and the tweedy archbishops of the Wilderness Society, who apparently feel they—and they alone, of course—have been endowed by their Creator with the inalienable right and responsibility to dispose of the wild lands that belong equally to all of us and to none of us."[11]

Bill Clark, Tree Hater

Liberal members of Congress were harsh in their assessment of Clark's qualifications for his new position. Congressman Sam Gejdenson (D-CN) said, "If there is anything good in this announcement, it's that Clark will no longer be our national security advisor, a position he was no more qualified for than he is for the position of interior secretary."[12] Congressman Edward S. Markey (D-MA) said that the Clark pick was proof that "the president plans to continue his environmentally dangerous, often incompetent and uninformed pro-industry policies."[13]

Such words were a mere warm-up for the attack from green groups. Said Geoff Webb of Friends of the Earth: "Clark doesn't know any more about national parks or endangered species than he did about Angola or Zimbabwe."[14]

Carl Pope, the political director of the 350,000-member Sierra Club, stated, "We're dumbfounded. Mr. Clark has no visible record on environmental issues. I've spoken to people who were involved in those issues in Sacramento when Ronald Reagan was governor, and Clark never showed any interest in those affairs."[15]

For the record, this was not true, as the *New York Times*' Philip Shabecoff demonstrated with a quick phone call to Norman B. "Ike" Livermore, California's Secretary of Resources under Governor Reagan and Chief of Staff Clark. Livermore, noted Shabecoff, was "generally

---

[11] Smith Hempstone, "Public Lands: RR is Serious", *The Washington Times*, October 14, 1983.

[12] "What They're Saying about Clark", *The Denver Post*, October 14, 1983, p. 10A.

[13] Philip Shabecoff, "Environmental Groups Angered by Reagan Choice for Interior Job", *New York Times*, October 14, 1983, p. 4.

[14] "What They're Saying about Clark", *The Denver Post*.

[15] Ibid.

held in esteem by environmentalists", and he said that Clark had been "a tower of strength" in implementing friendly environmental policies; he had been particularly helpful in the 1968 decision to set aside lands for the Redwoods National Park. "I will be very surprised if Bill Clark doesn't do very well as Interior Secretary", Livermore remarked.[16]

Nonetheless, the claim that "Clark never showed any interest" in the environment as Governor Reagan's chief of staff, or ever, for that matter, would not go away. "William Clark has no environmental record",[17] said Sierra Club's Polly Freeman, while the club's president, Denny Shaffer, joked: "Secretary Watt was bored by the Grand Canyon. I worry that Judge Clark may not know where it is."[18] William Turnage, executive vice president of the Wilderness Society described Clark as "a very right-wing person" who had "never demonstrated any kind of interest in or concern with the environment".[19] Added Turnage: "It is the third time that President Reagan has appointed Mr. Clark to a job for which he has no apparent qualifications.... It's a preposterous appointment."

Such *claims* were preposterous, given that this lifelong rancher had spent more time in the wilderness and had at least as much appreciation of it as did any of his detractors, but Clark's experience was dismissed as irrelevant. "The fact that somebody owns a ranch is only a reflection that he has the money to own a ranch",[20] said National Audubon Society president Russell Peterson.

In addition to congressmen, lobbyists, and environmentalists, there were journalists attacking Clark, such as John B. Oakes, a former senior editor of the *New York Times*. "There you go again, Ronald Reagan", he wrote. "It didn't seem possible for you to appoint a secretary of the interior less fitted for the job than James G. Watt. But now you've done it.... Mr. Clark won't even know what he's doing."[21]

---

[16] Philip Shabecoff, "Clark Praised and Assailed on Environmental Issues", *New York Times*, October 15, 1983, p. 9.

[17] Robert Sangeorge, "Watt Reaction", United Press International, October 14, 1983.

[18] Dale Russakoff, "Environmental Groups Prepared to Oppose Clark at Hearing", *Washington Post*, November 1, 1983, p. A2.

[19] Philip Shabecoff, "Environmental Groups Angered By Reagan Choice for Interior Job", *New York Times*, October 14, 1983, p. 4.

[20] Sangeorge, "Watt Reaction".

[21] John B. Oakes, "Clark's Low Wattage", *New York Times*, October 18, 1983, p. 31.

Clark also took it on the chin from editorial cartoonists. Bill Schorr drew Clark disguised as Smoky the Bear creeping into the woods with a can of gasoline and a box of matches, ready to torch the forest. In the *Los Angeles Times*, Paul Conrad had the nominee in a baseball uniform heading to the batter's box in place of Jim Watt, except Clark held a giant axe rather than a baseball bat. Another Conrad cartoon was captioned "Environmental Primer for William Clark" and featured a picture of a landscape with labels: birds, mountains, rocks, trees, and fish.

Once again, Bill Clark was getting hammered. None of that surprised his Uncle Chet, Lakeview, Oregon, rancher. "Every job he's gotten they've raised hell about", said Chet in a 1983 interview, "but he seems to thrive on that kind of stuff."

Chet cautioned that his nephew was a good learner, harkening back to a summer day in 1947 when he helped Butch, his own special name for his nephew, saddle a wild horse at the ZX Ranch in northern Lake County. The young green gelding bucked hard, throwing fifteen-year-old "Butch", leaving him with a limp that persisted all the way into the halls of the Department of the Interior. "Never let 'em buck once you're on board", Chet had advised—but young Clark had not been able to control the wild horse fully at that stage in his life. He did respect his uncle's opinion, however, and with age came the ability to control most challenges—particularly of the horse variety. "Once in a while I get a call from him", said Chet, "wanting an opinion about some damn thing." [22] It meant a lot to the old wheat farmer that his nephew still considered him worth consulting.

Among the criticisms of Clark moving to Interior was the claim that Reagan picked him to mollify conservatives. "I guess the appointment will play well with the right wing", said a high-level Department of Interior official. "God help us all over again." [23] William Turnage somehow concluded that the pick was "made as a sop to the extreme right wing of the Republican Party". [24]

[22] Lee Juillerat, "Washington Winds Shift Lakeview Power Base", *Herald News* (Klamath Falls, Oregon), May 21, 1984.

[23] Dale Russakoff, "Watt's Heir Apparent Stokes Fires of Protest: Bafflement, Rage and Skepticism Greet Selection of William Clark", *Washington Post*, October 14, 1983, p. A7.

[24] "What They're Saying about Clark", *The Denver Post*; and Russakoff, "Watt's Heir Apparent Stokes Fires of Protest".

In fact, conservatives were unhappy with the move. They had lost their man at the NSC, and at a time when the issue was the Russian Bear, not the spotted owl. Howard E. Phillips of the Conservative Caucus and Richard A. Viguerie, whose national direct-mail operation reached two million activists, expressed disappointment. Said Viguerie, "Moving Judge Clark to Interior gets a strong conservative anticommunist out of the foreign-policy making process and allows the moderates and liberals in the White House and State Department to assume total control of foreign policy. This appears to be a victory for Jim Baker and George Shultz."[25]

The *Times* noted that conservatives found it "astounding" that Clark was willing to walk away from his position as "the administration's most influential foreign policy official. . . . That's got a lot of people in the administration worried", said a senior foreign policy official. "There's a lot of unhappiness. . . . The hardliners are demoralized. A lot of us felt, no matter how bad things got for us, you could always call Bill."[26]

In a Page One piece entitled, "MISTAKE", the *Washington Post* quoted U.S. Ambassador to the U.N. Jeane J. Kirkpatrick, who said the Clark move was a "disastrous mistake".[27]

Hearings

Clark did, however, have some supporters. A young Republican congressman from Wyoming by the name of Dick Cheney, who himself had been a top prospect for the job given to Clark, called the Judge "a surprising but excellent appointment", as did Senators Paul Laxalt (R-NV) and Barry Goldwater (R-AZ).[28] Senate Majority Leader Howard Baker (R-TN) said he was confident that Clark would be confirmed.[29]

---

[25] Russakoff, "Watt's Heir Apparent Stokes Fires of Protest".

[26] Steven R. Weisman, "Clark's Move to Interior Makes External Waves", *New York Times*, October 16, 1983, p. 1.

[27] John M. Goshko, "'Mistake'; Kirkpatrick Thought Clark Should Stay", *Washington Post*, October 22, 1983, p. A1.

[28] See Lou Cannon and David Hoffman, "Reagan Adviser Clark Named to Succeed Watt; Decision Made Suddenly", *Washington Post*, October 14, 1983, p. A1; and "What They're Saying about Clark", *The Denver Post*.

[29] Shabecoff, "Clark Praised and Assailed on Environmental Issues".

Clark's confirmation hearings were scheduled for November 1 and 2, 1983, before the Senate Committee on Energy and Natural Resources. Here again, he received heated opposition, particularly from Senators Dale Bumpers (D-AR) and Howard Metzenbaum (D-OH). On the other hand, he was treated graciously by other Democrats, including Senators Paul Tsongas (D-MA) and Bill Bradley (D-NJ). Overall, this hearing was nothing like the humiliation of February 1981. There was no Joe Biden on this committee to ask Clark to name the state bird of Utah.

Clark's appearance went much smoother this time around. As a rancher, rider, and more, Clark had lived his entire life as a steward of the environment. He could simply talk about his experience and convince the senators of his passion for the job, and that was precisely the approach he employed in his confirmation hearings.

He recalled the two-room schoolhouse he attended as a child, as well as his home on "the most beautiful ranch in Ventura County", both now under thirty feet of water in a reclamation project known as Casitas Dam. He told the senators about his ranch in Shandon: "I look upon it as somewhat of a wildlife refuge." He noted that he had laid three miles of dirt road in the bottom of the canyon rather than cutting the top of a ridge. He developed his own springs on the property, from which he pumped all water for his home via a windmill up the hill, from where it flowed down to the house, warmed in part by the sun. "We plant ... only half of that farm each year," Clark continued, "letting the other half lie fallow, and we raise barley and cattle. We have quail, dove, ducks, and deer. We take no game. We allow none to be taken."

Clark told the committee that the ranch is officially a preserve. "My wife and I have retained two acres, including the house and an orchard where I planted two of every variety of fruit tree that will grow in the region." Clark talked on and on. If there were no further questions on ranching, said Clark, he would proceed to other areas. There were no further questions. Bill Clark was eminently qualified.

The Judge's tendency to treat all people, including political antagonists, with respect came full circle during the confirmation process: Clark received a wonderful surprise when former President Jimmy Carter called him to say that he was glad to hear that Clark would be heading to Interior, where he would be a "fair wind" after Watt, whom Carter declared a "disaster". Carter foresaw the troubles ahead for Clark in his hearings and graciously offered to telephone some wildlife groups to vouch for Clark. "You may have a hard time after Watt", he told Clark. "I'd like to call some of my green friends and tell them you're okay."[30] Clark said he would very much appreciate the help, and he credited his easier road this time around in part to Carter's intervention.

The hearings revealed another example of Clark's past coming back to help him: Clark had been told to expect some resistance from the 525 tribes of American Indians who were still steaming over James Watt. The Bureau of Indian Affairs was one of the ten bureaus within the Department of Interior, and the most confrontational. Clark prepared heavily for questions related to that area.

When he walked into the hearing room, he glimpsed six or seven Native Americans seated in the back row. Clark thought they looked somewhat familiar. As it turned out, these were indeed friends, having flown to Washington from San Diego at their own expense, to testify on Clark's behalf. Clark had gotten to know the group in the 1950s, when they were embroiled in a serious legal problem over a land dispute. They'd not been able to find an attorney willing to give them a hand until Bill Clark, Oxnard's new attorney, took their case, pro bono.

"I did not expect them", said Clark, who did about a third of his lawyer work pro bono. "That was a surprise. Their testimony ended all debate on me and the Indian issue."

Clark finished his testimony by thanking the senators. The committee voted in his favor by 16 to 3, with three Democrats opposed— Tsongas, Bumpers, and Wendell H. Ford of Kentucky.[31] On November 18, the full Senate gave its consent by a vote of 71 to 18—all of the 18 were Democrats.

The New Secretary of the Interior

Three days later, on November 21, Bill Clark was sworn in as secretary of the Interior at a ceremony in the Oval Office attended by the President and about a half-dozen others, including Joan, Jacque Hill, Joe Bullock, Helene von Damm, William French Smith, and Jim Baker.

---

[30] On this, see William E. Farrell and Warren Weaver Jr., "Birds of a Feather", *New York Times*, February 23, 1984.

[31] "Senate Panel Supports Clark to Succeed Watt", *New York Times*, November 10, 1983, p. A15.

"Judge Clark wanted to be sworn in privately and quietly, and he was", said Larry Speakes. Clark had now had a private swearing-in for seven of the eight positions he held under Ronald Reagan. (The exception was when he became a California Supreme Court justice.) The press said it was the only private swearing-in of a Cabinet officer in "recent memory".[32]

It did not take long before Clark started winning over foes, primarily because of his openness. In a gesture of supreme goodwill, he sat across the table from the very people who portrayed him as a gargoyle. This was a sharp departure from the style of James Watt, especially when Clark met with leaders of two major environmental groups whom Watt had called "extremists" and members of a "left-wing cult", namely Jay D. Hair, the National Wildlife Federation's executive vice president, and National Audubon Society president Russell Peterson, both of whom Clark invited to his office to air their grievances. This move by Clark startled conservationists.[33]

Clark promised to review Watt's record and to meet regularly with conservationists as well as industry groups. "It's clear from this meeting that ... Clark is a decent human being, and certainly not the arrogant, abrasive personality Jim Watt was", said Hair, whose four-million–member group was the nation's largest conservation organization. Said Hair: "We now have a guy there who will listen to you."[34]

Added Peterson: "It was such a contrast to our few—very few—other contacts with this administration. Clark didn't challenge us, and he didn't tell us we didn't know what we were talking about. That's not much of a test, but it is quite a contrast." Peterson said Clark was "certainly a different kind of human being than Watt". They concluded that Clark had made "a very good impression" and was a "refreshing change".[35]

Another example of the contrast between Watt and Clark was the relationship that Clark quickly developed with Congressman Morris

---

[32] Dale Russakoff, "Clark, Taking Over, Terminates One Watt Ritual", *Washington Post*, November 22, 1983, p. A3.

[33] See "Conservationists Pleased by Style of Watt's Successor", *San Jose Mercury News*, October 22, 1983, p. 13A; and Dale Russakoff, "Two Startled Conservationalists Take Clark up on Invitation to Talk", *Washington Post*, October 22, 1983, p. A6.

[34] "Report from Watt Sees '83 Success", *New York Times*, November 23, 1983, p. 16.

[35] "Conservationists Pleased by Style of Watt's Successor", p. 13.

Udall (D-AZ), the longtime chair of the House Committee on Interior and Insular Affairs as well as the Interior Subcommittee on Energy and the Environment. Udall and Watt had stopped speaking. Udall, a legend and political icon, was Mr. Interior on Capitol Hill, and the big question was whether Clark would get along with him. "They expected our first meeting together to be a shout out", recalls Clark. "Well, our first meeting together was scheduled. I walked up to the Hill with my staff, which was trembling, wondering if I could handle the situation—which was a good question. . . . We waited in the congressman's waiting area. Once he was ready, I told the staff to stay seated—which made them even more nervous."

The introductory meeting was scheduled to last fifteen minutes. Clark and Udall exchanged ideas for an hour and a half, while the new secretary's staff squirmed and paced outside. The two had a "wonderful meeting", says Clark. "It went so well." They talked about their backgrounds, about family, about their fathers, and early frontier life. Udall was tall, like Clark's father, and, likewise, was suffering from Parkinson's. "We were on a first name basis after that, 'Mo' and 'Bill' ", says Clark. "We were on opposite ends politically but not philosophically, because we both had love and concern for both our environment and natural resources. And the personal relationship became close and productive." Indeed, Udall would ultimately ask Clark to preside over the dedication of his official portrait at his retirement ceremony. Clark was honored to do so.

Clark kept reaching out. One of his first public moves as the new secretary was to give an important speech calling for an end to partisanship over conservation issues and offering to make his department more accessible to environmental groups, Congress, and the media. Speaking at the National Wildlife Federation, he challenged environmentalists to propose policies that kept in mind the nation's security and economic needs. He called for an armistice in the running conflicts between Interior and green groups. There could be a "convergence" of America's environmental, national security, and economic needs, he said, but "it takes two or more to converge."

Jay Hair called the speech a "symbolically important" departure from Watt. Some, however, were unappeasable: William Turnage said that while Clark was "cordial", cordiality would not protect America from Reagan's "devastating" policies.[36]

A week later, for the first time since President Reagan took office, the Interior Department's Fish and Wildlife Service invited environmentalists to its annual Christmas party in the agency cafeteria. Jay Hair said he did not even know the service had held Christmas parties during the previous two years. "I certainly appreciate the invitation",[37] he added.

Clark's offer of goodwill did not stop with the Christmas season. Two months later, he telephoned Congressman John F. Seiberling (D-OH), to ask his opinion about the pending resignation of the director of the Office of Surface Mining. In three previous years, said the Democrat, he had been ignored or assailed by Clark's predecessor; he was never once consulted on a policy or personnel decision. The congressman said he was "amazed" and gratified by the phone call.

The New York Times noticed the change in relations between the Interior Department and the environmentalists. Moreover, it gave the credit for the improvement to the efforts of Bill Clark. "Apparently", reported the newspaper, "a new day has dawned at the Department of the Interior."[38]

Changes at Interior

Secretary Clark changed much more than the tone at Interior; he also changed personnel. Clark replaced department Solicitor William H. Coldiron, a key figure in controversial Watt policies involving stripmining regulation, offshore oil development, wilderness protection, and coal leasing. The Coldiron removal brought to six the number of Watt's political appointees that Clark had replaced since taking office. He earlier replaced Under Secretary J.J. Simmons and the chief architects of Watt's offshore oil- and gas-leasing programs, Dave C. Russell and William P. Pendley. Watt was incredulous. "I can't believe that",

[36] Philip Shabecoff, "Watt Successor Offers Olive Branch to Critics", New York Times, December 8, 1983, p. A24.

[37] Pete Earley and Dale Russakoff, "Christmas Spirit Rises", Washington Post. December 14, 1983, p. A21.

[38] Philip Shabecoff, "Calmer Seas with Clark at Helm", New York Times, February 21, 1984, p. B8.

he reacted when told of the dismissals. "It doesn't make sense. They are outstanding people."[39] Clark also selected Ann McLaughlin for the number two post at the agency, which was reported as one of the highest-level appointments of a woman in the administration.[40]

Clark made some significant policy modifications with respect to the natural resources under his management. The Clark Interior—in "a major policy swing certain to have an election-year impact in the West"—backed away from two tough stands that the Reagan administration had taken against subsidies for beneficiaries of costly federal water projects. In a letter to western senators, signed by Reagan, Clark's department outlined a revised administration position on financing irrigation and flood-control projects and, reversing a previous position, stated that the federal government would pay the full cost of repairing unsafe dams.[41]

On a related matter, the new Interior Secretary removed the Grand Canyon from the government's list of potential dam sites, ripping up a fifty-year-old piece of paperwork that was considered one of the most unpopular development ideas of all time. The Grand Canyon had been listed as a possible dam site during the 1930s, when government surveyors were scouting possible spots for hydroelectric plants. First proposed by the Roosevelt administration, the potential use of the Grand Canyon was supported as recently as the 1960s by President Johnson, when it had run into opposition from environmentalists. The wall of the dam would have been seven-hundred-feet high. "Like so many disastrous plans, it seemed like a good idea at the time", said an Interior official.

Environmentalists still found fault with Clark's action on the Grand Canyon. "Generally speaking, this is a good sign", said David Conrad of Friends of the Earth. However, he cautioned, "The question that

---

[39] "Watt Surprised by Interior Department Dismissals", *Tulsa World*, December 24, 1983, p. D1. For the record, Watt had been delighted with the choice of Clark. "Bill's an extremely capable and fine man", he said. "He's a tremendous guy and we happen to have a close personal friendship. I just couldn't be more pleased." Watt called Clark "a prince". "Couldn't Be More Delighted Says Watt of Nomination", *News Press* (Santa Barbara, Calif), October 14, 1983, p. A1.

[40] "Clark Names a Woman to No. 2 Post at Interior", *USA Today*, December 23, 1983, p. 7A.

[41] Dale Russakoff and Ward Sinclair, "Cost Allotments to Change; Reagan Revises Water-Project Policy", *Washington Post*, January 24, 1984, p. A1.

still remains is, what about the 100 sections of land that are on the Hualapai Indian reservation?" [42] Soon enough, Clark covered that, too. He returned 132 thousand acres, more than 200 sections, of canyon land to the Hualapai Indians.

Clark's environmental achievements were acknowledged in an important election-year piece that appeared in a February 1984 *U.S. News & World Report*. "In swift moves that may steal the thunder of critics, President Reagan is breathing fresh air into his environmental policies", the article reported. "Confrontations that marred Reagan's dealings with environmentalists have faded." Credit for the peacemaking went to Clark for prosecuting polluters with renewed vigor, slowing an apparent rush to develop energy and mineral resources on public lands, reviving federal acquisitions of parklands, and opening the way for adoption of a plan to protect ground water that reportedly had never come up for consideration under Watt.

"All these changes leave critics foundering", said *U.S. News & World Report*. Bill Clark was "disarming" the critics.[43] In the process, he was not only turning Interior around, he was removing the environment as an issue against Reagan in his re-election campaign.

There were additional policy implementations of existing Congressional actions by Clark's Interior.[44] He even proved to be an advocate of wildlife conservation, which, he told the National Wildlife Federation, was "not a liberal or a conservative challenge", but "common sense." [45]

---

[42] Cass Peterson, "Grand Canyon Finally Sheltered from Hydroelectric Developers", *Washington Post*, February 15, 1984, p. A17.

[43] Ronald A. Taylor, "Environment: A New Leaf for Reagan", *U.S. News & World Report*, February 27, 1984, p. 59.

[44] See David Smollar, "Clark Intensely Reviewing Watt's Policies at Interior", *Los Angeles Times*, December 31, 1983, p. 1; "Interior's Clark Seeks $150M for Park Lands", *USA Today*, December 30, 1983, p. 7A; Mary Manning, "Clark to Push Plans for Doubling Power Capacity at Hoover", *Las Vegas Sun*, December 30, 1983, p. 1B; Ronald Reagan, "Remarks at Dedication Ceremonies for the New Building of the National Geographic Society", June 19, 1984, p. 875; and Ben A. Franklin, "Settlement to Require U.S. to Enforce Strip-Mine Laws", *New York Times*. October 14, 1984, p. 26.

[45] Clark said this to the National Wildlife Federation in a March 17, 1984 speech in Atlanta, located in the binder "William Clark's speeches/statements" at Clark's office in Paso Robles, CA. Also see: Ronald Reagan, "Remarks at a White House Ceremony Marking the Golden Anniversary Year of the Duck Stamp", ceremony at the White House Rose Garden, Washington, D.C., July 3, 1984.

Not long after the *U.S. News and World Report* article, Clark received some favorable coverage in certain environmental publications. *Audubon Action*, for example, listed some of Clark's accomplishments in an editorial entitled, "William P. Clark: A Few Good Things". The piece concluded, "In case anyone was wondering, it is now clear why William P. Clark remains one of President Reagan's most valuable aides." [46]

Though Clark impressed some environmentalists as a Republican who would at least consider their concerns, others continued trying to undermine him. The March 21, 1984, *Washington Post* reported on an attempt to pin something on Clark. "An environmental group contends that baits treated with a controversial poison known as Compound 1080 were scattered on a California ranch owned by Interior Secretary William P. Clark last year to kill ground squirrels without proper state and county permits." The group was mistaken in its claims, however, as demonstrated by state and county officials who found no evidence that any regulations had been violated, or that anyone had acted improperly. [47]

A continued source of contention between environmentalists and the Department of the Interior was the fact that Clark did not agree with everything on the green agenda. He believed that the government's environmental polices must be prudent and take into consideration the needs of the nation's security and economy.

Citing the threat to world oil supplies posed by conflict in the Middle East, Clark called for an end to congressional restrictions on the sale of federal offshore oil and gas leases. Congress had earlier in the year passed a moratorium on selling drilling rights in areas off the coasts of California, Florida, and Massachusetts, and was now hoping to extend and expand the moratorium. Clark told a group of U.S. businessmen, "I do not think that that approach is in the national interests." He said the nation needed to tap much more of its offshore oil and gas reserves. [48] "The American public won't think it funny when they start lining up in gas lines", said the secretary. [49] Clark was

---

[46] "William P. Clark: A Few Good Things", *Audubon Action*, April 1984, p. 3.

[47] Pete Earley, "Environmentalists Find Poison on Clark Ranch", *Washington Post*, March 21, 1984, p. A21.

[48] "Clark Would End Restrictions on Offshore Leasing", *Washington Post*, June 8, 1984, p. A21.

[49] Philip Shabecoff, "The Quest for Offshore Oil Wanes", *New York Times*, October 7, 1984, p. A8.

very concerned with America's dependence on foreign oil. Ultimately, his biggest disappointment at Interior was not being able to secure offshore drilling.

Clark made numerous statements and speeches as secretary of the Interior, whether testifying before the Senate Committee on Energy and Natural Resources or speaking to groups such as the California Farm Bureau Federation, the National Wildlife Federation, or to the National Press Club.[50] Between November 1983 and November 1984, he gave nearly sixty speeches and testimonies, an average of more than one per week.

The Personal

Clark stamped his own style upon Interior, reflected in the way he decorated the secretary's suite on the sixth floor of the Main Interior Building. He created a western ranch-style work environment—displaying western paintings and family memorabilia. He could often be found working at his desk after hours with a fire roaring in the fireplace.

Clark's new colleagues took note of the calm secretary's busy schedule, which began at home at 4:30 A.M. with some reading. Right after that, at 5:45 A.M., came the highlight of his day: a thirty-minute horseback ride while Washington slept.

Most mornings, Clark galloped through Washington with his park police friends and the occasional ambassador. Clark called his daily adventure a "marvelous break" from a difficult routine.[51] In addition, Clark and the President rode together occasionally at Quantico Marine Base in Virginia.

Clark's favorite horse was a Lippizaner stallion, a gift to Ronald Reagan from the Austrians. Nancy Reagan and the Secret Service feared the spirited animal was a risky mount for the President, so regularly exercising the horse was a task given to Clark. "Of course, I performed this duty at great inconvenience and sacrifice", says Clark with a grin.[52]

---

[50] "William Clark Speeches/Statements". Located in Clark files/binders at Clark Office in Paso Robles, California.

[51] Clark quoted in an article titled, "Shandon's Clark Recalls Work on Reagan Team", written by reporter Cynthia Neff for local paper, The Tribune (photocopy in Clark's files contains no date or full citation).

[52] Cynthia Neff, "Shandon's Clark Recalls Work on Reagan Team".

Joan chose to name the horse "Amadeus", in recognition of her fellow Austrian, Wolfgang Amadeus Mozart, a favorite of both Joan and Bill. Joan notes that *Amadeus* is Latin for "Beloved of God".

After Bill's morning ride, he gave Joan a kiss and hopped into a chauffeur-driven car. As a Cabinet secretary, Clark had a regular driver, Joe Bullock, a native of Georgia, who had moved to Washington fifty years earlier looking for work during tough times. Joe first found employment as a mule driver. He eventually traded in the animal to become a driver for various senior people in the federal government.

Some of Joe's former bosses did not treat him well. In fact, one Cabinet secretary from the previous administration did not speak a word to Bullock in three years. Thus, the driver was taken aback when Clark began talking to him, asking Bullock about his life and family. Even more surprising was Clark's request to ride up front, beside his driver. Joe agreed, so Clark rode "shotgun" for the rest of his term in Washington. Clark and Bullock discussed many topics, and Joe developed an interest in political matters and began reading the *Washington Post* every morning in anticipation of their conversations.

Clark's appearance in the front seat turned heads. It also caused a stir the first few times he and Bullock approached the front gate of the White House. The security people were disturbed by this informality, since Clark remained on the Libyan hit list. A special level of security had been ordered for the former national security advisor. Not a problem, thought Driver Joe, who secretly took the initiative to look after his new friend by concealing a .38 Special inside his coat.

One morning Bill's father was visiting. He, too, liked Joe, and gave him a gift: a western-style belt, with a kind of a "John Wayne silver belt buckle", as Bill describes it. Joe put it on right away and from then on always proudly displayed it by allowing his blue suit jacket to remain unbuttoned.

That belt and buckle led to a most unexpected honor for Clark's driver. It so happened that there was an upcoming state visit by England's Prince Philip, and, as was the custom, the White House needed to present a gift. Clark, Reagan, and a few others brainstormed following Clark's morning briefing. Clark suggested a "western belt" and had a certain belt in mind from Si Jenkins, a Santa Barbara friend of the President, from whom Reagan and Clark purchased western apparel.

"Well, what does it look like?" asked Reagan. Clark explained that he had a model waiting in the car—Joe, who was wearing the belt. "Send him up", ordered the President. They called down for Joe, who entered via the door of Reagan's personal secretary Helene von Damm.

Joe had worked for the government for nearly fifty years, but he had been nowhere near the Oval Office, nor within fifty yards of a President. When he walked in and saw Clark, the vice president, the senior aides, and the President of the United States, he shook with emotion, and the proud, six-foot-four man began to cry. He had come so far since the hardships of the Great Depression and the Jim Crow South.

No one in the room was prepared for Bullock's reaction, and all fell silent. No one knew how to respond—except Ronald Reagan, who quickly rose, walked over to the driver, extended his hand, and said matter-of-factly, "Mr. Bullock, I understand you have a belt to show me?" Reagan's grace put Bullock at ease, and the driver showed off his belt. Soon he and Reagan were swapping stories. "The rest of us just faded away", says Clark; "the two got along famously." Bullock left that day with a story to tell his fellow drivers, and his grandchildren.

Bullock "was a wonderful companion", says Clark. When old Joe died, several years after Clark left Washington, Bill returned to pay his respects at the funeral.

Clark Says Goodbye—For Good

In November 1984, Ronald Reagan crushed Democratic nominee Walter Mondale in a re-election landslide. Reagan won 49 of 50 states—losing only (and barely) Mondale's home state of Minnesota—and sweeping the electoral college 525–13. If Clark had come in as a troubleshooter to help Reagan politically, he succeeded; and now, after over a year on the job at Interior, the family and ranch in Shandon beckoned—this time irresistibly.

On January 1, 1985, Clark told President Reagan he was resigning his post to return to California. "My task at Interior is substantially complete; it's time to go home." The two were in Palm Springs, where the President was vacationing during the New Year holiday.[53]

---

[53] Lou Cannon, "Secretary Clark to Resign; 'It's Time to Go Home to California,' Interior Chief Says", *Washington Post*, January 2, 1985, p. A1.

Interviewed a few hours later on ABC's *Good Morning America*, Clark explained: "I've been here for four years now and I want to get back to the family." [54]

As he had in job after job, Clark exited with accolades. In his letter accepting his resignation, President Reagan wrote:

Dear Bill,
It is with very great regret that I accept your resignation as Secretary of the Interior, effective February 7, 1985.

First as Governor of California, and then as President, I have turned to you many times to fill the hardest assignments. In every case, you have taken the job and succeeded in just the way I knew you would. No one has given me more faithful service above and beyond the call of duty than you, and I want to thank you now for many jobs well done during the past eighteen years.

As you return to California, it is with my deepest thanks.

Sincerely, Ron

Clark received approval from some surprising places. "Even Clark's critics . . . have praised his performance at the Interior Department", reported Lou Cannon in the *Washington Post*.[55] Environmental lobbyists who had opposed his nomination, said the *Post*, "grudgingly acknowledged that they were sorry to see him go".[56] Louise Dunlap of the Environmental Policy Institute said: "We were pleasantly surprised with Secretary Clark. We found him to be very fair. . . . We're disappointed that he's leaving." Dunlap had testified against Clark at his confirmation hearings.[57] Paul Pritchard, president of the National Parks and Conservation Association, said Clark "left his mark, a good one".[58]

On Capitol Hill Clark received some praise from the other side of the aisle. "I must say, Mr. Secretary, you put out fires very quickly", said Congressman Sidney R. Yates (D-IL), who had been one of Watt's most outspoken critics and a Clark skeptic. Congressman Udall told

---

[54] "Clark to Quit Interior, Says Job Completed", *Spokane Chronicle*, January 2, 1985.

[55] Cannon, "Secretary Clark to Resign".

[56] Cass Peterson, "Clark's Announcement Stuns Interior Staff: Ex-Critics Regret His Plans to Quit", *Washington Post*, January 1985.

[57] Dunlap quoted in Philip Shabecoff, "Clark to Stay on for 2 or 3 Months", *New York Times*, January 3, 1985, p. A19; and Peterson, "Clark's Announcement Stuns Interior Staff".

[58] Peterson, "Clark's Announcement Stuns Interior Staff".

reporters that it had been "great" to deal with someone of such "common sense and fairness and judgment".[59]

The press was equally flattering. Editorial boards from the *Arizona Republic* to *USA Today* praised Clark.[60] The *Chicago Tribune* editorialized: "Applying honesty, fairness and common sense, Mr. Clark revived the department from the trampling it had received under the bizarre leadership of the controversial James Watt. Working quietly, he ... won the grudging respect of some of the administration's most shrill environmental critics."[61] The editors of the *Washington Post* added: "Clark worked with considerable skill to turn down the heat in that big building. He ended the daily fireworks displays and, in general, got the place back to work."[62]

The *Post* also noted that the loss of Clark was keenly felt by his staff. In an article titled, "Clark's Announcement Stuns Interior Staff: Ex-Critics Regret His Plans to Quit", the *Washington Post* reported that the mood at Interior was "a tad surreal", as employees absorbed the news that Clark was leaving a post in which he "seemed perfectly at ease".[63]

Lou Cannon noted in the *Post* that Clark was part of an exodus of three Californians whose careers were entwined with Reagan's, the other two being William French Smith and Mike Deaver.[64] "Reagan is losing his ties to the past", said an influential Republican. "He's going to find the White House a lonelier place."[65] In a personal letter to a friend, Reagan wrote, "I can assure you I'll miss Bill Clark ... Bill has stayed on about two years more than he wanted to and now feels he must get back to the ranch. You know I'm responsible for his being in public service eighteen years. His ranching is not vacationing as mine is. It's a working ranch and he feels a real need to get his hands on the reins."[66]

---

[59] Peterson, "Hodel, Laxalt Possible Successors", *Washington Post*, January 2, 1985, p. A1.

[60] The *Arizona Republic* editorial ran in the January 3, 1985 edition; the *USA Today* piece ran on January 4, 1985.

[61] "Bill Clark Goes Home", *Chicago Tribune*, January 12, 1985.

[62] "Secretary Clark Resigns", *Washington Post*, January 3, 1985, p. A18.

[63] Peterson, "Clark's Announcement Stuns Interior Staff".

[64] Lou Cannon, "Changes Near the Top", *Washington Post*, January 7, 1985, p. A2.

[65] Bernard Weinraub, "Help-Wanted Sign Goes up at the White House", *New York Times*, January 6, 1985, p. 2.

[66] The letter was dated January 7, 1985.

In his final weeks on the job at Interior, Clark made a number of decisions, including one that ended a controversy that had raged since the 1940s.[67] Clark signed a plan to reduce dramatically the Garrison Diversion project in North Dakota, one of the largest federal irrigation works under construction.[68] Four days later, he established a private foundation to seek donations for the U.S. Fish and Wildlife Service, which would channel private efforts to assist and expand the 444 wildlife refuges operated by the service. It would be called the National Fish and Wildlife Foundation.[69] Also before he left, Clark made recommendations for the 1986 fiscal budget.

When the time came for Bill Clark to say goodbye, President Reagan offered a few thoughts in his press conference, waxing philosophical about what he put Clark through for so many years: "I'd like to point out that Secretary Clark at my behest was in public life longer than I was because, between being governor of California and being president, I had a few years as a civilian. He didn't." When Clark left the governor's office, he went to the California Supreme Court and gave "18 years to public life, away from his private life", Reagan explained. Clark had told him two years earlier that he wanted to go home, Reagan said, but "I urged him at that particular time" to "stay on". This time, however, it looked like Ronald Reagan was letting Bill Clark return to the ranch.[70]

Riding Off

Perhaps the most unexpected farewells were two human-interest stories in the *New York Times* and the *Washington Post*, each of which served as a testimony to the friends Mr. Clark had made in Washington.

The *New York Times* piece was brief, only 216 words, and was entitled, "Comes a Horseman". It stated: "On many a morning, just before sunrise, a man on a white horse can be seen taking in the sights around Washington." This man, said the report, had been spotted on Capitol

---

[67] Dale Russakoff, "Compromise Approved on Huge Water Project; Long North Dakota Controversy Ends", *Washington Post*, January 19, 1985, p. 8.

[68] Ibid.

[69] "Wildlife Foundations Set Up", *Washington Post*, January 23, 1985, p. A21.

[70] "Text of President Reagan's News Conference", *Washington Post*, January 10, 1985, p. A14.

Hill, along the Ellipse and even in Georgetown. "This is no masked man, but a homesick Californian, Interior Secretary William P. Clark", said the *Times*. "After all these mornings of riding into a Washington sunrise, Mr. Clark ... is looking forward to galloping off into the sunset." [71]

The gem of tributes, however, was a piece in the *Washington Post* Style section on February 11, cleverly entitled, "Mornings on Horseback", borrowed from the title of a recent biography of Teddy Roosevelt. A Clark friend from the Washington press corps telephoned to tell him to enjoy the piece because such articles come only once in a political lifetime and nearly always as the public figure exits the national stage for good. Adorned with a huge picturesque photo of Clark riding Amadeus through Rock Creek Park, the piece was almost poetic:

> At dawn, when no one was looking, he would take in the capital from the back of a horse. He liked the solitude of the Washington Monument, the curious shadows in the Hirshhorn sculpture garden, the pink glow of the Commerce Department building, the silhouette of the Capitol.
>
> These rides were among the secrets of William P. Clark, the longtime intimate of President Reagan who left Washington quietly last week after four years as deputy secretary of state, national security advisor and, until last Thursday, interior secretary.
>
> He was an enigma to many, a private man who hugged the shadows, revealing nothing of himself or his influence. But to the U.S. Park Police officers who rode with Clark at 6:30 every morning for the past 15 months, he was simply a fifth-generation California rancher who came into his own in the saddle of the president's royal white Lipizzaner stallion named Amadeus, cantering confidently through Rock Creek Park.

The article quoted Park Police Sergeant Major Denis Ayres, Clark's riding companion, who said of the Judge: "If you can control 1,100 to 1,200 pounds of a horse who has a mind of his own, and get him to work for you, almost to perform for you like a ballet artist, well, that says a lot about a person.... [Clark is] an exceptional rider."

---

[71] Phil Gailey and Warren Weaver, Jr., "Comes a Horseman", *New York Times*, February 5, 1985, p. 20.

The *Post* writer, Dale Russakoff, noted that Clark on horseback was a contrast to Clark as Cabinet secretary. While the public Clark spoke tersely, without emotion, measuring the impact of each word, on Amadeus, "he was expansive, even lyrical." Asked which part of his ride he liked best, Clark, said the reporter, responded not with a place but with a feeling: "I love the solitude, the loneliness. It is the most ideal of circumstances. No phones, no interruptions."

Russakoff recorded how the handsome horse whinnied as he caught his image in the window of a Georgetown boutique, admiring himself. "He has a big ego, maybe the biggest in Washington", quipped Clark. "This horse, to use an Al Haig phrase, is 'in charge'." Clark talked about conversing with Amadeus. When asked what information he has shared with the stallion, Clark joked, "I'll never tell." When asked if Amadeus was privy to any state secrets, Clark said, "He's full of them."

As his ride with Amadeus ended, Clark conceded somewhat of a "hollow feeling" at leaving Washington, but no sadness at leaving his seat of power: "It has been a tremendous privilege. It's not the power that made it that way; it's a matter of duty. Ronald Reagan wanted people around him who did not necessarily look upon government as a way of life. I've kept that in mind through the 18 years."[72]

*   *   *

Bill Clark headed home, Amadeus with him, as Ronald Reagan had named Clark Amadeus' trustee, requesting that his friend take the stallion to the ranch in Shandon. The pastures of the Clark ranch would be the stallion's, and likely his rider's, final home.[73]

---

[72] Dale Russakoff, "Mornings on Horseback; Interior Secretary Clark's Final Canter in the Park", *Washington Post*, February 11, 1985, p. B1.

[73] There, the horse fathered two offspring that today enjoy the pasture and occasionally jointly pull a wagon of excited kids. Amadeus died at the age of twenty-three from cancer, two years short of the average life expectancy for his breed. Each year his Austrian caretakers flew to the Clark ranch to visit the stallion.

CHAPTER 14

Double Duty

Clark's Non-Interior Work at Interior

While at Interior, Bill Clark was on call to advise Ronald Reagan or to travel for him when requested to do so. In January 1984, for example, Interior Secretary Clark played a decisive role in the President's choice for attorney general. "President Reagan named his longtime counselor, Edwin Meese III, as attorney general after Interior Secretary William P. Clark urged the appointment of Meese rather than White House Chief of Staff James A. Baker III", reported the January 24 *Washington Post*. Said one administration official: "There is no doubt that [Clark] tipped the scales." [1]

This was the second Baker promotion opposed by Clark in three months, the first being the national security advisor position. Clark says he thought there were better people for those positions, individuals more dedicated to fulfilling Reagan's objectives.

Looking to a Second Term

In January 1984, Clark and Reagan discussed whether the President should consider running for a second term. Reagan had on several occasions broached the subject of his retirement with Clark, who acted as his sounding board. Clark followed this discussion with a personal

---

[1] Lou Cannon and David Hoffman, "Clark Backed Meese for Attorney General", *Washington Post*, January 24, 1984.

letter to Reagan stating, "You've done what you set out to do—tax cuts, budget reform, a year of steady economic growth, a revitalized military, communism disgraced, and nuclear terror confounded by the Strategic Defense Initiative. Another few months of 'standing tall' should restore the arms balance in Europe and very likely influence the rise of a less dangerous Soviet leader than the dying Andropov, and, yes, the Berlin Wall is crumbling under our policy of Peace through Strength."

In his last statement Clark was prescient, foreseeing the possibility of what was to most people then unthinkable: the fall of the Berlin Wall. He also foresaw the rise of a less dangerous Soviet leader, who was indeed in the works: a man named Mikhail Gorbachev.

Reagan and Clark also discussed the positive aspects of running again. In the first place, the President enjoyed his job. Secondly, he considered his work unfinished even though the economy was soaring, and American morale had been turned around from its "malaise".

Reagan made his decision: He would capitalize on the optimistic mood created in his first term and finish the race begun with the Soviet Union. As his re-election campaign would celebrate, it was "Morning in America" again.

Meeting with John Paul II

In keeping with his role as the President's special friend when called, Clark attended a meeting far beyond the realm of the usual duties of secretary of the Interior. In May 1984, Clark and Reagan came together again with Pope John Paul II, this time in Fairbanks, Alaska, largely due to a series of scheduling coincidences. Interior Secretary Clark was returning from an important inspection visit to Prudhoe Bay. The Pope was stopping to refuel on his way to Seoul, South Korea, to celebrate the 200th anniversary of Catholicism on the Korean peninsula. Reagan was returning from an historic visit to China.[2]

When asked by Alaskans what he had said to the Chinese, Reagan stated: "I tried to explain what America is and who we are—to explain to them our faith in God and our love, our true love, for

---

[2] Kris Capps, "President, pope will meet here", *Daily News-Miner*, March 20, 1984.

freedom."[3] He had indeed. On April 27, Reagan had stood next to Chinese atheist-communist leaders and publicly stated, in front of all the cameras and microphones, that "America was founded by people who sought freedom to worship God and to trust in Him to guide them in their daily lives."[4] Three days later, in a speech to students at Fudan University in Shanghai, he explained those great lines in the Declaration of Independence: "We hold these truths to be self-evident, that all men are created equal, that they are endowed by their Creator with certain inalienable Rights ..." Faith in the Creator is "very important to us", he said of his fellow Americans, adding that "most Americans derive their religious beliefs from the Bible of Moses, who delivered a people from slavery; the Bible of Jesus Christ, who told us to love thy neighbor as thyself, to do unto your neighbor as you would have him do unto you."[5]

John Paul II learned of Reagan's spiritual message to the Chinese and was pleased. He had always wanted to visit China to talk about Christianity, but had not been permitted by the communist authorities to enter the country. The Chinese would not allow the Pope to come, but they welcomed the U.S. President with open arms. The Pope, therefore, commended Reagan for turning the trip into an opportunity to preach the Gospel in China.[6]

Reagan and the Pope did not have much time together, but the local press dubbed their visits to Alaska as "probably the most remarkable 39 hours in Fairbanks history", touching "the lives of many of its people—some profoundly". For half an hour, noted the cover story in the main daily, "the heads of two of the mightiest forces on earth—one secular, the other spiritual—were face to face in Fairbanks."[7]

Alaskan authorities were nearly overwhelmed, fearing how they would provide security for two world leaders, both of whom had been shot

[3] Stan Jones, "Thirty-nine Hours of History in Fairbanks", *Daily News-Miner*, May 3, 1984.

[4] Reagan, "Remarks to Chinese Community Leaders", Beijing, China, April 27, 1984.

[5] Reagan, "Remarks at Fudan University", Shanghai, China, April 30, 1984.

[6] Reagan, "Remarks at a Welcoming Ceremony for Pope John Paul II", Fairbanks, Alaska, May 2, 1984.

[7] Stan Jones, "Thirty-nine Hours of History in Fairbanks".

three years earlier. They were expecting as many as forty thousand people at the Fairbanks International Airport to greet the jet carrying John Paul II. Protesters, made up mainly of union groups and the local chapter of the National Organization for Women, added to the chaos, shaking placards that read, "The Pope meets the Dope" and "Reagan is a BAD boy" (held by a young boy).[8]

The meeting between President Reagan and Pope John Paul II was the first since Reagan had established formal diplomatic relations with the Vatican. A photo from the meeting, which ran in the May 3 Fairbanks *Daily News–Miner*, shows Reagan and the Pope sitting together on a sofa in a conference room at the airport. Reagan, dressed in a dark business suit, is half out of his seat, speaking with animation, while the Pope, adorned in white to Reagan's left, listens pensively, with his left pointer finger on his temple. A crucifix hangs behind them. Clark sits to Reagan's immediate right. Secretary of State George Shultz is also there, as are the current national security advisor, Bud McFarlane, and Chief of Staff Jim Baker.

Bill Clark took no notes. "I regret that I was not able to record the details of the meetings with the Holy Father", says Clark, adding that his meeting ten years earlier with Cardinal Mindszenty also remains unrecorded. "But note taking would not only have been distracting, it would have affected the wonderful spontaneity of such meetings." Pope John Paul and Clark later said a prayer together, after which the Pope blessed him and the rosary ring Clark still carries in his right vest pocket.

The press was told that the President and the Pontiff discussed "east-west relations", arms control, and "regional and humanitarian issues". It was 1984, and there was a great deal to talk about: Solidarity members were still repressed, and the Church was still persecuted throughout Eastern Europe and the Soviet Union.

Pope John Paul and President Reagan had many concerns in common, but all the *New York Times* religion editor, Ken Briggs, could see was a photo-op for the Reagan campaign. "It's another phase of [Reagan's] election-year strategy", he cynically told a reporter for the Fairbanks newspaper.[9]

---

[8] Ibid.
[9] Ibid.

Secretary Clark Goes to Berlin

Clark accepted another important assignment unusual for a man in his official position. The same month he met with the President and the Pope in Alaska, he headed a U.S. delegation to West Berlin, where two days of ceremonies would mark the 35th anniversary of Stalin's decision to end the 1948–1949 blockade of the city.

On June 24, 1948, in one of the acts most responsible for initiating the Cold War, the Soviets blocked all of the overland routes to the Allied-controlled sectors of Berlin. Their intention was to starve out the Allies and make them surrender their sections of the city to the Soviet Union. In response, U.S. military advisors urged President Truman to crash the barriers. Fearing World War III, Truman instead opted for an unprecedented airlift. American and British pilots flew countless sorties, twenty-four hours a day, seven days a week, ferrying more than two million tons of food, fuel, and other supplies into West Berlin. Some pilots—the so-called "candy droppers of Berlin"—dropped bubble gum and chocolate bars with tiny parachutes to German children.

The airlift kept the western side of Berlin alive for eleven months until Stalin agreed on May 5, 1949, to lift the blockade. The supply flights continued another four months in case Stalin changed his mind.

Though the Soviets did not attack the Allied planes, there were twelve fatal crashes. Clark—along with city officials and others representing America, Britain, and France—laid wreaths at a memorial for the seventy-eight pilots and crewmen who lost their lives in the Berlin airlift.

Clark's speech in Berlin was a noteworthy statement, not just on the past but also on the present, clarifying what the Truman administration had done in standing up to the Soviet Union thirty-five years earlier and where the Reagan administration stood at that moment.

He began by stating that President Reagan had asked him to extend his personal greetings, as well as those of the American people, "to this . . . commemoration and celebration of freedom, justice, and liberty". As Reagan's personal representative and leader of the U.S. delegation, he was there to reaffirm America's "lasting commitment" to Berlin's freedom and "deep admiration" for the people of that "great city". He said that Americans were proud to have helped preserve the "democratic spirit" of the city during those "grim days in 1948 and 1949".

On Easter Day 1949 alone, said Clark, 1,398 Allied aircraft reached Berlin—a truly remarkable feat. He called the airlift "a mission of peace and compassion carried out with the tools of war" and said it demonstrated that the West would not back down in the face of tyranny and extraordinary pressure. The airlift was "proof of the tenacity of free men".

Americans served in Berlin "never as occupiers but always as guardians of the freedom of West Berlin and its brave people", Clark said. "Americans remain proud to stand shoulder-to-shoulder with Berliners." He called Berlin "a remarkable cathedral of democracy" and "an unmistakable symbol to the whole world of what is at stake and what is at issue between East and West". Occasionally sprinkling German lines in the speech, he said that if anyone had any doubt about the difference between freedom and oppression, between hope and despair, between justice and injustice, then, *"Lass sie nach Berlin kommen"*— "Let them come to Berlin."

Notably, Clark made a significant gesture in this speech, one not acknowledged by the press back home: He called for eventual German reunification, saying that the Western allies did "not accept the ugly division of this city or of the German nation". At that point, no one was talking, openly at least, about the reunification of Germany, nor of the dismantling of the Berlin Wall.

Clark noted that two years earlier, Ronald Reagan had visited West Berlin and called upon the Soviets to make a "significant reduction" in nuclear arms. Clark said he was there to reaffirm that challenge. "If the Soviet leadership rises to the challenge", said Clark, "they will find the United States more than willing to meet them halfway."

Clark closed with a "small personal footnote":

My wife found herself in Berlin shortly after World War II. After having been displaced from her native Sudetenland in Czechoslovakia, her first safe haven in the West was Berlin—West Berlin. She was received as a free human being, cared for and set on her way to America. It was in Berlin that Johanna, now Joan, fully understood and felt the real meaning of democracy. Thus, it is a special pleasure for my wife and me to be here with you today.

He finished with a "God bless you and *Danke schön*."

The address was a hit. The U.S. Army publication *The Stars and Stripes* reported that the Interior secretary was "frequently interrupted by bursts of applause".[10] Clark's talk, and visit generally, made the front pages of all major German dailies and was the lead story on all the news broadcasts, where it was universally hailed.[11]

Though it received less press back home, his visit was commended in an editorial by Marvin Stone in *U.S. News & World Report*, who noted that the "massive and skillful operation that was known as the Berlin airlift" was a story "that needs retelling as a reminder and a lesson", as Clark had done. Stone wrote: "To signify America's determination to keep West Berlin free, President Reagan sent Secretary of the Interior William Clark.... But it was more than just another commemoration. Clark's presence was meant to convey to the Kremlin that we still care about this outpost and the 7,000 Americans stationed here. The message was the same as it was 35 years ago: 'Hands off what isn't yours.' "[12]

Clark also got a brief write up in the "Washington Talk" section of the *New York Times*, which noted that the top man at Interior was not so preoccupied with mesquite and wild chaparral that he had lost touch with foreign affairs. The *Times* added that *Pravda* had attacked Clark's trip. Said *Times* reporters B. Drummond Ayres Jr. and Phil Gailey: "Americans may think Mr. Clark is concerning himself with public lands and offshore oil leases, but *Pravda*, the official Communist Party newspaper in the Soviet Union, isn't buying that." *Pravda* regarded Clark's presence in the divided city as a "provocative act", and accused him of conducting a crusade against socialism and promoting confrontation between the superpowers. "No one is sure what Mr. Clark did to bring on such an attack," remarked Ayres and Gailey, "but it probably has nothing to do with his attitude towards the coyote."[13]

The *Times* reporters saw the bigger picture—that the Berlin trip revealed Clark's broader service to Reagan: "The Berlin trip is only the latest indication of Mr. Clark's continuing foreign policy role. At

---

[10] "Clark challenges Soviets in marking Berlin blockade", *Stars and Stripes*, May 12, 1984.

[11] A long list of examples were collected and transcribed by the May 14, 1984 *Daily Press Review*, published by the United States Information Service.

[12] Marvin Stone, "Staring Down the Kremlin", *U.S. News & World Report*, May 21, 1984, p. 88.

[13] B. Drummond Ayres Jr. and Phil Gailey, "The Clark Attack", *New York Times*, May 24, 1984, p. B16.

the Administration's request, he recently debriefed several American ambassadors assigned to Central America, and the speculation is that President Reagan still relies on his old friend from California for foreign policy advice."

Secretary Clark Goes to Spain

A few months after Berlin, Clark was given another foreign assignment: he was sent to represent the United States at a ceremony in Mallorca, Spain, honoring Father Junípero Serra. The ceremony marked the 200th anniversary of Serra's death. King Juan Carlos was there, as was his wife, Queen Sophia. Clark gave an address in Castilian Spanish, which required him to stay up much of the previous night practicing the accent.

At the time, there was a movement afoot, spearheaded by Reverend Noel Moholy, a Franciscan, to canonize Serra as California's first saint. Moholy was a longtime friend of Bernice Clark, who supported Serra's cause, as did her husband and son.[14] Serra's advocates pushed the U.S. Postal Service to issue a Serra stamp, part of their publicity campaign to raise the priest's profile. Bill Clark publicly lobbied for the stamp. Now, in Mallorca, he had the joy of informing the audience that the commemorative stamp would be issued the following year.

Clark noted in his speech that Serra had extended Spain into the New World and that as a result, six generations of Clark's own family had lived "within the shadow" of Mission San Buenaventura, "where we have been christened, married, and buried". The memories of his youth, said Clark, "ring with the stories" of the early days of that mission and the "dedicated works" of the Spanish Franciscan Fathers.[15]

The Interior secretary informed the group that a statue of Serra stood in the Capitol Building, and the Bible carried by Serra in his travels was kept in California. "It was my privilege," relayed Clark, "little knowing I would have occasion to tell the story here today, to have been present when the oath of office was administered eighteen

---

[14] Bill Sr. said this during a May 15, 1969 talk he gave to the Ventura County Historical Society. See: Wally Smith, "Oxnarder Credits a Faithful Scout for Father Serra's California Success", *Ventura County Star-Free Press*, May 18, 1969, p. A8.

[15] "Remarks Prepared for Delivery by Secretary of the Interior William Clark at the Father Junipero Serra Ceremony", Mallorca, Spain, October 11, 1984.

years ago to Governor Ronald Reagan in Sacramento, with his hand placed on that very same Bible."

Two hundred years after Serra's death, said Clark, his teachings, work, and spirit remained "with us in our daily lives in the United States. . . . As Christopher Columbus expanded the physical dimensions of our planet, Father Serra extended the frontiers of Christian civilization." Clark said that Father Junípero "followed the light of his abiding faith in the perfectibility of man, a light he saw in his mind and heart, and one which he passed to his spiritual heirs in both the Old World and the New". Serra and the Catholic missionaries who followed him into the vast unknown territories of the New World "sought to establish the moral bases on which the new lands would be built".

At the end of the speech, Queen Sophia, a beautiful woman, looked over and gave him a smile, a wink, and American baseball's thumbs-up. "That made my day", acknowledges Clark.

Re-Electing Reagan

That summer saw both the Republican and Democratic national conventions, and Clark assisted Reagan on the campaign trail, while keeping things running smoothly at Interior.

The summer was not entirely about politics. There was time to look back as well as ahead. On June 23, the priests (along with alumni) at Villanova Prep, who once let a young Bill Clark work for his tuition in the kitchen, now honored Secretary Clark with a roast.

After the invocation by Father John Glynn, the evening saw some good-natured ribbing by Ambassadors Gavin and Dailey, from the class of 1948, as well as from emcee and former classmate Chuck Doud and former teacher Father Charles Flynn. It was a gala event marking the 60th anniversary of the founding of Villanova Prep. After jokes and accolades, the evening wound down with Clark presenting Headmaster Reverend Gerald Watt with a crucifix that had been banned and later smuggled out of Poland to be given to President Reagan. In return, the school showed its appreciation by presenting Clark with a 19-by-30-inch mural featuring the prayer for peace of Saint Francis. Clark later had the mural installed on the wall of the chapel in Shandon. The Augustinian who chose that particular gift could not have known its special meaning to both

Clark and Reagan.[16] It was a memorable evening, a way for Clark to reconnect with his roots.

With the November election only four months away, Clark was eager to assist the presidential campaign. He gave a number of speeches for Reagan on the campaign trail. Some of these talks advanced the Reagan record on the environment, as would be expected from the secretary of the Interior. Others related to Reagan policies generally, from tax cuts to the Soviets.

There were also less routine campaign tasks. For instance, in July, Clark, with Vice President Bush and Attorney General Meese, met with Evangelical Christians who supported Reagan. For the secular media, it was scandalous that some ministers were supporting Reagan. On CBS's Sunday morning news show *Face the Nation*, liberal activist-journalist Leslie Stahl badgered Jerry Falwell: "How can you tell us here on this broadcast that you don't tell your congregation who to vote for? Aren't you a strong supporter of Ronald Reagan? Don't you have a Biblical score-card that rates—?" Falwell jumped in: "Oh no, no, we don't, except that I publicly state what I believe, and for whom I'm voting. The World Council of Churches has been doing that for fifty years." [17]

The *Washington Post*, in a news article titled, "Spurred by White House Parley, TV Evangelists Spread Political Word", tried to portray the Evangelicals' enthusiasm for Reagan as the product of White House political maneuvering. Surely their political activism is the result of efforts by Clark and Meese, stated the *Post*, and not of a heartfelt Christian embrace of Reagan, this "strange" President who "speaks so much about the importance of religion and yet rarely goes to church".[18]

Final Round of Campaigning

Many of Clark's campaign speeches were delivered in California, where the audiences knew Clark well and where the secretary had his strongest influence. The focus on California may have reflected Nancy Reagan's concern that her husband was vulnerable in the state. To this

---

[16] See Chris Woodka, "Secretary of Interior Clark honored", *San Francisco Chronicle*, July 7, 1984. Other details taken from event program, which is held in Clark's files.

[17] See Dudley Clendinen, "Spurred by White House Parley, TV Evangelists Spread Political Word", *Washington Post*, September 10, 1984.

[18] Ibid.

day, campaign manager Ed Rollins is convinced that if Mrs. Reagan had not forced him to pour so much money into California, he could have devoted more resources to Mondale's home state of Minnesota, and Ronald Reagan would have swept all fifty states.[19]

Many of the cities in which Clark campaigned for Reagan had populations with deep interests in environmental issues. A typical Clark message underscored how the Reagan administration entered office only to find America's national parks in disrepair. The administration then embarked on "the most massive park-repair effort in history—a five-year, $1 billion project", Clark told an audience in Sacramento. The project would be finished in 1985, one year ahead of schedule.[20]

The Untold Story of Campaign '84: Clark, Carter, and Mondale

Clark's work at Interior came to have a crucial impact in the 1984 campaign, in a way that no one could have anticipated. As noted, beginning in 1982, Clark met with former President Carter to brief him on security issues. This developed not only into a working relationship, but a friendship that continued after Clark left the NSC for Interior. Indeed, in a gesture of goodwill, Carter—in the same phone call in which he welcomed Clark's nomination to Interior and offered to call his "green friends" to encourage them to support Clark—invited the Judge to Georgia to go quail hunting. Though enthusiastic, Clark assumed Carter would probably not follow through. "I thought he was simply being kind," said Clark, "and then, after two weeks on the job, he called and said, 'When are you coming?'"

Clark was nearly overwhelmed with his new duties, but he could not resist the generous invitation. On the weekend of February 17, 1984, Clark embarked on another of his quiet visits to Plains, Georgia, but this time to hunt quail. The hunt itself was a "real ritual", says Clark. Carter employed all the traditions: he had the customary horses, guns, and attendants Southern gentlemen used in such hunts. The two men rode side by side through the Georgia pines; each bagged

---

[19] See Ed Rollins, *Bare Knuckles and Back Rooms* (New York: Broadway Books, 1996).
[20] Veda Federighi, "Clark defends Reagan record on the environment", *Sacramento Union*, October 31, 1984.

the legal limit of twelve birds.[21] Back at Carter's residence, the two men talked about life, politics, and faith; they enjoyed a Vodka and orange juice, like old friends. Carter "couldn't have been more gracious", says Clark.

The Carter-Clark friendship paid political dividends. As noted, Carter had told environmentalists to refrain from attacking Clark during his Interior hearings, but that is not the whole story. The Democratic nominee for president, Walter Mondale, Carter's former vice president, had planned to blast the Reagan administration's environmental policies as a major issue in the campaign, and yet for some mysterious reason, the issue never heated up nor was the James Watt record attacked. The Reagan campaign was baffled: Why had Mondale not hit them hard on the environment? Clark got an answer two years later in a chance encounter at a dinner party in Tel Aviv.

Walter Mondale and Bill Clark both happened to be at the same dinner party hosted by Israeli President Chaim Herzog. Still smarting from the election, Mondale was cool at first, but about halfway through the dinner, he stunned the guests by stating, "Secretary Clark, I could very well blame my loss of the presidency on you." An awkward silence enveloped the room. One person laughed, not sure if Mondale was joking; he was not. "How so?" Clark asked. "When I approached President Carter on campaign strategy," Mondale answered, "I told him that my strategy included running hard against Reagan and the Department of Interior on the environmental legacy left by James Watt." However, Carter reproached Mondale: "Don't you touch Bill Clark. He's the only person in the Reagan administration that has been decent to me and Rosalynn. Besides, he's doing a good job at Interior." Mondale honored the wishes of his former boss, and a key issue of his campaign was taken away from him.

Looking to the Second Reagan Term

When Reagan began his second term, Clark's name was bandied about for high-profile jobs, including the chief of staff position, which was still filled by James Baker. Only two days after the election, Lou Cannon

---

[21] William E. Farrell and Warren Weaver Jr., "Birds of a Feather", *New York Times*, February 23, 1984.

reported in the *Washington Post* that conservatives were demanding that Clark be "heavily involved" in the second Reagan administration.[22]

The oldest conservative weekly in the country, *Human Events*, began running a series of articles calling upon Reagan to return Clark to right-hand-man status on a daily basis. "The first thing President Reagan should think about now is how to best restaff his administration, not only for the purpose of completing the able beginning he has given this country, but ensuring his role in history", stated the November 10, 1984 issue. "The key to success will start with his choice of a new chief of staff." Clark, said the conservative weekly, was the best man for the job—he "would command instant respect".[23]

Conservative columnist Jeffrey Hart, a professor at Dartmouth, agreed. In 1968, Hart was a speechwriter for Reagan during his brief presidential campaign. Throughout all the crises of that momentous year—Berkeley riots, burning cities, Black Panthers in Oakland, the assassinations of Martin Luther King Jr. and Bobby Kennedy— "Clark remained a pillar of sanity and common sense", wrote Hart. "[W]hen a homosexual scandal rocked [Governor Reagan's] staff, Clark stepped in, completely unflappable, and got the Reagan operation on the tracks." Hart also noted Clark's ability "to deal with and reconcile very different sorts of people", which "comes from not only his intelligence but from his palpable good nature".[24]

The write-in campaign for Clark as chief of staff was noted by other journalists. In the December 5 *Wall Street Journal*, Fred Barnes reported that Clark "may return to the White House as Mr. Baker's successor, but not for many months".[25] In fact, the chief of staff job was never offered to Clark, nor did he seek it or any other position.

There was another major post for which Clark was suggested during this period. A piece in *Time*, entitled, "Next in Line for the Nine", speculated on Reagan's next appointment for the U.S. Supreme Court. The article displayed pictures of the leading three candidates: Robert

---

[22] Lou Cannon, "President Wants to Keep His 'Winning Team' Intact", *Washington Post*, November 8, 1984.

[23] "In Wake of Re-Election, Reagan Should Make Clark His New Chief of Staff", *Human Events*, November 10, 1984, p. 1.

[24] Ibid.

[25] Fred Barnes, "The White House's Power Broker", *Wall Street Journal*, December 5, 1984.

Bork, Antonin Scalia, and Bill Clark.[26] While two of these men were ultimately nominated for the high court, Clark, again, declined consideration.

Clark's Advice for the Second Term

As Reagan's second term commenced, instead of assuming a new post, Clark continued to advise the President from the Department of the Interior. Only weeks after Reagan's re-election, Clark provided him with a five-page six-point handwritten letter in which he presented an assessment of the President's achievements so far and the goals they shared that remained to be fulfilled.

The letter was personal, but more generally expressed Clark's concern for the President's role in the world and his place in history. Reflecting the worries of many conservatives at the time, the letter was pessimistic regarding the U.S.-USSR relationship, arms control, and the likelihood of war, issues that Reagan was always more optimistic about than any of his advisors. Some of Clark's fears turned out to be unwarranted, whereas in other cases his advice was correct. In any event, Clark was attempting to reach Reagan on behalf of fellow conservatives, such as Jeane Kirkpatrick, Bill Casey, and Cap Weinberger, who knew Clark had the boss's ear.

The letter began, "Thank you, Mr. President, for the trust and confidence you have placed in me the past 19 years. I shall attempt to express some year-end observations to you as simply and candidly as I can."

Point One consisted of two sentences on Interior: "The policies begun by Jim Watt are going well and I hope to make them your quiet legacy. I find deep satisfaction here—it's not unlike running a very large ranch."

Point Two, labeled White House, was more personal and touched a raw nerve: "The terrible process of eating our young has gone unabated for four years. It can be stopped and I fully trust you understand the problem—not unlike the one we knew in Sacramento. My only real regret in the two-year stay at the White House was the deterioration in my relationship with Nancy and Mike who—I am told—found me

---

[26] "Next in Line for the Nine", *Time*, October 8, 1984, p. 32.

too 'hard line,' which translated to abrasiveness. I prayed my moving on would somehow restore the old relationships—that has not occurred. I apologize to Nancy and to you for the discomfiture caused."

Clark's third item was a long paragraph on the State Department. He and Al Haig had been able to "gain control of the State structure and to produce your Central America and East-West policies". He expressed concern that under George Shultz, "the nuclear arms issue has become paramount, [while] our duties towards other regions are suffering." Clark was chiefly concerned about communist expansion in America's front yard.

Then came Point Four, the heart of the letter, seven paragraphs long, nearly half the text, and headed: The Soviet Union. To remind the President of the nature of the communist enemy, Clark mentioned that during the previous evening he and his family had watched *The Truth about Communism*, a 1963 film series that Reagan had narrated.[27] The film focuses on the Hitler-Stalin Pact, the Comintern, the massacre in Poland's Katyn Forest, Moscow's desire for world revolution, the words of Marx in the *Communist Manifesto*, and much more.[28] Clark owned a rare copy of the videotape, which he enclosed for Reagan.

With the tape Clark sent a warning: "Mr. President, I submit no key person exists at State willing to concede the true nature of our adversary who—not inevitably but most probably—will wage total war on us in the lifetimes of our sons." Such fears were not uncommon; they were shared by the President and countless others on both sides of the political spectrum who thought the Cold War could turn hot and possibly trigger a nuclear war.

"Improving relations with the Soviet Union and arms control are critical, as you have noted; however, if arms control becomes the overriding priority or an end in itself, our other important goals may be distorted or lost. . . . We do not want to accept a bad arms agreement and the Soviets will probably not accept one that meets all the standards we have proposed—particularly 'deep reductions' [in missile arsenals] to equal level

---

[27] The documentary was a presentation of a group called The National Education Program, the president of which was George S. Benson of the American Heritage Center in Searcy, Arkansas. I watched part two of the video at the Reagan Library. The library is not in possession of part one. P. K.

[28] Ibid.

with real verification. The Soviets have never agreed to deep cuts in key strategic areas, nor have we, for that matter. The Soviets will never roll over, giving up elements of their superiority or accede to strategic equality for an arms control agreement with us."

Even if the Soviets and the Americans could agree on arms reductions, verification of treaty compliance would remain a serious problem. Verification was always the most difficult challenge of any arms agreement with the USSR. As Clark noted, the Soviets were notorious for cheating on treaties; Bill Casey had expressed "grave doubts" about America's ability to verify compliance. "Some wonder why we even discuss new limits at a time when the Soviets are violating existing ones."

Clark mistrusted the Soviets' motives for seeking arms negotiations. "The Soviets consistently push to place arms control front and center because this posture downplays their regional misbehavior and their relentless military buildup around the world; puts them into a position of equal status and importance with the United States (a position they do not deserve); and helps legitimize the regime internally, enhancing its stature internationally." The Soviets, Clark reminded Reagan, had behaved deceptively in the 1970s with respect to the Helsinki accords and détente, both of which Reagan had publicly denounced as "shams".

In summing up, Clark returned to the video. "As you stated so well in the film, the main problem we have with the Soviet Union is not that they refuse to sign agreements with us, but rather that they have a brutal totalitarian regime internally, and an expansionist policy internationally. Arms control agreements cannot resolve these two big problems. They can make them worse if we allowed 'making progress' on arms control to quiet us on Soviet misbehavior in human rights and expansionism (Nicaragua, Poland, Afghanistan, Suriname). Since the election, many of our staunch supporters have become concerned that 'peace through strength' may be overshadowed by State's 'peace through arms control'. That was Mondale's approach of course. I know you recognize these elements, but I feel compelled to restate them in light of State's clear rush."

With Point 5, Clark ended his heavy assessment on a sunny note, with reflections on his friend and confidant, Amadeus. "This type of letter usually saves the best for last. What began as an early morning routine to exercise horse and rider has grown to a great friendship between animal and man." Clark then suggested, on behalf of himself and his friends among the park police, that the President exit his car to ride Amadeus during the final portion of the upcoming inaugural parade. The recommendation was considered—Reagan loved it—but it was not executed; the parade was canceled because the streets had iced over.

Point 6 concluded the assessment affectionately, "Finally, Mr. President, your ten-foot-tall integrity—matching my own father's—is an inspiration to us all—that's what your twenty-year mandate has been all about. Sincerely, Bill Clark."

*   *   *

With Clark's advice dispensed, he would continue to help his President in every way he could, with one exception: Believing his tasks at Interior to be complete, he asked the President to accept his letter of resignation. Ronald Reagan knew there was no dissuading his old friend this time. Bill Clark would retire once and for all from full-time employment in Washington, but he would not leave Ronald Reagan entirely—far from it.

CHAPTER 15

Reagan's Quiet Emissary

Citizen Clark's Work at Home and Abroad

Once Clark left Interior, he left full-time service in the Reagan administration—for good. He did not, however, abandon Ronald Reagan. Although the formal account of the Reagan years lists Bill Clark as reporting for duty primarily in the first term, this is not the full story. The President still had much in store for his longtime friend, calling upon him again and again, for this issue or that crisis or some sensitive mission.

Initially, Clark returned to private life—to law. In March 1985, William P. Clark became counsel to Rogers & Wells, a prestigious international firm with offices in Washington, New York, Los Angeles, London, and Paris, headed by former Nixon Secretary of State William P. Rogers, with whom Clark became good friends.

Clark worked with Rogers & Wells on a part-time basis, depending on the case. He traveled to Washington at least once a month while operating mainly from his home office in Paso Robles. "So, it'll be life on the ranch", said Clark. "And of course, I'll be available to the President." [1]

An Emissary for All Seasons

Clark became involved in many disparate activities during this time, but his life revolved around the ranch and the ranch office. In March

---

[1] Phil Gailey and Marjorie Hunter, "Briefing: Clark and His Links", *New York Times*, March 4, 1985.

1985, he was named vice chairman of the Terra Museum of American Art in Chicago, as an accommodation to his friend Ambassador Dan Terra. In his position as vice chair, Clark assisted in founding the Musée d'Art Americain in Giverny, the home of Monet. The Musée is reputed to be the first museum of American art in France. A month later, in April, Reagan appointed him as a special presidential envoy to settle a land dispute between the Hopi and Navajo Indian tribes, a difficult assignment that was an extension of his Interior work.[2]

President Reagan also asked Clark to serve on various commissions. In March 1985, in compliance with the President's Executive Order 12499, he headed a high-level presidential group to study the management of nuclear weapons. The President's Blue Ribbon Task Group on Nuclear Weapons Program Management included James R. Schlesinger (Vice Chair), Harold Agnew, Alan C. Furth, Jeane Kirkpatrick, Frederick Kroesen, and William J. Perry. The group issued its report in July 1985.[3]

Clark immediately followed this chairmanship by serving on another committee from July 1985 to February 1986. The President's Blue Ribbon Commission on Defense Management, known as the Packard Commission, as named for Chairman David Packard, received a great deal of attention because its purpose was to reduce cost overruns in the Defense Department, an aspect of government spending receiving a lot of scrutiny in the media. The sixteen members included Ernest Arbuckle, General Robert H. Barrow, Nicholas Brady, Louis Cabot, Frank Carlucci, Barber B. Conable Jr., General Paul Gorman, Carla Hills, Admiral James L. Holloway, William Perry, Charles J. Pilliod Jr., Brent Scowcroft, Herbert Stein, James Woolsey, and Rhett B. Dawson. The commission issued its report on February 28, 1986.[4]

---

[2] For more, see: "Settlement in Indian Dispute Isn't within Reach, Aide Says", *Associated Press*, August 29, 1985; and Iver Peterson, "Tribal Positions Harden in Indian Land Dispute", *New York Times*, September 15, 1985.

[3] The task group, wrote Clark in his July 15, 1985 cover letter to the report to the President, found that "the relationship between the Departments of Defense and Energy for managing the [U.S.] nuclear weapons program is sound", while listing some areas for improvement.

[4] The report concluded that "there is a great need" for improvement in the way the U.S. government "thinks through and tie[s] together" security objectives and how much it spends to achieve those objectives. "The entire undertaking for our nation's defense requires more and better long range planning", it said.

Before Clark finished serving on one committee, a term of duty on another began. In March 1986, Clark was appointed counselor to the American Bar Association's Standing Committee on Law and National Security. The group was chaired by Robert F. Turner of the Center for Law and National Security at the University of Virginia School of Law, and involved thirty-six members in all, not including consultants and counselors. Clark was among a select group of nine counselors, which included Max Kampelman, Eugene Rostow, William French Smith, and William P. Rogers.

In May 1986, Clark served on an even more select group called the Commission on Integrated Long Term Strategy, cochaired by Fred Ikle and Albert Wohlstetter. This Commission included only ten other members, among them: Ann Armstrong, Zbigniew Brzezinski, W. Graham Claytor, Jr., General Andrew Goodpaster, Admiral James L. Holloway III, Samuel Huntington, Henry Kissinger, Joshua Lederberg, General Bernard A. Schriever, and General John W. Vessey. The commission included working groups on regional conflicts, technology, offensive and defensive forces, and the Soviet Union. The group studied subjects ranging from NATO to the proliferation of chemical weapons.[5]

Interventions

During this period, Clark also exercised the liberty of offering quick interventions when he thought necessary. For example, conservatives were worried that Cap Weinberger was not getting the support he needed from the White House. Clark sent a quick two-sentence note to the President on July 9: "Mr. President: When he was your secretary and I was your advisor, Al [Haig] would complain that he was being allowed to 'twist in the wind' if you or I had not called him by 0900 hours. Mr. President, Cap is twisting but not complaining—Bill Clark." Such a brief, handwritten note from Bill Clark alerted the

---

[5] In January 1988, the group issued a glossy sixty-nine-page report titled "Discriminate Deterrence", a term that never acquired recognition commensurate to the resumes of its distinguished members. The commission concluded vaguely, "Our strategy must be designed for the long term. . . . Our strategy must also be integrated." The report was a sterling example of the art of saying nothing. Blue ribbon commissions seemed to lose a lot of their luster in the years that followed.

busy President to something needing his attention. These infrequent messages, Clark says, usually referred to "someone's omission—or failure to appropriately acknowledge" certain personnel.

Regarding U.S. policy toward Nicaragua, on May 20, 1986, Clark sent a four-page letter to Reagan from the ranch. Not unlike the letter about U.S.-Soviet relations that he sent shortly after Reagan's re-election, the missive warned Reagan that his State Department was not implementing the President's Central America policies.

Reagan wanted to pressure the Sandinistas ruling Nicaragua to move away from communism and toward a democratic system. This effort called for funding the anti-communist forces within the country. Clark pointed out, however, that the State Department had adopted the view that while democratic reforms were desirable, they were neither realistic nor feasible. "Therefore, State has consistently ... sought a 'political solution' recognizing the communist regime in Nicaragua as permanent and stationary." Clark worried that accepting the Sandinistas as permanent and discontinuing aid to anti-communist guerillas would "reverse the good progress already made, likely resulting in a communist Central America".

The way Clark saw matters, State was on the brink of shaking hands with the Sandinistas, contrary to President Reagan's direction. He listed several examples to back up his assessment, among them: (1) Without the President's knowledge, State sent a representative to Nicaragua to establish a "separate track" for negotiations; (2) State never implemented the President's directive aimed at persuading Mexico to stop supporting the Sandinistas; (3) State never followed up on Senate-approved funding for the anti-communist guerillas, hence no current aid was forthcoming; (4) To the alarm of friendly nations in the region, Secretary Shultz had already visited Nicaragua to open direct bilateral negotiations; and (5) State drafted its own treaty for Nicaragua, which Defense, CIA, and NSC found inconsistent with the President's policies. Clark might have preferred to attend to his own personal business on the ranch, but who else cared as deeply as he did whether or not the President's goals were being fulfilled?

Clark not only sent letters of his own on topics of concern, but also, from time to time, sent along the letters of others who understood that Clark was a conduit to the President. The director of the Arms Control and Disarmament Agency (ACDA), Ken Adelman, had advice for the President on arms negotiations, summit talks, and Reagan's ideas about sharing the Strategic Defense Initiative with the Soviets.[6] He sent Clark a letter, dated April 7, 1987, for Reagan and attached this note: "Bill—some nice, simple, direct points for our mutual friend, as we discussed last Friday. Thanks, guy, for your help. This is truly important stuff. Fondly, Ken." Even though Clark had been out of office for four years, to get to Ronald Reagan—to get his quick attention on critical issues—Bill Clark remained the most effective channel.

Reagan's Emissary

In May 1985, a few weeks after Clark joined Rogers & Wells, Reagan sent him to Asia, specifically to South Korea, Taiwan, and China. In Seoul, Clark met with a number of high-level officials, including South Korea's President, Chun Doo-Hwan, with whom he discussed a host of topics, including closer economic relations between South Korea and China. In Taipei, Taiwan, Clark and President Chiang Ching-Kuo discussed a variety of matters, including military aid to Taiwan and trilateral relations with China. They also discussed the Achille Lauro incident and the importance of working together to deal effectively with terrorism.[7] The purpose of the China visit was to examine a China-U.S. business proposal, and Clark's participation saved the Reagan administration from a possible boondoggle on the Yangtze.

Clark Goes to China

Bill Clark arrived in Beijing with Secretary of Commerce Malcolm Baldrige on May 11. The main focus of the visit was the proposed Three Gorges Dam on the Yangtze River. After visiting the massive

---

[6] Adelman's letter to Reagan began: "I know how busy you are, so I'll keep this short. There's an old saying that people do not listen to advice unless they pay for it. Anyhow, here's some free, unsolicited advice." The letter both complimented Reagan for his past wisdom on arms control and the Soviets but warned him about future initiatives. Among his points, Adelman challenged "the conventional wisdom ... that nuclear weapons are bad in and of themselves". He acknowledged that, as Reagan had said, nuclear weapons had ominously hung over the world like the "sword of the Damocles". At the same time, said Adelman, that threat of Armageddon had helped keep the peace since World War II.

[7] This information is recorded in an October 23, 1985 telegram to Assistant Secretary of State Paul Wolfowitz, written by Clark's assistant, identified only by the last name "Thayer".

construction site, Clark met with Chinese authorities, along with representatives from five major U.S. construction firms, to discuss an American role in the project, as proposed by the Chinese at their highest level. An undated, unsigned summary of the meeting noted that China was "eager to proceed with construction" of the dam, which would "likely be the largest civil work attempted in this century".

Upon Clark's return to the States, Reagan's NSC, now headed by Bud McFarlane, looked carefully at the issue, using Clark's work as reference. Roger Robinson, NSC's top financial analyst, estimated that the hydroelectric dam would cost between twenty and thirty billion dollars. Although skeptical about the project, he acknowledged that it could be "very important to the development of central China and therefore to the success of China's overall modernization program." The project, said Robinson, was viewed by the Chinese "as one of the most significant in their history", not only because of the energy the dam would produce but also because of its potential to stem the periodic and destructive flooding of the Yangtze River. Robinson noted the financial benefits of the project not only to select Chinese citizens but also to American workers: Phase I alone would provide the U.S. economy with one to two billion dollars in contracts for services and equipment, and direct employment for 25,000 to 50,000 U.S. workers.

Such a project, noted Robinson, had been discussed as far back as 1943, when China under Chiang Kai-Shek was a close U.S. ally. That was before communist Mao Tse-Tung took over in 1949 and killed sixty to seventy million of his own people during the so-called Cultural Revolution.[8] Perhaps the time had come for the United States to partner with the Chinese in a project of this size and consequence.

As further studies were made in the months ahead, however, the risks of the project came to light. The early euphoria gave way to serious doubts. In the end, after much research and discussion, Clark advised Ronald Reagan against U.S. participation, and American capital and industry backed away. Clark has no doubts as to whether he decided correctly. "No one knew for sure at the time whether we were right or wrong", says Clark. "Later, however, the decision for the U.S. to pass was lauded by all."

---

[8] On this, see Stephane Courtois et al., *The Black Book of Communism* (Cambridge: Harvard University Press, 1999).

There have been endless problems—financial, mechanical, and ecological—in constructing the Three Gorges Dam. Local communities have been disrupted by the project, and there have been reports that the Chinese government has unjustly arrested and imprisoned citizens who have spoken out against it. The dam has not been completed, and is not scheduled to be finished until 2009.[9] In short, the project has been a disaster, and Bill Clark was largely responsible for averting America's involvement. Canada was more than happy to jump into the void, to its later consternation and disappointment.

Further Foreign Activities: 1985–1986

During 1985 and 1986, on behalf of the Reagan administration, acting as both troubleshooter and liaison, as well as private attorney and sometime tourist, Clark made trips to Ireland, London, Austria, and Switzerland, as well as additional visits to China, South Korea, and Taiwan. He was busier with overseas travel now than he had been as deputy secretary of state, but he was operating from the ranch rather than from Washington, D.C.

In regard to Taiwan, Clark continued to carry out high-level talks, becoming a liaison between President Reagan and President Chiang Ching-Kuo. One especially important example took place during a five-day trip in October 1985, which included an hour-long meeting

---

[9] Scientists are concerned that because of the construction of the Three Gorges Dam, worms will be able to spread the fast-spreading and potentially deadly schistosomiasis, which infects snails and humans; the effects on humans include fatigue, fever, internal lesions, distended organs, and death. The project threatens the survival of many different species.

Also, construction is destroying a beautiful region which features numerous priceless archaeological remains, which cannot be excavated as quickly as the water rises.

The massive amount of silt built up will most likely mean that the amount of energy produced by the dam will be far less than expected.

The project has even adversely affected water flows. The initial promise of flood control could fail because of estimates that the dam will cause an increase of speed and volume of water downstream. Surrounding tributaries have become severely polluted and useless. The construction has created a new lake that has become filled with domestic and factory waste. Numerous landslides have occurred since the project has begun. China has spent $990 million dealing with serious geological incidents in the reservoir area of the Three Gorges Project.

In regard to the mechanical and engineering problems, many large cracks have already appeared in the dam. If one of these cracks would give way, tragedy would ensue.

This is actually a short list of the problems.

with Chiang. Clark's visit was intended to counter-balance the recent visit of Vice President George Bush to China, a visit that had concerned Taiwan, which looked for a measure of reassurance, a sign from the Reagan administration that Taiwan was still an important ally and was not being abandoned in favor of China.

Clark was chosen for this mission because his credentials with the Republic of China had already been established at the highest levels in the first days of the Reagan administration. Also, as Reagan's close friend and trusted advisor, he was viewed by the Taiwanese as having the necessary authority to speak for the President. Reagan knew Clark thought about the U.S.-Taiwan-China relationship in the same way he did; he knew Clark would accurately represent his thinking. Further, Reagan had confidence in Clark because Asia policy, and the delicate China-Taiwan balance in particular, had gone smoothly in the first term, when Clark was at State and then at the NSC. Reagan trusted that Clark would be able to reassure Chiang of the American government's goodwill, of its "legal and moral commitments" to Chiang, his government, his country, and his people, "especially those commitments relating to security".

Clark did not disappoint. According to an October 23 telegram to Assistant Secretary of State for East Asian and Pacific Affairs Paul Wolfowitz, President Chiang told Clark that he had "appreciated President Reagan's efforts", most notably in assisting Taiwan in the development of fighter aircraft. Chiang was deeply concerned with recent efforts by the Chinese communists to intimidate Taiwan "by using the threat of war". He hoped that Clark would convey that message to President Reagan. He and other leaders in Asia looked upon President Reagan, not only as the leader of the United States and of the "free world", but also as their "faithful friend".

Chiang did not stop there. Clark understood, Chiang said, that the Chinese communists "would never change, despite tactics to disguise their enmity". He warned Clark that war could break out at any moment over the Taiwan Straits, and that Taiwan must be prepared for the worst. Clark answered that Reagan appreciated the precariousness of the situation.

Clark's activities in Asia continued throughout the remainder of the Reagan administration, with trips to Seoul again, in March 1986, and back to Taipei in May 1988, this time with Cap Weinberger and Bill's son Colin. Clark's involvement with Asia would extend beyond the Reagan years, as Clark became chairman of the USA-ROC (Republic of China) Business Council, a group to which Clark delivered addresses in November 1989 and November 1990.

He also gave the keynote address to the Asian Business League's Pacific Rim Forum in Los Angeles on April 26, 1990. In his remarks, Clark criticized China over its use of military force to disperse pro-democracy demonstrators in Beijing's Tiananmen Square, killing hundreds of people and wounding thousands more. The incident, he said, offered a "startling contrast" between Taiwan and communist China. The latter hosts a "massacre", while the former stands "as a beacon of light outside the China mainland, showing the Chinese people a successful alternative to the communist system". Taiwan, Clark insisted, had become both an economic and political model for developing nations everywhere.

Clark's Meeting with Saddam Hussein

Most everything that Bill Clark did for Reagan during his second term managed to find its way into the press, but there was at least one important exception: a meeting with Iraq's Saddam Hussein in January 1986.

Clark's objective in Iraq was to meet with government officials, including Saddam Hussein, on certain legal issues for a client. By protocol and custom, Clark informed current National Security Advisor Admiral Poindexter of his Middle-East travel plans in the event he might assist U.S. interests in any way. Clark was asked to see as many top Iraqi officials as possible to gather information on certain aspects of Iraq's war with Iran, now in its sixth year, with devastating loss of life on both sides. He was also asked to obtain, as appropriate, views on several other bilateral governmental and commercial issues.

On January 24, along with the occasional Iranian Scud missile, Clark and his team landed in Baghdad. He met over several days with a number of key Iraqi officials, including Senior Vice President Taha Yasin Ramadhan; Foreign Minister Tariq Aziz; Iraq's Ambassador to the United States, Nizar Hamdoon; as well as the ministers of interior, industry, petroleum, and trade.

For Hamdoon and Clark, this was the start of a longterm friendship. Also, Aziz and Clark, according to the memo of the meeting prepared by a U.S. embassy official who accompanied Clark, "established a very friendly relationship".[10] The fact that Aziz and Hamdoon were Catholic Christians, or Chaldeans, who both had attended the Jesuit-run Baghdad College, may have contributed to the rapport. During their long discussions, Aziz assured Clark that Iraq "was in no way harboring or support[ing] terrorists", including Abu Abbas.[11] This was probably incorrect and Clark suspected as much.

After his meetings with Aziz and Hamdoon, Clark spent two hours with Saddam Hussein. Also in attendance for the January 25 meeting were Abud Ihood, Hussein's chief of staff; an Iraqi interpreter; and a U.S. embassy officer. Clark and Hussein chatted amiably about several bilateral issues before Hussein proceeded to blame Iran for starting the war. The accusation was patently untrue, and Clark replied, calmly, that the Reagan administration wanted the war to stop. "It is serving neither side to continue this conflict", said Clark. "There can be no positive outcome, just further death on both sides—and casualties are already approaching one million men, women, and children."

Clark then urged Hussein to cease supporting Palestinian terrorist training camps operating inside Iraq. "We knew they were there," says Clark, "and they were effective." Saddam agreed, saying that neither Abu Abbas nor any other Palestinian terrorist would be welcome again in Iraq.[12] Clark pressed Hussein further on terrorism: There recently had been a terrible bombing at the airport in Rome. Clark told Hussein that the Reagan administration knew that the explosives used in the incident had passed through the airport in Baghdad. Hussein conceded that he, too, knew the material had passed through Baghdad, but said this was due to the lack of explosive detectors at the Baghdad airport, and claimed that the explosives would have made it through JFK airport for the same reason.

Hussein then made his requests: first of all, he confessed to a void of knowledge regarding the West, the United States. "All I know", he said, "is the Arab world—Iraq". Clark replied, "We can work on that."

---

[10] The memo, dated January 31, 1986, today in Clark's possession, was initialed by the author as "DRC".

[11] January 31, 1986 memo.

[12] This was a promise that, if kept, was not kept indefinitely. Sixteen years later, in April 2002, for instance, Saddam publicly upped his payment from $10,000 to $25,000 for the families of Palestinian suicide bombers who blew themselves up in the service of killing Israel's Jews. As for 1986, however, Clark believes that Saddam honored his pledge.

Secondly, Hussein wished to see "normalization" of relations between his country and the United States—not just in the commercial arena, but in the political arena as well.

Finally, Hussein raised the subject of the proposed oil pipeline from Iraq to Aqaba, Jordan. It had been put out for bids; however, Hussein thought the U.S. company's bid was too high. He was concerned that if the American bid were not accepted by Iraq, bilateral relations between Iraq and the United States could suffer, given that several high-ranking U.S. government officials had previously been associated with the company. Clark assured Hussein that his choice of bid would have no bearing on his country's relationship with the United States. Hussein was relieved and deeply grateful to Clark for this assurance. In the end, the pipeline was not built.

One of Clark's companions on the trip says Hussein saw Clark as "a man of honor—Iraq's hope for normalization of the political relationship between the U.S. and Iraq". Unfortunately, Clark was no longer in a position to take advantage of this opportunity, but his report urged those in power to do so. Although Hussein welcomed U.S. commercial ventures into his country, there was never the wished-for political concomitant. "Had that happened", says the companion, who wishes to remain anonymous in light of the current political situation, "the history of our world might have evolved very differently".

A claim made during and after the first Gulf War was that the United States in the 1980s assisted Iraq in the development of its weapons of mass destruction (WMD). These claims live on regardless of the lack of credibility. "We never armed Hussein," states Clark categorically, referring to the Reagan administration policy on Iraq, "and to my knowledge, we certainly did not give him anything like WMD technology, or assist him in developing WMD." In his conversation with Clark, Hussein neither asked about nor sought armaments.

At this point, the United States had not yet started providing Iraq with military intelligence. "We eventually agreed, some time after this meeting with Hussein, to supply important intel on Iran, in the form of imagery", says Clark, clarifying the nature of U.S. support. The satellite imagery pictured Iranian troop movements, including armored troops and tank columns. "We wanted a stalemate [in the war], a stand-off", says Clark. "A ceasefire between Iraq and Iran was our clear objective, and that ultimately did occur."

Clark's clear sense from his meeting with Hussein was that the Iraqi leader "wanted to be a friend" to the United States.[13] Their meeting was congenial; their discussions, civilized. However, political "normalization" failed to materialize and even may not have been attempted. Five years later, and following his possible misinterpretation of the U.S. ambassador's ambiguous signals to him, Saddam Hussein invaded Kuwait in August 1990.

There remains a valid question whether the two countries could ever have achieved a workable relationship, but the meetings in 1986 held hope for a healthy bilateral relationship between the United States and Iraq.

As a friendly gesture to his visitor, Hussein gave Clark a gift—an Italian Beretta 9mm pistol made under license in Iraq. The gift was placed in a glittery gold and blue box, also containing one carton of ammunition and a cleaning rod. Clark held little expectation the weapon would make it through security inspections on the trip home.

Soon after Clark departed Iraq, the Beretta began its own story. On their way home, Bill and Joan stopped in Israel, where they were feted by Israeli President Chaim Herzog. (This was the same party that included former Vice President Walter Mondale.) As Clark prepared to board a plane for Vienna, where he would stop to confer with Helene von Damm, U.S. Ambassador to Austria, his gift from Saddam Hussein became an item of interest to security personnel at the Tel Aviv airport.

A tall Israeli soldier holding an Uzi said, "Judge Clark, I'm sure I don't have to ask you the usual security questions because I know you had dinner with our President last night." Clark corrected the soldier: "No, ma'am, I think you better ask the usual questions." She did, adding, "Of course, you are not in possession of any weapons?"

Clark handed over the gold and blue box. The soldier inspected it closely, and gruffly commented that it came from Israel's enemy, Iraq. Clark explained the weapon's history and offered to give it to the guard. She said she would hand the box to the pilot, who would hold it until Clark got off the plane. Even then, the gun was not home free. It was confiscated again at the Vienna airport, where Clark reiterated the pistol's interesting tale. The guard smiled and told Clark, "Okay,

---

[13] Admiral Poindexter believes this was an optimistic appraisal; he states: "We did not draw the same conclusion."

you can take it, but if you pull it out [in the airport], you will, of course, be shot on sight." Both gun and owner made it safely home to Shandon, California, where arrangements were made to place the weapon at the Reagan Library.

Other Clark Travels

Bill and Joan made a number of trips to Europe during this period, including a stop in London, where on February 22, 1988, they attended a small dinner at No. 10 Downing Street hosted by Prime Minister Thatcher in honor of former Secretary of Defense Cap Weinberger. Thatcher was honoring Weinberger for his assistance in the Falklands War. Clark was seated next to Thatcher, on her left; and Cap, to her right.

A few months later, Bill and Joan visited Zagreb, Croatia, in a stopover that influenced Clark's later opinions on President Bush's policy in the Balkans and on the war in the region authorized by President Bill Clinton ten years later. While in Zagreb, Clark was asked by Croation President Tudjman for advice and counsel in structuring his new democratic government. Clark extended his stay by a few days to accommodate the new President's request.

Clark delivered an important address during an official 1987 trip to Austria, where he represented the United States at the Western Europe-U.S.A. Dialogue Congress. He first gave a statement on behalf of President Reagan and then followed with an analysis of the U.S.-Western European relationship, giving his answer to the question addressed by the congress: "Relations between the U.S.A. and Western Europe: Alienation or Partnership 40 Years after the Marshall Plan?" Clark's talk, marking the official opening, analogized the U.S.–Western European relationship to a healthy marriage. "In most marriages there are squabbles and misunderstandings", he said. "Frequent communication is the key to resolution."

In a previous discussion with President Reagan, it was decided that Clark should mention Soviet leader Mikhail Gorbachev in his address. Gorbachev had arrived on the scene two years previously, after Clark had left State and NSC. Clark held out the possibility that Gorbachev could be a reformer. "Mr. Gorbachev and the government he represents now have the opportunity and incentive for a change in conduct", said Clark. The Reagan administration stood ready to cooperate with him, Clark added, and was not, as some Europeans maintained, "a posse of Cold Warriors seeking a shootout at some O.K. Corral". Nonetheless, said Clark, "peace comes only through strength", and "strength and realism are the watchwords for dealing with the Soviet Union. As we view the Kremlin with continuous optimism, let it be remembered that four decades ago, the Soviets rejected participation in the Marshall Plan." [14] Mikhail Gorbachev may have come to Moscow, but the Cold War was not over yet.

Two Deaths

Sadly for Clark, the year 1987 was marred by two losses. When he returned from Europe, he received word that his friend Clare Boothe Luce had little time left on this earth. Having returned to politics to help Clark and Reagan in their fight against communism, Luce had been living in Washington for six years. That autumn, at the age of eighty-four, Luce died of a brain tumor at her Watergate apartment. Clark and the others who knew and loved Clare hoped and prayed that she was at long last reunited with her beloved daughter, Ann. Bill accompanied Clare's body to Saint Patrick's Cathedral in New York for the funeral Mass and then to a Trappist monastery in South Carolina, where she was buried.

Clark had suffered another great loss earlier that year, the passing of his friend and colleague William J. Casey. Casey was no longer a young man, but he was still active in public service at the time of his death, which had not been expected.

His premature death was made all the more bitter by his disturbing funeral Mass in Roslyn Harbor, New York. The celebrant was Bishop John McGann, whose homily was more of a political statement than a message of consolation. The mourners, who included President Reagan, were offended, and R. Emmett Tyrrell Jr., editor-in-chief of the *American Spectator*, noted that the gruff, cynical Casey would not have been surprised that at his funeral, in the presence of grieving family and friends, "an obtuse Catholic prelate" would rebuke him for "adhering to the same values that saved the West from Nazism in

---

[14] The Clark quotes come from a transcript of his July 8, 1987 address. President Reagan's remarks, on White House letterhead and dated June 24, 1987, were reproduced, placed in a binder, and circulated to every attendee at the July 7–11, 1987 conference in Austria.

the 1940s and have thwarted Communism ever since". Despite the expressed wishes of the Casey family, the Bishop had permitted himself to give a lecture on global politics, added Tyrrell. "Everyone was appalled", said Casey's daughter.

Clark wrote a letter to McGann, telling him it was "totally inappropriate to use the death of a great patriot to spread his own political views". He felt deeply for Casey's family and, in a coincidence a year later that found Clark on the same flight as Casey's widow and daughter, he approached the two women as they disembarked from the plane and pulled Bill Casey's memorial card from his pocket. "I carry it with me always", he said. Casey's wife and daughter were deeply moved. "My mom was thrilled", said Bernadette (Casey) Smith. "It was so considerate. We cried." [15]

Clark always includes Casey's name in any discussion of credit for winning the Cold War. Were Casey alive today, he would most likely do the same in regard to Clark. "He thought the world of Bill Clark", says Bernadette Smith. "They were on the same page—same wavelength. They came from the same religious background with the same commitment to country." Casey also shared Clark's enthusiasm on meeting Ronald Reagan for the first time. Bernadette remembers her father going to Colony Hill on Long Island to hear presidential candidate Reagan speak: "Dad came back and was very excited by Reagan's vision. 'He may be our best hope', he said." [16]

In his files, Clark keeps a July 1987 tribute to Casey written by R. Emmett Tyrrell Jr. The piece calls Casey "a great man", and also notes that he was one of the "best read men in modern American government", as his massive personal library attested. He was a crucial player in Ronald Reagan's political career, helping him win the White House and assemble his staff, and then assisting him in the fight against communism as the head of the CIA. "I had the highest regard for Bill Casey", says Clark.

---

[15] Interview with Bernadette Smith, November 15, 2005.
[16] Ibid.

CHAPTER 16

Tried but Failed

Stopping a "Political Travesty"

December 18, 1986 found former Secretary Clark back at the Department of the Interior, for an event in his honor hosted by the grateful secretary he had suggested as his replacement, Don Hodel. A portrait of Clark by renowned artist Everett Raymond Kinstler was to be unveiled. The mood of the moment was soured, however, by the fact that Ronald Reagan was in the most serious political danger of his career: a scandal had erupted, one that would forever be known as Iran-Contra. The issues remain little understood by the public, by reason of the confusion created by the media.

Charges in the press alleged that the Reagan administration had secretly and illicitly sold arms to Iran and had used the profits to help the Nicaraguan Contras in their war against the communist Sandinistas ruling their country. An arms deal with Iran, reported the press, violated a U.S. trade embargo against that nation. The primary purpose of the deal, which was to gain the release of hostages being held in Lebanon by Hezbollah, a Shi'a jihadist group funded and often directed by Tehran, was also problematic, as stated U.S. policy forbade negotiations with terrorists. Diverting the profits to arm the Contras was also a grave matter because Congress had passed legislation forbidding the Defense Department, the CIA, and other governmental agencies from giving them military assistance—so stated the media.

The reporters in attendance at the Department of the Interior that December were more interested in the Iran-Contra affair than in former

312

Secretary Clark's portrait, as revealed by their pointed questions. Clark was unable to answer their queries; he had left the NSC in October of 1983, three years before the purported events would have occurred. He did state, however, that he hoped for a quick conclusion to the uproar. "Ronald Reagan is wiser than his Cabinet and staff combined", stated Clark. "He does know what goes on around him, on the one hand; on the other hand, he never attempted to micromanage the White House tennis court." Clark advised: "Let's trust him, support him, and in this holy season"—it was one week before Christmas—"pray for him." [1] Not in the praying business, the press did not back down; it saw another Watergate on the horizon.

The connection between Iran and the Nicaraguan Contras began in June 1985, with the second major American hostage situation in seven years. On June 14, TWA Flight 847, en route from Athens to Rome, was hijacked by Lebanese Shi'a Muslims associated with Hezbollah, demanding the release of Shi'a prisoners held in Kuwait, Israel, and Spain. A U.S. Navy diver, a passenger on the aircraft, was tortured, murdered, and his body thrown from the plane to the tarmac. Hezbollah shuttled the remaining hostages from place to place, sporadically releasing a few, before sequestering some in Beirut and transferring the remainder elsewhere for "trial".

As the sequence of events unfolded, memory took American citizens back to 1979, nine months following the ascension of the Ayatollah Khomeini as Iran's "Supreme Leader for Life". Khomeini's ardent Shi'a followers seized the U.S. embassy in Tehran, taking sixty-three American citizens hostage, and demanding that the U.S. hand over their former ruler, Shah Mohammad Reza Pahlavi, to stand trial for "crimes against the Iranian nation". [2] The government of the United States responded by imposing an embargo on any domestically produced goods to be shipped to Iran. It also urged its allies to discontinue trade with Iran. After being held for 444 days, 52 of the American hostages were released on the same day Reagan took the oath of office: January 20, 1981. Many attributed President Carter's decisive defeat to his failure to rescue the hostages during the previous fifteen months.

---

[1] Guy Darst "Clark-Reagan", *Associated Press*, December 18, 1986.

[2] "Iran Hostage Crisis", *Columbia Encyclopedia*, Sixth Edition, 2001–2005.

Shortly after assuming power, Khomeini called for Shi'a revolutions across the Muslim world. Saddam Hussein, a Sunni Muslim and a secular dictator, perceived a Shi'a uprising as a threat to his power. With the encouragement of Saudi Arabia, the Gulf States, and others, and with military backing from the Soviet Union, Hussein launched a full-scale invasion of Iran. The struggle lasted eight bloody years, claiming the lives of more than one million people.

For Hussein, an Iran militarily weakened by the collapse of the Shah's government offered an opportunity to redress the treaty of 1975, forced on Iraq by a then more powerful Iran to settle a territorial dispute over, among other things, the Shatt al-'Arab waterway separating the two countries before emptying into the Persian Gulf. An Iraqi victory would also give Hussein control over more oil fields and bolster Iraq's standing and leverage within the area and beyond.

The 1985 hijacking of TWA Flight 847 occurred two years before the war's end, when Hezbollah had been seizing various individuals—most of them Americans who had chosen to remain in West Beirut despite repeated advice from the American embassy not to do so. Families of these hostages began to exert pressure on the administration through public statements and periodic meetings with the President. Reagan was emotionally drained by the pleas of the distraught families, as well as by the failure of the U.S. government to protect its citizens from terrorists.

Some in the administration thought that the current hostage situation, short of the U.S. military action being planned, could only be solved by dealing one way or another with Iran. Secretary of Defense Weinberger has stated that when he and Secretary of State Shultz were consulted on these matters they voiced their disapproval of arms deals with the Iranians.

While it remains unclear to what extent he had the support of President Reagan, National Security Advisor Bud McFarlane made an arrangement in 1985 with the Israelis, who had offered to sell the Iranians some of their American-made anti-tank missiles, which in turn were replaced with purchases from the U.S. Defense Department. Presumably, the transaction would result in the release of hostages. It was also hoped by Israel and the United States that the deal would strengthen elements in the Tehran government less hostile to

Israel and America, prevent Iran from turning to the Soviets for military assistance, and keep Iraq's ambitions for conquest in check.

The executive branch was in effect lifting the embargo on goods to Iran, placed as a result of the earlier hostage situation, and it had valid reasons for believing it had the legal right to do so, according to CIA officer Duane Clarridge, who was charged in the Iran-Contra affair.

"What many writers on the Iran and Contra issue fail to acknowledge, or even understand", says Clarridge, "is that an embargo is imposed or lifted by the executive branch of our government without need for or reference to either of the two other branches." [3] It was the prerogative of the executive branch not only to impose and lift embargos, but also to change foreign policy, Clarridge says. While some disagreed with the change in policy, it was within the authority of the executive to negotiate with Iran.

Admiral John Poindexter, appointed national security advisor in 1986 following McFarlane's resignation, explained the administration's position on Iran in the November 1986 *Wall Street Journal*. "We were overtaken and overwhelmed by the Iranian revolution and its aftermath", stated Poindexter. "We were traumatized by the new regime and its virulent anti-American posture." How could America, he asked, not try to shape the new Iran? The costs of waiting for change would be too exorbitant.

The decision had been made, with Reagan's approval, continued Poindexter, for the U.S. National Security Council to supply arms to Iran.[4] There was no hope, nor was there the intention to establish a pro-U.S. leadership to invite us back into Iran. The intention was to build "peace and stability in this region"; maintain "a bulwark against Soviet expansionism"; and end "a brutal war whose hideous consumption of human life—especially a nation's precious youth . . . [was] almost without precedent".[5]

The gains would be bilateral: The Iranians wanted a demonstration of presidential involvement and support; as only the President could authorize sale of military material, the arms constituted that support.

---

[3] Interview with Duane Clarridge, September 10, 2006.

[4] John M. Poindexter, National Security Advisor, "The Prudent Option in Iran", *The Wall Street Journal*, November 24, 1986.

[5] Ibid.

The U.S. demanded signs of Iranian opposition to the use of terrorism and assistance in gaining the release of U.S. hostages in Lebanon.

The timing was perfect to reestablish rapport with Iran, argued Poindexter. By the mid-1980s, Khomeini was ill and his control of his fiercely Islamic anti-American isolationist theocracy was wavering as his health declined. The moment was ripe to send out feelers to "pragmatic elements in the Iranian leadership", those who had "begun to search for ways to reduce their international isolation and establish more normal relations with the outside world."[6]

Poindexter concluded his remarks with:

> Those who now question us owe the country an explanation of how they would have acted differently given the stakes, the opportunities and the dangers. They need to tell us how they would have turned aside the kinds of overtures we were receiving. They need to tell us how they would have gone about protecting such an obviously sensitive mission. And they need to tell us how they would safeguard our interests in circumstances where the future stability of this vital region may hinge on the unfolding drama in Iran today.[7]

Aid for the Contras—whom Reagan had supported throughout his presidency and regarded as "the moral equivalent of our founding fathers" as well as the means of foiling Marxism's advance in Central America— was an altogether different matter. Beginning in 1982, a Democratic congressman from Massachusetts, Edward Boland, succeeded in attaching amendments to Department of Defense appropriations bills prohibiting the Department of Defense or the intelligence agencies from furnishing "military equipment, military training or advice for the purpose of overthrowing the government of Nicaragua". President Reagan was left with the choice of vetoing the omnibus bills, which would shut down the government, or signing them with all their imperfections.[8]

---

[6] Ibid.

[7] Ibid.

[8] Interview, John M. Poindexter, August 29, 2006. These omnibus or "Barnacle" bills were so called as many of their provisions could not have passed on their own merit. Poindexter states, "When I became National Security Advisor, I got the President to agree that I could go to the Hill and tell them that if there was another bill including restrictions on his Central America policy, the President would veto it no matter whether it was a single appropriations bill or an omnibus bill. I did that and that year there was no Boland amendment."

Boland amendments were again passed in 1983 and 1984, and during the latter year, Congress forbade any U.S. government aid that "would have the effect of supporting, directly or indirectly, military or paramilitary operations in Nicaragua". Congress permitted, however, the solicitation of funds from other sources, so long as they were not used for weapons. Determined to continue its military support of the Contras, the Reagan administration found a loophole: the National Security Council was not explicitly named in the Boland amendments. Funds were raised from private individuals and foreign governments and then directed by NSC staffer Lieutenant Colonel Oliver North into covert operations maintaining the Contras. Also, "several of the President's NSC staff were involved in . . . the plan, conceived by Amiran Nir, counterterrorism advisor to the Israeli Prime Minister, and in contact with Oliver North, to place a surcharge on the price of the missiles being sold to Iran", says Clarridge. "It was further proposed, and clearly the intention, to use these excess funds to underwrite Contra activity." [9]

Bits of information on Oliver North's activities leaked out here and there, but without raising any serious alarms. "Anyone who was breathing within the Washington, D.C., Beltway and even beyond knew that NSC fundraising was being used to arm the Contras", says Clarridge. Then on October 6, 1986, a plane carrying three Americans and lethal supplies for the Contras was shot down by Nicaraguan anti-aircraft guns. The only American survivor of the wreck inaccurately claimed that he had been working for the CIA. The press jumped on the story: Was the administration violating U.S. law by giving military aid to the Contras? A month later, the Iran arms deal came to light; and in December Lawrence Walsh, a former federal judge, was appointed independent counsel to determine whether illegalities had been committed, and, if so, which individuals should be prosecuted. A big question concerned Reagan's personal knowledge and involvement in the affair: *What did Reagan know?* became the buzz.

Congressional hearings began and were broadcast all day long on network television during the long, hot summer of 1987. The nation was riveted by the spectacle, especially by the sight of NSC figures such as Ollie North, testifying in his decorated Marine uniform, and Admiral John Poindexter, speaking slowly to interrogators between

---

[9] Duane Clarridge, interview.

pauses to puff on his pipe and listen to whispers from his attorney, Dick Beckler. Following this live coverage, the evening news gave their reports on the hearings.

The subject of the Boland amendments was never addressed, to Poindexter's disappointment. "None of the formal charges brought against me or Ollie included violating the Boland Amendments", he says. "I was seriously disappointed as we had a ruling from the President's Intelligence Oversight Board that Boland did not apply to the NSC staff—only to the Department of Defense and the intelligence community. All charges were secondary to that issue. Of course, this did not prevent the media from claiming that we had violated the amendments." [10] Clarridge adds: "The closest Walsh got to Boland was considering bringing the charge against North for 'conspiring to violate the Boland amendment', but the matter was dropped when he found the U.S. government would not make classified material available."

Clark Urges Pardons

Bill Clark was disturbed by the proceedings and especially by the outcome: criminal charges were brought against Oliver North, John Poindexter, and several others. Clark and others say Poindexter "took the fall" for his predecessor, who had brokered the deal with Israel and Iran and then left the questionable affair in Poindexter's hands. Clark volunteered to assist the principals charged in Iran-Contra, all of whom were close friends and members of his former staff. He urged President Reagan to pardon them.

Clark always had "great regard" for Admiral Poindexter, who possessed the necessary intelligence, moderation, and calm for the job of national security advisor and yet did not want the post. He would have preferred returning to sea at the command of a fleet, says Clark, but he had stayed on at NSC at Clark's request and out of loyalty to the President. He had served his country, and now he was threatened with fines and jail time, as was Lieutenant Colonel Ollie North, a decorated war hero Clark hired to serve on his NSC staff. Both Poindexter and North were distinguished Naval Academy graduates. Clark viewed the entire situation as a "political travesty".

---

[10] Ibid.

Clark made his view clear in an August 6, 1987 letter, sent from the Washington law office of Rogers & Wells, urging Reagan to pardon Poindexter and North.

Dear Mr. President,

As you well know, John Poindexter and Oliver North each served us with professional skill, integrity, and loyalty as staff members while I was your National Security Advisor.... During and since that time they participated in many successful programs, including the defense budget, economic summits, Suriname, Grenada, Achille Lauro, Libya, Philippines and Haiti. History will judge these programs well.... But after almost a year of intense official and media attention the most apt description of National Security Counsel [sic] staff conduct is that it was directed by overachievers who, in too enthusiastically implementing your policies, exercised judgments which in hindsight are claimed to be faulty....

It is abundantly clear that John and Ollie undertook their initiatives in what they deemed to be the national interest at considerable professional risk and without consideration for personal gain....

There is nothing in my judgment to be accomplished in the criminal prosecution of John or Ollie which would begin to justify still another review of events. More important national concerns must be addressed.

A pardon is not necessarily a recognition that any criminal conduct has occurred. It would simply be an expression of your conclusion that the story has been told, that the people involved have suffered enough, and that neither they, the Office of the President nor the country should be forced to endure an extended criminal trial in which the central issue relates to the creation and implementation of your foreign policy.

Except for those few who never like anything you do, the American people have overwhelmingly expressed their feelings that there should be no criminal prosecution and they will support a decision to pardon. They will perceive you as a man who, as in the past, stands behind his people in good and in bad times.

Taking all of the above into account, I strongly recommend that you grant presidential pardons for John and Ollie now, before the independent counsel concludes his investigations.

Sincerely, William P. Clark

Clark also understood that with the prosecution of Poindexter and North, President Reagan's entire foreign policy program would be on trial. He and many other observers saw Iran-Contra as a classic war-powers dispute between the executive and legislative branches over which had the right to make foreign policy. Reagan defenders argued—not unreasonably—that the Boland amendments were unconstitutional. Through the amendments, Congress had attempted to legislate foreign policy in a way that exceeded its authorization, infringing on the President's national security prerogatives as spelled out in the U.S. Constitution. In other words, the Reagan Administration, if it had violated the law at all, had "violated" a law that itself was unlawful. However, this was a moot point, as the Reagan administration argued that no law had been violated because Boland did not apply to the NSC.

Congress and the presidency have wrangled over foreign policy authority since the country's founding, according to political scientists Ryan J. Barilleaux and Christopher Kelley, who carefully studied the issues. The wording in the Constitution delegating responsibility for foreign policy is in places so unclear and contradictory that the courts have stayed out of the dispute. The Iran-Contra controversy is "an illustration" of a longstanding quarrel, they wrote, and "ought to be viewed in light of the larger struggles between the president and the Congress that began with the Vietnam War and Watergate".[11]

Democrats argued—also not unreasonably—that the law is the law. Congress makes laws. Congress passed the Boland amendments, and certain people in the Reagan Administration had violated them and then obstructed the lawful search for the truth of the matter. While a compelling argument, no one stood accused of violating Boland, except for a few CIA officers who were found to have stumbled into a legal thicket while trying to carry out their assigned duties. One was forced to retire from the CIA for ordering the evacuation from Nicaragua of two seriously wounded Contras. As the officer used an agency-controlled helicopter for the evacuation, the operation was deemed a violation of Boland. In the end, except for a conviction for income

---

[11] See Barilleaux and Kelley in Kengor and Schweizer, eds., *The Reagan Presidency*, pp. 122, 127.

tax evasion, most of those involved in the Iran-Contra affair were charged with obstruction of justice, lying to Congress, misspeaking, and so forth—charges all brought by a failed prosecutor.[12]

With his letter to the President requesting pardons, Clark included his draft of a suggested public announcement for the President, along with a one-and-a-half-page write–up on the constitutional authority for presidential pardons, including relevant court cases.

Now that the two select committees established by the Congress have completed public hearings of the sale of arms to Iran and the transfer of funds to the Nicaraguan Freedom Fighters, I think it is appropriate for me to speak out.

First I am not here to tell you that mistakes were not made. I think it is clear that they were. It is also clear that as President, I am ultimately responsible for every action taken by my assistants whether or not I know of them in advance. No matter what anyone else has told you, the buck can only stop here.

Second, the American people have heard from all the current and former members of this administration who know anything about the Iranian initiative and the transfer of funds to the Nicaraguan resistance. I realize that there has been some conflicting testimony but we should not be surprised that these people have somewhat differing recollections regarding events that occurred as long as two years ago. I have worked with and know most of these people quite well and firmly believe that they have recounted everything that they could honestly remember. Now the American people can decide if what was done was right or wrong.

It is also clear to me that none of these individuals made any decision or took any action which they did not sincerely believe to be in the best interest of the national security of this country. There can be no doubt that it has been and will continue to be the policy of this Administration to support the cause of freedom in Central America, to secure the release of all American citizens held hostage in foreign lands, and to encourage the establishment of a more moderate regime in Iran. This does not necessarily mean that I approve of the idea of selling arms for hostages or of sending the sale proceeds to the Nicaraguan resistance. That is not the issue.

---

[12] Duane Clarridge, interview.

The issue is whether the members of my staff who made these decisions should be subject to criminal prosecution. I believe that the answer is no. This does not mean that I think that any crimes were committed by my former advisors. What it does mean is that I have decided that neither they nor the country should be forced to endure the ordeal of an extended criminal trial in which the central issue is the manner in which the foreign policy of this Administration was created and carried out.

Therefore, pursuant to the powers vested in me by the Constitution, and without concluding that any crimes have been committed, I intend to pardon these individuals for their conduct while they served in the Administration.

Clark did not intend for his letter to become public, but it was leaked by someone in the White House and became front-page news.[13] Asked by a *New York Times* reporter to share Reagan's response to the letter, Clark said, "In 22 years, I have never discussed a presidential communication."[14] He was not about to change that policy.

Reagan did take Clark's pardon suggestion seriously, but it was quashed—by a source close to the President. Despite that unsuccessful overture, Clark did not let up. He wrote again to Reagan—a January 7, 1988 letter in which he continued to urge pardons.

Dear Mr. President:

I write you in the national interest.... Do the American people really want to see a third run of this ordeal, to now include revelation of our most sensitive intelligence sources and methods? Mr. President, you have the power and I believe the duty to end this matter by exercising your authority under the pardon clause of the United States Constitution. My predecessors, Dr. Kissinger and Dr. Brzezinski, add their concurrence to this recommendation.

Sincerely, Bill Clark.

On January 17, 1989, three days before Reagan left the presidency, Clark wrote again urging pardons, this time to the new national security advisor, Colin Powell, and asking him to present his request to

---

[13] Philip Shenon, "Time Is Running Out for a Decision on Pardons", *New York Times*, November 23, 1988.

[14] Richard L. Berke, "Reagan Confidant Urged Pardons in Iran Case", *New York Times*, November 18, 1988.

the President. He included a handwritten appeal by General John W. Vessey, Chairman of the JCS. Time was running out for Reagan to issue pardons.

When Reagan and his team left office, the controversy over Iran-Contra continued. While the chance to impeach Reagan had now passed, the opportunity remained for his opponents to leave an indelible stain on his presidency. Also, Reagan's vice president, George H. W. Bush, was now president. Had *he* been involved in Iran-Contra? Could he be implicated? Could his presidency be brought down by the scandal? *What did George know?* became the new mantra.

Clark was incensed by the never-ending escalation. He was infuriated by the shocking announcement the weekend before the November 1992 election that Cap Weinberger and others were about to be indicted. After an intense battle, President Bush had finally, somehow, pulled into a tie in the polls with Democratic presidential nominee Governor Bill Clinton. Then came the announcement of the impending indictments. New York Governor Mario Cuomo went before the television cameras to warn Americans that, in light of the announcement, a Bush re-election might result in a presidential impeachment. Between the weekend announcement and the Tuesday vote, Bush slipped six points in the polls. He was defeated.

A week later, on November 13, 1992, Clark sent a letter to former President Reagan at his Los Angeles office, informing him of press reports stating that because Weinberger was being drawn into the affair Reagan himself, as well as President Bush, might be called to testify on Iran-Contra.

Dear Mr. President:

Beginning in 1966, I have always attempted to give my best counsel toward protecting both you and the nation. Working together, we were usually successful. I further recognize that since leaving your Administration, you have neither requested nor required my counsel. However, in concern for both your personal interest and that of our nation, I point out the following critical situation.

In response to my 1987 pardon recommendation (attached), other advisors urged you to allow the Iran-Contra matter to "take its course." It has. I have spent hours with Judge Walsh discussing (former judge to former judge) dismissal of the action in the interests of justice. . . .

Mr. President, it is my considered judgment that you and President Bush will be called to testify in this political travesty come January, resulting in unjust and grievous harm to the national interests as well as to your own. The only correct solution is for President Bush to exercise his Constitutional power of pardon. Were he here, I am confident Bill [William French] Smith would concur. We would recommend you call George Bush.

With great admiration and gratitude, Bill.

As Weinberger's pro bono legal counsel, Clark had gone to Oklahoma to meet with Walsh. According to Weinberger's account of the meeting, Clark tried to persuade the independent counsel that "the course he was pursuing was both absurd and terribly damaging." Clark concluded that Walsh was interested in only one thing: some kind of admission of guilt by Weinberger, "preferably something—*anything*—that implicated President Reagan or even Vice President Bush". Weinberger was promised "no indictment and a light sentence" if he were "cooperative" with Walsh and his lawyers as they pursued the President. This promise, Weinberger was told by Clark, was accompanied by a wink and a nudge. Clark objected, telling Walsh that Weinberger would be lying if he pleaded guilty to something he had not done.[15] Walsh's actions were "despicable", says Clark, because "[h]e wanted to get the President and the Vice President by making a deal with Weinberger. It was analogous to extortion."

Clark's assessment of the political landscape was correct: Reagan was called to testify, and the results were embarrassing. By that point, as we later learned, Alzheimer's had begun to cloud the mind of the fortieth President. During his testimony, Reagan could not remember the simplest facts and details, whether related or unrelated to Iran-Contra. The President's enemies had a field day. Editorial cartoonists caricatured him with a quizzical look rattling off a number of "Gee, I don't recall's".

Clark had wanted Weinberger pardoned to spare not only the former President, but also Weinberger himself, who now faced five felony charges for allegedly lying to congressional committees. Weinberger was accused of concealing a private diary that prosecutors, according

---

[15] Weinberger, *In the Arena*, p. 357.

to the *New York Times*, said contained incriminating evidence—a claim that was made without having read the diary.

In Clark's view, Weinberger was being railroaded. Weinberger's supporters maintained that even though there was no illegality in lifting the embargo on goods to Iran, Weinberger had questioned the wisdom of dealing with Iran and opposed the missile sales in internal administration deliberations. With the decision to go ahead, however, he did his best to enforce the administration's change in policy. For his role in keeping the operations secret, he was scheduled to go on trial January 5. His legal costs to lawyer Robert Bennett could exceed $1 million. Clark, along with Jeane Kirkpatrick and Frank Carlucci, led an effort to help Weinberger pay those fees.[16]

The Nancy Factor

When Clark first urged pardons back in August 1987, Reagan appeared to be leaning in that direction. "He was inclined to pardon everybody," says Clark, "a blanket pardon to all for acting in the best interests of the country." If that were so, what stopped Reagan from following through? Or rather, *who* stopped him? According to Lou Cannon and other sources, it was Mrs. Reagan, along with Ken Duberstein and Stu Spencer, who "opposed all pardons for former aides on grounds they would blemish [Reagan's] presidency".[17] Mrs. Reagan reportedly believed that these men had embarrassed her husband; they would not be permitted to hurt his presidency further.

The Reagan Legacy

Some, including Weinberger, say that had Clark remained as national security advisor, there might never have been a connection between Iran and the Contras, or if there had, events would have unfolded much differently. Yes, the prudence of Bill Clark would have deftly steered Reagan away from any actions that even had the appearance of illegality. Speculation aside, we do know that Bill Clark tried and failed to limit the damage done by Iran-Contra to his friends, to their

---

[16] "Weinberger Friends to Help Pay Legal Fees", *New York Times*, September 24, 1992.
[17] See Lou Cannon, *Role of a Lifetime*, p. 3, 2000 edition.

reputations and their finances, by urging the President to pardon all of those implicated in the affair. These men had performed, however imperfectly, their duty to their country; they were not criminals. As far as Clark is concerned, they, and the President they served, did not deserve to leave public life in disgrace.

As time passes, the vision portrayed by the media of an incompetent president and a staff run amok recedes, and Reagan's true stature begins to materialize and to be recognized. Despite Iran-Contra, Ronald Reagan left office in 1989 with the highest approval rating of any president since Franklin Delano Roosevelt.[18] In a recent poll, organized by the Discovery Channel and AOL, more than 2.4 million Americans cast their votes, declaring Ronald Reagan the "greatest American of all time", edging out old standbys Abraham Lincoln and George Washington as well as comparative newcomers Franklin D. Roosevelt and Martin Luther King Jr. Perhaps the most telling and eloquent individual tribute comes from Marcin, a common citizen of Ronald Reagan's "suffering Poland":

> Great man, great leader, great American. He was the one who had torn down the wall dividing peoples of Europe into slaves and free men. If not for Ronald Reagan, Poland would still be under Soviet-Russian occupation. Thanks to Mr. Reagan I can now write these comments on my laptop, here in Warsaw. Thank you Mr. President. May God bless you and may God bless the United States of America.[19]

Clark celebrates this recognition as just due for his old friend—and for his country as well.

---

[18] Wolf, Julie, "The Iran-Contra Affair", *American Experience*, PBS Online.
[19] "Reagan voted 'greatest American'", *BBC News* in video and audio, June 28, 2005.

CHAPTER 17

Endings and a Beginning

Bill Clark's ongoing service on behalf of the Reagan administration was abruptly interrupted on Monday, March 7, 1988, as the fifty-six-year-old Clark attempted to lift his small plane from the dirt entrance road on his ranch.[1] His soul was the only thing that came close to lifting off the earth that day—the aircraft didn't get that far.

Ronald Reagan was three thousand miles away, in Washington. Not a year had passed since Bill Casey died, when the President came close to losing his other Bill, his top hand; but, it was not to be, thanks to Jesús Muñoz.

The narrow canyon where the plane went down, Jesús explains, is surrounded by hills that swallow up sound. Muñoz was driving his all-terrain vehicle up the lane, a road that sees only one or two cars per day, one of which is Clark's, when he noticed the wreckage near the machine shop. As he got off his ATV to investigate, he heard nothing over the noise of his vehicle. His eyes moisten as he tells the story, and he shakes his head to signal that he prefers to say no more about it.

After a moment, Muñoz recovers enough to deny the credit for saving Clark's life. "No, not me," he says, "the doctors saved him."

---

[1]Dating the incident required some digging. At Clark's ranch, Kengor had dated the incident as having occurred on March 14, 1988, and therewith labeled some audiotapes he made (as backups to Clark's original copy). Upon further investigation, including the discovery of an Associated Press article on the incident, filed with a dateline out of Shandon of March 8, and run in the *New York Times* on March 10, it became clear that the event occurred on March 7. The March 8 AP piece said that the event had occurred the day before, which was Monday, March 7.

The Clarks view the matter differently. They see the timely arrival of Muñoz as an act of Providence. For Clark, there were pages still remaining to be written in the Divine Plan.

The ranch hand from Mexico has been with the Clarks for twenty-five years and is treated as a member of the family. He has his own apartment, which Bill and Joan have told him he may consider his home for life.

Among his duties, Jesús maintains the contents of the barn, housing an interesting assortment of items, including five restored horse-drawn wagons still used by the family. In addition to the usual farm equipment, the building shelters an array of riding gear and all kinds of mementos. There is a framed Western Union telegram, dated June 15, 1949, 3:53 P.M., from Bill Jr. to Bill Sr., care of the Oxnard Police Department, requesting that his saddle, blanket, canteen, rope, chaps, and spurs be sent to him "immediately" in Northern California. There are also framed photos of Clark riding horses with presidents, and not just Ronald Reagan: one of them features Clark riding with Reagan's predecessor. The signed inscription reads: "Best wishes to Judge Bill Clark, my South Georgia hunting partner—Jimmy Carter 3/84." Another photo shows Clark as a boy sitting on the lap of Tom Mix, wearing the white Stetson given to him by the famous silver screen cowboy.

The door to the tack room rubs against the floor due to a recent earthquake. In a far corner of the handsome room is a small shrine with the Blessed Mother holding the Christ child. Clark had found the statue in the back of an old warehouse in Dublin, Ireland, years earlier. "It was a desecration," he says of the statue's discarded and neglected state, "no excuse for it." Clark brought the Madonna home and commissioned an artist to repair it, then he mounted her in a place of honor in the tack room, where Jesús Muñoz has been known to remove his hat and pay the Lady and her Son his respects.

*   *   *

While the accident caused Clark to take stock of his life, it did not move him to give up flying. Soon afterward, he flew over daughter Nina's ranch house, dropping bags of popcorn to his grandchildren playing in the yard. Occasionally, he flew his antique military T-6 over the ranch, executing loops and barrel rolls overhead. One afternoon he was joined by the father of his daughter-in-law Linda. "I was scared to death watching them do aerobatics up there!" Linda says.

His old NSC friend David Laux talks about being picked up by Clark at the San Luis Obispo airport. The Judge led Laux out of the small terminal, through the parking lot, and then through a hole in the fence back onto the airport parking apron for small planes. Laux asked, "Bill, where are you going? Have you got a car parked in here?" Clark said only, "You'll see."

Stationed among the private planes was a World War II "Bird Dog", a small but powerful "tandem seat" spotter plane used to guide artillery onto targets. Clark tossed Laux's suitcase into the back and said, "Get in; this is your taxi to the ranch." After a take-off roll of about 150 feet, they flew up and over the low hills. As they got closer to Clark's ranch, Laux asked, "Where's the airstrip?" Again Clark answered, "You'll see." As they got lower and lower over the dirt road that constitutes Clark's driveway/runway/landing strip, Laux's former boss ordered him, "Lift your feet; we're going to land." They settled down on the canyon bottom and taxied up the hill to the car/airplane parking garage at the top of the road.[2]

Something Beautiful for God

In his retirement from public office, Clark was able to give wing to his capacity for joy—and even frivolity—that he seldom had been able to indulge during his years of government service. He could take more pleasure in his family and his varied interests now that he was based at the ranch, but Clark also had serious work to do. He had a chapel to build, and that project became his top priority after the plane crash.

By the early 1990s, construction of the chapel was in full swing. During the construction period, the Clarks' home and barn became repositories for the statues and relics they had been collecting for the chapel. Bill's sisters, Molly and Cynthia, would tell their friends that the living room of their brother's home looked like an office in the Vatican.

---

[2] David Laux, interview.

Clark initially wanted to build the chapel on the campus of Villanova Prep in Ojai, but the school rejected his proposal as impractical because of the medieval feel he wanted, which required, among other things, no electricity. Also Clark and the school had a few differences of opinion regarding Church matters: Clark had grown more traditional than his alma mater, or was it the school that had changed over the years?[3] A location in Ojai, a more populated area, might have brought more attendees. In retrospect, however, the chapel needed to be on the ranch, near to Clark's home and heart, where he could visit and tend to the structure and grounds daily.

In spite of its remote location, Chapel Hill is not short of worshippers, or visitors. Roger Legreid, a Franciscan University graduate who attends Mass there weekly with his wife and children, explains the chapel's success in remote Shandon somewhat mystically by borrowing a line made famous in a film: "If you build it, they will come."[4] They have. There has never been reason for promotion.

The chapel sits atop the hill overlooking the entrance to the Clark ranch, thus receiving the unofficial name Chapel Hill by the community. Dedicated to the Blessed Mother and Junípero Serra, the chapel, twenty-six miles east of Paso Robles, is visible off in the distance as one drives along Route 46. It is high enough to be a navigation point for pilots inbound to Paso Robles.

The trail up the hill is lined on each side by ten-foot-wide rows of grape vines, from which the Clarks produce a cabernet sauvignon, the proceeds of which go to the Augustine Foundation, established to fund the upkeep of the chapel. Another seventy-five acres of vineyards—planted with a special variety of grape cultivated at the University of California, Davis—lie across the road from the chapel and are leased to another vintner. The Clarks also grow a family orchard of pomegranates, citrus, apples, nectarines, red pears, and avocados. They have nearly eight hundred olive trees—Manzanillo type—from which the Clarks produce Chapel Hill olive oil.

Outside the chapel is a small Italian fountain featuring a plaque comprised of fifteen sections of ceramic tile, white and blue, inscribed with the Peace Prayer of Saint Francis, given to Bill by his Villanova

---

[3] Tom Behan, interview.
[4] Interview with Roger Legreid, July 31, 2005.

classmates. To enter the building into the transept, the every-day entrance, one must duck through a five-and-a-half-foot limestone archway, which once served as the vestry door in a twelfth-century Trappist monastery. Imported by William Randolph Hearst in the 1920s, the stonework complements other ancient pieces, such as the fireplace and altar, which characterize the building. To accommodate large events such as the annual Mozart Festival, the fourteen-foot doors across the front of the chapel can be propped open, allowing additional seating for four hundred on the tile-paved courtyard.

Encased in the floor in the nave is a bone relic of Blessed Junípero Serra, the Spanish Franciscan priest who in the eighteenth century founded nine missions in California. In a shrine to the left of the altar, worshippers glimpse a three-foot-high copy of the San Damiano cross, from which Saint Francis heard the voice of the Lord asking him to "rebuild his church". Hanging above the altar is a three-hundred-year-old wooden crucifix. On either side hang six-hundred-year-old crosses bearing images of the two thieves who were executed with Christ. High up on the left is the angel of death, with skull and wings, a symbol of human mortality.

To the right of the altar is a statue of Mary—serene, peaceful, graceful—a replica of Our Lady of New York in Saint Patrick's Cathedral. Before he died, John Cardinal O'Connor gave permission for two copies of the statue to be made, one for Chapel Hill and the other for Thomas Aquinas College in Santa Paula.

The ceiling is made of colorful thirteenth-century tiled panels from Moorish Spain. Clark purchased the three hundred panels, no two alike, from the Hearst family. William Randolph Hearst had acquired them when building his San Simeon castle in the 1920s. The panels had been stored in boxes, unopened. Joan spent three months with cotton and cleaner, removing centuries-old grime from each tile, before Clark pieced the panels back together in the crawl space above the chapel ceiling.

Even with these precious items, the Clarks felt something was lacking in the chapel. Bill enlisted the help of Pat O'Leary, an Irish journalist and friend, to help him purchase from Ireland a tabernacle in which the Blessed Sacrament would repose. With the assistance of Father John Galvin of County Cork, where Clark's ancestors departed for America in January 1858, O'Leary located a tabernacle from a closed orphanage chapel. He also found a monstrance and a sanctuary lamp.[5] The true Presence transformed the chapel, Clark says.

Although the chapel had been blessed—but not consecrated—by Bishop Sylvester Ryan, "Something was clearly lacking that we did not fully notice until after the tabernacle was placed in the center of the altar on the axis", said Clark in an interview with an Irish paper. "Since then, something mystical has taken over. The ambience of the building has been transformed, almost inexplicably, but quite real to almost everyone who comes."[6]

For the Community

Clark financed the chapel and its furnishings from his own assets, and to this day no donation plate is passed during Mass. By custom, the Spanish service is an exception; congregants insist on passing a straw sombrero to pay the padre, to which Clark adds the customary stipend.

The chapel is available to those of all faiths in the community. The community, in turn, takes pride in the picturesque chapel, as well as in its builder. Clark displays discomfort when the focus is placed on him. He says he does not feel worthy to have built the chapel in the first place. Daughter Monica teasingly tests his humility: "Dad, you must have been quite a sinner when you were younger to need to build a church now!" Clark accepts the good-natured jab, and tells her with a smile: "You're right about that."

Throughout the year, the chapel hosts a number of regular services and events. There are two Masses on Sunday, one in Spanish and the other in English, a Protestant service (frequently) on Saturday, and a Friday evening Bible study and prayer service in Spanish. Each year during Holy Week, several Mexican immigrants who attend services at Chapel Hill do penance by crawling up the twelve-hundred-foot crushed stone path on their knees.

Aside from religious services, many other events take place at the chapel. For example, each year around Christmas time, Chapel Hill hosts a local Mormon choir that leads the congregation in a sing-along version of Handel's Messiah. Chapel Hill also hosts part of the

---

[5] Pat O'Leary, "Cork Tabernacle for U.S.", *Irish Catholic*, July 19, 2001.
[6] Ibid.

San Luis Obispo Mozart Festival each July. The chapel "is truly the best acoustically of any space I've been in", says Clifton Swanson, director of the Mozart Festival and head of the music department at nearby Cal Poly. In an interview with a San Luis Obispo paper, he said the sound inside the chapel "just purrs and reverberates in a beautiful way".[7] Swanson added, "It's a very magical spot. The musicians just love playing up there. . . . It's always more than a musical experience."[8]

It is no accident that the acoustics in the building are superb. "We're . . . music lovers", says Clark of himself and Joan. Structurally, there is a two-and-a-half-foot floor rise along the seventy-foot tile floor, the same proportion as a Christopher Wren church in London the two admired and later attempted to adapt for their chapel. "I loved the acoustics there, and they're here", says Bill.[9] "We had Mozart very much in mind when we laid this all out", he adds.[10]

A cleverly entitled article in the San Luis Obispo paper said that the chapel was "Built for the Spirit."[11] Clark did indeed build the chapel to lift the human spirit, and not only through worship services, but also through the spiritual impact of beautiful music. "I wanted to leave a place that would have spiritual value for the community," he said, "and music is spiritual."[12]

Clark also points to Saint Augustine, who wrote: "He who seeks Him has found Him." He said he hopes that the chapel will help seeking souls find God.[13]

The judgment among many in the local community is that Clark has succeeded. Said Jean Beck of the music at Chapel Hill, "When you sit there and listen, it's like being out of this world. You get a whole different feeling. And the chapel itself—it is glorious."[14]

---

[7] Ann Fairbanks, "Built for the Spirit", *San Luis Obispo County Telegram-Tribune*, March 30, 1994.

[8] Joe Brekke, "Made for music of the soul", *Tribune News* (San Luis Obispo), July 14–20, 2000.

[9] Fairbanks, "Built for the Spirit".

[10] Brekke, "Made for music of the soul"; and Marvin Sosna, "Chapel Hill—A Mountain's Acoustic Marvel", *PLUS magazine*, July 2002.

[11] Fairbanks, "Built for the Spirit".

[12] Brekke, "Made for music of the soul"; and Sosna, "Chapel Hill—A Mountain's Acoustic Marvel".

[13] Ibid.

[14] Brekke, "Made for music of the soul".

Clark often says that Ronald Reagan's Rancho del Cielo, his "Ranch in the Sky" hovering above the Pacific, was the President's "open cathedral". Well, Chapel Hill is Shandon's cathedral, especially when the huge front doors are flung open in the summer and the hills are filled with the sound of Mozart.

Endings—Joyful and Sad

As Clark made the transition to his new avocation, of being a benefactor to his local community, he witnessed the climactic unraveling of the Soviet Union, the very end his policies at the National Security Council had been designed to achieve. Throughout 1989, like dominoes, the East European countries that constituted the communist bloc fell away one at a time from Soviet domination. The unstoppable trend began in June with elections in Poland, where not a single communist won. The demand for freedom spread to Joan's native Czechoslovakia, then to Hungary, Bulgaria, and finally to East Germany, where in November the Berlin Wall was dismantled piece by piece by the citizens of the city. Christmas Day brought the stunning demise of Romania's Nicolai Ceausescu, the region's most brutal dictator.

Two years later, also on Christmas Day, came another historic event: Mikhail Gorbachev resigned his position as leader of the Soviet Union. Gorbachev's grip on that post was the only thing holding the Union of Soviet Socialist Republics together. It began to unravel when he resigned on the day the western world celebrates the birth of Christ.

Clark had often doubted the President when the Great Communicator made his dramatic predictions forecasting the end of communism. Reagan had confidently expected communism to collapse "in the near term ... in his lifetime", Clark says, and to the surprise of almost everyone, it did.

* * *

Another end in 1991 was not joyous. In that year Bill's parents passed away. The father he so admired went first, on January 30, 1991. After struggling for years with Parkinson's, William Pettit Clark died of heart failure at the age of 83.

Only a few months later, Bernice, Bill Sr.'s devoted wife of fifty-five years, joined him. The two of them had been one, and Bernice was not complete without him. "She remained as feisty as ever," says niece Pat, "but she had spent her life defending him; her main purpose in life evaporated when he died."

When Bill Sr. suffered those final years—the pain from Parkinson's was exacerbated by the discomfort of vertebrae he had cracked during a lifetime of riding horses—Bernice anguished with him. When he died, Bernice lost her own will to live. Each year, Bernice had marked the anniversary of the first kiss she shared with her husband. Apparently, her own frail heart could not bear commemorating those anniversaries alone.[15]

Yet, this close of one chapter in Bill's family life merely led to the opening of another. Bill Clark had not only his own children to cherish but grandchildren as well.

Preparing for Another End

It was also during this period that Bill began to brace himself for another difficult goodbye—to his old friend and President.

Bill Clark and Ronald Reagan spoke to one another infrequently during the late 1980s and into 1990 and 1991 as the Reagan Library and Foundation were underway. They met at Reagan's office in Century City to discuss the construction of the library, both financially and architecturally. Clark also continued an annual tradition Reagan especially enjoyed, sending him uncirculated silver dollars for his birthday.

The two were together on November 4, 1991, at the dedication of the Reagan Library. Reporters directed some questions at Reagan's confidant, requesting his thoughts on the library in particular. "It ends an era", said Clark of the formal opening. The press noted that Clark

---

[15] The love letters long ago exchanged between the two would have been a gift to their children and grandchildren—a chronicle of a wonderful romance. Reflective, perhaps, of the guard she had always kept around her personal side, Bernice decided that no one other than she and Bill Sr. would ever read the letters. She asked her daughter Cynthia and niece Pat to burn them. "It was a crime," says Pat, "but we had to do it, as it was her wish." Cynthia and Pat took the liberty of reading one of the letters before throwing it into the fire; Bernice sent it to her man while he was away at St. Mary's College in the 1920s. In the letter, Bernice described the changes that had happened in Ventura since the big man on campus left. "It was a priceless piece of history", says Pat.

was the longest serving Reagan appointee in successive years without interruption.[16]

That was indeed the case, from his work on the Reagan campaign in 1965, through the gubernatorial years, the court appointments, and on to three different jobs in Washington through 1985, not to mention subsequent appointments to commissions, as an emissary abroad, and more. In all, Clark faithfully served Reagan for nearly thirty years, with still more unofficial service to come.

Characteristically, Clark did not give a speech at the opening of the library, deferring the spotlight to Reagan: "It's his day, not mine."[17] It was Reagan's day all right, and it was also, yes, the end of an era— Clark had that right as well, but in more ways than he had in mind. Clark's contacts with his longtime ally were about to become considerably less frequent.

Clark recalls seeing Reagan just once more after the library opening, again in Century City. He does not recollect the exact date, though the year was probably 1993. He remembers a sense of sadness between the two of them, as if they somehow knew it was the last time they would ever sit down together. Both were a bit teary-eyed.

Though the experience was sad, Clark was spared the kind of agonizing final meeting with Reagan endured by others as the darkness of Alzheimer's descended upon him. Certain friends and associates who visited Reagan around this time suffered the former President not remembering their names. Reagan biographer Edmund Morris, who had met monthly with the President for years, sensed that his subject no longer recognized him.[18] The same happened with Mike Deaver, who by that point had known Reagan for nearly thirty years.[19] Mercifully, Reagan had not forgotten Clark. The former President recognized his top hand when they met for the last time, and the two chatted about the typical things.

---

[16] "William P. Clark Jr., Festivities close adviser's career". A copy of this November 1991 newspaper article (without acknowledgment of the source) sits in Clark's personal files.

[17] Ibid.

[18] See Morris, *Dutch*, p. 667.

[19] Deaver writes of this in *A Different Drummer*, where he also makes the point that Reagan himself saw his lifeguarding as a parable of his larger life. Deaver, *A Different Drummer*, pp. 14–15.

As the physical and mental distance increased between them, Reagan still remembered Clark. Edmund Morris writes about interviewing Clark, who told him about a mutual friend from the Cowboy Hall of Fame who had recently called to say that Reagan was "kind of confused these days". The friend said that he asked the former President why he did not see Bill Clark anymore. There was a tear in Reagan's eye as he mustered a shake of his head and said simply, "Ah, Bill and I go a long way back." At this, wrote Morris, Clark put his hands to his eyes and wept. Morris said it was quite some time before Clark was able to regain his composure.[20]

Clark still communicated with Reagan after their final face-to-face meeting, but only by mail or phone. In December 1993, for instance, he sent Reagan a note and a book of spiritual meditations by a Jesuit priest. Reagan responded by sending Clark a thank-you note the same day. "It was nice to hear from you and very kind of you and Joan to think of me in this way", he wrote. Clark also sent along a photo of the new chapel at the entrance of his ranch. "Just seeing it", said Reagan, "and that grand rolling hill has me counting the days until my next trip to Rancho del Cielo."

Because of what happened in the year that followed, Ronald Reagan would have precious few returns to that beloved ranch of his, and would never make another trip to Clark's own ranch, or to Chapel Hill. On November 5, 1994, Reagan informed the world in a touching handwritten letter that he had Alzheimer's, a disease that he said was about to carry him into the "sunset" of his life, a strikingly optimistic metaphor.

The next day, Bill sent his own handwritten letter addressed to both President Reagan and Nancy. "You have done the brave thing", he began, commending Reagan's candor. "But then, you always have." He noted that his own struggles with Parkinson's had kept him close to the ranch. The Judge told his two friends since the Sacramento days, "I dream and pray of you both often, hoping there might be another moment together someday." He thanked the President for the "privilege" of having served him for so many years, before adding, in a line that seems to have been directed mainly to Mrs. Reagan: "And

---

[20] The Morris interview took place, according to Morris, eight years after Clark left the White House, which would be 1991. See Morris, *Dutch*, p. 663.

I would ask your forgiveness for my shortcomings." He concluded by stating that Joan, Monica, Pete, Nina, Colin, and Paul all joined him in sending their love and prayers.

The prayers followed, but not "another moment together". Clark and others were discouraged from seeing Reagan again because of the justifiable fear that he might not remember his old friends and associates, and would get frustrated and saddened. Though Clark would not again see his President, he would serve him in yet another way.

Reagan's Defender

A year after Ronald Reagan informed the world of his illness, Bill Clark took on a new role—that of chronicler and defender of President Reagan's faith in God and reverence for the sanctity of human life. This new role was evident in an October 1995 speech he delivered to the Center for Security Policy's "Keeper of the Flame" dinner in honor of Ronald Reagan.

The Center for Security Policy wanted to give Clark its first annual Keeper of the Flame Award, but Clark declined, saying it should go to Cap Weinberger instead. He said "it wasn't appropriate" to give it to him ahead of others. Accepting Clark's refusal of the award, the Center asked if he would nonetheless give a talk at the dinner. He did so.

Clark underscored a side of Reagan that not many in that room knew about—his prayerfulness. He cited never before reported examples of Reagan privately praying: after being informed of the downing of KAL 007, upon each time he learned of another Marine killed in Lebanon, when being told of the assassination of Martin Luther King, Jr.

He also spoke of Reagan's respect for human life and his abhorrence of abortion. This foreign-policy and national-security audience was not surprised when Clark began talking about the Evil Empire speech, but it did not expect him to extract the famous speech's forgotten but powerful statements on the scourge of abortion.

The audience roared in approval when Clark noted Reagan's outrage over the injustice of *Roe v. Wade*, which wiped off the books of fifty states any statutes protecting the rights of unborn children. He quoted Reagan: "Human life legislation ending this tragedy will someday pass Congress, and you and I must never rest until it does." Clark told the crowd that Reagan believed that "Unless and until it can be proven that the unborn child is not a living entity, then its right to life, liberty, and the pursuit of happiness must be protected." Nearly all of the three hundred in attendance clapped wildly, some leaping to their feet. Clark ended the talk with a gracious gesture to Maureen Reagan, who remained seated nearby: "Maureen, please go home and tell him we love him and we're fighting the good fight. Thank you, ladies and gentlemen." Clark exited to raucous applause.

There would be more Clark defenses of Reagan over the years. The troubleshooter noticed some gaps in the stories being circulated about the President. Ronald Reagan's defense of the unborn was not being addressed, nor was his spirituality being recognized. Someone needed to set the record straight. Clark welcomed the role, and thereby found in retirement another way to serve his President.

CHAPTER 18

Sunset in California

In the 1980s, it had been Bill Clark's clear calling to serve his President in an effort to turn back the Soviet Union and win the Cold War. Now, with the Evil Empire sinking into the ash heap of history, and Ronald Reagan sadly drifting away, Clark was beginning to settle back into the rural life of central California. In yet another parallel between Reagan and his top hand, of the Californians who went to Washington, Reagan and Clark escaped the Beltway bustle—returning to their California ranches far removed from the glare of civilization's spotlight—westerners 'til the end.

For President Reagan, that end came June 5, 2004, at his home in Bel-Air, outside of Los Angeles, at age ninety-three. A public statement followed from William Clark's office. The Judge extolled Reagan's commitment to life, from defending the voiceless in the womb to the 300 million voiceless in communist Eastern Europe and Russia. Clark called Reagan "a defender of the innocent, young and old alike".[1]

After their separation, Clark's next time with his friend came Thursday, June 10, as Reagan lay in state in a closed casket draped with the nation's flag in the Capitol Rotunda. As Clark drew near the President's body, surrounded by a military honor guard, and the paintings and statues of America's other heroes, he was deeply moved.

Later that evening, Clark and roughly forty to fifty other Reaganites gathered at the Executive Office Building. "These were the forever

---

[1] "Statement from Judge William Clark Regarding Ronald Reagan's Passing", issued by the Young America's Foundation, June 5, 2004.

true believers, the old hands", says Bill. "Paul Laxalt attended as did Ed Meese, Dana Rohrabacher, and the truest Reaganite of us all, his son Michael Reagan." Joan accompanied Bill, as did Jacque Hill and Helene von Damm.[2]

Clark was one of the few who spoke briefly from the dais, referring to Reagan's faith in God, and of the next life. He emphasized the spiritual Reagan more than any other speaker. "He's in a better place", Clark concluded softly, removing his clouded glasses. Said Kimberley Bolt, one of those in attendance, "It was short and sweet—poignant."[3]

The next day, Bill and Joan joined the other invitees at Reagan's funeral service at the National Cathedral. Clark spoke with many old friends there, including former President George H. W. Bush and former Prime Minister Margaret Thatcher, delivering her eulogy via video presentation, though she mustered the strength to rise and walk over to Clark to shake his hand. Later, both Clark and Reagan returned to California. The following Saturday, Ronald Reagan's earthly body was laid to rest in a crypt at the Reagan Library in California.

The next morning, Sunday, June 13, Clark was alone preparing Chapel Hill for Mass. Father Ray Roh arrived early and observed him hosing off the tile. "Gee, Bill," said Roh, "there you were, the last few days, around all those famous people in Washington, all those world dignitaries at Ronald Reagan's funeral, and now you're here cleaning up bird droppings." Clark said simply, "Yeah, that's about right."

As Clark fulfilled his duties as "chapel janitor", people the world over were digesting a column he had written for the *New York Times* two days earlier. The context of the piece, entitled "For Reagan, All Life Was Sacred", was that mere days after Ronald Reagan's death influential but misled people were arguing that if he were still alive and of sound mind, he would support funding for human embryonic stem-cell research, which advocates claim can lead to cures for degenerative diseases like Alzheimer's and Parkinson's. That is, those who favored embryonic stem-cell research were attempting to reshape the extremely popular President into their own image.

---

[2] We thank Kimberley Bolt, who attended the gathering, for sharing this information.
[3] Interview with Kimberley Bolt, February 28, 2006.

"At Reagan's core was his faith in the power of personal experience", wrote Jonathan Alter in *Newsweek*. "His own personal experience revolved around Nancy, of course. If she passionately favored stem-cell research, it might have taken him a while, but he probably would have come around." [4]

There was no evidence for supposing that Reagan would have supported the creation and destruction of human embryos in order to obtain their stem cells for research—quite the contrary, as Clark established in the *New York Times*, with the assistance of Clarke Forsythe of Americans United for Life. Reagan respected the dignity of pre-born human life, even in its earliest stages of development. He championed the Human Life Amendment, which defined life as beginning at conception. Reagan as President had vetoed the type of research that some were claiming he would now support.

Clark began the piece with this powerful introduction: "Ronald Reagan had not passed from this life for 48 hours before proponents of human embryonic stem-cell research began to suggest that such ethically questionable scientific work should be promoted under his name. But this cannot honestly be done", wrote Clark, "without ignoring President Reagan's own words and actions."

Those words and actions, Clark continued, emphasized "the truth of human dignity under God" as well as "respect for the sacred value of human life". Clark then laid out the former President's unyielding opposition to abortion and embryonic stem-cell research in point-by-point examples, excerpted from Reagan's speeches, executive actions, letters, and other writings. [5]

It was the first and only column by Clark in the *New York Times*, though he was mentioned thousands of times in the newspaper over

---

[4] For a response to this, see George Neumayer, "Estranged No More", *American Spectator*, June 16, 2004.

[5] He noted that Reagan supported the Human Life Amendment, which would have inscribed in the U.S. Constitution "the paramount right to life is vested in each human being from the moment of fertilization without regard to age, health or condition of dependency." Clark noted that Reagan favored bills in Congress that would have given every human being—at all stages of development—protection as a person under the fourteenth amendment of the Constitution. Clark also noted that after the charter expired for the department of Health, Education and Welfare's ethical advisory board—which in the 1970s supported destructive research on human embryos—Reagan began a de facto ban on federal financing of embryo research, which he maintained throughout his presidency.

the years. His irrefutable exposition of Reagan's views on the sanctity of human life was, to Clark's regret, printed on the day of Reagan's funeral, not the day that Clark would have chosen. However badly the essay was needed, he says, "This was a time for mourning." In a conversation between Clark and Mike Deaver shortly after the article was published, Clark learned that Nancy Reagan had read the piece and was upset by it.

The piece was widely quoted and reprinted all over the world—in local dailies, in Catholic newspapers, and in prominent papers such as the *Washington Post*. It was reprinted by the National Right to Life Committee and picked up by numerous websites and blogs. It became the subject of Christian evangelist Chuck Colson's June 16 *Breakpoint* broadcast, heard by millions.

"Ronald Reagan, Lifeguard"

The *New York Times* column was a continuation of Clark's work to spread the word about Reagan's regard for the sanctity of unborn human life. In fact, Clark's writings and statements on Reagan and human life have been so influential, and so widely circulated, that a Google search on the phrase "Clark Reagan life" yields a staggering five-million hits.[6] Yet, there are still many people who are ignorant of Ronald Reagan's position on abortion. Few know, for instance, that he wrote a small book as president entitled *Abortion and the Conscience of the Nation*, which Reagan supporters maintain is the only book ever written and published by a sitting president.[7] Clark, more than any other single source, promotes and distributes the book, published in 1984 by the Human Life Foundation, and featuring afterwords by Dr. C. Everett Koop, Reagan's surgeon general, and British journalist and Catholic convert Malcolm Muggeridge.

Certain members of Reagan's staff wanted him to delay publication until after the 1984 election, fearing it would upset Republicans who

---

[6] The exact total, the results of a Google search done on July 22, 2006 at 7:15 PM EST, was 4,940,000. Most of these hits refer to three articles: a June 7, 2004 *Washington Times* piece titled "God's plan guided Reagan's life"; a June 10, 2004 *Newsmax* piece titled, "Reagan Championed Pro-Life Causes"; and the *New York Times* op-ed, "For Reagan, All Life Was Sacred".

[7] "The Pope and the President", pp. 54–55.

do not want abortion outlawed, but Reagan refused. The 2000 edition of *Abortion and the Conscience of the Nation* has a foreword by Clark himself, entitled "Ronald Reagan, Lifeguard"—connecting Reagan's life guarding as a young man with his later protection of human life as President. That summertime employment, in which he saved seventy-seven people from drowning, wrote Clark, first taught Reagan "the value of each person's life". Later, said Clark, those views were strengthened by the traumatic loss of his infant daughter Christina, who died in 1947 after living only three days. At the time, Reagan was fighting for his own life—battling pneumonia—in another hospital.[8]

Another instance of Clark's work on behalf of Reagan's dedication to life: he has a one-page write-up on file that he faxes upon request to the press, from hometown papers such as the *Ventura County Star* to national papers like the *Wall Street Journal*. Clark also has forty-five single-spaced pages of Reagan quotes on abortion, as prepared by the Reagan Library. These Clark keeps handy for people making inquiries about Reagan's thinking on the issue.[9]

"No American—and certainly no American president—", said Clark in an interview with a Catholic magazine, "has spoken out more forcefully and frequently on this subject than Ronald Reagan." Reagan "rarely missed an opportunity" to raise the issue of the sanctity of human life, he said, and would be "gravely disappointed" by the politicians who have tried to walk away from "this predominant issue of his agenda, as they did from the issue of slavery a century and a half ago, contending that the issue had been settled by the court, or acknowledging that it was an evil, but rationalizing that it was a necessary evil".[10]

Freedom Fighter

In addition to maintaining Reagan's pro-life legacy, Clark continues to help those reaching for freedom, as he had first done with the Polish officers at the CIC in the 1950s continuing into the 1980s with the Shostakoviches. One striking example: he came to the assistance of a good friend he had met in 1986 at the pinnacle of Iraqi leadership, Nizar Hamdoon, Iraqi ambassador to the United States.

---

[8] Ibid.
[9] Ibid.
[10] Ibid.

Hamdoon was an interesting man, Clark says, an architect by profession. He was always careful to represent the interests of his country without sounding either anti-American or pro-Hussein, a delicate task. Hamdoon was perhaps one of the few Iraqis able to offer advice, perhaps even criticism, to Hussein—without being eliminated. Middle East observer Daniel Pipes called Hamdoon "probably the most skilled diplomat I ever encountered".[11] Pipes clearly liked him, referring to him by his first name—as did Bill Clark.

Hamdoon and his wife visited the Clarks at the ranch for a pleasant weekend before the climate change in the mid-East following the Iraqi invasion of Kuwait. A Chaldean Christian, he later sent an English translation of the Koran for the bookshelf at Chapel Hill. When the Clarks were leaving Washington in the late 1980s, Hamdoon, along with Iraqi Foreign Minister Tariq Aziz, hosted a luncheon for Bill and Joan at the Waldorf, attended by Bill Casey, among others.[12]

Hamdoon disappeared from view in 1998 following his second stint in the United States, this time as ambassador to the United Nations, where he was a key player in the arms inspection negotiations between the United Nations and Saddam Hussein. Not long after, Bill Clark tried to help him and his family get to the United States. The effort included preparing passports for his daughters, but the Hamdoon family, to Clark's knowledge, did not leave Iraq. Hamdoon did come to the States to undergo chemotherapy in March 2003, returning to Iraq and his family in June, following treatment. He died on July 4, 2003, just three months after American troops entered Baghdad.

Over a year later, in September 2004, Clark came to the rescue of another major political figure: Solidarity's Lech Walesa. The Reagan team had supported Walesa in his fight for Poland's freedom from Soviet domination; yet, Walesa was having trouble securing a visa to enter the United States. After having served as Poland's President in the 1990s, Walesa was now quarreling with the country's current political leadership. U.S. officials feared that by allowing Walesa an American platform for his views, they would be seen as choosing sides and thereby

---

[11] Daniel Pipes, "Obituary for Nizar Hamdoon (1944–2003)", *Middle East Quarterly*, Fall 2003.

[12] The luncheon occurred in either 1986 or 1987.

hurt relations with the government in Poland, now a crucial ally in the war on terror in Iraq.

Clark was not happy about this treatment of a genuine hero for the cause of liberty. Walesa had done more to bring down the Berlin Wall than any other East European, with the exception of Pope John Paul II. Clark first telephoned the deputy secretary of state—his old office— and asked, "Is this how we treat our old friends?" He was also in communication with a high-level contact at the White House. Eventually, thanks in part to Clark's intervention, Walesa was permitted into the country that had supported him and his movement in their darkest days. During his stay, he met with members of Congress, the deputy secretary of state, and had several speaking engagements.[13]

In addition to helping the well-known find freedom and justice, Counselor Clark, now in his mid-seventies, takes on cases for those not so well-known. His pro bono clients around the state span the full spectrum—a Paso Robles teen in trouble, a young lady from Mexico, a group of nuns. All appreciate having a former state Supreme Court justice working on their side—one who, as Joan states "has a hard time saying no".

Clark's Other Causes

As would be expected from a man who "has a hard time saying no", Clark serves many non-profit organizations. He was one of several founding trustees for the Ronald Reagan Presidential Foundation and Library, devoting substantial time to locating an appropriate site. He sits on several national and international boards and also devotes a great deal of time and energy to educational and religious efforts, a few especially close to his heart.

Thomas Aquinas College, which offers a unique Great Books curriculum in Santa Paula, California, has long received the support of Judge Clark. Founded in 1971, the Catholic college employs the Socratic method to study the greatest thinkers of Western civilization. There are no textbooks, lectures, or majors. All students read from original sources and attend small seminars led by faculty. Thomas Aquinas presently ranks among the top 104 liberal arts colleges in the nation and

---

[13] Interview with Tomasz Pompowski, July 28, 2006.

also numbers among the top 40 for value; that is, the quality of the program compared to the cost of tuition.[14] Bill and Joan are good friends with Thomas Aquinas president, Tom Dillon, and his wife, Terri. Among other gifts, the Clarks contributed a seventeenth-century Spanish ceiling from the Hearst collection for the college's St. Bernardine Library.

Clark also supports Father Frank Pavone's Priests for Life and served as one of the founding members of the Ave Maria School of Law, of Ann Arbor, Michigan, founded in 1998 by the former owner of Domino's Pizza, Tom Monaghan.

He supports and serves on the board of the International Theological Institute for Studies on Marriage and the Family, located in Austria. Christoph Cardinal Schönborn, archbishop of Vienna, is chancellor of the institute, as well as one of the youngest members of the College of Cardinals, and rumored to have been among those receiving consideration as successor to Pope John Paul II. The institute, initiated by Pope John Paul II, is dedicated to advancing the Church's teachings on love and marriage in Central and Eastern Europe. A large number of the students are from the former communist bloc, which is particularly gratifying to Clark.

Among the major secular causes Clark supports is the Young America's Foundation, devoted to preserving Ronald Reagan's Rancho del Cielo and his legacy. He is co-chairman, with Ed Meese, of the Reagan Ranch Board of Governors, saving the ranch from commercial development. One of Clark's recent gifts to Rancho del Cielo, an antique Amish Phaeton-style doctor's buggy, is a favorite display inside the tack barn.

Propositions 73 and 85

On the political front, Clark likewise has not retired. He is engaged in fights to defend and protect life—from abortion to embryonic research—at state and federal levels.

In California, he was deeply involved in efforts spearheaded by two people he greatly admires, Katie Short and Jim Holman, to obtain voter approval for a parental notification law. In California, a child

---

[14] *America's Best Colleges 2006*, U.S. News & World Report.

under the age of eighteen cannot be issued an aspirin at school, have a tooth pulled, or get her ears pierced without the consent of her parents. Yet, she can have an abortion without her parents being notified.

Clark was the lead signatory on the official argument in favor of Proposition 73 (2005) and with two others, presented the official "pro" arguments for Proposition 85 (2006), for the Voter's Guide and the ballot. Both measures failed to win a majority of votes from the citizens of California. In spite of these and other setbacks, Clark is optimistic on the abortion issue. Thanks to the window into the womb provided by modern technology, more and more people are admitting the truth about the unborn child. "We're going to win this one", he says with the same assurance Ronald Reagan predicted the downfall of the Soviet Union.

The "FIP" and "The Formers"

Clark, who would never refer to himself as a VIP, instead jokingly describes himself as an FIP—a Formerly Important Person. Even formerly important people continue to be important to those currently in government. For example, while he was Secretary of Defense, Donald Rumsfeld frequently asked advice from Clark and other former high ranking defense and security officials, such as Cap Weinberger, Henry Kissinger, James Schlesinger, Frank Carlucci, and Harold Brown. Rumsfeld refers to his counselors who have served in Washington as "The Formers". Rumsfeld held several meetings with the Formers in his office at the Pentagon. The meetings were not *pro forma*, says Clark, but involved a genuine exchange of ideas with such VIPs as Secretary of State Colin Powell, Vice President Dick Cheney and National Security Advisor Condoleezza Rice.

The Road Not Taken

What would Bill Clark have become if he had never met Ronald Reagan? Clark says he probably would have proceeded happily as a "cow town lawyer" and a rancher, of course, "like the other Clarks". Providence—the Divine Plan—had something else in store, however, and William Patrick Clark became, quite unintentionally, the most famous Clark of them all, and yet not as famous as he could have been, had he dedicated himself to his own self-promotion.

"You talk about a dark horse in history," says former NSC aide Roger Robinson, "there may have never been a greater dark horse than Bill Clark. . . . He was *the* keyplayer, nearly the whole show regarding the Soviet takedown. [Clark] and his President were all about setting some three hundred million people free. And isn't it poetic, isn't it fitting, that this quiet rancher, this unassuming guy, gave everyone else the credit? He wanted no credit for himself. And then he just walked away."

The Clark tale is quintessentially American: a son of ranchers, sheriffs, and pioneering Irish immigrants who went as far west as they could go rising through honest, hard work to walk the halls of national power. His story is an American tale of the triumph of the underdog, the strong, silent guy who is doubted, questioned, ridiculed, but perseveres and wins.

The Ranch Life

Bill and Joan are pleased with the way their children's lives have turned out and enjoy a close relationship with all of them. All but one reside in California, and all, Bill emphasizes with great satisfaction, appear to have good marriages. Asked to give a snapshot of each of them in a sentence or paragraph, he hesitates—he needs pages, not paragraphs, but he gives it a try.

An accomplished ballerina in her younger days, Monica, the firstborn, most resembles her mother. She and her husband, Lee, live in Half Moon Bay where Monica works as a legal assistant.

Pete, eldest son, competently runs the real estate business, Clark Land and Cattle, as well as the home ranch operation with the able assistance of wife, Elena. Pete's ability in the rodeo arena would make Bill Sr. and great-grandfather Bob proud to claim him.

Then comes Nina, partner in the law firm Clark, Negranti and Cali, with her husband, Mark, and youngest brother, Paul. Nina balances the duties of motherhood and successful lawyering with a competence that makes her father proud. Her oldest son, Colter, studies veterinary medicine at the University of Colorado as does daughter Ashley at UC Davis. Young Clark is a star athlete and student in grammar school in San Luis Obispo.

Colin, next in line, was most active on the campaign trail with Reagan. Colin is now an entrepreneur in the telecommunications industry. He and wife Linda, a teacher, live in Colorado with son Garrett. Their oldest son, Connor, is a student at Grove City College.

Finally, the youngest, Paul, is an attorney in the firm of Clark, Negranti and Cali. Paul and his wife, Gigi, had the good sense to name their first-born Robert Emmett Clark, pleasing their father more than they could have anticipated. The Paul Clark family lives on the ranch, close to Bill and Joan, where Paul is active in the maintenance and programming of Chapel Hill. The little Clarks are four: Robert Emmett, Maiya, Jane, and Patricia, christened "Jelly Bean" by her grandfather.

"They are a credit to their mother", says Clark. "We are both proud of all of them, all that they have done, and even more, that they get along so well. They are a great blessing to both of us."

The Physical Takes Its Toll

2005 was a tough year for Clark. Like his President and close friend, Joan, his wife and dearest companion, began suffering from what Bill describes as "forgetfulness". One of the more moving notes Bill received following Joan's diagnosis came from Don Rumsfeld in which the sitting Secretary of Defense, overwhelmed with an intense war and bitter criticism all around him, took time to write:

> Dear Judge, I heard the unfortunate news that your dear lady has been diagnosed with a tough disease. I sure hope that the world will find ways to deal with it because it is a difficult one. You know that I am thinking of you and wishing you the very best. You are a dear friend and a patriot.
> Warm regards, Don.

In that same year, Clark was definitively diagnosed with Parkinson's—the disease that disabled his father. Clark's family was upset by the news of his diagnosis, and all it portends for a man they love and admire. Though tough on the outside, eldest son Pete hugged him and cried, as did Jesús Muñoz.

The disease frustrates Clark. Occasionally, Parkinson's slows his gait and slurs his speech. "Sometimes my face freezes", he says. "I can't always smile. It's like a mask at Hallowe'en. My father suffered it, which was unfortunate, because he was a smiler." Clark needs to think about walking before going into action; motion no longer simply happens.

At times, there is a neurological disconnect between the mind and the will and the legs and the feet. "If you don't think about it ahead of time," he says with a laugh, not losing his sense of humor, "you lock up sometimes and the legs don't move. It's a funny thing but it really doesn't slow me down."

Neither Joan's diagnosis nor his own Parkinson's has changed Clark's position on the stem-cell issue. He supports promising research with adult stem cells, which can be obtained without harming or killing a human being, but he continues the fight against using embryonic stem cells, which requires taking human life. "The former can cure," Clark says, "the latter kills."

Nor has his health diminished the work ethic he developed as a kid on a ranch—he remains eager to work any day of the week, except Sunday, sometimes from 4:30 A.M. until 9:00 P.M.

Goodbyes to Dear Friends

While reconciling with certain rivals from the White House and Sacramento days, Clark has recently made painful goodbyes to close Reaganites who were there with him from the very beginning of the Reagan revolution.

Lyn Nofziger and Clark joined forces in 1965 to elect Ronald Reagan governor—indeed, it all began at that table upon which Lyn sat while Bill stood inside the storefront office on Wilshire Boulevard in Los Angeles. The hard, no-nonsense Nofziger suffered throughout 2005 and 2006 with liver cancer, as well as Parkinson's. Lyn got the news halfway through 2005 that his condition was irreversible; he had little time left. Clark spoke with him almost daily, counseling him, giving him a shoulder to lean on.

Bill and Lyn frequently talked about God and cited Scripture to one another, and this period was hardly an exception. Nofziger appeared to have become very spiritual in his later years. During a July 19, 2005 phone conversation, as they discussed God, Clark was struck by the peace the tough Nofziger seemed to have found. "He's prepared to die", Clark said that day. Three days later, Clark learned the disheartening results of Nofziger's latest tests: his doctors said he had only sixty days to live.

Lyn's decline was made worse for Clark by the onset of difficulties from his own medications to slow the progression of Parkinson's, adversely affecting him at the time. He wanted to fly to Washington to be with Nofziger, just one last time, but wanted to do so with the dignity of being able to walk steadily. He would never make it, even though Nofziger was able to live beyond the predicted sixty-day period.

This was also the period when another of those intimate Reagan allies from as far back as the gubernatorial campaign began slipping away, one whom Clark also wanted to visit one last time: Cap Weinberger.

Weinberger and his wife, Jane, considered Bill and Joan their closest friends, and the Clarks felt similarly toward them.[15] Clark and Weinberger (along with Bill Casey) were the men most responsible for helping President Reagan confront the Soviets—and, in the minds of many, win the Cold War. Clark and Weinberger remained close from 1965 through 2006, kindred spirits, always allies—and always speaking, once or twice a week through the 1990s and into 2006, a stretch when Cap's health progressively declined. In 2005, Weinberger began dialysis. Then, in March 2006, he contracted pneumonia and ended up in intensive care. This indeed seemed to be the end.

Bill was on the phone often with Cap and Lyn throughout that March. Then, on the morning of Monday, March 27, 2006, Lyn Nofziger went first. Only hours later, at roughly 2:00 A.M. on Tuesday, March 28, Cap joined him.

As Cap's time was running out, his wife, Jane, called Bill, on standby three thousand miles away, to say that his old comrade-in-arms was ready to go and wanted to say goodbye. She told Clark, "You'll need to shout into the receiver, Bill. He can't hear very well." Clark said, "Jane, I've never shouted at Cap in my life!" She chuckled slightly and then held the phone to Cap's ear. Clark shared with his friend those famous words of Our Lord that Pope John Paul II echoed on his first trip to his homeland as the new Pontiff: "Be not afraid"—the most prevalent exhortation in both the Old and New Testaments. He told Cap he was going to a better place. "God willing," said Clark, "we'll all be together again soon." Cap whispered simply, "I know." Those were his final words to Bill.

Bill had lost Cap and Lyn, both like brothers to him, within the span of a single day. He was up most of the night that followed. "You

---

[15] Weinberger, *In the Arena*, p. 173.

think you're ready for this", he said the next day, without the benefit of sleep. "I've been talking to them, keeping up their spirits, speaking with their wives.... But this eventually comes to all of us. We're here for just the blink of an eye." Only Clark and Ed Meese remain from the Sacramento years—the California conservatives who went to Washington and back carrying the Reagan torch.

The Final Pages in the Divine Plan

As he heads into the sunset of his life, Clark still struggles spiritually with the desolation Saint John of the Cross called the "dark night of the soul". He often finds himself asking aloud if God is there, all the while knowing that such an act presumes that He is present and listening to all. Mother Teresa endured the same tribulation for decades, even in her most productive days of ministering to the destitute of Calcutta. Therein exists the paradox of the condition: Faith is strongest when the faithful are lacking consolation, but nonetheless persevere through the darkness with complete abandon and trust.

Why did Clark always so long for that ranch? Why, before each job, no matter how important or interesting, including managing the nation's foreign policy at one of its most crucial times, did he always need to be talked away from the ranch?

In a sense, there is no puzzle: Naturally, ranching is Clark's inheritance; it is in his genes, from Robert Emmett through William Pettit, Uncle Ned, and all the Clark men. The ranch takes him back to his youth, close to those he loved, and misses most.

More than that, though, there is a spiritual dimension to his longing, one that transcends family roots. Like Saint Francis, he connects with God through nature, first among those vistas at the Chismahoo, then at Red Bluff and Slagger Camp. Engulfed by the beauty and majesty of the mountains, he felt close to God. At the ranch in Shandon, once more in the one-on-one isolation between man and Maker, Bill Clark walks among the citrus trees behind the ranch house in silent meditation.

He finds solace in the eighteenth-century classic *Abandonment to Divine Providence* and in books and tapes by Father Benedict Groeschel, C.F.R., one of his spiritual mentors and a good friend. When the New York Franciscan priest was arrested in Westchester County for saying a rosary in front of an abortion clinic, the judge was summoned to rescue him from prison.[16] Father Groeschel has regularly visited Chapel Hill, where he celebrates Mass and gives talks and annual retreats.

Another source of great consolation for Clark in his struggles, spiritual and physical, is Chapel Hill itself, where he is a participant in each Catholic service. In addition to his duties as do-it-all maintenance worker, he arranges for the weekly celebrant, who comes from one of the surrounding parishes to celebrate Mass. Joan cares for the altar linens. Clark welcomes worshippers and makes any necessary announcements before Mass begins. As the priest elevates the host, Clark or one of his sons rings the tower bell, heard throughout the valley. Occasionally, one of Clark's longtime friends, such as Father Frank Pavone or Father Benedict Groeschel, is on hand and the congregation is treated to a sermon by one of the luminaries of today's Church.

Why can he not rest on his laurels, in the knowledge that he has raised a fine family, achieved his goals of owning his own piece of land, of helping roll back the Evil Empire all the while serving his President, his country and his God to the best of his ability? The answer is simple. Despite all his accomplishments, there remains in Bill Clark's heart—to borrow from Saint Augustine—a God-shaped vacuum—that same God-shaped vacuum informing his life since his days in the seminary in upstate New York—that same God-shaped vacuum compelling him to recite the prayers of the Mass while herding sheep in splendid isolation on the northeastern slopes of Mount Shasta.

Finally, hanging in his closet in the back of the ranch house are the black overcoat given him by his godfather, the far-traveled U.S. Army uniform, the well-worn judicial robe, and a long-held friar's robe presented him by Father John Vaughn, O.F.M., former Minister General. But—unlike the overcoat, the uniform, and the judge's robe—the robe of Saint Francis has not yet been worn.

---

[16] When Clark arrived, he found the bearded Franciscan monk wearing an orange prison jumpsuit instead of his gray robe, and curiously smiling. Clark asked him, "Father, what's so funny?" Groeschel told him of the words of comfort he had just received from an elderly African American in the walkway: "Blessed are they who are persecuted." The priest blessed the gentleman, who was still on his knees.

ACKNOWLEDGMENTS

There are many people to be thanked for their participation in making this book possible. At the risk of neglecting some who deserve mention, we would like to express our gratitude to a few individuals.

"As far as support, encouragement and wisdom are concerned, no one provided more to me than my wife, Susan," says Paul Kengor, "particularly in the final days of working with Bill to complete this project." Pat Clark Doerner adds, "Working on this book may have made a saint of me, but it made a martyr of my husband, Richard. Not only has he supported my participation in the project from the beginning, he has remained on call to read and add his perceptive 'outsider' comments on the manuscript whenever asked."

Bill's sisters, Molly Krebs and Cynthia Heffner, reviewed the early chapters, contributing anecdotes and crucial comments. The younger siblings enjoy teasing their relatively famous brother, but both are proud of him and say as much.

The Clark children and their spouses were also helpful, not only in providing insights, but in offering hospitality whenever the Kengor or Doerner families visited the ranch at interview time. This is also true of Joan Brauner Clark, a lady in the truest sense of the word; her unfailing encouragement and good humor buoyed us through the process from start to finish.

The most inspirational of all would have to be Bill, himself. Paul adds: "I've learned from Bill Clark something more personally enriching than historical knowledge: I learned humility, observed in its purity from a master—one who so mastered the craft that he would never acknowledge that very humility."

We are grateful for the assistance of the students at Grove City College who helped in the research and editing process. Among them, Colin Swearingen did a super job in collecting every article with Bill

Clark's name from the *New York Times*, the *Washington Post*, the *Wall Street Journal*, the Foreign Broadcast Information Service, and other sources. His "Google" searches filled Paul's office with boxes of articles relating to William P. Clark. Also helpful were Allan Edwards, Betsy Christian, Jennifer Moyer, Andrew Larson, Rachel Bovard, Margie Dudek, Eric Tinstman, Shawon Jackson-Ybarra, Leah Ayers, Ashley Falzarano, Kelly Schoeffel, Megan Maley, and Shelly Mohr. Among them, Betsy Christian was particularly helpful, and Megan Maley clearly had a role in the DP, most notably through her input at the Clark ranch in July 2006. Also, a former student who is now a friend and a colleague, Cory Shreckengost, was a huge help.

Also from Grove City College, we appreciate the kind interest and support of Lee Wishing, John Sparks, Dick Jewell, Sam Casolari, and David Porter. Both the current president of Grove City College, Dick Jewell, and the previous president, John Moore, took special interest in this book and its subject.

From Bill's office, his secretary, Jayne Halley, was obliging, accepting our sudden intrusions and demands on her office computer and her time. Her recent successor, Liana Rostro, is efficiently filling Jayne's shoes, speeding the process along. Also, Tracy Hough performed the tedious task of transcribing many hours of tape-recorded interviews.

Our thanks to Dr. Gabriele Lusser Rico and Curtis Patrick for their helpful comments on the gubernatorial period.

The assistance of Dan McGovern and John Murphy was indispensable for the chapter on the California Supreme Court. Among the many interviewed, David Laux, Roger Robinson, and the late Cap Weinberger were extremely insightful.

The Suriname chapter was repeatedly read and worked over by the participants. It went through multiple drafts before we got it right—a real burden, but worth the investment. Reviewers included Clark, Paul Gorman, Dewey Clarridge, John Poindexter, and others who were not there but learned about the operation in detail, such as Tom Reed. A special word of thanks to Dewey, who reliably stepped in to help ensure our facts were correct on issues ranging from Suriname to Libya.

David Laux was essential in compiling information on the Pacific Rim, as well as elsewhere throughout the book. Laux's attention to detail and his memory for the telling anecdote paid great dividends in telling Bill's story. We look forward to more of Laux should he decide to put the rest of his story into print.

We also thank Ron Robinson, of the Young America's Foundation, for his insights on Clark and for his encouragement. "You may be the only writer in the country", wrote Robinson to Paul, adding Peter Schweizer's name as well, "who could get him to tell his tale." Tom Reed was also essential in convincing Clark to move ahead with this project.

We appreciate the work of the staff at the Reagan Library: Duke Blackwood, Mike Duggan, Cate Sewall, Ben Pezzillo, and Kirby Hanson. Mike especially expedited the declassification process as best he could.

Then, of course, there is the publisher:

To our knowledge, this is the only memoir of a Reagan official published by a religious press. It had to be so, since the story of Clark's life has a strong spiritual component—a distinctly Catholic one. Of course, as Clark might say, the choice was never our own doing: we were but the instruments in the DP. That being the case, Father Joseph Fessio, S.J., was the conductor. Father Fessio, the founder and editor of Ignatius Press, has long been a friend of Bill Clark, and from the outset offered to publish this book. In short order, we had an arrangement.

We are also grateful to a number of others from Ignatius, especially Mark Brumley, Tony Ryan, and Nellie Boldrick, who joined Paul for the roller coaster ride of working out the details of the contract, plus much more. Vivian Dudro was of great help in editing the overall manuscript as was Jo Baeza, a friend of Bill's from his days at Stanford.

We are deeply indebted to John Raisian of the Hoover Institution, who generously came through with crucial funding to help cover the costs for this book. John and his organization are a blessing, and continue to carry on a legacy of great scholarship.

Paul adds his thanks to his agent, Leona Schecter, indispensable, as she has always been. Likewise, Leona's husband Jerry was again a reliable source of wisdom.

Finally, though it is hard to say exactly when the idea to approach Clark for this biography first popped into Paul's mind, he believes the source was Floyd Brown of the Young America's Foundation, who, as Paul worked on his books on Ronald Reagan, kept telling him: "Of all the Reagan people, Bill Clark is the one with the best story. You should write a book on *him*."

"Good advice, Floyd. I hope I did okay", says Paul.

INDEX